D0812162

IMPERIAL
Saint

IMPERIAL
Saint

THE CULT OF
ST. CATHERINE AND THE
DAWN OF FEMALE RULE
IN RUSSIA

Gary Marker

NORTHERN ILLINOIS UNIVERSITY PRESS

DeKalb

This book is dedicated to the memory of

Lindsey Hughes (1949–2007),

a dear friend and generous colleague.

Information regarding the images found in this volume is on p. 309.

Library of Congress Cataloging-in-Publication Data

Marker, Gary, 1948–

Imperial saint : the cult of St. Catherine and the dawn of female rule in Russia / Gary Marker.

   p.   cm.

Includes bibliographical references and index.

ISBN-13: 978-0-87580-375-3 (clothbound : alk. paper)

ISBN-10: 0-87580-375-X (clothbound : alk. paper)

1. Catherine, of Alexandria, Saint. 2. Catherine, of Alexandria, Saint—Cult—Russia—History. 3. Christian women saints—Cult. I. Title. II. Title: St. Catherine of Alexandria and the justification of female rule in Russia.

BX4700.C45.M37 2007

272'.1092—dc22

2007013001

Contents

Illustrations

Preface

• The topics upon which this book dwells—gender and religion, queenship, the political veneration of saints, court ceremonials, religious processionals, the construction of the feminine in political life—are familiar elements of contemporary late medieval and early modern European historiography. They are also familiar to early modern Russian historians, in fact increasingly so over the past decade. As a practical matter, though, most histories of Christian sainthood and European queenship tend to take rather little notice of circumstances east of the Vistula, although events since 1989 have begun to ease this barrier a bit, sometimes pushing it as far as the Dnieper, but rarely to the distant Volga. This is an old and familiar complaint among Russianists, intoned with righteous and not infrequently bibulous indignation in the company of like-minded sufferers, gathered around cramped tables in hotel bars during annual conventions in search of comradely understanding. So far as I can tell, no one else has noticed. One day, perhaps, the field of early modern European history may advance all the way to Chukotka, but until then it remains the task of specialists in our field to demonstrate the resonance of our writing to a wider scholarly community.

Although not explicitly comparative (except perhaps in chapter 2 where the Russian image of St. Catherine of Alexandria is placed alongside the Catherine cult elsewhere), the study draws widely on the scholarship on religion and gender in late medieval/early modern Europe, both Byzantine and western European, and it asks many of the same questions. I would hope that it adds some new perspectives out of the east (or at least an occasional wrinkle) to the larger and very rich scholarly literature on the cult of St. Catherine, and more broadly, the cult of saints in European political discourse.

Be that as it may, the narrative focuses squarely on Russia, what might be called the long prehistory of eighteenth-century female rule and the texts and practices upon which it came to rest. Just to underscore the importance of these phenomena for Russia and the jarring discontinuity that they constituted prior to 1725, the year in which Peter the Great's widow, Catherine I, ascended the throne, female rule had been virtually unknown in Russia, limited to the tenth-century Princess Olga of Kiev, the first baptized Russian ruler and the grandmother of St. Vladimir, the Kievan prince who presided over the conversion of the Rus' to Orthodoxy in 988. Otherwise, female political authority had been instituted only during two brief regencies, that of Elena Glinskaia in the sixteenth century and Sofia Alekseevna in the seventeenth. Between 1725 and 1796, however, the Russian throne was occupied by women for all but five years, and women ruled as regents for much of the rest of the time. So great had been their cast on the throne that Paul I (1796–1801), the dyspeptic son of Catherine the Great, the longest-tenured Russian empress (1762–1796), rewrote the laws of succession in 1797 so as to all but guarantee that a woman would never again rule Russia. In this, if in little else, he was successful. To this day, Catherine the Great remains as the last woman to preside over the Russian state or government.

As had been true in Great Britain, the Holy Roman Empire, Sweden, and other Renaissance states that accepted female crowned heads, Russian authorities relied heavily on precedence to explain and justify the presence of a woman on the throne. When the case otherwise appeared weak they, like their counterparts further west, proved adept at inventing precedence or at creatively re-presenting it so as to create an illusion of seamless continuity. They relied upon Scripture so as to demonstrate the consistency with Christian teaching and divine sanction and on both religious poetry and carefully orchestrated ceremonials to celebrate it, as in the versified processional for Elizabeth I of Britain. In this endeavor, secular power brokers depended upon the acquiescence of the clergy, and the approving words and gestures of clerical pronouncements, without which the divine unction would ring hollow. Again, no differences here between west and east. For all these reasons, I go somewhat against the convention of our field and view the background to elevation of Catherine I in 1725 partly through the lens of European queenship, even though I refrain from using "queen" in a Russian setting.

Russian historians tend to avoid words that are commonplace in the histories of other European states, such as "royalty," "king," and "queen," in discussing the tsar and tsaritsa, or after 1721 the emperor and empress, and for good reason. There are several justifications for this lexicographic particularism, but some are particularly germane here. The Russian language distinguished "tsar" from "king" *(korol')*, a term that is associated with other European crowned heads. "Tsar" could be applied to non-Russian rulers—the Byzantine emperor, the Tatar khan—and most importantly to God. But when mortal rulers bore this title it implied some sort of domain over Russia itself, even though no doctrine existed to proclaim such a linguistic relationship explicitly. Homogenizing terminology tends to obscure this specificity. Russia also lacked the complex legal formulae, or even simple legal constructs, that other states employed to explain the lawfulness of a given person's rule, male or female. In fact, during the period in question Russian succession relied on a single legal premise, Peter's decree of 1721 stating that the reigning monarch chose the successor. Although the law assumed that the heir would come from within the dynastic family, rank, age, blood, even gender gave way in this brief pronouncement to the will of the monarch, who answered to God and no one else for his decision.

Thus there are certain defining qualities to Russian practices and precedents that undergird their particular terminology. Nevertheless, the political and cultural background to Catherine's ascent looks rather like those in other parts of Christian Europe and drew upon much the same inventory of texts, gestures, and rationales. The narrative strategies were the same as were many of the sources of textual authority. Those who were called upon to explain the public celebration of Catherine I, her coronation, and her ultimate ascendancy to the throne, also saw these developments against the backdrop of Christian Europe, and often referred explicitly to queenship elsewhere. Moreover, Catherine reigned as an independent sovereign or autocrat *(samoderzhitsa),* a circumstance familiar to any crowned head even if the precise meaning of her (or any one else's) sovereignty was never spelled out. In short, one asks the same questions about the beginnings of female rule in Russia as of female rule in any other monarchic state. Hence "queenship" seems appropriate here.

Regarding the cult of saints, much the same observations apply. For those unfamiliar with Russian scholarship a brief précis may be in order here. There is an old and never-ending debate in the field, begun by Father George Florovskii over half a century ago, regarding what he called "the silence" of old Russian culture. It begins from the incontrovertible fact that Russian medieval texts rarely discussed abstract ideas or theology divorced from devotional practice. Canon law, as it is commonly understood in Catholic Europe, was transposed to Russian Orthodoxy primarily in a practical form, the *kormchaia kniga.* Doctrinal and speculative disputations about meaning and faith, as between the great theologians of western academies and cathedrals, did not take place very much in Russia, and when they did occur, as in the Eucharist controversy or the conflagrations over the retranslated service books of the seventeenth century, they focused on very specific issues of direct relevance to the church service or religious practice. The explanations for this "silence" are as varied, contradictory, and speculative as there are contributors to the discussion. Some have argued that Russia inherited Byzantine theology as a whole, thereby not needing its own speculative theology. Others have imagined that old Russia simply was too backward, too intellectually undeveloped to produce original thinkers or "great ideas" on its own. Still others believe that the doctrinal awareness was there, at least within the upper clergy, but that its understandings were consigned to oral rather than written communication. One or two of our colleagues have even turned to modern neuroscience to interpret textual silences!

I confess to being hopelessly ill-equipped to comment fruitfully on this controversy, temperamentally too wedded to documents to engage in abstractions at that ethereal level. Fortunately, a fairly large body of narrative and prescriptive texts, as well as occasional eyewitness or first-person accounts do survive, and one can look for what is present or absent (silences) in them. These sources become more common once we enter the seventeenth century, when Muscovite officialdom, both secular and church, embrace bureaucracy, a more systematic approach to keeping written records, and—not insignificantly—print, all in the service of expanding the authority of the center and moving the Orthodox flock toward a more uniform set of practices. In the eighteenth century such sources appear in veritable abundance. Once again, all of this is reminiscent of affairs in late Renaissance Europe, even if the belated or compressed timing of these practices are often special to Russia.

In large measure the narrative sources—chronicles, saints' lives, *chronographs*—have formats, functions, and contents comparable to those same texts elsewhere. Following the changes in these narratives over time and place, in particular being sensitive to alterations in a given saint's (in this case St. Catherine's) life text, demands a special level of scrutiny. Charting changes in iconography, or sudden appearance at key moments in the narratives—such as a chronicle account of Vasilii III's deathbed confession in 1535 in which, seemingly out of the blue, St. Catherine became the Grand Prince's heavenly intercessor—leans heavily on the methodologies used in studying cults of saints irrespective of geography or confession.

A central theme of this work is the intersection of gender, power, and religion, and the use of highly gendered imagery to associate certain attributes with masculinity or femininity. Once again, I have been influenced by western European scholarship, especially the works of Caroline Bynum *(Jesus as Mother)* and Peter Brown *(The Cult of Saints),* not only in sensitizing me to the microscopic reading of words and passages, but also in recognizing the transposition of masculine traits onto female objects. Bynum's noted essay, "Jesus as Mother," has proven invaluable in attuning me to the elasticity of cross-gendered language. The most consistent example of this type of gender transposition is the valorization of St. Catherine in Russian texts as brave and manly. The Russian word here, *muzhestvo,* is explicitly male, from *muzh/muzhchina* (man) in its root meaning, and in its application to female martyrs. Bravery, of course, was central to the persona of St. Catherine in western vitae as well, but it came to play a particularly prominent role in the politicization of her Russian vita as it evolved in the sixteenth through the early seventeenth centuries. Conversely, Russian texts and images muted or ignored altogether the theme of the bride of Christ until well into the sixteenth century, long after it had become foundational in Catherinean veneration in much of the Christian world. By the late seventeenth century, though, the mystical marriage had taken center stage in Russian texts and images. Gender transpositions do not explain these variations in toto, of course, but without attentiveness to gendered language they are inexplicable.

St. Catherine has received extensive and searching treatment in recent western scholarship, including Katherine Lewis's studies of St. Catherine in late medieval England, Julie Hassel's study of female autonomy in the so-called Katherine group of vitae, and the recent (2003) collection of essays edited by Lewis and Jacqueline Jenkins, *St. Katherine of Alexandria: Texts and Contexts in Western Medieval Europe*. As a newcomer to the subject I have benefitted immensely from the research and insights of these authors. Overall, their studies have emphasized St. Catherine's image as intercessor and exemplar for individual women, especially those in personally or socially vulnerable circumstances, whose private meditation and prayer, or pilgrimages to nearby St. Catherine chapels and monasteries, became common forms of veneration. As we shall see, this was not the case in Russia, at least prior to the late eighteenth century.

While I do address in some detail the place of Russia within the more general Christian world, in particular regarding the St. Catherine cult, I do so without an explicit concern over whether Russia was in any fundamental sense unique. Hence, those seeking didactic observations on the enduring and unresolvable Russia-and-the-West theme are likely to be disappointed. No *Sonderwegs* here. The Byzantine foundations play a central role in understanding the sources and practices of the Russian St. Catherine cult, and Russia's search for precedents within the early Byzantine church pervaded virtually every subject I encountered in researching this book. Elements of the Byzantine cults of saints radiated throughout Christian Europe in the late medieval period and the Renaissance, and most assuredly in providing templates for the veneration of St. Catherine. Russia shared in this wider efflorescence and drew from the same well of late Byzantine manuscripts, and to that extent at least participated equally, if not necessarily reciprocally, with the rest of Christian Europe. Thus, it is hoped that this study will help to bring Russia into that larger narrative.

A Note on Transliteration

In most instances this book follows the Library of Congress system for transliterating Russian and Greek words. No system is perfect, and I have chosen to use common English spellings of names, such as Peter, Sofia, Alexander, and Catherine, rather than transliterating the Russian equivalents. Reference material, however, transliterates strictly by the book. An additional issue relates to certain Russian names and their antecedents among Greek saints. Generally, but not uniformly, I will use the Greek variant for the saint and the Russian variant for the namesake when they are closely juxtaposed (e.g., Eudokia, Evdokia). The exceptions are Catherine and Sofia, who are referred to so often that I have resorted to common English equivalents for both saint and ruler. Although not strictly according to Hoyle, this mixture follows common conventions and will, I hope, prove not to be confusing.

Acknowledgments

As enjoyable as it has been to research and write this book, the study of
St. Catherine has involved a steep learning curve, one that has led me to
turn repeatedly to colleagues and learned friends for advice and assistance. Just as an illustration: several years ago, when I was first considering undertaking a research project on female rule, I saw a reference to Peter the Great's Order of St. Catherine, the subject of chapter 6. My first
reaction was to march to the office of a medievalist in my department
with the question: "Who was St. Catherine?" Out of that less-than-humble
beginning this book gradually emerged. I would therefore like to thank officially all the many medievalists and early modernists, both Russian and
western, who generously and continuously answered such naïve questions. My colleagues at Stony Brook have been a constant source of interest and stimulation: Sara Lipton, Joel Rosenthal, Ned Landsman, Kathleen
Wilson, Herman Lebovics, Nancy Tomes, Young-sun Hong, Robert Gold-
enberg, Christina Bethin, and several others. Equally, I should like to
thank the members of the international group on eighteenth-century
Russian studies. A warmer, more collegial, more engaging group of scholars would be difficult to find. Lindsey Hughes, Maria DiSalvo, Viktor
Zhivov, Tony Cross, Simon Dixon, Roger Bartlett, Gareth Jones, Alexander
Kamenskii, Evgenii Anisimov, Olga Kosheleva, Isabel de Madariaga, Andrei
Zorin, Janet Hartley, Joachim Klein, and Paul Keenan have served as willing audiences for my sometimes unorthodox, and often long-winded
declamations. Quite a few volunteered to become unofficial St. Catherine
scouts, sending me references, postcards, and photos from their journeys
whenever they saw a St. Catherine. Colleagues in the United States have
done much the same: Marcus Levitt, George Munro, David Griffiths, Jay
Alexander, Roy Robson, Irina Reyfman, Nadezhda Kizenko, Alexander
Martin, Barbara Skinner, Daniel Waugh, and several others. The staffs at
several libraries and archives in the United States, the United Kingdom,
and Russia have afforded me great help in finding materials. Among these
are the staff of the library of the State University of New York at Stony
Brook, the New York Public Library, the libraries of the University of Illi-
nois and the University of California at Berkeley, the Widener Library at
Harvard, the British Library, Cambridge University Library, the library of
the School of Slavonic and East European Studies of the University of London, the State Historical Library in Moscow, the Library of the Academy of
Sciences in St. Petersburg, and the State Public Library in St. Petersburg.
Among archivists are those from the Russian State Archive of Ancient Acts
(Moscow), the Russian State Archive of Moscow Oblast (Moscow), and the
Russian State Historical Archive (St. Petersburg), which tragically is closed
for the foreseeable future. From this large cohort of professionals I particularly want to thank three: Donna Sammis, the Inter-library Loan librarian
at Stony Brook, without whom this project would have never been com-

pleted; Chris Thomas, the now retired head of the Slavonic Division at the British Library; and Edward Kasinec, the head of the Slavic Division at New York Public Library.

As always, Mary Lincoln of Northern Illinois University Press has been a paragon of editorial professionalism. I wish to thank Nancy Kollmann and Daniel Kaiser for their thorough and searching readings of the entire manuscript. Several others read, heard, and commented upon portions of the work in earlier stages: Valerie Kivelson, Elise Wirtschafter, Greg Bruess, Ann Kleimola, Roy Robson, Diane Koenker, Bill Wagner, and Joan Neuberger, to name a few. I thank all of them for their assistance and suggestions, but of course the final product is my own, warts and all.

The American Philosophical Society provided much needed financial support during a sabbatical year in London, and the School of Slavonic and East European Studies, University College London, provided an academic home during my year there. The Russian State Humanities University in Moscow and the Institute of History of the Russian Academy of Sciences in St. Petersburg have been my welcoming sponsors over several trips to Russia.

I also want to give great thanks to my wife, Ann, and my son, Josh, for tolerating my monologues about St. Catherine and for hiking to obscure sites in search of yet one more little-known chapel, icon, or stained glass window. I promise it won't happen again.

IMPERIAL
Saint

1

The Problem of Female Rule

is this unlooked? [handwritten annotation]

• This book begins and ends with the vexing riddle of eighteenth-century female rule, its ideological underpinnings and the apparent ease with which Russia's deeply patriarchal political culture came to terms with it. In the words of Brenda Meehan, whose ground-breaking article on Catherine the Great inaugurated this issue some three decades ago, "there is no philosophical confrontation of the issue of female rule among most Russian writers; this was not an important problem. . . . A woman holding power poses few discernible psychic threats to the Russian men writing about her."[1]

Unlike most such studies, this book seeks to redirect our attention in several basic ways: first, it veers away from Catherine the Great, the most widely discussed female ruler, toward the formal beginnings of female rule, i.e., the reign of Catherine I. Chronologically it views the public presentation of Catherine, both before and during her reign, against the backdrop of the available tropes of female authority that Russian culture had come to accept during the several centuries prior to Catherine's ascent in 1725. Simultaneously, it concentrates primarily on religious and faith-centered expressions of legitimation, in particular those inscribed in the Russian cult of Catherine's name day saint, Catherine of Alexandria, whose representations fill several chapters in this book, rather than on the lay or secular representations that have drawn most of the attention from Meehan and others. More to the point, it treats these expressions as texts or symbols in their own right, with God and salvation at their core, rather than as midwives of secular statecraft.

The Case for Catherine I

The reasons for this refocus are straightforward. Catherine the Great was, after all, the very last female ruler in Russia, preceded by three female crowned heads during the eighteenth century, as well as two de facto female regents (Sofia Alekseevna and Anna Leopoldovna). By the time of her coronation in 1762 female rule had become almost commonplace, and the justifications and cultural narratives of female rule were already well established, if not exactly normative, so much so that they hardly required rearticulation. Hence the "silence" that Meehan observed. Some of these narratives derived from as far back as Sofia's regency and de facto sovereignty in the late 1680s. As Isolde Thyrêt has convincingly shown, others were derived from the publicly constructed images of the Muscovite tsaritsa, and thus originated still earlier.[2] But Peter the Great's destabilizing and reluctant decree on succession (1721), Catherine I's coronation in 1724, and Catherine's ascendancy to rulership in the following year collectively inaugurated modern female rule in Russia as an official, legal, and public, if unanticipated, fact. It stands to reason, then, that one should look here, at the beginning, for the most telling and acute expressions for and against female rule, rather than later.

Even a cursory look at the two Catherines reveals just how unlikely a path breaker the first Catherine was, and how bewilderingly improbable her ascent must have seemed to those at court with an eye for precedence. If Catherine II faced the daunting hurdles of gender, and both a non-Orthodox and non-Russian background in her ascendancy to rulership, Catherine I added to this list a great many more obstacles: the absence of an accepted Russian precedent,[3] her non-noble (to say the least) origin, an undocumented conversion to Orthodoxy,[4] a shady background, and especially her status as Peter's second wife.

Regarding Catherine's initial liaison with Peter, for example, and her conversion from either Lutheranism or Catholicism to Orthodoxy, there survive only legends born of rumor, hearsay, and demonization. A. A. Kizevetter, for one, argued that the two met and began cohabitating in 1703, at which time Catherine converted to Orthodoxy. But if Kizevetter saw any corroborating documents he kept them to himself. Slightly more expansive are the accounts offered by S. M. Solov'ev and Villebois, Peter's French aide-de-camp. Solov'ev maintained that Catherine was the daughter of a resident of Lifland, the peasant Samuel Skavronski, who placed Catherine in the Menshikov household in 1703 or 1704 as a companion to the Menshikov girls, Mariia and Anna. According to this account, based in part on archival records, Samuel was employed by Pastor Glück, the Lutheran archbishop of Marienburg, and it was the connection between Glück and the Menshikovs that brought Catherine to Peter's attention. Solov'ev deduced that by October 1705 Catherine had had two children by Peter, which would place the initial liaison in 1703, and Reinhard Wittram, the great German historian of Peter's reign, simply accepted Solov'ev's version.[5]

The detailed memoir of Villebois insisted—on what authority he did not say—that Marta (or Marfa) Skavronska, the future Catherine, was born in Dorpat (Tartu) in 1686, and that she came from a family of fugitive Polish peasants. Baptized a Catholic and raised as a Lutheran, she worked as a servant for Glück while her husband was away at war. When the household moved to Riga, it soon came under the authority of the Russian forces commanded by Prince Boris Sheremetev, who attacked and then occupied the city. Seven months later Menshikov arrived to take command, took an interest in Marta, and, in the words of Villebois, "introduced her to the tsar's bedchamber." Peter subsequently brought her back to Moscow and arranged for her to live in comfort, but separately from him for the next two or three years. Most recently, Paul Bushkovitch uncovered documents in the Prussian State archive that imply a liaison in spring 1704, which would be consistent with both Solov'ev's and Villebois' accounts.[6]

Several years prior to the official and highly public wedding of 1712, Peter and Catherine had almost certainly married privately at an unknown time and place, apparently not long after Peter had divorced his first wife, Evdokia, and forced her to take the veil.[7] Disgruntled traditionalists deemed the divorce and second marriage—hardly the first such circumstance for a sovereign in Russian history—impermissible in the eyes of Scripture and Russian law. In the words of the Third Pskov Chronicle, in its condemnation of Vasilii III for his divorce of his childless wife of many years, Solomoniia, in favor of the much younger Elena Glinskaia, "As the apostle has written, 'if you send one wife away and marry another, you commit adultery.'"[8] One accusation, particularly rife among Old Believers, maintained that the marriage amounted to nothing less than incest. Its proponents based their conclusion on the commonly held—but completely undocumented—view that Peter's son, Aleksei, had become Catherine's godfather when she converted to Orthodoxy. By this line of reasoning Peter had become Catherine's spiritual grandfather, a status that, in the eyes of many believers, was equivalent to or more venerated than a biological grandfather because of its sacral presence in baptism and first communion into the body of the church.[9] To bring grandfather and granddaughter together in matrimony, therefore, constituted a particularly grievous act of incest.

Whether by adultery or incest, traditionalist critics considered Peter to be living in sin, with Catherine being—at best—a mere lover or adulteress (*bludnitsa,* or something more vulgar) rather than a tsaritsa.[10] Some whispered that Catherine had already married (and never divorced) a Swedish corporal (Villebois referred to the husband as a horse grenadier in the service of Charles XII). Named Meijer in some accounts, Johann Trubachev in others, he was said to have married Marta in July 1704, i.e., at the very moment of her initial liaison with Peter.[11] The fact that Catherine bore Peter at least two publicly acknowledged children before their official marriage clearly did not help her reputation. The divorced and cloistered Evdokia survived and even outlasted Peter's marriage to Catherine (she died in 1730), a guarantee that the issue of the divorce would not fade away.

Perhaps the only advantage the first Catherine held over the second was the fact that the Peter whom she succeeded died a natural death, and one in which she was not implicated, rather than a violent one. And yet, Catherine I did reign as *samoderzhitsa,* however briefly, and with the full public acquiescence of the court, the guards regiments, and the clergy[12]. Finessing these daunting handicaps was complicated, and the careful and systematic reinvention of the persona of Catherine during Peter's last decade as a power in her own right instead of a mere consort and helpmate paved the way for her own accession and for the female crowned heads who came after her. This is not to suggest that Catherine's rule was in any sense premeditated or imagined before the fact. Peter's gradual elevation of his spouse after 1711 right through to her coronation in 1724 had everything to do with defining her position within Petrine court politics, and later, with guaranteeing her personal, political, and financial security once he was gone. But it was not, on the evidence, meant to provide a foundation for female rule. By all accounts Peter had initially expected his son Aleksei to succeed him in more-or-less traditional fashion. After Aleksei's disgrace, incarceration for treason, and death in 1718, the mantle passed to Peter's infant son, Peter Petrovich, and manifestoes proclaiming him the heir to the throne were ordered printed in 1718.[13] Unfortunately for an orderly succession, the young Peter died in childhood, leaving the tsar with no obvious male heir and obliging him to improvise new legislation with an unspecified outcome.

Religion and the Right to Rule

To the meager extent that scholarship has examined the political persona of the first Catherine in light of female rule, it has dwelt on the secular elements of specific ceremonies and rituals at court: the coronation proclamation, public assemblies, and Catherine's secular iconography. Her vaunted heroism, specifically her manly bravery *(muzhestvo)* at the battle of Pruth in 1711, is the most commonly cited justification for her coronation, and Peter made certain to proclaim this tale at every possible opportunity. It is in this context that Catherine became a warrior queen, a Semiramis, the image most frequently cited in the literature. Richard Wortman's searching description of the newly devised coronation ceremony, based primarily on the published *Opisanie koronatsii e. v. Ekateriny Alekseevny,* the engraved *Konkliuziia* by Ivan Zubov, and the diary of the Holstein envoy Friedrich-Wilhelm Bergholz, emphasizes the ceremony's statist and secular content, and it concludes that "the monarch no longer looked to the clergy for moral guidance. It was replaced by a sermon or oration *(Slovo Bozhiia)* . . . [in this case by Archbishop Feofan Prokopovich] and little in the message was religious."[14]

That classical myths accompanied Catherine I's coronation and the advent of female rule is undeniable and well documented. Beyond the fleeting references to Semiramis, the sculptures and bas reliefs of the palaces in Ekaterinhof and St. Petersburg (both the Summer Palace and the future Mikhailovskii Palace) presented the tsaritsa/empress as lavishly as Minerva and Diana, wise, truthful, and strong figures, but unmistakably pagan.[15] Church and faith extolled Catherine as well, however, and far more frequently, particularly for audiences and subjects who had no entrée to palaces and court spectacles (i.e., virtually the entire population), or those in attendance who had no first-hand knowledge of the coronation rituals of late Muscovy, and who therefore may not have been as familiar with old ritual as were the leading churchmen or Peter's researchers into protocol.

As visually dramatic as these court ceremonies were for those who witnessed them, they had a modest public afterlife as written texts, especially the coronation rituals. The *Opisanie*—which in any case did not include the text of Feofan's sermon—had two modest simultaneous printings in Moscow (three hundred copies) and St. Petersburg, and the *Konkliuziia* engraving had a single run of sixty, none of which entered general circulation.[16] More importantly, female legitimacy, especially one without any clear or acceptable precedent, could derive not from conquest or pagan myth, but from God and only from God, a fact resonant in both the language and the ritual of the coronation. So too, one might add, did virtually all of the qualities of feminine heroism that civic panegyrics very occasionally affixed to pagan amazons.

Every official, both foreign and native, who wrote for the record about Catherine's coronation in 1724 and her ascent to the throne a year later, employed a preeminently faith-centered discourse, and emphasized the divine inspiration for these two events. None except for Feofan referred to the likes of Semiramis at these moments of Catherine's legitimation, and he did so only the one time. Even the skeptical Old Believer community at Vyg sent congratulatory greetings to the new empress, as was their wont, referring to her as "the Most Radiant Divinely chosen tsaritsa, Most August Divinely Crowned Empress, all-merciful great sovereign Ekaterina Alekseevna" whose coronation "covers all of Russia in joyous happiness."[17]

Catherine herself underscored this immutable truth in a private letter written to Prince M. M. Golitsyn shortly after her succession (the letter is dated March 18, 1725). In it she inquired why she had as yet gotten no report that the standing army in Ukraine had sworn allegiance to her "for it is by the will of God that we have received the scepter of Russian power" ("ibo po vole bozhiei skipetr derzhavy rossiiskoi my poluchili").[18] Lest there be any doubt, patriarchs from throughout Orthodoxy sent Catherine letters of condolence at Peter's death and simultaneous congratulations at her ascendancy. In a letter of April 1726, for example, the patriarch of Constantinople conveyed his rejoicing at the news that "the most august and Divinely-crowned *("Bogovenchannaia")* Catherine" had received the throne from God and in Christ, and he expressed his hope that the empire would thrive in the hands of such a monarch. A month later the patriarch of Antioch sent a similar message.[19] Peter's court may have mocked religious ritual and its valorization of the clergy, but it respected the centrality of faith, out of pragmatism if nothing else. It pursued a "cult of the civic," in Viktor Zhivov's words.[20] But that cult, as Zhivov shows, relied deeply on "the magic of old rituals," in order to link it to familiar and preexisting tropes of authority and thus forestall, or at least minimize, its repudiation.

One must not lose sight of the fact that the coronation was a church service, with a complete and elaborate liturgy, and that it took place in consecrated space, in the Moscow Kremlin's Dormition Cathedral, rather than out in public spaces *("publichno")*. The congregants and the dozens of clergy in attendance were surrounded on all sides by sacred imagery and were called upon to pray and bless the event repeatedly during the ceremony. Peter placed the crown on Catherine's head, but this act too represented, at most, a slight modification of the coronations of the empresses of Byzantium. As his researches into protocol had revealed, those rituals prescribed that, after the public confession of faith, a new empress would be crowned by the emperor, albeit with her marriage crown, as an extension of the ritual that crowned the new emperor.[21] In Catherine's case, the entire moment was first consecrated by a prayer read by the archbishop invoking God, Samuel the Prophet, and King David, i.e., the *biblical* roots of all coronations.[22]

We are not speaking here about 'tradition,' if that term implies something primordial or fixed in antiquity (most of the so-called traditional rituals were themselves of recent vintage, dating not much farther back than the reign of Ivan IV), but rather the continuity of faith within the otherwise fluid symbolism of Russian power. Still less are we suggesting a correspondence between public expressions of faith and private belief, or any symmetry between the legitimated public persona and the true facts of that individual's biography. Michael Flier has observed that, "A ritual is . . . a sequence of gestures, movements, utterances, whose very replication is at the heart of the mystery that sustains a community of believers. The familiar in this case breeds comfort rather than contempt. It generates fervor, promotes stability, *maintains* faith. *It is the known quantity in ritual that is all important, not the novel* [italics added]."[23]

The claim to reign, especially one so dissonant as—to paraphrase Feofan Prokopovich—the "Right of the–Female–Monarch's Will," had to have a Christian and churchly foundation, one that resonated within "real existing Orthodoxy." Otherwise it had no foundation at all.[24] Everyone knew this and accepted it, as one of the fundamental articles of faith, a body of public myth that bound imperial rulers with their Muscovite forebears. As before, it was the clergy's job to articulate the right to rule, and their essential and explicit referents for political discourse were not Pufendorf or other secular philosophers, but *Scripture*. Beyond fervent prayer, the speech acts of choice, as Wortman avers, were sermons, or *uchitel'nye slova,* which the heads of the Russian church had orated at every coronation since at least Aleksei Mikhailovich's ceremony of 1645.[25]

The vast majority of sermons, one should keep in mind, celebrated holy days in the religious calendar, and as a result the *slovo* as an oration (i.e., as speech act and *not* as literary text) remained preeminently an elaboration on faith in the expectations of those who heard them. Much like their western counterparts, Russian sermons of this era began almost invariably with a biblical inscription, which served as the organizing principle of the text, as well as the key to understanding the subsequent imagery. Even panegyric sermons, which constituted a small fraction of the overall number before and during Peter's reign, remained imbued with the sacraments, incarnation, resurrection, communion, and salvation during Peter's reign and beyond, even if this particular one may not have.[26]

a religion - centered society

Faith and Empire

This study, then, explores the use of that religious imagery and formal explanation, and in particular the recourse to Orthodoxy's pantheon of women of power, that were available as ideological buttresses for the unanticipated and unplanned advent of the formal rule of Catherine I in January 1725. In addition to confronting the riddle of Russian female rule within a politics and culture that remained overwhelmingly patrilineal throughout the eighteenth century and beyond, this book addresses two interpretive problems that have loomed large in contemporary eighteenth-century Russian studies: secularization and the nature of political sovereignty. Russia had its share of great men and women during the eighteenth century, but the wonder of imperial autocracy was that it survived and even prospered through a succession of ill-prepared and unimpressive rulers, male and female. Somehow, Russia's golden age of empire coincided with the reigns of an infant, a teen who died on the eve of his planned wedding, three assassinations, an illiterate Baltic peasant woman, and another who had spent most of her adult life in German-speaking Kurland. Four of these reigns lasted less than three years, and several times, in the absence of a designated successor, the new crowned head was chosen by guards' regiments and court parties. Yet, through all of these so-called palace revolutions, *imperiia* and *samoderzhavie* lived on, even thrived, as unshakable myths of rulership, renewed by successive generations of serving families, and rearticulated through the conventions of divine will. These myths endured presumably in no small measure so as to avoid a repetition of the *smuta,* the dark days of the Time of Troubles that engulfed Muscovy in violence and disorder in the early seventeenth century, the fear of physical and dynastic disorder that seems never to have been far away from the thoughts of Russia's political elites. That, and the utter determination to avoid formal oligarchy, i.e., the institutionalized sway of certain elite clans over the fortunes of their rivals. The durability of an imperial edifice in the face of weak rulers and perpetual "undergovernment" suggests that the minor reigns may well tell more about the quality of Russian autocracy than the major ones.

Most of the body of contemporary explanation remained distinctly medieval, in that it relied less on deductive reasoning than on analogies, the juxtaposition of images, and, above all, justification by precedent, typically from the Bible or from Christian antiquity. Roy Strong has aptly defined this typology of medieval reasoning as "the foreshadowing of present by past events, and it recurred repeatedly in nearly all verbal and visual representations of political authority."[27] Even Feofan Prokopovich's most didactic and politically innovative works, such as *Pravda voli monarshei* (*The Right of the Monarch's Will*), leaned heavily on precedent, or on the claim of precedent. As with western medieval argumentation, explications of Russian political authority meant situating modern, and in particular innovative, practices, *renovatio* perhaps, within the repetitive cycles of Christian time, be it annual, generational, or epochal. The goal, of course, would have been to connect modernity to a recurring and unbroken chain of human events that ultimately led back to the Old Testament foundations of monotheism, Abraham, David, and Moses. Visually, this idea was famously represented by the princely family tree (the transposition of the tree of Jesse, the father of King David who initiated divine kingship[28]), which showed the branches and twines physically linking the current ruler with the pantheon of glorious ancestors. Such images became more common during the latter seventeenth century, and while tsaritsy did occasionally appear, they never stood on a branch of rulership. The most well known is Semen (Simon) Ushakov's 1668 engraving, commissioned as a private issue for the ruling family, of the "Mother of God of Vladimir and the Tree of the Muscovite State," adapted from the biblical tree of Jesse.[29] At the top stood Christ and the archangels in heaven, and at the base, the tree trunk, was the Dormition Cathedral. In the center were the Bogomater' and the Christ child, and they were encircled by twenty bygone Russian princes and tsars. At the foot of the picture, standing just inside the Kremlin walls but unconnected to the tree, were Aleksei Mikhailovich on the right, and Mariia Il'inichna and *tsarevichi* Aleksei and Fedor Alekseevich on the left. Although wearing a crown, Mariia's role here is that of mother, both of the nation and of the anticipated future tsar. The organic unity of power, from God and nature, was thereby preserved as exclusively male.[30]

Simon Ushakov, Icon of The Mother of God of Vladimir, or the Tree of
the Muscovite State (1668) with Tsar Aleksei Mikhailovich, Tsaritsa Mariia
Il'inichna, Tsarevichi Aleksei, and Fedor standing away from the tree.

These associations with the continuity of divine authority remained central to political ideology in Peter's time. When panegyrics deemed Peter "the new Constantine," or "the new Vladimir,"—just as they had done for his father—they were claiming something much more for him: the mantle of godly kingship dating back directly to King David (with whom he was sometimes compared as well).[31] Nearly everyone who visited the Muscovite court came away with the same impression. Thus, Jacques Margeret, the French soldier of fortune who became embroiled in the Time of Troubles, observed in 1606, "This word *tsar'*, they say, is found in the Holy Scripture. Everywhere mention is made of David or of Solomon or of other kings, they are called *Tsar'* David, *Tsar'* Solomon. . . . Thus they keep for themselves the more authentic name of *tsar'* with which God was pleased to honor David, Solomon, and others ruling over the house of Judah and Israel in olden times."[32]

That Margeret had a less than perfect understanding of the etymology of "tsar'" is apparent, but in this case less salient than his reportage of the conventional understanding as conveyed to him by unnamed interlocutors. They *believed* that "tsar'" was reserved for Russian and biblical kings, even if that belief was wrong. This didactic use of precedence simultaneously revealed the virtue of the reigning monarch and the Christian essence of his greatness, its placement in the epochal cycles of God's time: what God ordained before he is ordaining again and, implicitly, will ordain in the future, thereby setting the stage for a succession of new Peters. Peter became what Strong has termed "the terrestrial reflection" of heroic and godly exemplars.[33] In the eyes of some he also became the head of a divinely sanctioned state religion.[34]

The determination to insist that female rule, much like all the rest of Peter's acts of cultural discontinuity, followed the paths trod by spiritual forebears permeated these texts. Such a strategy was in itself quite familiar. Russia's rulers had long ago learned the value of retrospective revisionism, as for example in the Moscow Nikon Chronicle's insistence that Ivan III's annexation of Novgorod during the 1470s merely continued a relationship dating back to Riurik. "'People of Novgorod, your land is my patrimony, and so it was beginning with our grandfathers and forefathers, since the time of Vladimir.'"[35] Making the case—any case—for Catherine required an equal measure of historical imagination, since within Russian worship biblical kingship was always masculine, and this was how Russian texts had always presented it. Zhivov and Boris Uspenskii's seminal essay, "Tsar' i Bog" ("Tsar and God") has detailed the Muscovite variant of the "king incarnate" *(Tsar' tlennyi)*, which emerged in the sixteenth century and proliferated during the reign of Aleksei Mikhailovich, as simultaneously connecting Russian kingship with God the father and differentiating the ruler's carnal or this-worldly kingship, from God's eternal power as the king in heaven.[36] In their conception, the earthly tsar, or *basileus*, took on a special charisma that was parallel to God's and divinely ordained, but not divine or magical in itself.[37]

Fundamental to this Byzantinization of Russian kingship, as they termed it, indeed so embedded that it rarely required verbal articulation, was patrilinearity, the assumption that the line of political authority was entirely masculine. Mother of God was continuously invoked to bless and protect the king, intercede for him perhaps, but not to be the anointer of his authority. Nowhere did this cosmology create any obvious space for independent female political authority, least of all for earthly queenship. Recent scholarship, especially Isolde Thyrêt's *Between Tsar and God*, has demonstrated that such spaces did exist at the apex of sixteenth- and seventeenth-century Muscovy but that they were conditional on the presence of male authority and often conveyed by subtle gestures, occasional iconography, and fleeting images, rather than through formal or didactic expression. Thyrêt's chapter "Sofiia Alekseevna, the Tsarevna as Ruler" and Lindsey Hughes's biography of Sofia have demonstrated just how far this imagery could be developed, to the point of supporting the de facto rulership of Sofia, and her intermittent use of the term *samoderzhitsa* (sovereign) between 1686 and 1689.[38] In Thyrêt's words, "As intercessor for the realm, defender of the faith, or the House of Divine Wisdom, she essentially derived her mandate to rule not only from God's grace, as the tsars did, but from her contribution to the religiously constructed body politic of the stardom. . . . Rather than insisting on the traditional gendered notion of the stardom, they placed the regent on an equal footing with her brothers."[39] My own work has benefitted immensely from these insights, particularly through the reading of iconography, and in the absence of documentary paper trails, by taking subtle gestures seriously as keys to political understanding.

The Limits of Precedence

Catherine's situation in 1725, however, differed in critical ways from those of her pre-Petrine female predecessors. Most important was the irreducible fact that she reigned as monarch, both legally and formally, and they did not. She alone passed from consort to official ruler. She had had a coronation, and they had not. Even Sofia, whose regency arguably paved the way for Catherine by making de facto female authority imaginable in Russia, never was crowned (unlike her brothers) and apparently was not formally proclaimed regent. She ruled, as the aphorism goes, but she never reigned, despite the consecration of *pomazanie* and its attendant ceremonials. By that standard, Sofia's modifications of gendered representation of legitimacy were relatively few in number and subtle in execution. Poetry and iconography may have gestured toward an independent authority, but these subtle acts produced no clear doctrine of female rule and, more importantly, no ceremonial anointing in Dormition Cathedral. Divine images yes, but without divine blessings to which the elites could bear witness. And, of course, she lost in 1689, thus immediately depriving those gestures of female rulership that were linked to her of any standing. Finally, whereas the other Romanov women had the familiar and deeply inscribed spaces of the Kremlin to help shape their identities along faith-centered lines, Catherine's persona was situated mostly in the palaces, cathedrals, and streets of St. Petersburg, brand-new physical spaces that in themselves were devoid of familiarity and precedent.

Constructing the political identity of Catherine as female monarch, therefore, required a much lengthier, more careful, visible, and textual orchestration than had been true for earlier tsaritsy and regents, even though little or none of this orchestration anticipated that she would reign. Finding and then articulating feminine equivalents to the unbroken chain or living tree of Christian kingship took work and theological dexterity, and it demanded signifiers that the occasional court spectacles of Amazon warriors could not provide. However dramatic they may have seemed to the few courtiers and foreign residents who witnessed them, they did not fit into anyone's notion of Christianity or divinely ordained authority. It demanded nothing less than the articulation of a female precedent. Russian Orthodoxy venerated many female saints, of course, but very few as rulers in their own right, and certainly no Russian female saints, save perhaps Olga, were situated on the ladder of kingly lineage, as a new David or new Constantine.

At first glance, the most accessible precedent of religiously strong female figures within Orthodoxy should have been Mary, Mother of God (*Bogoroditsa* or *Bogomater'*) and Holy Sofia (*Hagia Sofia,* the divine wisdom of God). Mary, primarily as Mother of God but also as the Holy Virgin, dominated Orthodox representations of the feminine in every medium—icons, church names, akathysts, supplications, miracle tales, all of which far outnumbered representations of other female exemplars. Marian references were ubiquitous in political discourse (as in the Ushakov engraving cited above) long before, during, and after Peter's reign, by blessings, protection, and intercession *(pokrov, zastupa)* with God on behalf of the weak and fallen. During Tsar Alexei Mikhailovich's first marriage to Mariia Il'inichna, for example, Simeon Polotskii employed Marian references repeatedly in his panegyric verse *(virshi)* to the tsaritsa, in spite of the fact that her name day saint was not (and could not be) Bogomater', but Mary of Egypt.[40] The writings of Karion Istomin, Silvestr Medvedev, Stefan Iavorskii, and most other ecclesiasts of the day are equally replete with allusions to the Virgin as both guide and intercessor to the many Romanov women for whom Polotskii composed panegyric verse.[41]

Bogomater' was invoked repeatedly in prayers on behalf of Catherine I, just as it had been for tsaritsy since at least the sixteenth century.[42] Long before her coronation, Catherine was widely esteemed as *"matushka-zastupnitsa"* (dear mother-intercessor), an identity that permeated the contemporary writing about her, private and public. Petitioners, friends, foreign diplomats, boyar families (men and women), even Peter's own entourage turned to Catherine to intervene with her husband on their behalf. Thus, a song supposedly sung by the people awaiting the emergence of "our mother on earth" *(zemnaia nasha mati)* from the Dormition Cathedral in the Kremlin after the coronation deemed her *"zastupnitsa"* (intercessor) at least four times, and rhymed it more or less synonymously with *"pomoshchnitsa"* (helper), *"prositel'nitsa"* (supplicant), and *"predstatel'nitsa"* (representative).[43] No doubt, their enthusiasm was enhanced by the anticipated 15,000 rubles worth of gold and silver coins that the empress, much like her male forebears, would toss into the crowd.[44]

Clearly, Catherine's political role as intercessor and loyal helpmate to the tsar and as the earthly counterpart to Mother Mary had, by then, become well defined and deeply inscribed on her official persona. A "mere" intercessor, however, by definition did not rule in her own name. One could argue that the Marian "echo" (to employ Alexander Panchenko's term)[45] negated female rule in that the queenship of heaven on which it relied presupposed the presence of a higher male authority with whom to intervene. Just as Mary intervened with God, so too did Catherine intervene with Peter. Legitimizing female rule, so it would seem, required a holy antecedent, the veneration of whom was not bounded entirely by familial authority. A Russian Joan of Arc, so to speak.

After Bogomater', Holy Sofia was arguably the most well known and accessible example of feminized, if not incarnate, secular wisdom and authority within Eastern Orthodoxy. Elizabeth Zelensky and others have shown that the trope of Sophic Divine Wisdom was used extensively in panegyrics and speeches in the political symbolism of the 1680's.[46] In Zelensky's view, Sophic Wisdom marked an important stage in the depersonalization of political power, since "St. Sofia" referred as much to the ideal of holy wisdom *(premudrost')* as to the personhood of Sofia Paleologue. More recently Thyrêt has argued that panegyrics identifying Sofia Alekseevna with St. Sofia emphasized the "sacred virginal womb," book learning, bravery, and the divine image of the sun, many of which qualities would later be transposed onto Catherine.[47]

But Hagia Sofia occupied an ambiguous role in the Russian pantheon, even at the height of the Sophic cult in the late seventeenth century. On one hand, her presence in visual representation was extensive and quite ancient, as the eleventh-century cathedrals in Kiev and Novgorod and numerous icons were consecrated as "Holy Sofia, Wisdom of God." On the other hand, the fact that she was a depersonalized object of veneration excluded her from service books and the compendia of saints' lives that might translate ethereal images into accessible carnal experience and attributes. A. I. Nikol'skii demonstrated long ago that Russian Orthodox worship included no specific services to St. Sofia before the seventeenth century, and even then a debate raged within the church hierarchy as to whether Sophic Wisdom related to God, Christ, humanity, or Mother of God.[48] In the Petrine era, references to Sofia and Sophic Wisdom or Sophic

Economy *(Sofiia-khoziaistvo)* disappeared from panegyrics, just as the personhood of the monarch made a roaring comeback. One of Peter's first decrees banned the circulation of portraits of Sofia Alekseevna, a proscription so rigorously executed that they virtually disappeared from view until the 1770s.[49] This enforced hiatus from the political pantheon, which absence guaranteed that she would continue to loom large in her glaring invisibility, is entirely understandable in light of the violent rupture between Peter and his half sister and former regent (she died only in 1704). Seven years after the bloodletting of 1682 (the notorious Khovanshchina) that enabled Sofia to become regent, Peter finally vanquished his half sister in 1689. But this victory came none too easily, and Sofia's withdrawal from politics and into a convent was hardly voluntary.[50] To many both at court and among the armed regiments, her name signified an alternative—and for several years a living one—to Peter, an embodiment of faith against which Peter's reforms were forever being judged.[51] The risk that Sophic veneration could regenerate support for a hardly domesticated opposition, whose bloody eruptions during the 1680s and 1690s had included several boyar families, *streltsy* (musketeers), and Cossacks, rendered St. Sofia unavailable as an example of empowered femininity in Petrine and post-Petrine political language. The only exceptions to this veil of silence came from Russia's St. Sofia cathedrals in Vologda and Novgorod, where the Likhuds revised the *Prolog* and canticles in her honor in 1707,[52] and from within Novodevich'ii Monastery, where the presence of Sofia Alekseevna (or Susanna after she took the veil) made a deep impact. Thus, on September 1, 1708, a *slovo* on Sophic Wisdom (apparently composed by one of the Likhud brothers) was orated at the St. Sofia Cathedral in Novgorod, but never made more public.[53]

The bruising struggle against his half sister included a clash of symbols and textual gestures that proved helpful in undermining Sofia in 1689, but they provided powerful religious arguments against female rule that could only make matters more complicated in the 1720s. Ernest Zitser explains that the necessity of showing that the 1689 coup explicitly removing Sofia from power conformed to divine order led apologists to interconnect succession with traditions of patrimonial and patrilineal inheritance. "[It] held that elder daughters were entitled to a share of the patrimony in the form of a dowry and could even act as guardians during the minority of their brothers but could not assume the inheritance for themselves. The 'scepter of rule' could be handed down only from father to son."[54] This, he argues, is linked to the explosive Eucharist debate that enflamed the court clergy in the late seventeenth century. "Evfimii Chudovskii defended the practice of taking communion as a priest behind the closed gates that hid the altar from the laity during the Eucharist service—a practice that was explicitly modeled on the coronation of Byzantine emperors. . . . Since a woman could neither receive a Communion at the altar nor be ordained as a priest, this practice also ensured and legitimated succession by primogeniture exclusively through the male line of the royal family. . . . Taken together, both could be used to challenge the legitimacy of Tsarevna Sof'ia's rule."[55] What constituted a useful theological gesture in 1689 turned out not to be helpful thirty-five years later, when the principle of the male line (which proved malleable but relatively firm) was, of necessity, divorced from the analogy of the Eucharist and primogeniture (no small paradox given Peter's own legislation of 1714 on property inheritance).

The Heritage of Female Saints and Name Days

Beyond Mary and Sofia, late Muscovite-century Orthodoxy offered few obvious alternatives. The pantheon did include noteworthy female saints (Barbara, Eudokia, Anastasia, Tatiana, Paraskeva, and others), of course, most of whom Russia inherited from the Greeks. St. Barbara, for example, attracted widespread veneration in Russia, as both intercessor and healer. An early fourth-century martyr, St. Barbara's relics, legend had it, had been transported to Kiev at the beginning of the twelfth century in honor of the marriage of Barbara Comnena, the daughter of the Byzantine emperor Alexius, to Sviatapolk Iziaslavich of Kiev. In all likelihood such a marriage never took place since neither Byzantine nor Rus' sources mention it, and those scholars who have examined the record find no evidence that Alexius had a daughter named Barbara.[56] Nevertheless, the transposition of the relics onto Rus' soil, or the belief in their transposition, helped to generate a significant cult of St. Barbara within Muscovite Orthodoxy. Supposedly placed in the Mikhailovskii Zlatoverskii Monastery in Kiev, the relics became objects of veneration and miracle worship. In subsequent centuries, St. Barbara developed a presence in both popular and court religion, especially in Ukrainian Orthodox dioceses, and her cult generated several miracle tales, akathysts, and special prayers, of which several survive from the seventeenth century.[57]

But few female saints, outside of the sainted Byzantine empresses, had a transparent association with political authority that would have been accessible during Peter's latter years and in the immediate pre-Petrine decades. Depictions of St. Irene, the former Byzantine ruler, did show her with a royal crown as well as a saintly nimbus, as in the icon of the saints of the tsarist family painted by Simon Ushakov some time in the early 1660s.[58] Such images were not produced with great frequency, however, and they were not matched by similar poetic or homiletic imagery. Given Irene's association with the restoration of iconophilia at the Byzantine court, hers was hardly an example on which Peter would look kindly given his well-known and oft-repeated aversion to the proliferation of icon cults.

An alternative strategy, one that fell well within the accepted practices of faith and princely tradition, looked to name day saints as celestial exemplars of powerful women. One's name day *(tezoimenitstvo* or *den' angela)* was an important cyclical holiday in Russian Orthodoxy, considered more important and more likely to be formally celebrated than one's actual birthday at least until the eighteenth century.[59] They had come into Rus' at the moment of the tenth-century conversion, and they were prominent in the earliest texts translated from Greek. One's saint, formally assigned at baptism, linked every believer directly with the sacred, a union that belonged to both the eternal (the angels) and the temporal (the Christian calendar) and that was symbolically renewed annually on one's name day. Name day saints were, thus, familiar, universal, and preeminently Christian. One's saint automatically became one's spiritual guardian, or angel (hence the term "day of one's angel"). The possibility that a prominent person, especially a member of the ruling family, might take on the virtues of one's saint, to transform one's self into the living image of one's angel, was a widely employed trope of Orthodoxy, at least from the sixteenth century onward.

Within the Novodevich'ii Convent in Moscow (established in 1525), a resting place of many elite women, tsarist name day saints were represented prominently both in wall paintings and on iconostases. One pillar from the late seventeenth century included an image of John the Baptist specifically as the name day saint of tsars Ivan Vasil'evich and Ioann Alekseevich. Elsewhere in the chapel there were clustered images of several name day saints associated with the families of Boris Godunov, and in another section those of Aleksei Mikhailovich.[60] A mid-seventeenth-century icon painted by the court iconographer, Simon Ushakov, similarly celebrated the heavenly blessing on the ruling family by composing a scene of all the name day saints of the living members of the family (Aleksei, Irina, Evdokia, Anna, Sofia, Fedor, Mary of Egypt, Catherine, Simon, Tatiana, and Martha).[61]

In this way and others, the men and women of Russia's ruling families had celebrated name days for generations, and these celebrations grew steadily more lavish and somewhat more public during the seventeenth century, more baroque perhaps, engaging the entire city of Moscow. Although they remained thoroughly religious in ceremony, these days increasingly became opportunities to celebrate the entire ruling family, by demonstrating that the virtues of the individual being honored, male or female, simultaneously expressed the virtues of Russia's rulership overall, and for an ever growing audience. In 1678, for example, Bernhard Tanner, the Prague-born Polish ambassador to Moscow, described the name day (June 20) celebration of Tsar Feodor Alekseevich as a "large festival."[62]

> No one in any profession went to work, even though during holidays and Sundays people in other locations usually did work. From morning until evening there was such a drone in all the churches that those whose ears were not used to this had a difficult time hearing. . . . On the streets people came up to us offering greetings on their tsar's name day, and they respectfully informed us, that as a symbol of his particular warm feelings toward ambassadors, he had ordered that the joyousness of this festivity be extended

to us. In return the ambassadors expressed their gratitude and their wishes for blessings of all sorts, and offered highest praise to Heaven for making it possible for their presence on the name day. At about noon cooks arrived [in the ambassadorial court] with a food cart and other implements, and, while preparing the table, expressed the hope that the fare would be very good. Since it was a Monday we all expected that they would serve us meat. But when we saw that it was Lenten fare, largely dairy dishes (in all 200), seasoned primarily with flax oil, we lost hope.[63]

Beyond public spectacle, the veneration of name day saints had the added virtue of androgyny, in the sense that they provided both male and female sources of holy authority and intercession and hence a potential complement to the exclusively patriarchal construction of kingship. During the seventeenth century and then during Peter's first marriage to Evdokia Lopukhina, Saint Eudokia, the fourth-century Byzantine empress and the name day saint of the first Romanov tsaritsa, Evdokia Fedorovna as well as several other Romanov women, had attracted a good deal of attention in poetry, iconography, and homiletics, both as a venerable and pious nun and as a queen. Had Evdokia remained married to Peter, there is every indication that St. Eudokia would have been elevated to even greater political prominence. But the divorce put an abrupt break, if not quite an outright prohibition, on the veneration of St. Eudokia, and ongoing rumors about tsaritsa Evdokia's aspirations to power ultimately made her name day angel nearly as taboo as St. Sofia.[64]

For both Catherine I and II, the name day saint chosen after their conversion to Orthodoxy was Catherine of Alexandria, the early fourth-century martyr and bride of Christ. St. Catherine had long been a familiar presence on the Russian religious calendar, and by the mid-seventeenth century her iconic persona (lik or obraz), and especially her name day, November 24 in the Russian calendar, had grown important. Not surprisingly, her image became still more prominent during the eighteenth century, with numerous churches and chapels being dedicated to her, and ever more aristocratic women being baptized as Catherine, a name that had been relatively uncommon before then.

Without belaboring the obvious, both empresses had originally been baptized outside of Orthodoxy, and with different Christian names (Marfa and Sophie respectively) and name day saints. The name changes in themselves were not new. As Russell Martin has shown, changing the names of royal brides was practiced, if inconsistently, in Muscovy. "[I]n some instances the entry of the bride into the Terem was accompanied by her assuming a new Christian name. Thus, Ivan Ivanovich's second wife, Pelageia Petrovna-Solovaia, took the name Feodosiia in 1575; Tsar Vasilii Shuiskii's (second) bride, Ekaterina Buinosova-Rostovskaia took the name Mariia in 1607; Mikhail Romanov's first and unfortunate bride-elect, Mariia Khlopova, took the name Nastas'ia in 1616."[65]

A contemporary popular Russian icon of St. Catherine

Each of the Catherines accepted their new names as young women, when they converted to Orthodoxy, so as to be made acceptable brides for their respective Peters.[66] In neither case was the choice dictated by birthdays (Catherine I's was in April, Catherine II's in early May). Rather, they reflected deliberate decisions of those in power (probably Peter for Catherine I, and most definitely the empress Elizaveta Petrovna in the case of Catherine II), presumably to connect them with saintly figures fitting for the companions and future brides of rulers. This book, then, rests on the premise that the Russian Orthodox veneration of name day saints provided the inventory of heavenly images and pathways to divine sanction upon which the justifications for female rule came to depend, both at its unplanned and ad hoc advent in 1725 and with subsequent ruling empresses through Elizabeth. What virtues did the veneration of St. Catherine of Alexandria display during late Muscovite times to make her the choice in the eyes of prominent hierarchs for such an elevated veneration in the eighteenth century? And how were those virtues mobilized on behalf of female political authority and, later, female rule?

In Search of St. Catherine

Rather than begin with the rulerships of Aleksei Mikhailovich, Fedor, and Sofia, when a court cult of St. Catherine emerged in full force, chapter 2 goes back to the beginnings of her veneration, both for Christendom overall and for Russian Orthodoxy specifically. The goal has been to provide a reasonably complete archaeology of the layers of meaning ascribed to her over the centuries. Against that backdrop one sees the advent of a Catherinian cult and then, in chapters 6 through 9, its politicization and bombast during the last fifteen years of Peter's reign.

This line of research brings one face to face with texts (chronicles, iconography, saints' lives, religious ceremonials) and modes of scrutinizing them that may be common fare for medievalists but are decidedly virgin land for historians of the imperial period. Where historians of the modern period (i.e., the Petrine era and after) have the mixed blessing of sometimes voluminous documentary paper trails generated by a robustly bureaucratizing state intent on making multiple copies of even the most minute transactions, medievalists in the main do not have this luxury. In the end they all make inferential leaps, of course, but some jumps are longer than others. For this study these inferences can be subsumed in the interpretive category of "gestures," defined as significant affinities that are deduced not from direct documentation but from political context. Such a strategy has become relatively common in historical iconography, as historians have endeavored increasingly to read visual materials as texts in themselves rather than as illustrations of points developed verbally. Only very seldom do icon painters or their patrons leave verbal traces of their motives or reasons for depicting a saint in a certain way or for juxtaposing specific saints in wall paintings *(rospisi)*, iconostases, or triptychs. It is only as gestures, therefore, that one can hope to ascribe meaning to them, whether as authorial intention, discourse, or as reception. Since visual texts were primary means for displaying the qualities of St. Catherine's holiness to Muscovite and imperial believers, this style of reading defines much of the argumentation for this book.

As important as the visual is, though, it ranks second to the meaning of names. A fundamental assumption underlying this entire project is the proposition that the assignation of "Catherine" or "St. Catherine" had political and cultural meaning, at least through the early eighteenth century. When a church, monastery, or chapel was consecrated in a saint's name, that act, presumably, constituted a conscious choice open to analysis and interpretation. So too was the naming of a daughter "Catherine" in an elite Muscovite family or the interpolation of St. Catherine or a church of St. Catherine in a chronicle account, in particular when added well after the fact (see, for example, the discussion of Vasilii III's deathbed soliloquy in chapter 3). The meaning, though, is never fixed or a priori, and it is never didactically explained in the texts themselves. Thus, the explication of "Catherine/St. Catherine" itself depends very heavily on the idea of gestures, situated within the text in thickly described contexts.

Although it relies very extensively on the language of encomia to St. Catherine, this query must begin with a caveat against placing too much emphasis on the specific biographical details of individual saintly vitae. Russian panegyrics and saints' lives made widespread use of the *mineia obshchaia,* or *The General Menaion,* a single and remarkably stable volume that might well be termed the Orthodox guide to the rhetoric of piety. Although apparently unknown among Greek manuscripts,[67] the *mineia obshchaia* had a long history in Rus', dating back centuries before the advent of print, although apparently not quite to the earliest East Slavic Christian texts.[68] With the establishment of the *pechatnyi dvor* in the early seventeenth century, the *obshchaia* became the menology of choice, circulating far more widely (at least fourteen Muscovite printings during the seventeenth century, with a combined run of 19,000 copies) than any of the other menologic texts.[69]

Often characterized as the poor parish's substitute for the expensive and multi-volume compendium of saints' lives, *chet'i minei,* the *obshchaia* was also intended for use as a supplement to the more abbreviated collection, *mineia mesiachnaia,* when the volume containing the *mesiachnaia* did not include a vita for the saint in question, a not infrequent occurrence given the proliferation of local saints.[70] In the place of biographically specific services, it provided templates of services and liturgical insertions in place of vitas, a ready-made body of hagiographic qualities in approximately twenty categories of saintly personae *(liki).* Among these were distinct guides to the praise of individual martyrs, groups of martyrs, martyred saints, and saintly monastic or "venerated" individuals, both martyred and non-martyred. Each of these was further differentiated by gender.

All individual martyrs, male and female, earned prayers for the blessings of the prophets and angels, and all were valorized for their steadfast commitment to faith in the face of corporal torment. A prayer for lay male martyrs proclaims: "Although the cruel tyrant gave thee over to be subjected to the most painful tortures . . . thou, O God-mindful [saint] didst not renounce Christ, neither did thou sacrifice unto idols."[71] Such language could apply equally to men and women. But women alone could bear the identity of "bride in the blood of Christ" *(zhenikha Khristosa kroviu)*. Both male and female martyrs drew praise for their wisdom, but only women, whoever they were and from whatever category of saintliness they emerged, were valorized at length for their chastity. And only female martyrs underwent gender transcendence, both by overcoming their feminine weaknesses to endure hardships for their faith, as bravely as would men, and by demonstrating "masculine wisdom" *(muzhemudrost')*.[72]

> Bearing in thy feminine body manly wisdom of the mind, thou, O glorious one, hast disdained the beasts that are in waters.
>
> Having manfully and wisely stood in thy mind against the rage of the tormentor and his insolent harshness, thou, O God-wise one, foresawest the ever and immovably abiding unto the ages delights of the future.
>
> Having adorned thy soul with the beauties of virginity and with the blood of martyrdom, thou hast, O glorious martyr (mentioned by name), handed thyself over unto thy Maker Who doth indeed preserve thee in incorruption for ever . . .
>
> Tied to the wheels, torn by ferocious beasts, tortured both by fire and water, having sharpened thy mind with the Divine Spirit, thou has manfully smothered the prince of darkness with the rush of thy blood and hast passed over unto the intellectual palaces, bringing unto thy Bridegroom, O Virgin, martyrdom as thy marriage portion.
>
> Having been sanctified with the blood of the Bridegroom, even Christ, thou hast, O most laudable one, adorned with thine own blood the garment of flesh; . . . Him supplicate that may be delivered from corruption and dangers those who in faith celebrate thine all-honoured memory.[73]

Caroline Walker Bynum has argued that "it is male biographers who describe women as 'virile' when they make religious progress. To men, women reverse images and 'become men' in renouncing the world."[74] As will be seen, the Russian St. Catherine and her living namesakes often took on decidedly masculine properties of bravery and reason in the writings of—invariably male—clerics, just as prescribed in the *obshchaia*. These were seen as enabling them to transcend their natural sex, but never quite getting to the point of becoming allegorical men. This formulation was reminiscent of Julian of Norwich, who maintained that her intellectual prowess was achieved in spite of her sex.[75] These literary formulations are important and they deserve attention, so long as one does not lose sight of their prescribed and formulaic phraseology.

Sainted nuns also were endowed with personal strength, a love for God, and an honest blessed femininity *("blagozhennaia chestnaia")*. As tonsured women, all had become brides of Christ when they took the veil, and they were recognized as such in their identities (*"prepodobnye zheny"* or venerable wives). But these betrothals derived from the veil rather than from extraordinary personal achievements, resulting in praise of their asceticism and their willingness to live piously "having therefore rejected the sweet things."[76] Instead, they were deemed "Bride [endowed with] a beautious goodness *["zhenikha krasnuiu dobrotu"]*, pure, and maternal." The service for martyred nuns *("sviashchennomuchenitsy"),* who "endured the breaking of teeth, cutting off of hands, feet and nipples, and being cut up by the lawless tormentors and suffering pains beyond endurance,"[77] elevated their standing as brides of Christ quite considerably. "What shall we call thee, O glorious one? A bride of Christ made illustrious through the beauty of virginity, an elect daughter of Jerusalem on high, cohabitant and associate of angels."[78] In contrast to lay martyrs, however, they did not undergo gender reversal, and were not praised as men or masculine. They struggled "incorruptibly," "invincibly," and "gloriously," but not "as men" *(muzhestvenno)*. Instead, their enduring femininity was repeatedly reasserted, made palpable through the opposition of purity and physical torment on earth, and their dual transformation into heavenly pleasure.

> Unto Thee, O my Bridegroom, I desire, and coupling love with the desire, I have given up my body unto torments for Thee, that I might find abode in the honourable habitations, wherein all the exulting abide.[79]

> First asceticism, secondly the blood of martyrdom, as an alabaster of myrrh, hast thou brought unto the Bridegroom, even Christ, for the sake of love, and as the reward hast thou received from Him, O wonder-worthy martyr (mentioned by name), divine and incorruptible crown and the grace of healing through the power of the Spirit.[80]

This subtle distinction between those who became brides of Christ, even as martyrs, by virtue of taking the veil, and those who betrothed Christ individually or biographically, through miraculous and personal intervention, would prove to be crucial during the late seventeenth century and beyond in feminine panegyrics, separating those Romanov women whose angels (Eudokia and others) belonged to a class of brides of Christ from those, such as St. Catherine, whose mystical marriage to Christ was singular and fundamental to her biographical narrative. The singular capacity of these brides to transcend their gender proved similarly crucial in the transfer of princely attributes from men to women in the eighteenth century.

Seventeenth- and eighteenth-century images of female bravery, wisdom, Godliness, and gender transcendence or reversal derived much of their phraseology directly from the *obshchaia*, not infrequently verbatim. Marvelously elastic, the generic language could be affixed to any number of saints, provided that what was known about the saint from the vita fit into the appropriate category. Sex was immutable, as was martyrdom, clerical or non-clerical status. The holy family, of course could not be adapted to fit living figures, and neither could the apostles. But otherwise the panegyrist (or his master) had the flexibility to deploy the hagiographic language provided by the *obshchaia* with what appears to have been considerable latitude. Thus, although the language of seventeenth- and eighteenth-century panegyrics often derived directly from the *obshchaia,* at times verbatim, there was still room for poetic licence to make the saint fit the living image, and vice versa.

Once these qualities were transposed from the martyr to her living image (Tsaritsa, later Empress Catherine), however, the particular biographical details of the saint became more important. These "facts" were set forth not in the *obshchaia,* but in the hagiographic vita, and by the seventeenth century the lives of saints were in print and changing rather little. It was equally important that there be a specific name attached to these virtues, and that the name be familiar and recognizable as saintly, since the entire exercise was intended to identify the living figure with someone whose holy martyrdom lay beyond doubt. Panegyrists could adapt these biographical accounts selectively and creatively, but they could not ignore them. Whether by coincidence or not, the life of St. Catherine, when the time came, provided an ideal template, a perfect angel, for the unfolding elevation of Catherine I (i.e., the *lik* rather than the flesh and blood human being) from consort to full political persona during the last dozen years of Peter's life. This symbolic reciprocity, in which saint and living image elevated each other to new heights of public veneration, encapsulated in microcosm the element of mutual reinforcement between state power and faith that characterized the exaltation of the Holy Family, the apostles, church fathers, and the angels in representations of imperial legitimacy.

Thus, although this study originated out of a curiosity regarding the religious explanations for female rule, and this remains the primary intention of the book, the process of discovery has broadened the focus considerably, both temporally and thematically. The object of scant scholarly attention in Russia, St. Catherine's presence began to emerge in all sorts of corners of Russian political and ecclesiastical culture, not just in the eighteenth century, but, more surprisingly, during the seventeenth and sixteenth as well. The tsaritsa's chapel in the Moscow *terem,* for example, was named after St. Catherine, as was an important monastery established by Aleksei Mikhailovich in 1658. The Muscovite court had extensive contacts with the St. Catherine Monastery in Sinai, and during protracted negotiations, it assumed a formal and exclusive protectorate over the monastery in the 1680s. Of equal moment were the various Russian Lives of St. Catherine and services to St. Catherine, both manuscript and in print, and their proliferation from the mid-sixteenth century onward.

With the onset of the Ukrainian, or Baroque, influence on the Muscovite court during the second half of the seventeenth and early eighteenth centuries, religious poetry and sermons extolling St. Catherine began to appear with regularity. Almost every poetizer or preacher of note, including Semen Polotskii, Karion Istomin, Silvestr Medvedev, Dimitrii Tuptalo (Rostovskii), Gavriil Buzhinskii, Stefan Iavorskii, Feofilakt Lopatinskii, and Feofan Prokopovich, composed multiple texts on St. Catherine, and these inform much of the analysis of the later chapters. Although many were written for the private appreciation of the ruling family, and hence remained in manuscript at the time, an equal number entered into print culture almost immediately. Most of these clerical authors, with the partial exception of Iavorskii and Lopatinskii, either directed presses personally, or they had an almost unfettered access to one. Polotskii, for example, had been given his own typography, the so-called Palace Press (Verkhniaia Tipografiia); Istomin and Medvedev had high and relatively well-paid positions at Pechatnyi dvor; Tuptalo had direct access to the press at the Caves Monastery in Kiev; and Buzhinskii and Prokopovich, as high-ranking clerics, all but presided over the leading presses in Moscow and St. Petersburg.

This confluence of original homiletics and burgeoning print culture transformed the landscape of praise for the tsarist family during the latter decades of the seventeenth century, both in tone and especially in visibility. It was one thing to praise the sacred womb of the tsaritsa in religious poetry seen by a select few at court, or to depict tsars on wall paintings (rospisi) in Kremlin cathedrals that were closed to all but the elite of Muscovite society. It was quite another to include such images in openly circulating publications. Even when the press runs numbered no more than a few hundred, once these editions made their way into monasteries, government offices, and private collections, the audiences became multiple, no longer exclusively familial or personal, and the cultural meaning was thereby transformed. No longer did one have to bear personal witness or to be granted special entrée in order to experience the majesty and power of the divinely ordained authority of living individuals. With such tools at their disposal Peter's clerical elite were able to bring their representations of St. Catherine/Catherine to the entire flock of believers, thereby transforming her from an object of court-based veneration into Russia's first female imperial saint.

PART ONE

The Saint

2

Vitae

• This chapter attempts to sketch the history of the veneration and cults of St. Catherine, and the sources upon which they were based, from their beginnings in Byzantium through the sixteenth century. The first half discusses the place of St. Catherine within Christendom overall, of which Russia was a part, and the emergence of St. Catherine cults in western Christendom. The purpose is to show how these cults evolved over time, how they added new elements to the standard vita, allowing for a fully articulated and multi-dimensional representation of St. Catherine by the fifteenth century at the latest. The second half of the chapter focuses specifically on Rus', beginning with the conversion to Christianity at the end of the tenth century and proceeding through the texts and images of the mid-sixteenth century. The purpose is to determine which features of the St. Catherine persona came to be featured in Rus' and when they appeared, and then to inquire how these compared to the patterns elsewhere in Christendom.

St. Catherine and Christendom

Honored as the patron saint variously of apologists, wheelwrights, lawyers, wet nurses, archivists, expectant mothers, sterile wives, dying people, maidens, Dominicans, school children, lace makers, spinners, spinsters, single women, students, theologians, philosophers, preachers, teachers, and scholars, St. Catherine of Alexandria's very existence is nevertheless widely challenged. Both Catholic and Protestant authorities have concluded that St. Catherine's vita was apocryphal, that such a person probably had never lived. The Presbyterian scholar S. Baring-Gould dismissed the vita as a "marvelous romance" founded on a "slender foundation," and the famous Anglican skeptic, Alban Butler, whose *Lives of Saints* gloried in exposing Catholic apocrypha, went even further, terming it "completely worthless."[1] In 1962 the Second Vatican Council drew similar conclusions, albeit in far more muted terms, and it included St. Catherine in the long list of popular saints (e.g., St. Christopher) whose days were withdrawn from the calendar, consigning her to the category of those for whom no clear documentation exists.[2]

Until rather recently western historians more or less agreed that the lives of saints, in particular potentially apocryphal ones, undoubtedly constituted inspiring guides for spiritual and ritual devotion but decidedly untrustworthy ones for biographical accuracy. In the words of the long-time president of the Society of Bollandists, the Jesuit scholar Hippolyte Delehaye, "the saints show forth every virtue in superhuman fashion . . . , they make virtue attractive and invite Christians to seek it . . . legend, like all poetry, can claim a higher ideal of truth than history."[3] Although not quite as skeptical of St. Catherine's vita as Vatican II proved to be, Delehaye did point out the fickleness of her many hagiographers and the elusiveness of her life.

> Everybody has heard the legend of the great St Katherine, whom her biographers connected with Alexandria, both by birth and by martyrdom. That did not prevent the Cypriots from annexing her . . . and this was contrived by means of a device that was as obvious as it was little creditable. Stephen of Lusignan asserted that he read at Famagusta the Greek text of a life of St Katherine, from which he learned that her father, the famous Costos, was not a king of Egypt, but of Cyprus.[4]

Within Eastern Christianity, however, the situation is quite different. St. Catherine remains today as a vital and unshaken object of veneration throughout Orthodoxy, and her relics in Sinai are considered both authentic and miracle working. For the revitalized Orthodoxy of post-Communist Russia the genre of saints' lives overall is in the midst of a robust rediscovery as sources of inspiration and guidance, both for ecclesiastical authorities and for individual believers. Enter almost any bookshop or kiosk in Moscow or any other Russian city and one sees numerous cheap paperback lives of individual saints, popular akathysts, or calendars of feast and fast days all bearing witness to the breadth of this resurgence. A stroll through the underground passageways of the metro confronts commuters with table after table of traders in icons, saints' medals and akathysts jostling with hawkers of other—decidedly more earthy—wares for the attention of passersby. Although not Russian, St. Catherine occupies a prominent place in this revival, featured in virtually every recent Russian-language compendium of saints' lives and holidays and available in most of the metro kiosks that sell icon reproductions or popular prints.[5]

Where, then, and on what basis did the enduring cult of St. Catherine originate? The apparent foundational source from which the later vitae or legends evolved is a brief passage in the mid-fourth century *History of the Church from Christ to Constantine* by Eusebius in which the author offers an extended lament over the fates of the early fourth-century martyrs of Egypt, particularly the women: "As for the women, schooled by the divine word, they showed themselves as manly as the men. Some underwent the same ordeals as men, and shared with them the prize of valor; others, when dragged away to dishonor, gave up their souls to death rather than their bodies to dishonor."[6]

The manliness of these women, their pious transcendence of the female body, soon became a hallmark of female martyrs, in Russia and elsewhere. Among these heroic figures one unnamed woman stood out, and it is she who, many argue, became the basis for St. Catherine: "Alone among those whom the tyrant tried to seduce at Alexandria, a Christian woman of the greatest eminence and distinction won the victory by her heroic spirit over the lustful and wanton soul of Maximin. Famed for her wealth, birth and education, she put everything second to modesty. In spite of his constant advances and her willingness to die, he could not put her to death, because desire was stronger than anger; but he exiled her as a punishment, and appropriated all her possessions."[7]

The name Catherine appears nowhere in the text of Eusebius, not even in the roster of Alexandria's martyrs that the author provided in an earlier passage.[8] The presumed affinity between the two, therefore, constitutes a retrospective interpolation and little more. The mention of a St. Catherine, so far as is known, can be dated only to the late eighth century, represented in several Coptic funeraries, and wall paintings in Naples and Rome, based presumably on an older oral tradition that has left no other traces.[9] The formal cult of St. Catherine emerged even later, some time in the tenth century, and the first datable and surviving texts of her life appeared only in the tenth, although there may have been written Lives or Passions a century earlier.[10] Simon Metaphrastes composed the first Greek life in the 960s, and this contained many—but by no means all—of the features of what became her standard biography, including the transposition of her remains to Sinai.[11] It is from this time that the first menologia, or calendrical accounts of St. Catherine's life, were written down, most importantly the *Menologium Basilianum* composed for the emperor Basil at the very end of the tenth or beginning of the eleventh century.[12]

The martyr Aikaterina was the daughter of a rich and noble chieftan of Alexandria. She was very beautiful, and being at the same time highly talented, she devoted herself to Grecian literature, and to the study of the language of all nations, and so became wise and learned. And it happened that the Greeks held a festival in honor of their idols; and seeing the slaughter of the animals, she was so greatly moved that she went to the King Maximinus and expostulated with him in these words: "Why hast thou left the living God to worship lifeless idols?" But the emperor caused her to be thrown into prison, and to be punished severely. He then ordered fifty orators to be brought, and bade them reason with Aikaterina, and confute her, threatening to burn them all if they should fail to overpower her. The orators, however, when they saw themselves vanquished, received baptism, and were burnt forthwith. She, on the contrary, was beheaded.[13]

Once put to paper (or parchment), her vita quickly expanded to become a more fully developed narrative, adding an ever growing list of biographical details and experiences. In this expanded form the vita spread widely and rapidly throughout Christendom, west and east. Her martyrdom, or *passio*, appeared in numerous extant compendia, such as the *Codex Palatinus*, from the eleventh and twelfth centuries, in both Greek and Latin, and in images and references throughout the Christian world.[14] By the thirteenth century major cults of St. Catherine had taken root in Germany, Italy, England, and France.[15]

Who, then, was this saint? Her life, or at least her nineteenth year, is described at some length in all the appropriate general collections of saints' lives, most importantly the *Acta Sanctorum* of the Bollandistes[16] and *The Golden Legend* of Jacobus de Voragine.[17] In the early fifteenth century John Capgrave, the prior of the Austin Friary, wrote a remarkable and widely read full-length biography in verse of St. Catherine, undeterred by the complete void of authentic sources and facts.[18] Nominally based upon a Latin translation of the mythical Ur text of St. Catherine, the undiscovered *Life of St. Catherine* by her contemporary and putative disciple, the future St. Athanasios (patriarch of Alexandria), Capgrave's biography reproduces (and often embellishes) nearly every legend affixed to St. Catherine, including many that were of relatively recent vintage.[19]

The primary outlines are these: Born to either a noble or royal family of Alexandria between the late third and mid-fourth century (most versions say her father was the aforementioned King Costus, but a few texts from medieval England make her out to be the daughter of Constantine the Great, while others claim that Costus was Constantine's half brother[20]), Catherine was converted to Christianity by a sacred vision. Most accounts maintain that she was secretly and mysteriously wed to Christ shortly thereafter, but some place the betrothal later, and others omit it entirely. At age eighteen, she presented herself to Emperor Maximinus, as in the St. Basil's version, or to his son Maxentius, the rival whom Constantine defeated in uniting the empire, as in most of the later versions. Still other vitae identify her tormentor as another eastern emperor from this era, Maximus.

This type of impreciseness is quite common in the lives of ancient saints, and Delehaye long ago cautioned against taking chronology or the names of the oppressing emperors literally. "No distinction is made between the emperors who ordered or those who allowed proceedings against Christians . . . they are all *impiisimus,* whether it be Nero, Decius or Diocletian, Trajan, Marcus Aurelius or Alexander Severus. All are equally inspired by the same insane hatred of Christianity, none has any concern but to destroy it."[21] By contrast, Katherine Lewis has emphasized that "the legend is firmly located in the period which saw the final demise of paganism as the primary belief of the Roman Empire and triumph of Christianity in the person of Constantine." Lewis also sees hagiographic meaning in the switch from Maximinus to Maxentius as Katherine's tormentor. "In fact, the legend of St. Katherine came to have special associations with the first Christian emperor. . . . Katherine's persecutor [Maximinus] was subsequently replaced by the more notorious Maxentius (Emperor of the West), who was defeated by Constantine in 312 AD and whose legendary 'bad end' was recounted in the story of the Invention of the Holy Cross."[22] In the end, almost all the lives written from the late medieval period onward did settle on Maxentius, and the temporal affinity with him and the Christian conquest of eastern paganism would prove fundamental to the subsequent Russian veneration of St. Catherine, particularly in the court cults of the seventeenth and early eighteenth centuries.

Irrespective of the name, the emperor was, as Delehaye rightly observed, invariably impious (as were all Roman emperors before Constantine, especially those who presided over the execution of Christian martyrs[23]), utterly evil, and, of course, male. St. Catherine chastised him for worshiping idols and for persecuting Christians.[24] In violation of his orders, she assisted in the burial of the Christian martyrs. Most texts credit her with secretly converting both the emperor's wife and Porphyrius, the head of his army, while others make no reference to an empress and, following Eusebius, suggest that the emperor wanted Catherine as his concubine or consort.

One of the earliest and most distinctive themes of the St. Catherine vitae was the valorization of her learning and intellect. Already in the early eleventh century the Passions characterized St. Catherine as being familiar with the most profound writings of the great pagan scholars of ancient Greece (the *Codex Palatinus* includes among them Hippocrates, Galen, Aristotle, Homer, and Plato).[25] Her grasp of secular wisdom in the service of her faith enabled Catherine to defeat fifty (sometimes more, sometimes fewer) leading philosophers or wise men (they, too, were always men) whom the pagan emperor had summoned in vain to refute her arguments. In the words of *The Golden Legend,* "albeit I was born to the purple and not ill instructed in the liberal learning, I have spurned all these things, and taken refuge in Our Lord Jesus Christ."[26] At first they were indignant that they had been summoned "for a trifling contention with a mere maiden, when the least of our pupils could have refuted her without effort."[27] To their surprise, the girl, touched by an angel and armed with the Spirit, vanquished the great men, who, in one version, converted en masse, and in another were immediately executed for their incompetence. Catherine was then imprisoned, subjected to a martyr's torture, scourged, starved, and condemned to death.

By the eleventh century the standard narrative had added a milling wheel (or, by Jacobus's account, four wheels), what came to be known as the "Catherine wheel" depicted in countless paintings and icons, an instrument of martyrdom studded with nails that would grind her to pieces.[28] Catherine prayed and through a miraculous intervention the archangel descended from the heavens, striking the wheel and destroying it. At this point the enraged emperor had her beheaded, and in most texts milk rather than blood poured forth from her severed neck. Angels then descended and bore her body to its ultimate resting place on Mount Sinai.

The Sinai monastery that has long borne her name and housed her relics dates back well before the first St. Catherine texts, perhaps to the late fifth century, but certainly no later than the time of Emperor Justinian in the mid-sixth century.[29] Its association with St. Catherine came several centuries later, possibly during the ninth or tenth century. In any case, the monastery did ultimately lay claim to St. Catherine's name and her miracle-working remains. Both the eastern and western church endorsed the authenticity of its reliquary, an embrace that took on great meaning throughout the Byzantine world, including Rus'.[30] Its carefully protected library houses some of the oldest known East Slavic religious manuscripts, most notably an early twelfth-century Psalter, described by Moshe Altbauer and Horace Lunt in 1978.[31] This early link with east Slavic Christendom would prove critical in subsequent centuries when the ties between Sinai and the Muscovite court grew quite strong.

This manifest layering and altering of biographical details and miraculous attributes enabled the remarkable elasticity and variation that has characterized the multiple modes of veneration of St. Catherine that have proliferated over the last millennium. From approximately the late eleventh and early twelfth centuries, a genuine cult, or perhaps a series of cults, of St. Catherine emerged within western Christianity, possibly as a byproduct of the Crusades and the growing awareness of the Holy Land in general, and Sinai in particular. Texts and images proliferated. English writers produced a burst of new accounts, what has come to be known as the Katherine group. In both England and northern France, St. Catherine chapels came to be built on hillsides so as to remind the faithful of Sinai and to function as nearby pilgrimage sites for local populations that had no possibility of journeying to Sinai itself. These chapels typically held im-

ages of the saint, to which people could come to pray.[32] The Dominicans
in northern Europe adopted St. Catherine as a principal patron saint in
the thirteenth century. At about the same time many aristocratic women
in Sweden chose the effigy of St. Catherine for their personal seals in spite
of the fact that few of them were named Catherine, owing to the rigidity
of Swedish naming practices.[33]

Most specialists believe that the audiences for this cult, and to some degree its prime movers, were women, both lay and clerical, and that from this
time forth St. Catherine became an intercessor specifically for women and
around women's concerns, at least in the western church. The proliferation
of rural chapels of St. Catherine in twelfth- and thirteenth-century England,
and the specific cult images that they contained, are taken as evidence that
women of lower status prayed to her to provide them husbands, to broker
marriages much as Mary had brokered her mystical marriage with Christ.[34] A
charter from Rouen dated 1084 donated land to the church "where the most
holy and revered virgin and martyr Katherine daily performs miracles and
her bones are venerated far and wide."[35] These were mostly healing miracles,
in particular curing sterility among young married women.[36]

A momentous addendum to the St. Catherine legend, the anointed
bride of Christ, has been identified by most of the scholarship as dating
from the second half of the twelfth century, a period that saw a sharp increase in cults of female saints throughout western Christendom.[37] The
earliest known tale of an actual wedding dates from a Veronese poem of
1251, "De Sainte Caterine."[38] This soon became a defining element of
her persona, leading to an ever more elaborate set of narrations of her
mystical marriage to Christ.[39] As expressed in countless subsequent Lives,
service books, and frescoes throughout Christendom, the mystical marriage took place through the intercession of Mary and an ever-changing
cast of other intermediaries at some time before Catherine's initial interrogation by the emperor. Against expectations and the pressure of her
family, according to the most popular versions, Catherine had rejected
numerous suitors, and finally she resolved never to wed. Only after
learning of Christ and then being introduced to him by Mary does she
embrace the idea of a marriage that maintains her chastity. Christ eventually accepts her and the two are wed in heaven in a mystical ceremony.
Thus, when confronted with the emperor's demands she responded that
she could be wed to no mortal man because she was betrothed to Christ
in heaven. In the words of *The Golden Legend,*

> "Fix what I tell thee in thy heart, I pray thee," said the emperor, "and have done
> with thy dubious answers. Not as a serving maid do we desire thee, but as a cho-
> sen and potent queen; and thou shalt triumph with honour in my kingdom." . . .
>
> "Whatever torments thou can devise," she said, "delay them not, for I de-
> sire to offer my flesh and blood to Christ, as He also offered Himself to me.
> He in sooth is my God, my Lover, my Shepherd, and My only Spouse."[40]

This added element of her vita became a commonplace of her visual representation, both in iconography and in secular art, and the conviction that she had undergone an actual wedding ceremony with Christ elevated St. Catherine above other lay female martyrs. As Lewis argues, "This development served to confirm her as the most powerful and important female saint, setting her apart from even the most popular of the other virgin martyrs. Katherine alone was worthy to be selected by the Virgin Mary as Christ's bride."[41] Anointed thus as Christ's beloved, St. Catherine became the prototype for female virgin martyrs within late medieval and early modern Christendom and an object of particular fascination among the faithful, men and women. But the meaning of her martyrdom was far from fixed. At the most transparent level she became a favored intercessor to Christ for individual women. Beyond this, the juxtaposition of Catherine's beauty and innocence, ubiquitous features of the Catherine Lives, as against the wisdom, learning, and intellect displayed in her rhetorical mastery over the philosophers, has led some to see her example as an implicit threat to subvert existing power and gender relationships—the young and fair maiden challenging the emperor and defeating his learned philosophers.

This power of intellect became inscribed in the visage of what is sometimes called "the reading saint," a picture of the composed and virtuous maiden sitting in quiet contemplation with a book in hand. Literate pious women, it has been suggested, could look at the image and imagine themselves as saints.[42] This image could have provided a personal link between the individual woman reader and spiritual valor, one that hinted strongly at female autonomy and independence. The image of a solitary St. Catherine implied an absence of flesh-and-blood male authority over her, a direct link between the carnal saint and God's words. The more common pose of Catherine, book in hand, standing or seated triumphant over the impious emperor, shows even more vividly her power over male temporal authority.

In written form, the Katherine-group writers, almost certainly men, presented her as brashly defying male authority, thereby providing "inspiring models of heroism for women."[43] Karen Winstead and others have shown that the severing of heads or breasts and the miraculous flow of milk are commonplaces in the lives of female martyrs.[44] "This conventional use of body parts and torture instruments as emblems is not merely a coincidence, for the ordeal associated with a particular emblem often was not unique to the saint that it came to signify—Juliana, for instance, was tortured on a 'Katherine' wheel in some accounts, while many a virgin martyr . . . had their breasts torn off."[45]

In one sense these adaptations conform closely to the features that Caroline Bynum, in a famous critique of Victor Turner, associated with what she terms the social dramas produced when medieval men wrote women's lives. "In the later Middle Ages, it is male biographers who describe women as 'virile' when they make religious progress. To men, women reverse images and 'become men' in renouncing the world. . . . So, when we take our stand with male storytellers, whether their tales be of women or of men, we find social dramas everywhere, with liminal moments expressed in images of gender reversal."[46] Hence Catherine's own transitions, her conversion, her mystical marriage, valorous spirituality and test of faith constituted archetypes of the genre. So too did her conversion of the queen, officers, and servants at court, her life-altering intervention in the trajectory of their time on earth.

The St. Catherine Chapel of Abbotsbury Abbey, England (circa 1400)

The independence and defiance displayed in the Catherine Lives might easily have been read in unintended and subversive ways, however, by the very anchoresses or solitary pious women whom the authors were trying to enlighten and possibly restrain.[47] Examples of chastity and resistance to temptation were, of course, prescriptions for self-discipline according to the values of the church. Similarly, the attention paid to Catherine's role as an agent of conversion conformed well to preestablished roles for women religious. The comfort that Catherine drew from prayer and the angels, especially while in confinement, corresponded closely to the idealized role of cloistered women at the time. One manifestation of this cloistered ideal was the proliferation of convents of St. Catherine in western Christendom, particularly during the late thirteenth and early fourteenth centuries.[48] But the solitary and unregulated reading of what had become a multi-dimensional Catherine legend could have veered in a different and more individualist direction.

In fact, during the fourteenth and fifteenth centuries the venerations of St. Catherine and the shrines connected to her grew more emotive, less restrained, and often deeply personal. The elusive Sir John Mandeville wrote of a visit to the Sinai monastery some time in the middle of the fourteenth century, an experience he described at some length.

> There [on Mt. Sinai] is the church of Saint Katherine, in which are many lamps burning. They use olive oil both for food and lighting, and that oil comes to them as if by a miracle. For every year rooks and crows and other birds come flying to that place in a great flock, as if they were in their way making a pilgrimage; and each one brings in its beak instead of an offering a branch of olive, which it leaves there; and in that way there is a great plenty of olive oil for the sustenance of the house. Now since birds, which have no reason, do such reverence to that glorious virgin, we Christian men certainly ought to visit that holy place with great devotion.
>
> Into that abbey neither fleas nor flies, or any other kind of vermin of corruption, ever come, by the miracle of God and His Mother Saint Mary and of the holy virgin Saint Katherine.[49]

Mandeville's wondrous apparition of God, Mary, St. Catherine, and nature, all joined together to bring forth a series of ever recurring miracles, conveyed a sense of awe and joy capable, he imagined, of touching the heart of any believer. For some pious women, these recurring miracles involved ongoing saintly visitations whose outcomes were explosive and even revolutionary. The strongest and most obvious example of the latter is Joan of Arc, whose interrogations of 1431 are suffused with the presence of St. Catherine. Under intense questioning Joan revealed repeatedly that St. Catherine and St. Margaret visited her virtually every day, spoke with her, and provided guidance directly from God on how to be strong, resistant, and true to the faith in the face of the English assault.

> Asked whether the voice which spoke to her was that of an angel, or of a saint, male or female, or straight from God, she answered that the voice was the voice of St. Catherine and of St. Margaret. And their heads were crowned in a rich and precious fashion with beautiful crowns. "And to tell this," she said, "I have God's permission."[50]

> Asked what sign she gives that this revelation comes from God and that it is St. Catherine and St. Margaret who speak to her, she answered: "I have told you often enough that it is St. Catherine and St. Margaret; believe me if you will."[51]

For Joan, St. Catherine offered not just divine intercession but detailed guidance in her actions and a foreknowledge of their immediate consequences.

Asked if she knew beforehand that she would be wounded, she answered that she did indeed, and she had told her king so; but that notwithstanding she would not give up her work. And it was revealed to her by the voices of the two saints, namely the blessed Catherine and Margaret.[52]

Asked whether the world was painted on the banner she carried, with two angels, etc., she answered yes, she had but one. . . . Asked what this signified, to paint God holding the world, and two angels, she answered that St. Catherine and St. Margaret told her to take the banner, and bear it boldly, and to have painted thereon the King of Heaven.[53]

Joan of Arc was not alone in this ethereal intimacy. The autobiographical confessions of Margery of Kempe, the fifteenth-century English mystic and bride of Christ, which were dictated just a few years (ca. 1438) after Joan of Arc's trial, also referred to conversations with St. Catherine. "Sometimes, too, our Lady spoke in my mind; or it might otherwise be St. Peter, Saint Paul, Saint Katherine, or whichever saint I happened to become devoted to."[54] St. Catherine of Siena, who was said to have patterned her life after her namesake, invoked the first St. Catherine's name in her letters, as in one describing her demeanor while awaiting the execution of an unnamed young man, "I waited for him at the place of execution. I waited there in continual prayer and in the presence of Mary and of Catherine, virgin and martyr."[55] The seventeenth-century Capuchin nun Maria Domitilla Galluzzi saw St. Catherine as an ideal of single-minded devotion to Christ, after whom she fashioned herself as "a kind of post-Tridentine Catherine of Alexandria . . . [Maria] maintained single-minded devotion to her heavenly bridegroom . . . [and] she leaves no doubt that she would have been as willing as Catherine to endure the wheel in order to avoid being given carnally to a bridegroom of this world."[56]

Each of the examples reflects the personal bonds that these women developed individually within the larger cult of St. Catherine. Some offered solace, the comfort of private prayer rather than disobedience in the face of pain. For Joan of Arc and Margery of Kempe, however, the intercessory presence of St. Catherine inspired socially and politically transgressive behavior. The unifying elements for all of them include awe for her piety and faith-based courage in the face of physical force and torture; veneration of her chastity and marriage to Christ; and, above all, her capacity, as the bride of Christ, to act as personal intercessor between God and mortal women. It was through her that they heard God's instructions and knew that God presided over their fate. With her reassurance each of them confronted the pains and opposed the iniquities of this world with the full confidence that they would prevail over their tormentors in the kingdom of heaven. These also became the abiding features of her iconography and her widespread secular portraiture during the Renaissance.

A number of Italian confraternities adopted St. Catherine as patron saint during the late Renaissance, once again to honor her role as intercessor for vulnerable women. The Roman Compagnia delle Vergini Miserabilei di Santa Caterina della Rosa, sponsored by the Jesuits, catered specifically to daughters of prostitutes.[57] Its mission was to raise them morally and spiritually to be prospective brides, and the residents prayed to St. Catherine to help make this possible. Although carefully cloistered, each year on St. Catherine's Day they were paraded on the streets dressed in virginal white behind a large float bearing an effigy of the saint. Nominally a prayer processional to local churches, the display also presented them publicly to families of prospective suitors. One seventeenth-century Jesuit maintained that Ignatius Loyola had placed these girls under the protection of St. Catherine because "she is among all the virgin queens . . . so worthy a patron for . . . maidens to copy."[58]

These very elements—youth, virginity, contested female authority, resistance, the body, and the Catherine wheel—formed the core of the Catherine enduring myth as it emerged into the modern (i.e., post-Renaissance) world. Even when transposed outside of the faith-and-salvation-centered discourses from which she emerged and into the pulp and decidedly secular novels of modern popular culture, St. Catheriniana maintained the virtues of female bravery and independence, as the taming of the Catherine wheel inspired a momentary frisson of rebelliousness in otherwise orderly women. For example, the popular literary figure of a slightly earlier generation, the thoroughly correct nanny Mary Poppins, discovered to her delight that embodying and controlling the Catherine wheel constituted a small and light-hearted rebellion against social conventions, to which the gazes of men and children bore witness: "And at that moment, before the children's astonished eyes, Mary Poppins did a curious thing. She raised herself stiffly on her toes and balanced there for a moment. Then, very slowly, and in a most dignified manner she turned seven Catherine wheels through the air. Over and over, her skirts clinging neatly around her ankles, her hat sat tidily on her head, she wheeled up to the top of the shelf, took the cake, and wheeled down again, landing neatly on her head in front of Mr. Turvy and the children."[59]

One final piece of the St. Catherine mosaic, her regality, deserves mention here, even though it occupied a less prominent place in western iconography than the elements already listed. Catherine was, in Voragine's words, "born to purple," that is, her father was a king. Capgrave included many pages demonstrating how Catherine was descended from kings ("Here may ye see of what men and of what place came this woman, this lady, this virgin"), not just of Alexandria but of Rome as well.[60] Her inheritance was the royal crown, and Capgrave devised an elaborate coronation ceremony entitling her to be queen.[61]

Her royalty recurs repeatedly in her iconography, signified primarily by her pointed crown, and it became part of the inventory of saintly attributes available to the female crowned heads of Europe, especially those named Catherine. The courts in early modern Sweden and Denmark also employed her as a figure of veneration associated with specific women of the ruling family. She was closely associated with the English ruling family, as "an intrinsic part of the conception and practice of English queenship for the rest of the middle ages."[62] The wife of Henry V, Catherine of Valois, repeatedly invoked St. Catherine during her coronation in 1421, and Catherine of Aragon was greeted by a player dressed as St. Catherine ("a faire yonge lady with a wheel in hir hand in likness of Seint Kateryne") as part of the formal pageant when she entered London in 1501 to marry Prince Arthur.[63] In a ceremony that eerily prefigured several aspects of the courtly celebration of St. Catherine in Petrine Russia, Saints Catherine and Ursula approached the arriving princess and addressed her.

> I, Kateryn, of the Court Celestiall,
> Where as is joye and pardurable lisse,
> From whens all grace and compforte doeth and shall
> Always procede, for very love, iwisse,
> Am come to you, faire lady, sithe that this
> Into this cytie is your first resorte,
> To welcome you, ayde, assiste, and compforte. . . .
>
> And as I holpe you to Crist your first make,
> So have I purveyed a second spouse trewe,
> But ye for him the first shal not forsake;
> Love your firste spouse chef, and aftir that your newe,
> And thise rewardes therof shall ensue;
> With the secunde honour temporall,
> And with the first glory perpetuall.

This was but one fragment of a long and elaborate courtly pageant, but it conveyed the combined regality and intercession of St. Catherine, looking down as the bride of the king of heaven upon her namesake, the future earthly queen. Through St. Catherine, Catherine of Aragon had gained Christ as her first bridegroom, one whom she was instructed not to forsake even while wedding the mortal Arthur. In this way, she was a palpable embodiment of her celestial angel, who thereby provided a feminine and pure link between the kingdom of heaven and the Court of St. James. These very themes of saint and living image will resurface, and with far greater intensity, in the queenly cult of St. Catherine that arose in the Russian court under Peter the Great.

The Russian St. Catherine

St. Catherine probably entered Russian faith and culture as part of the original conversion of the Rus' in the late tenth century, or shortly there-after, that is, more or less conterminously with the emergence of the Catherine cult in western Christendom. That she emerged into Russian worship not long after her maiden appearance in Basil's *Menologium* at the end of the tenth century and simultaneously with the early St. Catherine cult in England, France, and Italy means that Rus' to some extent partici-pated, if not necessarily reciprocally, with the rest of Christian Europe in the early European elaborations of the St. Catherine legend outside of Byzantium and Rome.

Like the others, Russian Orthodoxy drew its primary textual inspirations from Byzantium, at first through simple translation, and subsequently through subtle and not-so-subtle adaptations. Prayers to Catherine were in-cluded among the very first transpositions of Byzantine saints into Russian consciousness, and supplications to her appear on November 25 in some of the earliest surviving Slavonic translations of Greek service books, specifi-cally a *Gospels* held by the National Library in Rheims from the first half of the eleventh century[64] and one of the manuscripts of 1095–1097 of *sluzheb-nye minei* analyzed and published by Vatroslav Jagic in 1886.[65] Although not a vita, the service for November 25 does include extensive prayers to St. Catherine, along with prayers to Pope Clement and Bishop Peter of Alexan-dria, with whom she shared the day.[66] These canticles constitute an evoca-tive and highly descriptive act of martyrology, and they assume, perhaps pre-maturely for Rus', a familiarity with the details of her life. They note her martyrdom in Alexandria and at the hands of Maxentius's ungodly power and false knowledge, her purity, divine wisdom, and reason (*"premudrosti"* *"bozhii razum," "premudryia dobryia muchenitsa Ekateriny verny"*[67]), virginity and youth (*"devitsa mlady"*[68] and *"Otrokovitse slav'na"*), beauty, and bravery (*"krepko i muzheski khrabrovavshi"*[69]). They offer prayers of intercession to use her mercy and to intervene with Christ to save their souls and to open the gates of heaven to them.[70] They openly associate her with Mt. Sinai and speak of the miracle that spirited her remains there. Throughout the service, the canticles refer to her as queen and as one who wore a crown (*"tsesaritsa,"* *"i ven'ts'm tsarstviia ven'cha sia"*).[71]

In light of the scholarly consensus on the advent of the story of the mystical marriage, it is somewhat surprising to discover in this service at least three passing allusions to St. Catherine as a bride of Christ (*"Nevesta sviataia, Ekaterino preslav'naia," "zhenishche moi,"and "zhenikh premudraia"*), which beseech her as such to open the gates of heaven (*"Otver'z priemlet tia v dveri raiskiia zhenikh premudraia"*).[72] These phrases are fleeting and they include no biographical or narrative content. Since many female martyrs and sainted (as well as unsainted) nuns were in some sense brides of Christ, these references could have reflected nothing larger than a relatively common generic use of the term without implying the specific mystical marriage that came to be a fundamental element of St. Catherine's vita during the thirteenth century. They conform in a general way to the phraseology of the *mineia obshchaia* for female martyrs (*"zhenikha Khristova kroviu," "khristos nevestu," "premudraia nevesta,"* and others). But the earliest recorded *mineia obshchaia* dates from a later period. Moreover, the early Slavic menologic texts contained very few such generic prayers in the services for female saints, and the fact that the phraseology recurs in three separate prayers reveals at the very least that her unspecified role as bride of Christ was of some importance rather early.

Mystical marriage or generic phraseology, the language of this service demonstrates that eleventh-century Rus' was drawing its images of St. Catherine simultaneously from the same corpus of Byzantine sources as the rest of the Christian world. The service also assumes, perhaps misleadingly, a preexisting familiarity with the details of the life of St. Catherine. This implied familiarity may have simply reflected the circumstances of its point of origin prior to being translated into Slavonic, rather than evidence having to do with Rus' per se. That is, the audience on Mt. Athos or in Constantinople for the Greek original may have been familiar with a St. Catherine vita, as were the Greek clerics who served in Rus'. The newly baptized flock in Kiev or Novgorod may well not have been, however. In any event, no Kievan-era *zhitie* of St. Catherine is known to have existed.

Once introduced, St. Catherine became a fixture in Russian liturgical worship, albeit no more so than other Byzantine saints of antiquity. Abbreviated versions of the name day service appear in several—but not all—early service books, including a twelfth-century November *mineia* and two twelfth-century books of canticles *(stikhirary),* and perhaps in other early manuscripts as well.[73] O. V. Loseva's recent study of early Russian religious calendars *(mesiatsoslovy)* shows that twenty-seven out of the 190 manuscript Gospels, Apostles, and *Obikhodniki* (canticles) from the late eleventh through the early fifteenth century that included the saints mentioned St. Catherine, albeit on varying dates.[74] Only in the sixteenth century do the Russian *mesiatsoslov* and *prolog* settle definitively on November 24 as her feast day, one day earlier than in most other traditions, including most of the other Eastern-rite churches.[75]

The primary textual fount for this service, in addition to Scripture, was almost certainly the tenth-century *Menologium Basilianum,* parts of which became known in Rus' no later than the early twelfth century. It is from this time that the earliest East Slavic *prologi,* or collections of abbreviated saints' lives, made their way into Rus', most likely by way of Bulgarian sources.[76] Whether these early translations included the St. Catherine text remains unknown, since the inventories show that the earliest surviving manuscripts all seem to be missing large sections of November. Thus, it cannot be stated with any certainty when the first actual St. Catherine *zhitie* appeared in Rus', or what it contained.

Those early service books that did include her disagreed on the date of her feast day, even though they all placed it in late November. This inconsistency, although not unusual, implies a certain lack of clarity as to who she was. Her initial iconography—or that which survives, all from Novgorod—gives a similar impression. The frescoes on the Church of the Savior (dated 1199 and built on the instructions of Prince Iaroslav Vladimirovich) included an image of St. Catherine in the bottom row on one wall, between Saints Timothy and Eudokia.[77] Placing her there announced to those who recognized her that she belonged in the pantheon of important saints and martyrs, but was not so important as to be placed higher, among the angels or church fathers, a celestial locus reserved for the most revered patron saints.

A twelfth-century icon from the Church of the Transfiguration depicting the apostle Peter and St. Natalia the Martyr includes a nondescript St. Catherine on the border, along with the Hetemasia, the archangels Michael and Gabriel, and saints Eudokia, Clement, and Nicholas.[78] Here again, her placement on the border implied a secondary level of reverence. Another Novgorod icon from the mid-thirteenth century in honor of St. Nicholas links him to the apostles and to the fourth-century Alexandrian martyrs. St. Nicholas is shown standing, framed by medallions of four saints, two on either side of his head. On the left are the martyred St. Athanasios of Alexandria, the putative author of the apocryphal early *Life of St. Catherine,* and St. Onesimus, the first-century Roman martyr, bishop of Ephesus, and follower of Paul. On the right are the apostle Judas and St. Catherine.[79] This image displays St. Catherine wearing a shawl or simple habit over her head, as would befit a sainted martyr who had taken the veil rather than the customary crown of rulership befitting such a well-born lay martyr. Although she holds a cross, there are no physical representations of her martyrdom, conquest over unbelief, or mystical marriage.

If even icon painters, presumably working under the direction of church officials, were less than certain of who St. Catherine was and why she merited veneration, one can imagine that she did not loom large in popular religious awareness at that time. Nevertheless, her name had become a presence in the religious world of Novgorod, if not necessarily throughout Rus', and at least two women from high-ranking families in the early twelfth century were named Catherine. The first of these, as recorded in the *paterik* of the Caves Monastery in Kiev, was the daughter of the mayor *(posadnik)* of Novgorod, who had married very well, becoming the wife of Prince Sviatoslav Ol'govich of Chernigov in 1136.[80] The second, also from Novgorod, is more intriguing. Her representation comes in the form of an illustration of St. Catherine on the last page of the so-called Panteleimon Gospel, a twelfth-century parchment codex. Here she appears standing in full regal attire posed next to St. Panteleimon, with the inscriptions identifying the two of them on the side.[81] Those who have studied this Gospel carefully have surmised that Panteleimon and Catherine were the patron saints of the couple for whom the Gospel was assembled. If so, this would imply a more elevated presence for St. Catherine than suggested by the surviving iconography. On the other hand, the name "Katerina" appears only twice (from the late twelfth or early thirteenth century) on the birchbark documents uncovered to date from the Novgorod region.[82] At the very least (and probably at most), these notations show that St. Catherine had penetrated the awareness of some urban elites already at the beginning of the twelfth century, although once again the evidence is limited to Novgorod.

Since traces of her in both word and image remain slight, it would be extravagant to postulate anything like a nascent cult of St. Catherine during the extended appanage period that followed the disintegration of Kievan Rus'. True, by the fourteenth century her abbreviated vita had become a standard piece in *prologi,* and it was included in all the subsequent manuscript and printed versions, as was her prayer service in all the *minei sluzhebnye.*[83] In addition, the first Novgorod Chronicle recounts that one of the temples destroyed in the town's fire in 1311 was a church of St. Catherine.[84] In the sixteenth century, Archbishop Makarii of Moscow made passing reference to a very old East Slavic homily on St. Catherine ascribed, like so many others, to John Chrysostom. There is good reason to doubt that such a text existed even in Makarii's time, however. It has never been found, and the attribution is certainly apocryphal since there is no evidence that Chrysostom had heard of her (hardly surprising if she never existed).[85] Catalogues of Chrysostom's works in Greek and Latin also fail to list any such homily. St. Catherine goes unmentioned in the various *khronografy,* such as the *Letopisets ellinskii i rimskii,* whose text O. V. Tvorogov has recently published, even though the reigns of Constantine, Maximinus, and Maxentius are discussed at considerable length in all of them.[86]

The St. Catherine that emerges from these early texts, although vague on specifics and falling well short of a full hagiography, remains generally faithful to the language of the *mineia sluzhebnaia* and to the prescriptions of the *mineia obshchaia.* A fourteenth-century volume of services for saints of the month of November praises her chastity and martyrdom, and concludes that all those who seek a marriage infused with the spirit ("I kto vsi syshyshese dukhovnogo braka") should pray to her.[87] A book of canticles from the fourteenth century included four verses to St. Catherine that expressed much the same sentiments.[88] A fifteenth-century volume praised her for her wisdom;[89] Canticles from the sixteenth century included the prayer, "Catherine, divinely wise martyr, let us pray to Christ to shine a light that my soul be led out of the darkness."[90] Another sixteenth-century prayer begins with the words, "Lord God in Heaven, hear me. I beseech your servant Catherine to pray for me."[91]

A nineteenth-century inventory of manuscripts held at the Trinity-St. Sergius Monastery in Sergiev Posad includes at least twenty-two St. Catherine entries from the late fifteenth and sixteenth centuries, and at least forty-one in the entire collection.[92] While hardly definitive, this relatively large number suggests that St. Catherine may have begun moving away from the figurative margins of Muscovite religious consciousness. A few of these entries provide marginalia that offer a small glimpse into what might have been taking place and specifically why individual supplicants prayed to her. A prayer to St. Catherine included in a codex of 1524 contained a passage, much like the one cited above, seeking intercession for the passing of a soul, a role that Russian supplicants were by this time applying to her more frequently. A hand-written notation at the end of the prayer concluded with the following plea, "Lord Jesus Christ, Son of God, these are our prayers to your most immaculate mother and to the holy martyr Catherine seeking mercy for your servant, the sinful and unworthy monk Galiseishko. Amen."[93] An early seventeenth-century collection of canticles apparently composed by Theofanes the Greek included the following reassuring inscription: "Whoever shall read this prayer every day will be saved from eternal torment."[94]

It is instructive at this point to compare these Russian supplications with the St. Catherine cult in the western church. They shared the idea of personal intercession between the individual sinner and God and they honored her martyrdom and chastity above all else. But Russia's individual supplicants (or those few who have left behind evidence of themselves) appear to come primarily from the monastic clergy, and all are male, rather than from the lay women religious of Britain and France who drew strength and guidance from St. Catherine. There is almost no trace of an appeal for healing, childbirth, and matchmaking, no recorded miracles, miracle cults, or local shrines, and only the one supplication on behalf of marriage. In short, Russia's veneration of St. Catherine may have emerged at the same time as the western one, and it certainly stemmed from the same literary roots and drew from a common understanding of her multiple saintly virtues. But otherwise the Russian cult was rather distinctive within Christendom overall—at least through the middle of the sixteenth century—less individualized, less linked to women, the carnal female body, or to the laity in general, and rather more closely associated with the individual search for grace and the salvation of the soul.

Notwithstanding the handful of inscriptions, then, the evidence for this-worldly personal intercession remains limited. So far as is known, there were few, if any, rural churches of St. Catherine and no Russian tales of miracle-working icons or visitations. There exist few manuscript akathysts to her, in contrast to St. Barbara, for example, for whom quite a few such texts survive (the overwhelming majority of akathysts were directed, of course, to Bogomater). Only occasionally does one see traces of something that might hint at individual intercession. A slightly later testament of 1653 by one Mikhailo Zakharov syn from Solikalamsk, donated an icon of St. Catherine to the Trinity St. Sergius monastery, a tantalizing but solitary hint of a household cult.[95] A peasant legend transcribed in the

Vologda countryside in the late nineteenth century does reveal a local miracle cult among villagers, and according to local lore the tale had originated long before its transcription by a regional ethnographer. But the tale does not suggest a personal intercession, and the transcription offers no clue to the legend's provenance or antiquity.

> Long, long ago, in a peasant field near a small hill by the mouth of a stream there appeared an icon of the great martyr Catherine. The peasants commenced building a chapel at that very spot in honor of the icon that had appeared.
>
> The first night of construction passed, and when morning came the peasants gazed upon a structure on the hillside, and they expressed amazement at the miracle. However, they continued their construction on the old site. The next night it happened again, just as during the first, and then a third time. The peasants thought about this and resolved that the hillside was the place that was fitting to God for building the chapel. And so they began to build it there.[96]

One explanation for the absence of intimacy may be that St. Catherine's vita did not include acts of physical healing or material uplifting among her miracles. By that logic, one would be more likely to turn to a healing saint during times of personal distress. Muscovites frequently prayed to Nicholas the Wonderworker to fulfill this role and—less commonly—to women saints Barbara and Paraskeva. During the late sixteenth and early seventeenth century local healing saints mushroomed throughout Orthodox Muscovy, often to the consternation of the new patriarchate. All of this provides clear evidence of the popular wish for supernatural intercession in bodily matters, an intercession that was not offered in the vita or services to St. Catherine. But the absence of healing tales from her hagiography had not prevented innumerable pious women elsewhere in Europe from turning to St. Catherine in personal supplication for healing, guidance, and assistance in childbirth, as the roster of groups for whom she has been patron saint clearly demonstrates. Western scholars typically have linked this role to the miracle of her martyrdom, particularly the assertion that milk flowed from her severed neck instead of blood. Sacred martyrdom was a part of her Russian vita as well, and it drew special mention in the hagiographies. The absence of a definitive healing miracle did not prevent St. Catherine from becoming a patron saint of Russian midwives from the early nineteenth century onward, summoned most commonly at times of difficult childbirth. And several nineteenth-century Russian hospitals for women and children bore the name of St. Catherine. In other words, it was not the vita per se (or at least not singly) that determined the trajectory of her cult up until the mid-sixteenth century but rather her relatively minor standing. To this point, although she was by now well entrenched in the calendrical cycle of worship, nothing in the history of Rus' had sufficiently linked her to important events or personages so as to elevate her in public consciousness.

Still, these literary gestures paralleled St. Catherine's slow and partial migration from the margins of Russian icons to the center. Judging by the surviving and catalogued iconography, St. Catherine was being included in a growing number of visual representations in Rus' from the fifteenth century onward.[97] Unlike the early Novgorod icons, these images tended to place her among a large group of saints and prophets surrounding or standing before the Savior or Mother of God. One late fourteenth-century icon from the Novgorod school now held in the Tretiakov Gallery in Moscow displays the Baptism with Christ on the throne *(deesis)* and six church fathers shown at the top. Around them on two sides are arrayed the visages of approximately a dozen saints, one of whom is St. Catherine, all standing by the River Jordan.[98] Another common placement is found in a late fifteenth-century Novgorod icon of St. Nicholas the Wonderworker, who is standing and holding a closed book in his left hand. Above him is a *deesis* with five figures: on the left stand Apostle Peter and St. Athanasios, in the center the Savior, and on the right Apostle Paul and Dmitrii of Salonika. Just below them stand St. Paraskeva (Piatnitsa), Archdeacon Stefan, and the martyrs Barbara and Catherine.[99]

During this time, St. Catherine is only occasionally portrayed singly or joined with just one other saint. An exception is a mosaic from Pskov of the second half of the fourteenth century that paired St. Catherine with another female saint, thought to be St. Barbara.[100] One other particularly intriguing image from this era is an early sixteenth-century wooden sculpture discovered in Perm. It shows a large carving of three female saints often grouped together: St. Paraskeva with much smaller figures of St. Catherine on her left and St. Barbara on her right. Both Paraskeva and Catherine are wearing crowns, and Barbara, who is frequently displayed with a crown, is here wearing a shawl and habit of a sainted nun.[101] The catalogues do not say what sort of structure (chapel, church, or cathedral) housed this sculpture, but the grouping suggests the possibility that a local cult of these female saints may have arisen in far off Perm. At the very least, it shows that the veneration of St. Catherine had spread quite far from the traditional centers of Moscow, Novgorod, and Kiev.

All of these images displayed St. Catherine with a crown, and several referred to her as tsaritsa, a clear indication that the crown signified both saintliness and queenship.[102] Otherwise, the images conveyed little from her vita or martyrdom, and they offered no obvious element that would signify a special standing above other saintly figures of veneration. Perhaps the first image in Rus' to afford her more prominence is a late fifteenth-century two-sided tablet from Novgorod depicting Christ's entry into Jerusalem. The back of the tablet presents her holding a cross with only two other saints, Merkurii and Jacob the Persian.[103]

An eighteenth-century wooden sculpture showing (l. to r.) St. Catherine, St. Paraskeva, and St. Barbara.

By the turn of the fifteenth-sixteenth century, St. Catherine began to figure more prominently in visual imagery, and on occasion to have images
dedicated to her alone. Several icons from Moscow, Novgorod, and
Kolomna conveyed her life through a series of scenes, typically about a
dozen, surrounding a central image of the martyred saint. Such so-called biographical or "life" (zhitiinyi) icons were well known throughout Christendom, and they constituted an effective medium of conveying selected biographical content outside of the liturgy and written texts. The appearance
of Catherinian ones as early as the first quarter of the sixteenth century
demonstrates, first, that the icon painters knew the details of her vita even
before Makarii compiled his massive Velikii chet'i minei, and, secondly, that
St. Catherine had become important enough to merit this kind of attention.

Perhaps the earliest of these is a shroud dating from the late fifteenth-
early sixteenth century from the Khutynskii Monastery in Novgorod. It
depicts St. Catherine in the center and twelve scenes from her life around
the perimeter, culminating with her martyrdom (beheading) and ascension.[104] A sixteenth-century example from Moscow presents fourteen
scenes of her vita, including her lecturing the pagans and the emperor, the
visitation of angels, the conversion of the philosophers, their subsequent
death by fire, Christ's visitation, and Catherine's martyrdom. In the center,
St. Catherine is shown standing before Christ, who is above her and to her
left, possibly (but not obviously) signifying the mystical marriage, and she
is adorned with a crown and royal garb. She holds a scroll on which are
the words, "Lord, my God, hear me as I pray to Thee. Yea, whoever recalls
my name Catherine in the passing of his soul from this world will be
brought forth in peace."[105] This prayer recurs in several subsequent icons
of St. Catherine.[106] Behind her stands the executioner, preparing to re-
move the sword from its sheath in anticipation of her imminent beheading. In front of her are people of faith on their knees, and in prayer.

This is a very powerful set of images, and it configures St. Catherine as a
central persona. Her faith, intelligence, spiritual intercession, and martyrdom are on full display here, the victory of divine intellect over pagan, as
well as her resistance to the ungodly authority of the Alexandrian king.[107]
What is missing or at least understated, as in most of the other zhitiinye of
this time, are depictions of the mystical marriage. But if this assemblage reflected an emergent cult, it was still in its earliest stages. Indeed, prior to the
mid-seventeenth century Muscovite icons only infrequently displayed her
alone, or in individual or personal juxtaposition with Christ. Far more commonly she remained as one of several martyrs in the presence of Mary, either gathered in prayer at her feet or following behind her. A sixteenth-century
Iaroslavl icon of the Mother of God of Kherson (Korsun), for example, included St. Catherine as one of five martyrs surrounding Mary.[108] A sixteenth-
century Moscow icon of Mother of God with a Golden cloth (pokrov) indicating her divine intercession includes many saints in prayer around

her and the Savior above. In the rear stand St. Catherine and Mary of Egypt, with Saints George and Dmitrii the Man of God observing them.[109]

How, then, does one understand her growing visual presence? The notes to the life icon with the prayer scroll suggest that the words on the scroll, particularly the phrase "in the passing of one's soul" *(pri iskhode dushi,)* connects this icon to the court, specifically to the chronicle account of the death of Grand Prince Vasilii Ivanovich in 1533 in which that exact phrase is repeated. If true, this is the first iconographic representation of a spiritual association between the saint and the court. A number of other sources also hint at a growing veneration beginning some time in the sixteenth century, most visibly at the courts of Vasilii III and his son, Ivan IV. Notable are the greater frequency of prayers to St. Catherine and individual manuscripts of her vita, as well as the occasional reference to specific churches or chapels of St. Catherine in Novgorod Velikii and Mozhaisk.[110] A chronicle fragment from 1563 also makes reference to her name day,[111] and a passage from 1582 in the third Novgorod Chronicle notes Ivan's gift of 500 rubles to "Mount Sinai for the Great Martyr Catherine."[112]

Perhaps the best illustration of this resurgence is the extensive vita included in Metropolitan Makarii's massive compilation of Christian history and saints' lives, the *Velikii chet'i minei* of 1556. In spite of its literary and ideological importance, the extant scholarship has uncovered precious little information regarding the methods Makarii employed or the sources he consulted. He began the work in Novgorod, several years before arriving in Moscow to serve as metropolitan, but his actual modus operandi is opaque. Even less is known about the specific motivation behind the compilation and the revised vitae, other than as a massive literary exercise and an effort to supply a systematic accounting of all saints authorized by the meropolitanate in the wake of proliferating local cults and rituals. Begun several years before the advent of Muscovite printing, the collection was far too large to be hand-copied in full with any regularity. Rather, clerical copyists transcribed specific lives, or sections of those lives, as needed and then recompiled them in bound monastic collections, or *sborniki*. Even after movable type arrived at the court of Ivan IV during the mid-1550s, the presses were too few and too primitive to enable them to publish such a monument. Who used it in the sixteenth century, and how, remains little understood.

That said, the *Velikii chet'i minei* contains quite a lengthy vita of St. Catherine, running to almost twenty column-pages and twenty-seven numbered paragraphs, far longer than any previous Muscovite account, and possibly the first full-length hagiography of her composed in Rus'.[113] Narrative girth does not by itself imply an elevated status for St. Catherine in Makarii's pantheon of saints, since the entries for most of the saints were considerably longer than previous Muscovite texts. There is no reason to believe that he paid particular attention to St. Catherine, or that anyone else did as a result of Makarii. Nor should one assume that her vita was read more frequently or attentively than before. Still, hers was one of the longer vitae in Makarii's compilation, and at the very least the narrative served as a thick textual resource that was now in some sense authoritative and that henceforth would serve as a new starting point for anyone who *did* seek to elevate St. Catherine in Muscovite worship, until Dimitrii Rostovskii rewrote the *chet'i minei* at the end of the seventeenth century.

This particular *zhitie* has generated no specialized scholarship, or even passing commentary in the existing literature. In the absence of an archival paper trail or careful textology, it is impossible to say what the sources were that allowed Makarii to write this expansive narrative. Two sixteenth-century *sborniki* from the Moscow Synodal library include *zhitiia* of St. Catherine of a similar length, and the first sentence in each of them is exactly the same as the first sentence in the *chet'i minei* text ("Leta tretiago desiat i piatogo tsarstvuiushchu nechistivomu tsariu Maksintiiu.")[114] Whether these two texts antedated or reproduced Makarii's text is unknown, but one of the Synodal texts and Makarii's, employing identical phraseology, identify the author as Athanasios of Alexandria, the apocryphal narrator of the Greek *passio* contained in the *Codex Palatinus* (number 4) as well as of Capgrave's *Life* written a century earlier[115] ("I mnogy videvshi proslavisha Boga, tu abie i az Afonasei, Borzopisets, rab syi g-zha sviatiia Ekateriny. I pisal sia pamiati rad").[116]

The similarity with the *passio* is surely not coincidental. The organization of the two texts is nearly identical, each containing twenty-seven sections, each citing the same dates and, introducing St. Catherine at the same point (paragraph 4 and then not again until paragraph 8), attributing the account to Athanasios at the same point (paragraph 26) and in the same way,[117] identifying the archangel Michael as Catherine's celestial intermediary (paragraph 10 in each), and praising St. Catherine for the identical set of virtues and for having studied the same roster of writers from antiquity. In many sections the phraseology is almost identical.[118] To give but one example, the first sentence of Makarii's *zhitie* is nearly word for word the same as the Greek.

Passio Sanctae Aekaterinae
1. Anno trecentesimo quinto, imperante impio et malo imperatore Maxentio, erat multa insania idolorum.

Muchenie Sviatyia Ekateriny
1. Leta tretiagodeciate i piatogo, tsarstvouiushchoiu nechistivomu Maksentiiu, be mnogo vl"khvovaniia kumirom.[119]

It seems very likely, therefore, that this *passio* constituted the fundamental antecedent, either directly or through an intermediary redaction, for Makarii. Makarii's version also bears a strong similarity to the organization and some of the phraseology of the St. Catherine vita (which, however, does not mention Athanasios) included in the fourteenth-century

Bulgarian *Bdinski Zbornik,* a Slavonic codex consisting of the Lives of twelve female saints and two other essays. The modern editors of *Bdinski Zbornik* have identified this text as a variant of the late medieval Greek *Passio* Number 30 reproduced in the *Bibliotheca Hagiographica Graeca,* a hagiography that itself resembled the *Codex Palatinus.* In any case, the basic source(s) for Makarii appear to have come directly or indirectly from this core group of medieval Greek texts.[120]

The account in the *chet'i minei* dwells at great length on Catherine's cerebral qualities, in particular her extraordinary rhetorical virtuosity. It begins with a lengthy description of the pagan rituals and sacrifices at Maxentius's court, among which was his command that his leading advisors *("boyars and voevodas")* present their offspring, male and female *("otroki i otrokovtsami")* at court. It is here that Makarii introduces Catherine. In her initial audience with Maxentius, she openly acknowledges her unparalleled learning and intellect, and avers that she has read "all the books of Virgil . . . , Galen, Aristotle, and Homer, and Plato, the Philistines," and many others.[121] She knows every word of seventy-two languages both spoken and written, and has seemingly mastered all available human knowledge. The text soon mentions that Catherine has already embraced Christianity, although under circumstances that the text does not relate, and is reluctant to enter into Maxentius's pagan temple. Makarii's account devotes almost no space to describing the mystical marriage per se, admittedly an uncomfortable element for medieval Russian Orthodoxy, although it does allude to its having taken place prior to the events described in the actual narrative. It also displays little of the physicality of other Catherinian vitae, both Byzantine and Catholic. Catherine's youth, purity, and chastity gain a good deal of mention, but not her vaunted beauty or Maxentius's desire for her. The wheel as the instrument of her martyrdom appears toward the end of the narrative, but the text says very little about the assault on her body.

Instead, it concentrates on wisdom and learning, Catherine's awareness of the inadequacy of knowledge born of humanity and the strength that all this provides her in her subsequent confrontation with the emperor's philosophers and then with the emperor himself. Knowing pagan learning so well, she is able to see through the clever fallacies *("prelesty")* of their reasoning. Already committed to Christ, she stands fearlessly before her adversaries and tormentors. Secure in her faith, she wins over the emperor's tribune, Porphyrios as well as the empress (paragraph 15), and thereby undermines Maxentius's standing from within.

These depictions of Catherine's faith and martyrdom, as cerebral, clear-headed, militant, and unshakably given over to Christ, were consistent with the visual images offered in the life icons of the era, even though the latter presented a more graphic representation of her martyrdom. Neither medium, however, gave prominence to her mystical marriage, although that too would emerge prominently in subsequent generations. This was now the

Early eighteenth-century Siberian icon (artist unknown) showing Christ (above) and (left to right, below) St. Antipa, St. Gregory the Theologian, and St. Catherine

Not terrible shiny

authoritative representation of St. Catherine for Muscovy, and it was one that proved increasingly attractive and accessible to the court over the next several decades, in particular when it wished to portray its own military campaigns as Christian crusades against unbelievers, as in the siege of Kazan, or as pious resistance against the armed forces of heresy, as in the Polish occupation of Moscow. In both cases, St. Catherine had become a politically useful saint, an increasingly visible element in the inventory of sacred symbolism available to the centralizing and increasingly expansive Muscovite state. It is from this political base that a genuine state-centered cult of St. Catherine would evolve over the next century and a half.

3

The *Terem* Chapel and the
Romanov Women

• The next two chapters explore the Muscovite veneration of St. Catherine as it unfolds during the sixteenth and seventeenth centuries. Both chapters are organized around specific consecrated spaces *(sviatyni)* and important historical events onto which St. Catherine comes to be inscribed. The overarching questions for both chapters are the same: how and when does the cult of St. Catherine come into being? The physical loci of the inscriptions are, for the most part, connected to the court, the ruling family, and the city of Moscow itself.

St. Catherine in the Field

Throughout the seventeenth century and beyond, Moscow itself housed at least two St. Catherine churches that merited the attention of eyewitnesses and historical record keepers. One of these, the church of St. Catherine in the Field *("na vspolie")*, was constructed probably in the late sixteenth century, but certainly no later than the reign of Vasilii Shuiskii. Recently reconsecrated, it stands in the Moscow river district on Bol'shaia Ordynka Street and operates, as it had for many years before 1917, as the parish church of Moscow's St. Catherine parish. I. Tokmakov, who wrote a brief history of the church in 1882, could not determine its date of origin, but he was nevertheless confident that it had existed for at least three hundred years.[1] Some accounts link its beginnings to Tsaritsa Irina Fedorovna, wife of Tsar Fedor Ivanovich and sister of Boris Godunov, who, they maintain, commissioned it to serve the recently established merchant community. Still others say that a wooden church of St. Catherine was opened there in 1611 and replaced by a grander stone one in 1657.[2] All of them agree that this church long held a relic of St. Catherine and several icons of St. Catherine. Its place in national memory, however, derives from the symbolically important role it is said to have played in Muscovite heroic lore during the latter months of the Time of Troubles.[3]

On August 24, 1612, the patriotic forces of Prince Dmitrii Pozharskii and Dmitrii Trubetskoi joined together to defeat forces loyal to the Polish hetman Jan Karol Chodkiewicz. These latter forces had moved out of the church of St. Clement on a small square between Piatnitskaia and Ordynka streets and, according to one version, barricaded themselves in the St. Catherine church. The *Novyi letopisets,* an early seventeenth-century chronicle devoted to the reign of Fedor Ivanovich and the Time of Troubles, described a major battle in which the patriotic forces of Kuzma Minin and Pozharskii aligned against the Lithuanian hetman. As a way of orienting the readers both in space and time, the account spoke of the Muscovite forces decamping on August 24, the Day of St. Peter the Metropolitan, by the Moscow River at the Church of St. Catherine.[4] They set up a fortification by the Church of St. Clement, "the Roman Pope," and fearing a bad outcome (implicitly because of the association with Catholicism, the faith of the Poles), they erected a temporary field church in the name of the Mother of God, the apostle and evangelist John the Theologian, and Metropolitan Peter, the Muscovite Wonderworker, and they wept and prayed that God deliver the Muscovite state from those who would destroy it. Eventually, they succeeded in driving the hetman and his forces out of the church.

Regardless of whether the author added the reference without self-consciousness or included it in order to draw wider attention to a newly politicized saint, it shows that the image of St. Catherine had begun to loom somewhat larger in political discourses of the sixteenth and early seventeenth centuries. Avraam Palitsyn, the famous monk-warrior of the Trinity-St. Sergius Monastery and a participant in the event, characterized the battle of St. Catherine's church as both fierce and decisive ("Prispeshivshim zhe vsem kazakom ko obozu u velikomuchenitsy khristovy Ekateriny, i byst' boi velik zelo i preuzhesen; surovo i zhestoko napadoshia kazaki na voisko litovskoe"), leading to many casualties among the enemy forces.[5] In the view of one nineteenth-century scholar, this battle marked the beginning of Moscow's liberation from Polish occupation.[6] However apocryphal the story may be, there is no doubt that serious battles took place at this time. August 1612 came to be accepted, both by eyewitnesses and later chroniclers, as the moment in which the combined militias dislodged Chodkiewicz and the Polish forces from much of Moscow.

Interestingly, both the chronicles and Palitsyn characterized the course of these events primarily in secular terms. None of the decisive victories were deemed miraculous in themselves. The Muscovites prayed to God, removed themselves from the church of the Roman pope, and wept for victory, but the deliverance, as described in the sources, came from their own forces in the field of battle. No divine signs appeared to them, and no holy shrines were constructed on the site or claims of divine or miraculous intervention asserted after the fact. Equally noteworthy was the decision to pray directly to God rather than to an intercessor. The impromptu field church summoned the Mother of God, St. John, and Peter the Metropolitan to join St. Catherine in bearing special witness to the battle, an implied gesture toward intercession perhaps. But this fell short of the direct supplications associated with *zastupa* and *pokrov*. The authors of these texts, then, chose to interpolate St. Catherine's church into their text, but without explicitly granting it—or her—miraculous agency.

Still, there was no doubt in their minds that final victory demonstrated God's favor on the Muscovites. Virtually all the texts of the era understood the Troubles apocalyptically, as divine retribution for Muscovy's sins, especially those of Boris Godunov, the widely rumored assassin of Tsarevich Dmitrii several years earlier. The liberation of Moscow, in particular the cleansing of the occupying infidel armies from the city's consecrated spaces (churches, monasteries, the Kremlin), demonstrated God's forgiveness, if not necessarily his miraculous intervention. From that perspective, the specific sites of liberation (or those so inscribed after the fact) were neither accidental nor incidental. If God had punished Muscovy because of Boris Godunov, then the choice of a church of St. Catherine formerly associated with Godunov's sister (and through her Boris's insinuation into the ruling Danilovich family) as a locus of deliverance could easily be read as wiping the slate clean, a purge in the most literal sense. Within the holy narrative, then, St. Catherine became the sacred vessel (or one of them), God's chosen angel of deliverance on this particular day at this decisive battle. As a site linked with the triumphant end of the Time of Troubles and the rise of a new dynasty, this St. Catherine's church became a frequent recipient of tsarist largesse, receiving numerous gifts from the Romanov family throughout the seventeenth century and even beyond.[7]

Even well after the court moved to St. Petersburg, the ruling family maintained an interest in the church in the fields, granting it substantial gifts and enlarging it. In January 1621 the young tsar, Mikhail Fedorovich, gave alms to a few prominent Moscow churches in memory of the deceased overseer of the state treasury, Mikifor Vasil'evich Trakhaniotov, and one of the churches was St. Catherine's.[8] By the mid-1650s, a stone church replaced the original wooden edifice (which had been destroyed at least twice by fire and warfare), and over a century later a newly crowned Catherine II had the church completely redesigned by the empress's favored Moscow architect, Karl Blank, and given a new iconostasis. The new church in the fields was consecrated in September 1767, at a time when most of the court could only take note since many of its members, including the empress, had moved temporarily to Moscow to preside over the Commission on a New Law Code.

The Household Chapel

Of far greater significance was the association of St. Catherine with the tsaritsa's private church (sometimes termed the *terem* chapel) in the household quarters *(Bol'shoi dvorets)* of the Kremlin. Begun according to some accounts in 1536, the wooden chapel was dedicated on January 8 (O.S.), 1587, possibly but not incontrovertibly already as the Church of St. Catherine.[9] After being destroyed in the Kremlin fire of 1627, the church was rebuilt in stone within the Bol'shoi dvorets by the English architect John (Taller) Taylor. Reconsecrated by the patriarch in the presence of the ruling family, the church was formally named (or perhaps reconfirmed) the St. Catherine chapel on November 17, 1627, as recorded in the *dvortsovye razriady,* the more or less official records of proceedings at the Muscovite court dating from the reign of Boris Godunov.[10] The wave of reconstruction included a second smaller private chapel of St. Evdokia, named in honor of Tsaritsa Evdokia Luk'ianovna, which stood just above St. Catherine's. Opened and consecrated at the same time as the rebuilt St. Catherine's, it seems not to have had its official dedication until 1654[11]. Within close proximity to the *terem,* the private quarters of the Romanov women, these two chapels and their shared refectory *(trapeza)* were intended for frequent use, and were thus fairly sizable and ornate for private chapels. St. Catherine's measures approximately seventy feet by twenty-one feet (ten *sazhen* by three *sazhen*), with a well-designed iconostasis that was initially created and periodically redone by a large staff of well-regarded artists and craftsmen, including the seventeenth-century court icon painter Simon Ushakov and his workshop of nine apprentices.[12] The church had a permanent clerical staff that grew from five in the early years to eleven in the 1690s.[13] It maintained its own choir and it served as the household chapel for more than a century.[14]

By the 1640s, the St. Catherine church had emerged preeminent as the chapel of choice for the Romanov women, attended far more frequently in the second half of the century than St. Evdokia's. The new tsar, Aleksei Mikhailovich, spent more time there than his father, and he took a more active role in prayer services there. The accounting books of the Secret Chancery show a regular flow of cash from the court to the St. Catherine church, to pay for repairs, vestments, new icons, and the like.[15] Individual members of the ruling family also gave alms on a regular basis.[16] Evidence of the intimate ties between the ruling family and this chapel comes from the testimony of Paul of Aleppo, whose reminiscence of his time in Moscow during the mid-1650s included a brief description (the only such seventeenth-century description so far as is known) of a service performed at the beginning of Lent. At the tsar's request Paul's master, Patriarch Makarios of Antioch, conducted the service in a Kremlin church that Paul identifies as St. Catherine's.

> On the morning of the Tuesday . . . the Emperor sent for our Lord the Patriarch in the *sania* [sanctuary], to say mass for him in one of the upper churches of the palace, dedicated to the Nativity of Our Lady and St. Catherine, in order to commemorate the birthday of his eldest daughter, named Eudocia. . . . We went therefore, and, ascending to the church, performed mass there, in company with the Patriarch of Moscow and the Archbishop of Servia [Serbia], before the Emperor and some of his nobles. The Empress and his sisters were in the porch; the door of which was closed, that none might intrude upon them; and they looked over us from behind the veils and lattices.
>
> The church is very small, of ancient structure, with a gilt cupola. On a request made by the Patriarch to our master, the latter held an ordination of Priests and Deacons. As this is the Emperor's private church for the winter, observe what he now did there. Descending from his seat, he went round, like a candle lighter, to light tapers before the images, whilst we were looking on in astonishment. After he had made the tour of the Sacrament, he approached the two Patriarchs; who gave him the usual benediction with the cross; and then passed to the Empress and her attendants, to bless them in like manner.[17]

Paul's wonder at the tsar's personal involvement in the service grew all the greater when Aleksei Mikhailovich repeated this scene the next day in the church's refectory.[18] Paul may well have been confused, as some scholars believe that the service took place not in St. Catherine's but in the newer St. Evdokia chapel just above St. Catherine's, a more appropriate location for celebrating the name day of Evdokia Alekseevna. This would account for his describing the church as "very small" (St. Evdokia's was far smaller than St. Catherine's), although Paul's sense of its ancient vintage is odd since the entire edifice had been completely rebuilt only a generation earlier, and the St. Evdokia chapel was quite new. Unfortunately, the relevant court records shed no light on this day's church services. If Paul did mix up the two *terem* chapels it would be understandable, and it would diminish the descriptive value of his testimony, one of the rare eyewitness accounts of such a service. In a larger sense, however, his possible confusion may well reflect what he was told at the time, implying that the entire complex had come to be known as St. Catherine's in court parlance, thus underscoring for Paul of Aleppo and others the preeminent standing of St. Catherine's among the Romanov women.

Although diminished in importance after the court moved to St. Petersburg and virtually destroyed by a second fire in 1737 (allegedly the only artifacts to survive were four icons: The Savior, the Mother of God, St.

Catherine, and St. Evdokia), the St. Catherine church continued to function as private chapel for the ruling family when they were in Moscow. No longer a working church, the structure still exists today as part of the residential complex of the president of the Russian Federation. A description from 1720 provides a clear indication of the earlier prominence and splendor of the St. Catherine chapel and the significant resources dedicated to its splendor. Both the iconostasis and the doors were made of gilded wood, with the latter including carved icons. In addition to ornate clerical vestments, the chapel contained a large silver cross that had fifteen images from the lives of Saints Martha and Mary of Egypt and bore an inscription indicating that it had been commissioned in 1682 for the Church of St. Catherine on the orders of the co-tsars Ivan and Peter and Tsarevna Sofia.[19] From the first half of the century it housed at least one icon case *(kiot)* of the Blessed Mother of God.[20] In the 1680s, a silver ladle was given to the co-tsars Ivan and Peter, presumably at the initiative of Sofia, with an inscription of the church of St. Catherine, as if to remind them even as they ate of the presence of blessed female authority.[21] The chapel contained an altar of St. Onufrii that was used for special prayers to the martyr to intercede when the tsar's children were ill or when there were difficult childbirths.[22]

The documentary evidence makes it clear that St. Catherine's saw frequent use throughout the seventeenth century, and that its clerical staff carried out important functions within the tsarist household. The tsaritsa, whose demanding schedule of church attendance obliged her to rotate among several Kremlin churches (fifteen in all), cathedrals, and monasteries, regularly attended mass at the St. Catherine chapel, sometimes alone but occasionally accompanied by other members of her family, including the tsar and his son, the future tsar Aleksei. Services of thanksgiving for newborn children of the tsar's immediate family took place there as well. The male offspring of the tsar were brought to the chapel to be blessed and cleansed in holy water, and on occasion to attend mass or matins.[23] Invariably, the tsaritsa would make a small offering to the church whenever she prayed there, and occasionally at other times as well. Important holidays or services tied to family celebrations were often held there, including in some years St. Nicholas's Day, St. Alexis's Day, Easter, the Nativity of the Mother of God, and the liturgy of Saints Peter and Paul.[24] For these important services the tsar and members of the court often would attend and the patriarch would officiate.[25] This ongoing entrée to men and boys of the court questions the old image of the *terem* as a rigidly cloistered locus and instead corresponds with Thyrêt's characterization of the *terem* (and Ivan Zabelin's data, if not his conclusion) as a site where the tsaritsy carried on active correspondence and engagement with the larger world of politics and court.[26] Throughout the seventeenth century the clergy of St. Catherine's served as so-called priests of the cross *(krestovye sviashchenniki),* that is, overseers of the chambers of venerated icons, within the tsarist household.[27] And unlike many of the other palace clerics, they managed to steer clear of the bloody political intrigues surrounding the *streltsy* in the 1680s, thus avoiding entirely the incarcerations and exiles that had brought suspicion upon the Kremlin clergy.[28]

At some point in the mid-seventeenth century the chapel became the primary locus for the court's increasingly elaborate celebration of St. Catherine's Day. Patriarchal records from the late seventeenth century delineated many of the special liturgies at which the patriarch or his designated representative officiated from 1668 until the end of the century. In 1879, N. I. Novikov printed these records, not always with perfect accuracy, in volume 10 of *Drevniaia rossiiskaia vivliofika* (the Ancient Russian Library), hereafter *DRV*. They show that the *terem* church of St. Catherine, often together with the Dormition Cathedral and the Ascension (Voznesenskii) Convent, celebrated the saint's day virtually every year.[29] Typically the patriarch conducted an evening mass at Dormition Cathedral in the presence of the saint's relics, and then he went to St. Catherine's to read the name day service. Another high cleric would conduct a parallel service at Ascension Convent.[30] Apparently the St. Catherine chapel was occasionally the site of sermons, still something of a rarity in the middle decades of the seventeenth century. A manuscript sermon in the archive of Karion Istomin, the poet and one-time director of the Moscow Pechatnyi dvor, includes the following inscription: "On November 23 of this year, 7197 [1689], I wrote this sermon in pen, and, once it was written, it was read aloud at the church of St. Catherine on the 24th during the liturgy, in the presence of the tsars, with the blessing of the holy patriarch Ioakim. Protopop Ioann Grigor'ev."[31]

From the outset, therefore, the church of St. Catherine took on the character of a family chapel. Others could and did pray there, both women and men, but always in the company of the tsaritsa. Palace records from the 1630s onward show that the tsaritsy brought their children to the St. Catherine church a few times a year for communion, a sacred ritual of Russian Orthodoxy reaffirming one's acceptance of Holy Mysteries.[32] Several of the children were baptized at St. Catherine's, including Mariia (1660), Feodosiia (1662) and Simeon (1665).[33] The children also attended vespers and other church services there as well.[34] In various years, starting no later than the 1630s, the tsaritsa and her children occasionally celebrated important holidays there as well as some family funeral services.[35] After each of these she gave additional alms to the chapel.

One particularly odd—and almost certainly erroneous—piece of documentation involving the chapel demonstrates that the inclusion of St. Catherine's in certain ceremonies had become automatic, so automatic that it was included at the appropriate point in a decree describing an event that never took place. A document dutifully recorded in the first volume of the *Polnoe sobranie zakonov* (Complete Collection of Laws), hereafter *PSZ* or the Laws, describes at some length the funeral cortege of

Tsarevna Tatiana Mikhailovna on August 23, 1658. According to the description, a large service was conducted on that date in Dormition Cathedral, after which a private funeral service for the tsarevna was conducted by the metropolitan of Siberia and two archimandrites at St. Catherine's before they proceeded to inter her body at Ascension Convent.[36]

What makes this proclamation startling is not the description of the service or the processional, both of which conformed to the norms of the day. Rather it is the year in which it allegedly occurred that raises wonderment. All the appropriate records list Tatiana's dates as 1636 to 1706, and a number of scholars of the Petrine era, S. M. Solov'ev among others, have recounted Tatiana's disagreements with her nephew, Peter, well after he ascended the throne.[37] The *dvortsovye razriady* mention her presence at numerous functions during the 1680s and 1690s, all of which confirm that she was very much alive in those years. No other tsarevny at the time were named Tatiana, other than one who had died in 1611, and none of the Romanov tsarevny are recorded as having died in August 1658. And yet here is the announcement in black and white, complete with some references that were appropriate to that specific time and impossible for 1706 (e.g., the observation that both the tsar and tsaritsa attended the funeral [there was no tsaritsa in 1706]), both in *PSZ* during the 1830s and decades earlier in volume 10 of *DRV*, published in 1789.[38]

Perhaps both Novikov, the compiler of *DRV*, and the nineteenth-century compilers of the Laws made a glaring mistake here by somehow interpolating the 1706 funeral into 1658, although the Laws were being worked on under the scrutiny of the famously meticulous Mikhail Speranskii. More likely, though, the mistake originated decades earlier and was unthinkingly reproduced in the later volumes. Even as simulacrum, what remains of interest is the funeral ritual that the announcement carefully describes and St. Catherine's place within it, almost invariably in connection with the *terem* and the convent as the three essential sites for the Romanov women. On St. Catherine's Day in 1686 the bond tying St. Catherine to the resting place of the Romanov women became stronger still when Patriarch Ioakim, in the presence of Ivan V and Sofia, dedicated a new church of St. Catherine within the Ascension Convent itself, adjacent to the Church of the Archangel Michael, Catherine's celestial herald in Archbishop Makarii's vita.[39] This association survived well into Peter's reign, until the formal move to the new capital at the earliest. When Tatiana Mikhailovna actually did die (or so it is thought) on August 24, 1706, the funeral service, although described in different words and referring to a different cast of participants than the 1658 entry, retraced the same route. The deceased tsarevna was carried down the stairs from the living quarters and out into the square by her official attendants. She was placed into a casket and laid down on a deathbed, draped with scarlet cloth and covered in gilded satin. The deathbed, as the decree relates, was then brought along a carefully defined route, "passing by the St. Catherine church that stood at the foot of the Golden Hall of the tsaritsy, past the back entry to the living quarters, and up to Ascension Convent."[40] At that point the casket was dressed further and taken to the burial site, at which point the liturgy was allowed to begin. By Peter's decree, a forty-day period of official mourning commenced, including a round-the-clock attendance at the casket, rotated among the wives of high-ranking serving men (boyars, *okol'nichi* and *dumnye liudi*).

Compare this route to the much less elaborate processional described in the announcement of the death and funeral of Tsarevich Alexander Petrovich in May 1692, in which the sacred images, Ivan V, and all the tsaritsy passed directly from the St. Catherine chapel to the burial ground without making the short detour to Ascension Convent.[41] Similarly, the ceremonial for the funeral of Tsarevich Aleksei Alekseevich on January 17, 1670, made no mention of the St. Catherine chapel when tracing the route of his cortege.[42] Clearly, these processionals constituted intricately choreographed—and carefully textualized—elements of the mourning ritual, a circumstance that makes the specific references to the St. Catherine chapel in the official announcements of events as sacred specifically to the Romanov women all the more noteworthy.[43] When the women did not appear prominently, or when a processional bore no intimate connection to the clan per se, St. Catherine went unmentioned. For example, the lengthy 1665 summary of the tsar's Palm Sunday ceremonial detailed the many churches and cathedrals visited by the tsar or his representatives, both within the Kremlin and elsewhere in Moscow. This list apparently did not include St. Catherine's, and instead it spoke vaguely of the tsar "deigning to depart from his private quarters" ("iz svoikh Gosudarskikh khorom izvolil") to the Dormition Cathedral, the point at which any reference to St. Catherine's would have appeared.[44]

This gendered affinity echoed anew generations later, long after the *terem* chapel had lost its importance, when a new St. Catherine's chapel was constructed (or possibly rebuilt) in Ascension Convent during the reign of Alexander I (completed in 1811 and consecrated in 1817), with a side chapel dedicated to the Kazan Mother of God. Perhaps in anticipation of the coming war with Napoleon (the sources do not say), St. Catherine and the miraculous Marian icon from the conquest of Kazan, Russia's most prominent heavenly intercessors with God, were being summoned one more time to guard over the resting place of the Romanov women, and by extension the mother church of Russian Orthodoxy.[45]

Why St. Catherine?

How this affinity between St. Catherine and the venerated feminine spaces in the Kremlin came into being and when it first emerged remain ambiguous. The sources remain frustratingly opaque both as to whether the *terem* church had been dedicated to St. Catherine from the outset, that is, in the 1530s or 1580s, or only after being rebuilt in 1627, or why it was named after St. Catherine at all. The *dvortsovye razriady* did not refer to a St. Catherine church prior to the pronouncement of 1627. They spoke instead of an unnamed "palace church," or sometimes "the church in the living quarters" *(verkh)*. Immediately after the reconsecration of 1627, the *dvortsovye razriady* also began to identify the palace church as St. Catherine's, and most of the scholarship has accepted 1627, probably erroneously, as its earliest date.[46]

On May 29, 1624, the court had received a number of gifts from Patriarch Theophanes of Jerusalem including an image of St. Catherine with a metal casing of silver and gold.[47] This icon would be prominently displayed in the reconsecrated church, and it may be that the chapel was reconsecrated in St. Catherine's name in acknowledgment of the holy gift at a time when relations with the more senior patriarchs were becoming quite important to the new Romanov dynasty. Of course, this is merely a speculation based upon chronological proximity, and it should be noted that, shortly thereafter, the court received equally precious gifts from the patriarch of Jerusalem among which were relics of St. Tatiana the Martyr.[48] Following this line of reasoning, the chapel might just as easily have been named after her.

There are some documentary hints that the chapel's naming took place earlier, either at the formal consecration of 1587, or perhaps when construction of the chapel was first begun during the 1530s. The accounting books of the treasury *(kazennyi prikaz)* detailed multiple purchases for "the church of St. Catherine the martyr in Christ, that is for the Lady [tsaritsa]" as early as November 1613.[49] If, as it seems, these were references to the *terem* church rather than the St. Catherine Church in the Fields, the naming could indeed have taken place well before 1627. Chronicle accounts provide no direct information on dating, although one brief reference vaguely seems to suggest a date of 1587.[50] Chronicles do offer a possible context, however, to address both the timing and, more importantly, the thinking that would have led the ruling family to name such a central family chapel after St. Catherine. Several chronicles written during the middle and later years of the sixteenth century made reference to St. Catherine, including at least one interpolation for the fourteenth century that had not appeared in chronicles composed earlier. The Nikon Chronicle, for example, noted that in 6907 (1399) Prince Andrei Dmitrievich, the son of the recently deceased Dmitrii Donskoi and the brother of the reigning grand prince, traveled to Novgorod, received many honors from the Novgorodians, and then returned to Moscow. It added, "In that same year a side chapel *(pridel')* at the stone church of the Blessed Mother of God was built in Novgorod dedicated to the martyr St. Catherine and to St. Alexis the Man of God."[51] This passing reference is of no great import in itself except for the fact that it did not appear in earlier accounts of Andrei's journey to Novgorod.[52]

The mention of Alexis the Man of God, namesake of the metropolitan of Rus' from 1354 to 1378 who was himself an important national saint of relatively recent vintage, arouses no surprise since by this time Aleksis had achieved a highly visible official veneration as a patron saint and protector of Moscow.[53] Viktor Zhivov has remarked that this was a time when Muscovy first began imagining itself as a geopolitical power (his term is "the imperial idea"), and later writings inscribed it so even more heroically. The symbols and the spaces (textually) in which this new self-fashioning was framed were religious and celestial, with saintly agency, such as St. Aleksei, given particular standing.[54] But placing St. Catherine alongside him was something new, at least insofar as she had occupied no comparable place in previously composed chronicles.

The transposition into a new medium bears comment because it marked the first time that the name of St. Catherine, a female Byzantine saint, had been interpolated into a narrative text discussing Rus' itself, other than one intended for a church service. In this case the text in question was offering a master narrative of national history. Dating this intervention, then, becomes critical to decoding its possible meaning and purpose. B. M. Kloss has established that most of the texts in the Nikon Chronicle were composed or revised in the second quarter of the sixteenth century, in large measure by Metropolitan Daniil of Moscow.[55] The beginnings of St. Catherine's elevation to a higher political status, thus, likely derive from the latter years of the reign of Vasilii Ivanovich or the early years of Ivan IV.

Other contemporaneously composed chronicle accounts reinforce the impression that the metropolitan, or other members of the immediate milieu of Vasilii Ivanovich, were likely responsible for interpolating St. Catherine into the national history. Vasilii's death in early December 1534 is described at length in each of the relevant chronicles, irrespective of when they were initially composed, and they dwell on his final instructions to the boyars, his sons, and his wife. Here, for example, is Tatishchev's account, assembled in the mid-eighteenth century but taken almost verbatim from an early redaction of the Nikon Chronicle, the so-called Akademicheskii 15 copy:

> 7042 (1534) On Sunday, September 21, the Grand Prince Vasilii Ivanovich left Moscow with Grand Princess Elena and their children to worship at the Trinity St. Sergius Monastery on the day in memory of the miracle worker. From there he went to relax at Volok[alamsk], where he began to feel some pain in his leg. When the pain became more severe, the grand prince ordered that he be taken from Volok to the Immaculate Mother of God, the Joseph Monastery, to pray. And from there he was brought to Moscow in a weakened state on Sunday November 23.[56]

Tatishchev then includes parallel variants of the text describing Vasilii's last days, in which the grand prince commands the boyars to serve Elena and his son and heir, Ivan. In the first version he orders them to safeguard the Rus' lands under Ivan's rule, with God's help, as well as "the entire Christian fatherland from misfortune, as well as from blasphemy, heresies, and from the offenses of powerful individuals."[57] At this point Daniil has him tonsured as a monk, renamed Varlaam, and he then administers the last rites. Soon after, Vasilii dies and enters into his eternal rest in heaven on St. Barbara's name day, as the chronicle duly notes.

The second text places the deathbed scene on September 21 and omits the references to the Christian fatherland, heresies, and St. Barbara. In their place it emphasizes the secular heritage of Muscovite princes, their unification of the Rus' lands, "from the Don in the south to the very border of Kazan in the east." It then connects this princely authority to Byzantium, by affixing "the seal of the Greek kings through his mother, the reclining eagle [orel plastanoi]," to the official proclamation of the grand prince's death.[58]

One notes the themes of true faith, heavenly intervention, and Christian kingship in the first, versus the emphasis on the state and Byzantine kingship in the other. These elements then become intertwined in Karamzin's reading of the chronicles written a few decades after Tatishchev's. Quoting the Rostov (or *Tipografskaia*) Chronicle, he relates that on August 24, 1534, a strange sign in the morning sky (possibly a partial eclipse of the sun) foretold the death of Vasilii despite the prince's robust health.[59] As in Tatishchev's first chronicle, Vasilii became ill a month later while celebrating the feast day of St. Sergius at the Trinity Lavra, and soon realized that he was dying. On his deathbed three of his boyars implore him to forego tonsuring, which had been his expressed desire, and be buried as a layperson.

> They said that Saint Vladimir did not wish to be a monk and was named equal to the apostles; the hero Donskoi also died as a layman, but his virtues assured him of repose in the Kingdom of Heaven. As they stormed about and argued Vasilii crossed himself and read his prayers. Already his tongue had grown heavy, his vision dimmed, and his arm fell to his side. He gazed upon the image of the Mother of God and kissed it humbly, and with a manifest impatience as he awaited his last rites. Metropolitan Daniil took the black vestment and handed it to Abbot Iosaf. Prince Andrei and Vorontsov wished to grab it away. At that moment the Metropolitan angrily uttered the frightful words [to Vorontsov and Prince Andrei]: "I will not offer you blessing either for this world or the next! No one shall take his soul away from me. The silver vessel is good, but a gilded one would be better." Vasilii rested. They hastened to complete the rite. The Metropolitan, having placed the epitarkhilion on Abbot Ioasaf tonsured the Grand Prince himself and renamed him Varlaam. In the confusion they forgot the head dress *(mantia)* for the new monk. The Trinity Cellarer, Serapion, offered his own. The Gospels and the habit lay on the breast of the dying one. Several minutes passed without a sound. Standing at the foot of the deathbed Shigona was the first to cry out

"The sovereign has expired!" And all of them wept. It is said that Vasilii's face suddenly grew bright; that instead of the stench of death, the room filled with a sweet fragrance. The Metropolitan cleansed the body and dressed it in cotton.[60]

In many of its particulars this deathbed scene conforms to what Dmitrii Likachev once termed "monumental historicism": summoning loyal boyars and heirs; handing down clear lines of obedience and succession; sharply delineating good from evil, godly from profane; ritual laments over the deceased; and so on.[61] Several of those scenes composed contemporaneously or slightly later, however, interposed an additional deathbed soliloquy in which St. Catherine, heretofore unmentioned, suddenly became a central presence. As recorded, with slight variations, in the *Tsarstvennaia kniga, Stepennaia kniga, Postnikovskii letopisets,* second *Sofiiskaia letopis',* and *Aleksandro-Nevskaia letopis'* the grand prince lay in his deathbed.[62]

Metropolitan Daniil then came to him, as did his brothers, Prince Iurii and Prince Andrei, and all the boyars and *deti boiarskie.* And the metropolitan told him to send for the sacred great wonderworking images of Vladimir, and Luke the Evangelist, and Nicholas the Wonderworker. The Grand Prince then summoned the sacred image of Nicholas the Wonderworker, which was very quickly brought to him. . . . And then [the Grand Prince] ordered his chancellor of the cross *("diaku svoemu krestovomu")* Danilka [Metropolitan Daniil] to chant the canticle of the great martyr Catherine and the canticle for the passing of his soul. And he ordered that he be given his last rites. And, as he began to chant the canticle, forgetting little and, as if awakening from his dream, he began to speak before the image of the great martyr in Christ, Catherine . . . "it is time for you to reign, Lady." And he grasped the image of the great martyr Catherine, and showing his affection for her, placed the image in his right hand, which had been in pain. And then they brought him the relics of the great martyr Catherine, and placed his right hand upon them. And, while he lay on his bed they summoned his boyar Mikhail Semenovich Vorontsov, and the two of them embraced and he forgave him. And from this moment he lay a long while.[63]

Even more than the tale of Andrei Dmitrovich of 1399, this passage attracts one's interest, both because of the newly inscribed central role of St. Catherine at such a critical juncture (the passing of a prince), and because of its association with Metropolitan Daniil, the putative author and a major figure in the account of 1532. The metropolitan himself, credited by Kloss and others with rewriting much of the history of the Russian church, may well have initiated the new court-centered prominence of St. Catherine, or perhaps the initiative derived from the wider circle of clerics out of the Joseph Volokalamsk Monastery from which he had emerged. Gail Lenhoff has shown that, beginning in the late fourteenth century, the Mother of God had taken on a particularly important role as protector of the emerging Muscovite state, the intercessor against its enemies and the protector of its princes.[64] This was as true during the reign of Vasilii III as it had been earlier and later,[65] and some scholars have seen her intercession as a defining element of Muscovite "national" consciousness. Yet in Daniil's accounts, the prince beseeched St. Catherine, rather than the Queen of Heaven, Mother of God, to act as his primary intercessor with God—once the wonderworking healing icons had failed to restore his health. Vasilii here was doing something new, certainly for Russian Orthodoxy.

Daniel Collins has argued that such deathbed testaments often "derive from similarities in what the author actually saw or expected."[66] In his view, the obligatory deathbed scenes—the anointing of successors, the admonitions to rule justly—were not merely literary devices but reflections of real concerns by the recorders and heirs alike.[67] If they were not in the original accounts, he maintains, they were added in subsequent redactions. From this perspective, however, the interpolation of St. Catherine appears superfluous, even slightly gratuitous, since the previous redactions already met the necessary criteria. Indeed, if accurately recorded—and Daniil had been particularly close to the grand prince and was indeed his confessor—Vasilii's deathbed exchange elevated St. Catherine far higher in the Russian pantheon than had any previous Russian text or image. The monologue imported in toto the Catherinian role of personal intercessor, by now common in western Christendom but heretofore little known in Muscovy, and transposed it from women to men, from pious commoners to princes. St. Catherine was granted celestial agency within Russian history, chosen by both God (implicitly) and grand prince to shepherd the prince's soul to heaven. At this moment in the chronicles, the veneration of St. Catherine had been given a standing within a nation's politics equaled elsewhere in Christendom, arguably, only by the tenth-century *Menologium* of Basil and perhaps the inquisition testimonies of Joan of Arc. The question, then, is why: why in Muscovy and why now?

One plausible place to begin inquiring is the calendar. Although Vasilii died on December 3, the Nikon and Alexander Nevskii Chronicles, among others, began the deathbed narrative on the morning of Sunday November 23, or the eve of the feast of St. Catherine.[68] None of the chronicles acknowledged the connection, however, even though the Nevskii Chronicle went on to ascribe immense celestial authority to St. Catherine at the prince's deathbed just a few days later. By contrast, both chronicles noted that Vasilii was tonsured as Varlaam and subsequently died on the eve of St. Barbara's Day (the Nikon Chronicle mentions the connection twice)[69]. From this account one might infer that St. Barbara's Day was recognized at the time as an important and familiar calendrical landmark while St. Catherine's Day was not. Another mid-sixteenth century chronicle not directly linked with Daniil, the *Letopisets nachala tsarstva tsaria i velikogo kni-*

azia Ivana Vasil'evicha, mentioned both November 23 and St. Barbara's Day but did not include the appeal to St. Catherine among the Grand Prince's last words.[70] From all of this it would appear that the time of year did not play a role in St. Catherine's presence in the deathbed soliloquy and rather heightens the suspicion that the soliloquy was interpolated deliberately and with specific purpose in mind.

Facticity aside, the primary myth-making role must be assigned to the chronicler, Metropolitan Daniil. A prolific theologian and author of sixteen homilies and many more epistles, Daniil is not known to have composed any meditations on St. Catherine.[71] However, his ongoing prosecution of both the Transvolgans and of Maksim the Greek and Maksim's confederate, Vassian Patrikeev, emphasized the superiority of Scripture and patristics over "the teachings of Hellenic scholars."[72] Hellenism had been a specific charge against Maksim, and his tracts and epistles, among other writings, were filled with references to Socrates, Plato, and Aristotle.[73] It is also true that he cited the Greek patriarchs of the early church, in particular Gregory Nazianzen and John Chrysostom, quite extensively, but this side of his writing drew relatively little comment during his interrogations. Maksim's questioners challenged him to recant his fondness for "Hellenistic and judaizing teachings . . . and those of other mortal heresies."[74] In the trial against Patrikeev, accused of following Maksim's heretical teachings, Daniil denounced both of them for relying too much on pagan wisdom of the ancient Greeks, Aristotle, Homer, Phillip, Alexander, and Plato and not enough on the sacred rules of the church fathers. "Up until this very day [said Daniil], Hellenistic teachings were not based upon the holy fathers or the seven [Patriarchal] councils, and you ["*ty*"] here and now have written teachings based upon these very Hellenistic sages, Aristotle, Homer, Phillip, Alexander, Plato. But it is written in the sacred rules that one must not rely upon them."[75]

St. Catherine's defeat of the emperor's Hellenistic philosophers, her transcendence of the wisdom of the pagan Greeks of antiquity, fit this argument perfectly. By strategically interposing her with St. Aleksei, and then by making her the tsar's deathbed intercessor with Christ, Daniil could have been employing her to connect the spirituality of the ruling family with the patristic ideology of the Josephites and the camp of the Possessors more generally. This strategy affirmed its Christian beginnings and ignored its Hellenistic ones, and thereby implicitly rejected the legacy of Maksim, who as it happened, made only occasional and fleeting references to St. Catherine.[76]

There is another, and equally plausible, reading of this chronicle account, deriving from Ivan III's and Vasilii Ivanovich's periodic resort to the tsarist title and their connection to the Byzantine throne through Ivan's marriage to Sofia (Zoia) Paleologue. Sigismund von Herberstein, who was in Moscow between April and November, 1517, described Sofia as "a very artful woman [who] had considerable influence over the activities of the grand duke."[77] Sofia's mother was Eikaterina Asanina Paleologue, the first living Catherine with any connection to the Muscovite throne, and, with the exception of Tsar Vasilii Shuiskii's second wife, Ekaterina Petrovna Buinosova-Rostovskaia, the only one until later in the seventeenth century.[78] She herself came from a royal family that lay claim to the recently vacated Byzantine throne. Whether or not he genuinely aspired to the Byzantine throne, as some accounts maintain, Ivan and his heirs surely coveted the title of "tsar," derived, as V. Savva and Michael Cherniavsky have demonstrated, as much from the Byzantine Basileus as from the Tatar khan, not to mention its obvious resonance of God, the King of kings *("Tsar' tsarei")*.

Herberstein maintained that Vasilii coveted the title of tsar, and hoped to prevail upon the pope and Holy Roman Emperor to refer to him as such.[79] This view gains some ex post facto support via a Moscow icon from about 1630, depicting the Fedorovskaia Mother of God and including images of saints associated with living members of the family: Evdokia, Mary Magdalene, Martha, and John the Baptist. Also included was St. Catherine even though none of the Romanov women of that time bore her name. The editors of the catalogue in which the icon is recorded also took note of her presence, and they confidently stated that "she was represented undoubtedly as proof of a direct family connection between Tsar Mikhail Fedorovich Romanov and the Riurikide tsars [sic] through Ivan the Terrible's first wife Anastasiia Romanova. St. Catherine was the namesake of Catherine, the mother of Sofia Paleologue, the wife of Grand Prince Ivan III. And she was particularly venerated by Vasilii III and Ivan the Terrible."[80]

Of course, this reading of St. Catherine's presence in the icon is entirely speculative and it assumes that the informed contemporary viewer would draw multiple connections to events and personages several generations removed from the living Romanovs. The well-informed viewer might, however, have recognized that this connection with St. Catherine had been entirely undeveloped during Sofia's own day even though other saintly images (Sergius of Radonezh, Gabriel) had been deployed both to express the divinity of Vasilii's claim to the throne and to intervene on behalf of a male offspring in the royal family.[81] Vasilii's first wife, Solomoniia Saburova, had been childless, and she had sought the intercession of St. Sergius as well as sorceresses to help her "untie her womb." As Thyrêt recounts, Solomoniia's brother Iurii admitted as much during an inquest that took place on November 23, 1524, that is, on the very eve of the feast of St. Catherine, the sometime patron saint of midwives![82] Had there been an intention at the time to engage St. Catherine on behalf of the blood line, surely it would have gained mention in the inquisition. It is just as likely, therefore, that the 1630 icon was representing St. Catherine's new, or recently rearticulated, role as a patron saint of the ruling family and protector of their chapel. But the idea that this also was a gesture of legitimation through Anastasiia is, in itself, plausible. When viewed against this political backdrop, the half-Greek

Vasilii's deathbed soliloquy, and specifically the references to St. Catherine reigning and his affection for her, may have constituted a less than subtle gesture of imperial pretension, an everlasting inscription in the chronicles of his direct matrilineal line to the Byzantine throne through his maternal grandmother.[83]

Nowhere else in the chronicles did St. Catherine rise to such heights as in the dying words of Grand Prince Vasilii, but these interpolations initiated a steady stream of continuing, but by no means commanding, Catherinian presences in Russian princely narratives. Her name appeared with increasing frequency in the accounts of Ivan IV and Fedor Ivanovich. Both the Nikon Chronicle and the *Tsarstvennaia kniga,* for example, included the veneration of St. Catherine in the account of Ivan IV's siege of Kazan in 1552. In each version Ivan ordered three field churches to be set up outside the city: the Archangel Michael, St. Sergius, and St. Catherine.[84] He then mounted his horse and prayed in front of the image of St. Sergius before going into battle. Both Archangel Michael and St. Sergius had long been associated with military victories, especially in battles pitching the faithful Rus' against unbelievers. This was a new role for St. Catherine, however—at least within Muscovy, and one must assume that her spiritual conquest of the unbelieving emperor of the east made her an important ally in the battle of the Christian tsar against Muslim Kazan.

The Nikon Chronicle followed up with two additional references to St. Catherine, one for 1558, and another for 1564. The former summarized a visit to Moscow by Patriarch Makarios of Alexandria, who bemoans the ravages to Sinai wrought by the unbelieving local authorities. His request for assistance was only the latest in a long history of such supplications dating, according to chronicle accounts, as far back as the fourteenth century. For the first time, however, Makarios made specific mention of St. Catherine, by pointing out that Sinai was the holy site of Moses and Aaron, Elijah the Prophet, "and the most wise great martyr St. Catherine." Moved by the plight of his co-religionists, Ivan issued a formal epistle offering material and moral support to Alexandria and Sinai.[85] Then, in 1564 the same chronicle noted that Ivan's brother, Iurii Vasil'evich died at the age of thirty-one at 2:00 a.m. on November 24, which, it proclaimed, "was the day in memory of the great martyr St. Catherine."[86]

St. Catherine's day, marked ubiquitously on the Orthodox calendar since at least the eleventh century, had not previously received any acknowledgment in the chronicles, in spite of numerous references to events that took place on November 24. Without putting too much emphasis on a passing citation, using St. Catherine's Day as a familiar landmark of yearly time, so as to situate Russian events in the template of the universal Christian calendar, was nevertheless new. It indicates either that St. Catherine's Day had become an accepted point of reference, or that the chronicler was endeavoring to make it so.

A Cult of St. Catherine

Whatever lay behind the founding moment, the association with the Romanov women was palpable, if not yet clearly defined. Its only equal at this time was the Kremlin Church of St. Evdokia, named, as previously noted, after the tsaritsa Evdokia Luk'ianovna and her name day saint, which had been consecrated at almost the same time as St. Catherine's.[87] Thus, on October 22, 1628, the tsaritsa ordered a special memorial service for her parents, for which she sent prayer offerings to three Kremlin churches: St. Evdokia's, the Church of the Nativity of the Mother of God, and the Church of St. Catherine.[88] By placing St. Catherine's on a par with those named after Bogoroditsa and one that the tsar had constructed in her honor, the tsaritsa's gesture conveyed the chapel's importance and linked it not just to the Romanov ancestors but to her own as well.

Further evidence of St. Catherine's political elevation came from the recording of saints' days celebrations. These began to be noted in court records only in the late 1620s, the first coming on March 1, 1628, St. Evdokia's Day, the day of the tsaritsa's angel.[89] Most subsequent notations were limited to name day saints of the ruling family, mostly the tsaritsa but occasionally her daughters Irina and Marfa as well, or to those of important male saints such as Nicholas the Wonderworker and Sergei of Radonezh.[90] The single exception to this pattern was St. Catherine, whose name day began to draw notice in 1627. Within a few days of the chapel's reopening, its clergy were participating in a previously unrecorded service at the Ascension (Voznesenskii) Convent in the Kremlin to commemorate St. Catherine's Day.[91] This service bears mention for several reasons. First, it highlighted St. Catherine's new importance for the ruling family, living and deceased. Representing the living Romanovs was Sister Marfa Ivanovna, now an elder of the convent but most importantly the mother of the tsar. Representing the ancestors was the convent itself, an old landmark of Muscovite power founded initially by Dmitrii Donskoi in honor of his wife, Evdokia. More to the point, the Ascension Convent had long been the preferred burial site for the women of the Muscovite ruling family.[92] This ritual was thereby openly associating the martyr, St. Catherine, with the convent whose very existence symbolized the continuum of Muscovite princesses, the feminine side of rulership dating back to the fourteenth century.

A year later the ceremony took on further solemnity with the addition of a processional of the cross and holy water proceeding from the Ascension Convent to the patriarchal church.[93] Archival records from 1632 reflect the growing link between the Russian crown and the saint by making reference to the tsar's public appearances on St. Catherine's Day, "a day to be venerated not just by the nation but also by tsars" ("etot den' chtilsia ne tol'ko narodom no i tsariam").[94] This sentiment was repeated in an *ustav* of 1634 delineating the ceremonies to be carried out, including those in the Dormition Cathedral.[95] In 1633 the tsar was recorded as attending both the matins and mass services at St. Catherine's.[96] Although the ceremony remained unassociated with any specific members of the ruling family until 1658, patriarchal records show that this ritual became an annual event,[97] and that it soon came to include a mass at the St. Catherine chapel.[98] True to tradition, the tsaritsa marked each of these celebrations with an offering to the St. Catherine chapel in honor of its patron saint.[99] After the birth of Tsarevna Ekaterina Alekseevna in 1658, the ceremony became considerably more elaborate. The entry in the daily records of the Privy Chancery for November 24, 1659, reveals that a vespers service and full mass took place at the St. Catherine chapel, conducted by Metropolitan Pitirim, after which the tsar distributed pirogi to the clergy in honor of his daughter's name day. The entry relates further that dignitaries from Georgia, Siberia, and other far flung places were in attendance, as well as members of all the upper ranks of serving men.[100]

With the exception of the patriarch and any other presiding priest, these entries dwell almost entirely on the women, both saintly and carnal. The centrality of the feminine in the processional, or at least in its recording, is noteworthy, and it seems to reflect the emergence of the persona of Evdokia Luk'ianovna, newly married to the tsar. This willingness to give the tsaritsa so much textual visibility was itself new, coinciding almost exactly with the (re)consecration of the chapels of St. Catherine and St. Evdokia. Prior to that time, relevant accounts made almost no mention of Romanov women, and none of Tsaritsa Evdokia, even in the recording of prayer services. The single exception was the tsar's mother, the aforementioned Marfa Ivanovna, who was represented as the mother of the new dynasty and the intercessor for the Russian nation, credited in the *razriadnye knigi* with having convinced a reluctant Mikhail Fedorovich to accept the throne.[101] As a persona of enormous prestige and as the elder of the Ascension Convent, she alone among the Romanov women earned mention in the prayer records for several years after 1613.[102]

Yet beginning in mid-1626 all the relevant sources begin to mention the tsaritsa by name and to include a log of her prayer routine, and to a lesser extent that of her daughters, as if to inscribe the female members of the ruling family into the formal record as the supplicants to God, to make the everyday function largely, but by no means exclusively, matrilineal. At the same time Evdokia Luk'ianovna became the primary female recipient of supplications, or was so listed in the *dvortsovye razriady*, thereby replacing her mother-in-law as the mother of the nation, even though Marfa Ivanovna remained alive until 1631. Thus, the consecration of a secondary *terem* chapel for the tsaritsa more or less coincided with Evdokia Luk'ianovna's emergence as the mother of the nation, the intercessor with God and the tsar, the accepted Marian role. That the name of St. Catherine stood overarching this new mantle led to her transformation from being one of several important female saints to serving as something of the patroness saint of the *terem* and the women it served. This elevation may also have been reflected, albeit faintly, in the appearance of the name Catherine, previously uncommon, at court among daughters and wives of elite families. A list of approximately fifty women from the Streshnev clan formally received by Tsaritsa Evdokia Luk'ianovna includes only one Catherine, Princess Katerina, the daughter of Ivan Mikhailovich Vorotyn-skii. A similar list of Miloslavskiis received later in the century by Tsaritsa Mariia Il'inichna adds to this the tsaritsa's mother, Princess Katerina Fedorovna, and Princess Katerina L'vova. A 1654 list of dignitaries assembled to meet the Georgian queen included Katerina Ivanovna Trubetskaia. One should not read too much into this, however, since the list of Naryshkins received by Tsaritsa Natal'ia Kirillovna included no Catherines, even though two of her children's nannies *were* named Catherine (the above mentioned Miloslavskaia and Katerina Ivanovna Buturlina).[103]

Similarly fragmentary confirmation of St. Catherine's ascent, both at court and within clerical institutions, comes from a variety of other venues. By this time, of course, all the newly printed *mesiatsoslovy* and *prologi* include at least a brief mention of her, and prayers and services to her began to appear in occasional manuscript collections *(sborniki)*. A 1650 inventory of the manuscripts in the Suzdal Spaso-Efimieva Monastery, for example, includes a "book of saints' days, troparion, and an easter service, including a sermon *(slovo)* of the martyr Catherine."[104] Other documents reveal that Abbess Evdokia (Sheremeteva) commanded that St. Catherine's Day be celebrated in Novodevich'ii Convent in Moscow annually between 1597 and 1604, throughout her tenure as abbess.[105]

Within lay society overall, however, there is scant trace of widespread popular veneration up to this point. Recordings of St. Catherine place names, churches, or chapels in the provinces are rare, and in the countryside (where admittedly there is little evidence of church names of this era) nonexistent. A tsarist charter of 1606 describes how Petr Blagovo came to Viatka uezd to the church of "Catherine, the Martyr in Christ."[106] Another document refers to the establishment of the Transfiguration Monastery in 1596 in the village of Ekaterininskoe, also near Viatka.[107] The monastery of St. Michael in Kiev, important, inter alia, because of the remains of St. Barbara said to be kept there, added a side chapel of St. Catherine some time between the late sixteenth and late seventeenth centuries.[108] Novikov's inventory of churches in Moscow and Moscow province (published in 1789) does list quite a few St. Catherine side churches, but with no indication of when they were built.[109] By way of comparison, the nineteenth-century ten-volume collection of materials on the diocese of Moscow listed not a single rural church of St. Catherine.[110] In 1612 local magnates established a Peter and Paul–St. Catherine Monastery in the town of Minsk, but as Minsk lay outside of Muscovy at that time, there is no way to know whether this had any connection with events in Moscow.[111] In short, Moscow's veneration of St. Catherine appears to have remained a preeminently closed and political rite, increasingly significant for the ruling family and within court circles, but not yet a popular celebration for the masses of Russian Orthodox believers.

4

Monasteries

• During the seventeenth century the Muscovite court developed strong institutional and cultural ties with two St. Catherine monasteries, one in Ermolino south of Moscow that was established by direct order of the tsar, and the other in Sinai, the most important site in all of Christendom devoted to her cult. These sites helped to define the court's newly ambitious place within Orthodox spirituality, while simultaneously strengthening and publicizing the connection between the ruling Romanov family and the veneration of St. Catherine.

Ermolino

About twenty-five kilometers south of Moscow lies the modern town of Vidnoe, an industrial settlement of about sixty thousand residents at the center of the Leninskii raion, a geographically large but sparsely populated expanse of nearly fifty thousand hectares with a population of about 130,000. In earlier times the landscape of this area looked quite different from today's industrial sprawl. Dominated by extensive woods, ponds, streams, and scattered fields, it teemed with birds, small mammals, and other wildlife. Its civilization claims a heritage as far back as the eleventh century when, it is said, members of the Viatka tribe of East Slavs looking for agricultural land

and land for hunting chose to settle there. So attractive was the local verdant flora that the area became a flourishing dacha belt at the beginning of the twentieth century, an identity that the current local authorities hope to revive. The town's publicity proudly refers to a clause in Ivan Kalita's will of 1339 granting the area to his son.[1] By the sixteenth century the area, then named Ermolino, had become a popular retreat for magnates from Moscow, and both Vasilii III and Ivan IV are said to have been frequent visitors. The early Romanov tsars came often to the region, especially after rebuilding the suburban palace at Kolomenskoe, from which a day trip to Ermolino was quite easy. Aleksei Mikhailovich, in particular, enjoyed assembling large parties there, where he and his invited guests would spend whole days hunting falcons, one of the tsar's passions.[2]

Nestled within Vidnoe, amidst a school, an old bakery, and some factories, lies a modest expanse of trees within which stands a small and unprepossessing cloister, the men's Monastery of St. Catherine. Never a major landholder—at its prime it owned under one hundred desiatins of land—or a hotbed of doctrinal controversy, the monastery has passed through most of its history quietly and in relative obscurity, one of hundreds of small monasteries scattered throughout the countryside with little national visibility. At the current time, perhaps twenty or so monks and novices reside and work there, scattered among a small number of partially restored buildings returned only recently to the Russian Orthodox Church and reconsecrated during the last days of perestroika. Even now, as Vidnoe tries to publicize itself as a historic and scenic locale on its attractive websight, the on-line brochures and photo gallery make only brief mention of the monastery, perhaps out of respect for the publicity-shy monks, or possibly because of a wish to project a dynamic, future-oriented profile to prospective visitors and investors.[3] Whatever the reason, the St. Catherine's Monastery does little, now as before, to attract the attention of outsiders.

Founded in 1658 by the order of Tsar Aleksei Mikhailovich, the St. Catherine Monastery was from its inception tied to the name and patronage of the ruling family. As such it became a site of occasional pilgrimage and local veneration in the late seventeenth and early eighteenth centuries. As these pilgrimages declined in the mid-nineteenth century, the monastery became a popular destination for day tourists seeking to take advantage of its field of birch and large fish ponds.[4] By the 1890s, those who wished to stay overnight could choose from two small hotels situated at the monastery itself, one made of stone, the other of wood.[5] Nineteenth- and twentieth-century descriptions, seeking to evoke a sense of past splendor in order to attract more would-be pilgrims and sightseers, commented on the striking gilded cupolas and columns of its cathedral, reconstructed in the late eighteenth century with funds supplied by Catherine the Great. It contained two altars, one dedicated to St. Catherine and the other to the Dormition of the Mother of God. Although frequently in poor repair, the cathedral's iconostasis was richly adorned with delicate carvings and finely painted icons.[6] Commentaries also spoke of the many gravestones and little monuments in and around the monastery and the interesting side chapels, named after St. Dimitrii Rostovskii and St. Sergius of Radonezh. The monastery possessed a few noteworthy icons, including one of St. Catherine, donated by Aleksei Mikhailovich himself, and for a time a relic of the saint.

Shortly after the revolution of 1917 the monastery closed, but it soon transformed itself into an agricultural cooperative and workshop, the Ekaterininskaia pustyn' (St. Catherine hermitage), and one of its churches continued to function as the local parish church. Over the next several years the hermitage became a private residence for 164 nuns, who among other things presided over a seasonal fair.[7] Finally, in 1931 the Soviet state closed the entire facility and expelled the remaining clergy. In the next few decades the buildings fell into the hands of the NKVD/KGB, which used them as a combination prison and interrogation center, by reputation a notorious and particularly gruesome place of torture and execution during the Great Terror. After World War II, the facility became a training center for agents of the Ministry of Internal Affairs, and it remained such until 1991 when the Orthodox church regained possession of the property. Officially reconsecrated, the newly reopened monastery held its first liturgical service on July 15, 1992, and it now conducts regular services as well as engages in local charity work. It is the monastery's beginnings that are of interest here, however.

In late November 1658, Tsar Aleksei Mikhailovich was relaxing in Ermolino, as he often did, accompanied by a large hunting party. Rather than returning to Kolomenskoe, on this occasion the party spent the night on site in tents. While sleeping, the tsar had a vision, and upon opening his eyes he saw a beautiful angel before him, dressed white as the snow. The pious tsar recognized at once that this was the Great Martyr, St. Catherine, and in awe he listened as she announced that God had granted him a new daughter whom he should name Catherine. The next day the tsar hastened to return to Moscow and was met en route by messengers from the Kremlin, who confirmed that the tsaritsa, Mariia Il'inichna, had indeed given birth to a daughter the previous night. As instructed, the tsar commanded that the daughter be named Catherine, the first so named in the Romanov clan or in the recorded history of Muscovite rulers. As an act of thanksgiving, he established a sanctuary barely a month later, at the very site where he had slept that fateful night.[8] This site, soon officially renamed Ekaterininskaia roshcha (the St. Catherine grove), quickly gained a chapel that became the first edifice of what would be, under the direct patronage of the court, the St. Catherine's Monastery. According to the records of the Prikaz Bol'shogo dvortsa (Chancery of the tsar's residence) from 1660, "In the vicinity of the hamlet of Ermolino an area measuring eight-and-a-half desiatins has been designated the St. Catherine's birch field, and in the field there shall be a church of St. Catherine and a ceme- tery, along with a garden plot measuring five desiatins in which vegetables shall be planted."[9]

This tale, in itself a minor landmark of the tsar's biography, is more por- tentous than appears at first glance. Miraculous visitations, although far from uncommon in the narratives of Muscovite and Imperial Russia, typi- cally did not guide the naming of children in the ruling family. And no comparable tales inform the naming of Aleksei's other offspring. Both cus- tom and canon law prescribed that children would be named after the saint of the appropriate sex whose feast day occurred soonest after the child's birth. Although not always followed to the letter, especially with girls because of a relative paucity of female saints,[10] this understanding provided the fundamental framework for naming practices. If not the next available saint, princely and tsarist offspring almost invariably received the name of a major saint whose day occurred within a week or so after birth.[11] Thus, Tsarevich Dmitrii Alekseevich, born October 22, 1648, was named for St. Dmitrii, whose feast day fell on October 26; Tsarevna Evdokia Alekseevna was born on February 17 or 18, 1650, and St. Evdokia's Day occurred on March 1; and so forth.[12]

Not so, however, for Ekaterina Alekseevna. Official sources differ on the date of birth—not uncommon for the seventeenth century, but most place it on November 27. The formal proclamation of her birth, preserved in the papers of the Oruzheinaia Palata (Armory), was dated November 27.[13] V. N. Tatishchev, the eighteenth-century historian, reproduced a docu- ment from the late seventeenth century listing the birthdates of all of the children of Aleksei Mikhailovich in which Catherine's birthday was given as the 27th.[14] P. M. Stroev, working from a wide selection of court records, employed the same date.[15] The so-called Mazurinskii Chronicle, penned in the early 1680s, also says she was born on the 27th.[16] Finally, two *bogo- mol'nye gramoty* (official letters of pilgrimage) published in 1836, dated re- spectively November 28 and December 13, 1658, stated explicitly that the birth took place on November 27.[17] If accurately recorded, this naming act was a singular and unprecedented occurrence among the ruling family for the seventeenth century and later in that the birth took place three or four days *after* St. Catherine's feast day, in direct contravention of accepted practice. By contrast, every other recorded birth in the ruling family fell, as prescribed, before the saint's day. Something other than the calendrical norms, it seems certain, was dictating the naming of this baby and the designation of her name day saint.

Penetrating the recorded dreams or spiritual sensibilities of a seven- teenth-century tsar lies beyond the interpretive capabilities of the histo- rian. Nevertheless, one cannot help but wonder what might have inspired such a vision on that late November night. Other than attending services at the *terem* church, Aleksei Mikhailovich is not known to have had any prior devotion to St. Catherine, and up to this point the name Catherine had been absent from Romanov lineage. From that moment on, however, "Catherine" became relatively more common among elites whose daughters were born in the autumn, first in the royal family, and then among courtier families. Similarly, St. Catherine chapels gained a degree of popularity, albeit far less than in the eighteenth century when the presence of Catherinian crowned heads inspired St. Catherine chapels in several confessions all over the empire. A document from March 1681, to give one example, records that the chancellery clerk Evdokimo Afonas'ev, along with all the peasants of the Kurostovskaia volost' in the diocese of Novgorod and Velikie Luki, had petitioned to rebuild their burned church and reconsecrate it as the Church of St. Catherine.[18] A similar petition from the diocese of Kholmogory and Viatka, dated 1709 (i.e., before the official recognition of Catherine as Peter's consort), requested permission to rebuild two damaged churches, one of St. Dmitrii and one of St. Catherine.[19]

Aleksei was neither the first nor the last prominent figure in Russian history to record a dream or to have portentous and miraculous visitations while sleeping. Dream-state visitations constituted a prominent feature of saints' lives, almost always as an introduction to the earthly miracles that would ensue. The Nikon Chronicle of 1520 and subsequent miracle tales recount that Tamerlane had fled from battle against Muscovite forces in 1395 and returned to his homeland after having a nighttime vision of the Mother of God, dressed in purple [as queen of heaven] and at the head of an army.[20] Among contemporaneous personages, Patriarch Nikon also recorded a dream of his own from the night of January 12, 1661, while he was residing at the Voskresenskii Monastery still unsure whether to return as patriarch. He had fallen asleep from exhaustion during a prayer service, and he suddenly found himself in Moscow's Dormition Cathedral.

> And he saw in the church a great light, not to be described in words, and he was astonished at that light with an unspeakable awe; and in that [light] he saw the whole church on both sides, and he saw rising from their tombs all the bishops (and metropolitans) who were buried there. . . . Afterwards he saw from within the altar, from the north side, a bright youth . . . going, with many light-bearers following, as they make the introit with the holy gospel: and that bright youth carried in his hand a royal crown; and with those shining forms all the bishops, having united, went up into the holy sanctuary, the great holy doors meanwhile standing open. And that bright youth set down the royal crown on the throne before the holy gospel.[21]

The dream continued with Nikon meeting Russia's first metropolitan, Peter, who stretched out his hand to Nikon and told him to go to the tsar and ask why he had enslaved the church and its holy possessions. Nikon protested that he had already done so, but Peter ordered him to try yet again. "It is thy duty to testify and to suffer for this even to blood. But if the tsar will not believe this our word, nor receive thy testimony . . . see what will be thereafter."

Much like the tsar's vision of 1658, this dream placed Nikon on the side of the saints and forefathers, in this case a beatific—and as such unassailable—verification of his ideological position, made manifest as in the tsar's dream by a saintly presence and radiant, pure light. It raised for him the spectre of Christian martyrdom, and by implication sainthood, in a scenario reminiscent of the fate of Metropolitan Fillip, famously sacrificed a century earlier by Ivan IV, whose remains had only recently been returned triumphantly to Moscow. As with the tsar's apparition, the fact of the dream (if it was a fact) was less important than its recording, which could then be made known within the immediate entourage almost immediately. Since no other mortal occupied his dream state, no one could dispute or censure its apparently divine contents except by claiming fraud or visitation not by a messenger of God but by a demon.

While working on the first volume of *Chet'i minei* in 1685, during the fast of the nativity of Christ (November–December), Dimitrii Rostovskii, who recorded at least three apparitions, had a dream-state visitation from the late third-century martyr St. Orestes, whose vita he had just completed. In the vision the saint "looked upon him with a joyful countenance" and displayed for Dimitrii all the wounds of his martyrdom in defense of the cross, many more than Dimitrii had described in the vita. "The writer began to wonder which Orestes the saint was, and thought that perhaps he was the soldier Orestes, one of the five martyrs of Sebaste. As if to answer his thought, the holy martyr said, 'I am not the Orestes who was one of the Five Martyrs, but he whose life you have just completed.'" The vivid apparition affected the writer so deeply that he included the experience as an appendix to the Life itself.[22] By recording it in the printed text Dimitrii was inscribing himself into the life of the saint and proclaiming a heavenly editorial intervention, a certification that superceded any fact checking that the technical correctors or church censors might seek to impose.

A second dream is described in his diary entry for Monday, August 10, 1685. Chastising himself for his habitual oversleeping ("due to my usual laziness"), he confesses that he had arrived at the morning service quite late, just before the reading of the psalter portion. During his sleep he had a vision *("videnie")* that he had been directed to look into some caves in which the relics of St. Barbara reposed. Looking into the crypt, he saw what appeared to be St. Barbara asleep, lying on her side. Wishing to feel the relics, he lifted them out of the coffin, and suddenly standing before him was St. Barbara as if alive! He prayed to God for his sins. The saint responded as if there were some doubt that she knew that he was praying in Latin *("po-rimski")*. Dimitrii immediately felt remorse and began to despair. St. Barbara told him not to worry, and she lay back down in her coffin. Once again Dimitrii remarks that it appeared as if the body were alive and completely white. At that moment he was struck by the inappropriately humble coffin in which the saint's relics lay and he commenced a search for a new and more elegant one into which the relics could be transposed. At that very moment he awoke, but he felt a joyousness in his heart, which he understood to mean that God saw what this dream signified and how the event would come to pass in real life. He then beseeched St. Barbara ("my patron") to pray that God give him direction in his life.[23]

Dimitrii did not include this experience in his published vita of St. Barbara, but it shared many of the features of the vision of St. Orestes. In both, the saint knew Dimitrii's thoughts and spoke to him as if in conversation. Both saints instructed him in his work, just as St. Catherine and St. Peter had earlier instructed Aleksei and Nikon, even though Dimitrii had not conveyed any particular torment or confusion prior to the dream. St. Orestes instructed him to revise the vita and St. Barbara made him see the importance of providing a new crypt for her relics. Through the act of transcription, therefore, all of these figures were inscribing onto themselves a direct heavenly, even divine, guidance in specific matters, beyond the power of men to challenge.

The third text, also recorded in the diary (April 3, 1689), involved not a saintly visitation but a divine one, albeit mediated through human visage. It recounts a dream Dimitrii had involving Lazar Baranovich, at that time the archbishop of Chernigov. In this dream, set in Lent of 1676, Baranovich was preparing to conduct services. In the dream Dimitrii found himself standing in front of the altar at which Baranovich was seated. Several of the brethren gathered together to prepare for the service and to read. Suddenly Baranovich became angry at Dimitrii, saying "I did not select you! I did not say the name to you. Brother Paul the Deacon shall remain, the rest of you I did not select!" Dimitrii bowed down and promised to do better and begged his forgiveness. "He forgave me, kissed my hand, and told me to prepare for the service." Dimitrii then opened the service book, where he found the same words with which Baranovich had chided him. He read them with fear and amazement and the words were burned into his memory. At that moment he awoke, and he decided that the apparition meant that through the person of the archbishop the Creator himself was punishing Dimitrii. He asked around about Deacon Paul, but no one, either in Chernigov or Kiev, knew of such a person. "But God himself knows what this Deacon Paul signifies. Oh my God! Give me a sign *(ustroi o mne veshch')* through your blessedness and merciful will for the salvation of my sinful soul."[24]

Several decades later, both Peter I and the tsaritsa Catherine had dreams recorded, and although the original transcriptions seem to have disappeared from the relevant archival collection (Kabinet Petra Pervogo in *RGADA*), M. I. Semevskii published a transcription of the ones he found in 1884. Nearly a century later, James Cracraft subjected several of these dreams to a searching, if unavoidably speculative, psychoanalysis.[25] Peter's texts are relatively spare and non-narrative snapshots, rather like the prosaic dreams everyone experiences. Dominated by beasts, spires, rivers, these texts are devoid of transparently religious or saintly intervention, with the possible exception of one in 1716 in which: "His Majesty the Tsar had a dream about the Turks. He saw many of them in rich dress on a field in [St. Petersburg], among which was the vizier, who came up to His Majesty, said nothing, and then held up [his sword] in the form of a Latin cross, as the others standing behind the vizier did with their swords. And the swordbelts were inlaid with many rich gems. And after the vizier and the others had taken off their swords with the richly inlaid belts, they surrendered them to His Majesty."[26]

Here, the vizier would seem to be submitting to the power of the—albeit Latin—cross, a symbol of Christianity, as the tsar vanquished the sword and ill-gotten jewels of the infidel. The theme of the cross defeating the infidel from the east was a commonplace in Peter's Russia, as it had been in earlier reigns. This particular account appears to integrate many of the elements of the vaunted battle of Pruth in 1711 (jewels, laying-down of arms, the power of the cross), but it radically—and miraculously—reverses them, so that the vizier lays down his weapons before Peter and the cross, rather than vice versa, which would have been much closer to the actual outcome.

Dream texts, then, constituted expressive and powerful genres for political discourse and struggle, ways of mobilizing the otherwise unworldly and non-verbal pantheon of saints to one's cause. What, then, can one make of Aleksei's dream? Was there anything noteworthy about naming his daughter Catherine beyond the visitation itself (need there have been)? One can say that Aleksei drew specific examples and inspiration from the era in Byzantine history in which St. Catherine was said to have lived, and he referred to it in several writings, personal and public. A decree from July 1655, for example, offering praise and extra financial compensation to serving men spoke of how Russian forces had defeated the Poles and Lithuanians by fighting under the banner of the true cross "with which cross the ancient Pious King (tsar') Constantine defeated King Maxentius for having banished the Orthodox faith."[27] This identification of the Muscovites with Constantine and the true cross recurred on several occasions during and after Aleksei's reign, even though the role of latter-day Maxentius shifted depending upon the enemy of the moment. But here, and in most such analogies, there was no mention of St. Catherine.

In the absence of any entrée into the tsar's psyche, one can at least reconstruct the external context in which the dream occurred and then inquire whether or how St. Catherine might have been a part of it. The mystical visitation took place at a particularly difficult moment in church-state relations, just a few months after Nikon's apparent abdication as patriarch, an act that placed Aleksei in the awkward position of de facto head of the church for the next several years. By all accounts, he was preoccupied with religious affairs at this time, actively intervening to promote bishops sympathetic to the new prayer books and rituals and to compel reluctant ones to accept them. He had been in communication with several Orthodox patriarchs, including those of Gaza, Antioch, and Alexandria, whose intervention he eagerly sought, and which was fully provided.

A crucial figure in mediating these relations was the controversial and even notorious Arsenios the Greek, one of the most important translators working at the Muscovite court in the 1650s and 1660s—translators who collectively were preparing allegedly corrected Slavonic renderings of Greek texts. For someone entrusted with such an important mission —Arsenios served for several years as the de facto chief corrector at the Pechatnyi dvor—he had a particularly complicated past. Born in northern Greece around 1610, he had studied in Venice and then at the Collegium Athanasianum, or Greek College, in Rome. While in Rome he probably converted to the Uniate faith in order to be allowed to continue his studies. Upon returning to Greece he renounced Roman Catholicism, became a monk, and traveled to Constantinople for further study. Sent to the Peloponnesus as a representative of the Constantinople patriarch, he was soon arrested by the vizier under suspicion of espionage. While in prison he was subjected to torture until he agreed to be circumcised and converted to Islam.

Once free, Arsenios fled to Wallachia, confessed, and reconverted to Orthodoxy. He then traveled to Lviv and Kiev, where he had a chance meeting with Patriarch Paisios of Jerusalem, who was en route to Moscow to solicit alms from the Russian court. Paisios invited Arsenios to accompany him, and they arrived in Moscow in late January 1649. Because of Arsenios's apparent facility with Greek, Latin, and Slavonic, the Russian patriarchate asked that he be permitted to remain in Moscow to teach Greek and to assist in the important work of retranslating liturgical texts.[28] Shortly thereafter, however, Paisios learned of the dubious past of Arsenios and dutifully informed the Russian authorities. Arsenios initially denied everything, but under the threat of a physical examination he acknowledged the truth. Confronted with an awkward dilemma, the tsar ordered him sent to the Solovetskii Monastery so that he might be immersed in true Orthodox practice. Arsenios remained confined to Solovki for three years, but soon after ascending the patriarchal throne, Nikon brought him back to Moscow early in 1653. For the next several years, Arsenios occupied a position of considerable authority in the Moscow Printing Office, translating several important texts from Greek into Slavonic, albeit from fairly recent Greek sources rather than ancient ones. Once Nikon abdicated in July 1658, Arsenios's position became increasingly vulnerable. Deprived of his primary patron and under polemical attack as a heretic from Ivan Neronov among others, he continued translating, but with reduced authority, until September 1662, when the tsar sent him back to Solovki, after which the sources lose track of him.[29]

In addition to being the personification of everything that the Old Believers considered anathema about the church reforms, Arsenios holds particular interest as perhaps the primary translator of Greek patristic and liturgical writings into Slavonic. Everyone who has studied his primary publications— the revised *Sluzhebnik* of 1655, *Skrizhal'* (*Sacred Tablet*) of 1656, the *Khronograf* of Pseudo-Dorotheos, and a collection entitled *Anfologion* (1660)[30]—has concluded that Arsenios's relative discomfort with Slavonic resulted in a great many awkward and occasionally impenetrable neologisms. More importantly, scholars such as A. I. Sobolevskii and V. P. Adrianova-Peretts long ago determined that, in the main, his sources were not ancient manuscripts at all, but relatively modern editions published mostly in Venice and employing vernacular Greek, many of which had been brought to Moscow by Arsenii Sukhanov as part of his search for books and manuscripts during his not quite official visit to Mount Athos.[31] These editions in modern Greek contained numerous variances from the original ancient manuscripts, in many cases more than the Slavonic translations supposedly in need of immediate correction. Their recent vintage was known to many of the churchmen in the reform party on both sides of the Nikonian divide, and this fact merely confirmed to the Zealots of Piety the sinful nature of the project of retranslation.

The revised *Sluzhebnik* and *Skrizhal'* have attracted extensive commentary, and both of them have left a long paper trail on sources, translation, assessment, and subsequent approval by the church council of 1656 for publication and distribution.[32] To this one can add only a small inquiry regarding their publishing history. Arsenios's *Sluzhebnik*, the first corrected edition of the basic liturgy, had a press run of twelve hundred, rather typical for service books of its day. One should note, however, that each succeeding modification—and there were several during the late 1650s—had a comparable press run, thus guaranteeing maximum confusion since each edition differed slightly from the previous. *Skrizhal'*, by contrast, was a one-time publication, and probably not intended for circulation directly to parishes. The question, though, is just how widely did the patriarchate want to distribute *Skrizhal'*, that is, was it meant simply for a learned elite or did they want it to penetrate to monasteries and dioceses? Unfortunately, the relevant archival inventories relating to *pechatnyi dvor* are less than clear. There is no listing entitled "*Skrizhal*" in the inventory for the year 7164, or any years near it. The inventory does have a listing for 7164, however, for twelve hundred copies of something entitled "A Book of the Liturgy of John Chrysostom and on the Mysteries of the Church in the East, also some works [prepared] by Afanasii of Alexandria on various matters relevant to the banner of the cross."[33] If this pithy title indeed refers to *Skrizhal'* (and mercifully, such a title recurs nowhere else in the inventory), then the intended circulation was rather extensive. This commitment of time, labor, and material resources to a very large and bound edition spoke volumes about the doctrinal importance that both Nikon and the tsar ascribed to the book, and by extension, the authority that they were willing to grant Arsenios as, at the very least, the primary overseer of translation work.

The text of interest here, however, is *Anfologion,* the lengthy compendium of patristics and selected saints' lives on which Arsenios labored for several years and finally published in 1660. Once again, the inventory is opaque, but there is a listing for 7169, the year of its publication, for something described as "Books of Florid Works" *("Knig tsvetosloviia"),* which received a massive printing of 2,400 copies. In the absence of further documentary clarification, these identifications are by no means certain. But, once again, such a title does not appear again in the inventory and the timing is right. It is reasonably likely therefore that 2,400 copies of *Anfologion* were produced, an indication that the patriarchate endowed it with considerable importance indeed.

In that light, it is surprising that, with the exception of Adrianova-Peretts's analysis of the life of Aleksei the Man of God contained within it, *Anfologion* has been rather little studied. Extracted in part from three works by the contemporary (he died in 1660) Greek monk Agapios (Athanasios Landos) of Crete and Mount Athos, the originals, entitled (in Greek) *The Salvation of the Wicked, The Book of Paradise,* and *The Treasure,* had their first publication in Venice in the early 1640s.[34] They included a large selection of saints' lives and patristic writings on worship, ritual, and salvation. The precise circumstances behind the translations are not known, but the frontispiece says that Arsenios had compiled and translated these texts on instructions from the tsar.[35]

Although published in October 1660, the press's work on *Anfologion* commenced well before then. As one point of reference, work on translating and augmenting *Skrizhal'* may have begun as early as 1654. The manuscript text was completed in October 1655, and then approved for publication only in June of the following year. The Russian *Skrizhal',* a massive volume over eleven hundred pages long, included several original Slavonic texts not found in the Greek original: a long epistle of Patriarch Paisii on the correct forms of liturgy and ritual, an essay by Maksim the Greek, and some commentary of Nikon's.[36] Production required several months of intense work in a publishing house with many other demands on its resources, and its actual publication date came some time in the year 7166 (1657 or 1658).[37] *Anfologion* was slightly more than half that size (660 pages), but in its case the entire text had to be translated. And yet the press completed production by the end of 1660, a sign that considerable labor went into getting it into print with all deliberate speed. The nineteenth-century church scholar Makarii included it, along with the newly translated *Triod', Mineia obshchaia,* and *Mineia mesiachnaia,* as one of the texts that the church council of 1658 approved for publication, from which one might deduce that a manuscript translation had already been prepared by that time.[38] In all probability, therefore, the decision to translate had come while Nikon still occupied the patriarchal throne, and certainly well before the tsar's miraculous vision in Ermolino.

St. Catherine. Stroganov school, seventeenth century. From the chapel of the Intercession at Rogozhskoe cemetery, Moscow

This latter piece of timing is possibly important, or at the very least curiously coincidental. Arsenios's anthology borrowed or retranslated from many sources in addition to Agapios, making the final compilation and organization of the volume as original as would have been true for a manuscript codex of the day. The specific selections and their order of placement in the compendium, thus, offer potential hints of the compilers' priorities and concerns. Although not as fundamental as *Skrizhal'* or Semen Polotskii's *Zhezl pravleniia* (The Crozier of Governing) in establishing official church doctrine against the Old Believers, *Anfologion* did emerge out of the same context of doctrinal and liturgical correction, and it was expected to fulfill the same general purpose of articulating and enforcing liturgical uniformity, the authority of the Hellenic-based texts emanating from the patriarchate over those in use in the monasteries and dioceses. Chronologically, the fact that it was published in 1660 made it the first approved non-liturgical text to appear in print without any visible reference to Nikon. In both its narrative composition and its timing, therefore, it was an artifact of officialdom and it would have been scrutinized as such by all those in the hierarchy looking for any modifications in tone now that Nikon was—perhaps—no longer patriarch.

A quick review of the table of contents makes it clear that the ideological reliance on the Hellenistic church fathers remained unchanged. All the texts came from or described the history of the early, mostly fourth-to-sixth century, Byzantine church. Although not commenting on Russian ritual per se, these selections rearticulated by their very presence the unchallengeable authority of Christian antiquity: Gregory of Nazianzen, Chrysostom, St. Maximus, and others, unleavened by a single modern or Muscovite voice. Whether anyone at the time actually read the essays (apparently few did, given the absence of any seventeenth-century inscriptions or marginalia on surviving copies)[39] was almost beside the point. The collection announced the obvious simply by coming into being: Russia's faith was and would remain Greek, and at one with the rest of the Orthodox world. In this light, it is particularly interesting to note that the volume's first contribution was a newly translated vita of St. Catherine, prepared for the above-mentioned 1641 Venice edition by Agapios.[40] As expressed in the frontispiece,

> Contained herein are commentaries upon this world *("tsvetoslovie"):* the sufferings and martyrdom of Saint Catherine, the great martyr; and the [life of the] great martyr, Saint Feodor the stratilate; and the life of the venerable saint Aleksei the Man of God. In addition, it contains selected and useful chapters and instructive writings from religious and spiritually wise church teachers. By order of the most pious and blessed great lord tsar and grand prince Aleksei Mikhailovich . . . and with the blessing of the most holy metropolitans, archbishops, and bishops, and of the entire holy council of patriarchs.[41]

> This account of the suffering of Saint Catherine the holy martyr, and the great martyr Saint Feodor the stratilate, and Aleksei the Man of God, along with four essays by Gregory the Philosopher and chapters from Maxim the Confessor on love, were translated from Greek into Slavonic by the monk Arsenios the Greek.[42]

Unlike *Skrizhal'* and many manuscript *sborniki* that contained similar theological and liturgical miscellany, Arsenios's anthology provided no lengthy introductions or explanatory notes except for this summary. It is not known who among the likely participants chose the specific selections, or why he did so. Somehow, though, between the tsar, the patriarch, and Arsenios, a decision was made during the late 1650s to include St. Catherine and to feature her prominently in the title page. Whereas her vita fell in the middle of Agapios's original (and was not mentioned on the Greek title page), it was placed first in the Russian *Anfologion,* a re-placement that implies a deliberate choice.[43]

Records from the tsarist and patriarchal court shed no further light on the subject, but the mere fact of its publication and presumed distribution to leading church repositories conveyed an association between tsar and saint well beyond the physical confines of the Kremlin. One need not have read the text, but merely the title page, to see the link. From that perspective the publication of *Anfologion* was a decidedly public act, for the educated clergy if for no one else. Although not directly cited at the time, and perhaps not often read since,[44] this vita proved consequential in another way for Russian Orthodoxy, because it provided the narrative template for what would soon be the standard Russian hagiography of St. Catherine, composed by Dimitrii Rostovskii (Tuptalo) a few decades later.

Simply by inclusion in this collection, St. Catherine's life was implicitly being deployed in defense of a modernized Hellenism, that is, the very opposite of its anti-Hellenic iconology in the writings of Metropolitan Daniil a century earlier. The vita, in fact, differs markedly from the account in Makarii's *Velikii chet'i minei, Bdinski sbornik,* or any other Slavonic accounts that had circulated in Muscovy up to that point. Rather than beginning with Catherine's biography and personal virtues, the *Anfologion* text began with a lengthy meditation, or moral prelude, on the wishes of all those who trod the earth to enter the gates of heaven, the hopes of people from all stations in life that their humble deeds and earthly sufferings will grant them eternal peace. Only after several pages of reflection does the text even mention St. Catherine, her beauty, wisdom, and bravery, "and her many other virtues. Tsarevna Ekaterina, I sing the praises of your truth and divine wisdom."[45] The use of "tsarevna" presumably referred to St. Catherine's own royal birth, since the very next paragraph identified St. Catherine as the daughter of the prior king Constantine. Appearing so soon after the birth of Ekaterina Alekseevna, however, the expression "Tsarevna Ekaterina" almost certainly elided the two tsarevny for readers at court.

With the preamble complete, the author offered a lengthy vita, emphasizing Catherine's secular Hellenistic learning ("Homer, Aristotle, Virgil, Plato"), the temptations of Maxentius, her protection of her chastity, and most especially the mystical marriage, on which the text dwelled for several paragraphs. Reflecting perhaps the influence of baroque literary styles, this elaboration of the mystical marriage constituted something of an innovation for Muscovy, at least insofar as no previous (or previously recorded) Muscovite texts had given it narrative space. One supposes that the idea of the mystical marriage must have grated against Muscovite sensibilities, for whom women became brides of Christ by their office, through taking the veil, rather than via an individual, and almost anthropomorphic, betrothal and wedding ceremony. While the Muscovite church was obliged to accept this aspect of St. Catherine's vita as a given once it had gained the imprimatur of the patriarchs, it did not have to write about it in the native language or discuss it in the service. With the printing of *Anfologion,* this language barrier was now breached, as was the tight control over the contents of her vita.

The author directed special attention, both in the vita and in the appended prayers, to Catherine's martyrdom on behalf of the one true God (in this setting a transparent reference to Byzantine patristics), and the power of her unshakable faith to serve as an example that bound others to it (an ideal that Aleksei Mikhailovich espoused and openly emulated at court). At the very dawn of the church schism, then, the tsar was embracing St. Catherine as his own, much as Vasilii III had done on his deathbed, as a kind of talisman of the singular purity of the words and rituals of true belief, a feminine equivalent to the Byzantine church fathers whose authority legitimated the recourse to current Greek practice. By implication, her life and martyrdom, her refusal to submit to false wisdom and superstition, all re-presented in an approved translation of a 1641 vita published in modern Greek in Venice, were now boldly and openly claimed as their own by tsarist and patriarchal authority, the alliance of princely rule and the Council of Patriarchs, whose imprimatur was needed before the edition could see the light of day.

In this environment of swirling religious conflicts, the miraculous nighttime visitation, the naming of Tsarevna Ekaterina Alekseevna, and the establishment of the St. Catherine Monastery took on a decidedly political cast. The angel of God and the newly inscribed avatar of Hellenic purity had spoken directly with God's anointed one in the naming of a royal daughter, a sign perhaps that heaven was there to provide direction through the current troubled waters, and that this guidance would, or at least might, pass through the most pious and serene tsar. Henceforth the tsarevna, the new monastery, and by extension anything Catherinian that emanated from the court, served as constant physical reminders of the palpability of heavenly intervention, evidence of the mystery and might of divine coronation, the act of *pomazanie.*

The confluence of these multiple gestures transformed St. Catherine during the 1650s and 1660s from an intimate and rather privately venerated patron of the women of the tsar's family into a major political icon with public visibility. It is not at all surprising, therefore, that the tsar poured money into the building of the monastery and into the sacred images that it would hold. By 1664, Aleksei had resolved to use stone in the initial construction, an expensive commitment to be paid for out of the tsar's own funds. As a founding act, as if to demonstrate the momentous nature of the Catherinian visitation, the tsar donated a miracle-working icon of St. Catherine, presumably from the *terem* chapel, adorned with precious stones.[46] During his latter years he often visited Ekaterininskaia roshcha, typically in the company of a large retinue. At least one document records that he celebrated St. Catherine's Day there, along with two Moscow archimandrites, the secretary and undersecretaries of the Secret Chancery *(Tainyi prikaz),* and other dignitaries.[47] The iconostasis in the sanctuary's church was completed at the very end of his life, in 1674, and it is described as having gold and silver ornamentation and being extensively devoted to the life of St. Catherine. The sanctuary itself housed an icon with relics of the saint that had been donated to Muscovy some time earlier.[48] To honor the new iconostasis, Metropolitan Pavel of Sarsk was sent from Moscow to celebrate St. Catherine's Day there.

The consecration and formal dedication of the new cloister took place during the reign of Fedor Alekseevich on October 11, 1679. The new tsar, less enamored of the hunting fields than his father, traveled from Moscow along with the magnates V. V. Golitsyn, M. G. Romodanovskii, and several other high-ranking serving men specifically to participate in the dedication of the sanctuary's new church, named after St. Sergius and St. Nicholas.[49] The calendar of patriarchal celebrations, begun in 1668 and printed in volume 10 of *Drevniaia rossiiskaia vivliofika,* records that in 1679 the patriarch celebrated St. Catherine's Day with a midnight mass in the Dormition Cathedral and sent the archimandrite to read the liturgy in Ermolino immediately afterwards.[50] This appears to have been a singular event, inspired in all probability by the tsar's recent visit. According to the official log, subsequent official celebrations of St. Catherine's took place within the consecrated Kremlin spaces, as described in the previous chapter, circumscribed by the Dormition Cathedral, the Voznesenskii Convent, and the St. Catherine *terem* church.[51] Still, in 1687 the archbishop of Kolomenskoe, whose diocese included Ermolino, was sent to Voznesenskii Convent to celebrate the St. Catherine's Day mass there, an indication that the newly dedicated St. Catherine Monastery shared in the Kremlin's otherwise spatially circumscribed celebration of her day.[52]

Because it had been established in a patrimonial forest, the monastery initially lacked both arable fields and peasants to till them. Consequently it was maintained by a dedicated account out of the Kremlin's Bol'shoi dvorets, granting it foodstuffs and cash. In addition, the ruling family made certain that it was adorned with old and precious icons, and that the ark in which St. Catherine's local relics lay was equally rich and magnificent. The account books of the Secret Chancery reveal a great many allocations for the monastery, in particular during the 1670s and 1680s, an indication of its special standing at court.[53] Eventually a village and parish did grow up around the monastery, which at least until the secularization of church land in 1764, had ninety-nine desiatiny of its own land, mostly birch and nut trees. Over time the monks and peasants developed various local rituals venerating St. Catherine and her miraculous visitation to the tsar. On important days, and especially on the Day of St. Catherine, they would carry the miracle-working icon out of the church in a processional of the cross and take it into the woods and around to the homes of the nearby peasants.[54] Even there, however, the absence of recorded miracle-working tales suggests that Catherine seems not to have evolved into a popular or folk saint. She may have been venerated locally, but she did not become a source of individual intercession in peasant ritual, at least not in Tsar Aleksei's time. The monastery in Ermolino never became the proverbial chapel on the hill, and never served as a recognized substitute pilgrimage site for Sinai, as the St. Catherine chapels of England and Normandy had done in late medieval times. Even after the miraculous visitation, for which all of Muscovy rejoiced, the ceremonial cult of St. Catherine remained largely within the confines of the court even as the textuality of that cult was becoming more open.

Sinai

Parallel to these stormy happenings and perhaps interrelated with them, the Muscovite court was dramatically refashioning its ties to the St. Catherine Monastery in Sinai. Founded around the site of Moses' burning bush in mid-sixth century by Emperor Justinian, the monastery came to be associated with St. Catherine some time in the ninth or tenth century.[55] Since then the monastery has held St. Catherine's relics in a series of ornamental caskets, as well as housing numerous icons and wall paintings of the life of the saint. A major tourist attraction, the modern monastery contains approximately two thousand Byzantine icons, some dating from the monastery's founding, an extensive collection of religious art, hundreds of precious artifacts and vestments, as well as 3,500 illuminated manuscripts, one of the largest such collections in the world (by some estimates second only to the Vatican's). For many centuries it held the fourth-century Sinai Codex that now is housed at the British Museum in London.

From its earliest recorded history, the Sinai monastery dwelled in a desert region not far from the sea. Its outer walls stand up to two hundred feet tall and are several feet thick in some places. Ancient watchtowers still stand at its corners, as does the old reinforced gate and portcullis, the only point of ingress until the twentieth century. Despite these symbols of impregnability, as the position of the Greek authorities in Constantinople became ever more perilous, the monastery's overseers recognized their potential isolation, and they began to seek material support and physical protection from other corners of the Orthodox world, including eventually Rus'. Several Russian chronicles refer to the monastery's chronic shortage of money and loss of protection, especially after being sacked by the Egyptians in 1366, two concerns that directed the monastery's gaze increasingly northward.[56] The need to rebuild led to many journeys to raise alms, the first one by Bishop Markos to Novgorod in 1376, as reported briefly in the second Novgorod Chronicle.[57] "In the year 6884, Metropolitan Marko came to Novgorod from the

Holy Mother of God Mount Sinai." Chronicles relate that the monastery returned the favor by sending artifacts, icons, and even a tooth of St. Catherine to the Russian princes. The latter gift would appear to be unlikely, however, since there are no known Muscovite miracle-working tales involving relics of St. Catherine on Russian soil, and there are no further references to this tooth in Russian sources.

The fall of Constantinople in 1453 permanently altered the relationship between the Byzantine church and the Russian court. Rightly or wrongly, the monasteries of the Holy Land felt themselves to be particularly vulnerable, and they turned with increasing frequency to Muscovy for material assistance. Added to this was the marriage of Ivan III to Sofia Paleologue, the daughter of the now deposed Byzantine ruler, in 1459. As N. Kapterev showed long ago, these twin reversals of political fortunes reverberated broadly in Russian political self-images, as did the image of Muscovy in the Orthodox world.[58] For Sinai, it amounted to an open door.

By the early sixteenth century Russian clerics were making periodic pilgrimages, both political and spiritual, to Sinai, and deputations from Sinai came regularly to Moscow. In 1519, Grand Prince Vasilii Ivanovich met with two elders from the Sinai monastery, granting them six hundred items of gold, sable, squirrel, and other valuable objects. A similar mission in 1558 yielded a promise, repeated in 1581, from Ivan IV to provide extensive material support.[59] These generated a considerable flow of alms, and in 1582 Ivan dispatched two merchants, Trifon Korobeinikov and Iurii the Greek, to travel to Constantinople, Antioch, Alexandria, Jerusalem, "and to Mt. Sinai, and to Egypt, to the patriarchs and archimandrites and abbots, and all the common fraternity" to present alms. And with them he sent nine hundred rubles in cash "for the church on Mt. Sinai named after the Great martyr Catherine and where her honored relics lie."[60] According to another account he commissioned an eternal flame for the monastery to burn above the reliquary. A few years later, in 1593, the Muscovite court sent an additional 430 gold pieces to Sinai to commemorate the new Moscow patriarchate.[61]

There are at least three published versions of Korobeinikov's journeys to the Holy Land (and several republications), one printed in 1783, another in 1789 in Nikolai Novikov's *Drevniaia rossiiskaia vivliofika,* and the last a century later in *Pravoslavnyi palestinskii sbornik.*[62] On the initial trip, Korobeinikov's party arrived at Sinai in June 1584 (7092), but stayed only three days at the St. Catherine Monastery.[63] They returned in November and celebrated St. Catherine's feast day at the monastery, an event that Korobeinikov described in some detail: "After vespers the Patriarch opened the crypt with the relics and kissed the holy relics on the head himself, as did we unworthy sinners. And the relics lay there, collected in the crypt and covered with a cotton cloth and an iron casement above that. A blessed aura and goodness emanated from the holy relics and the cloth. And then the Patriarch picked up the cloth and blessed it. But the holy relics themselves were not given to anyone. And this is how the honored holiday was carried out."[64]

The second pilgrimage, carried out on behalf of Tsar Fedor Ivanovich in 1593 shortly after the Moscow Patriarchate's establishment (7101), constituted an extended expression of thanksgiving and largesse by the Russian court to the more ancient but now captive co-religionists to its south. As the tsar's official envoy, Korobeinikov distributed alms everywhere he went—to a very large number of religious offices and individuals—as well as charity for destitute Christians. Many of these benefices honored the memories of church figures, both Greek and Russian, thereby proclaiming the oneness of their faith and the benefaction of the Muscovite tsar. At the St. Catherine Monastery, Korobeinikov distributed forty-four gold pieces to the hegumen, thirty elders, and assorted other figures in residence.[65]

It is also from about this time that other Russian pilgrims, primarily clerical officials, began to pen their impressions of the Holy Land, including St. Catherine's. An envoy for Metropolitan Paisii, for example, described two such trips, in 1577 and 1592, in which he spoke of his sense of awe at the saint's crypt, at that time made of white marble and gold. Here lay "the relics of the redeemer (izbavatel'nitsa) Catherine, the martyr in Christ the Savior, the divinely wise and saintly maiden, who silenced the rhetoriticians with her Godly speech. Like precious treasures, her relics are kept under three locks."[66]

These were not the first Russian travelers to the Holy Land, to be sure, and they were not the first to describe their experiences. An early twelfth-century abbot, Daniil of Chernigov, is thought to have journeyed throughout the Holy Land between 1113 and 1115,[67] and several fifteenth-century copies of his journeys survive. The abbess, St. Efrosiniia, the daughter of Prince Briacheslav of Polotsk travelled to Jerusalem and was buried there in 1173. Stefan of Novgorod allegedly traveled there in the mid-fourteenth century; Ierodeacon Zosima of the Trinity Monastery did so around 1420; a wealthy Moscow merchant (gost') in 1466; and deacon Arsenii Selunskii did the same at an unknown time before the sixteenth century.[68] None of these accounts afforded St. Catherine or the monastery any unique standing or importance to the Russian faith, no hint at a special cult of St. Catherine. Indeed, the earliest recorded journeys make no mention of St. Catherine's Monastery at all, even though their accounts consist of little more than travel logs. At most, the early descriptions—such as Korobeinikov's—articulated a connection between St. Catherine and the Russian court as one of many such growing ties with Holy Land sites, along with Mount Athos, Jerusalem, Alexandria, and a number of other monasteries. In the seventeenth century, however, the cash flow grew wider, and the Sinai monastery began to loom larger in the official Orthodoxy of the Romanov court. In 1630, Tsar Mikhail Fedorovich sent an official charter to the Sinai monastery that permitted representatives of the monastery free passage through Moscow once every four years to seek alms. Although the charter conveys the heightened visibility and importance of the St. Catherine Monastery to the Russian crown, this patent should not be seen as singular, but rather understood in a broader context of Moscow's growing assertiveness within Orthodoxy. Charters of this type, as Kapterev has shown, were becoming relatively common, with ever more monasteries and bishoprics in the Orthodox world turning to the new Romanov dynasts for financial support. Moscow, in turn, saw alms giving as a way of enhancing both the prestige of its newly patriarchal church and the court's ambition to be the protector of Orthodox Christianity. Thus, the terms granted to the Sinai monastery were offered as well to other foreign monasteries and bishoprics in Macedonia, Jerusalem, Alexandria, and elsewhere.[69] Several Russian monasteries were granted similar patents for periodic travel within Muscovy to gather alms. In return for cash, these sites were more than willing to shower Muscovy with holy relics, literally hundreds of which, including the putative heads of St. Gregory and St. John Chrysostom, poured into Russia during the seventeenth century. Among these holy relics was one of St. Catherine's fingers.[70]

Be that as it may, the Sinai monks continued to look to Moscow with increased urgency, as reflected in the regular flow of delegations from the monastery to Muscovy, including three between 1625 and 1636.[71] There is some evidence, in the form of the monastery's memorial book, to suggest that this interest was reciprocated. This record, Codex Sinaiticus Slavonic 49, lists the supplicants from Russia and the surrounding territories (especially Ukraine) who requested that special prayers be read on their behalf and on behalf of their kin. The earliest of the records, consisting almost exclusively of Muscovite supplications, date from the 1630s, and the entries continue for about a century.[72] The vast majority of the entries came from the elite ranks of Russian society, including the ruling family, lay serving men (boyars, okol'nichi, etc.) and high-ranking ecclesiastical officials, including the patriarchs. Some came from commoners, but these were relatively few and most of these were individuals, such as choir singers *(pevchie)* connected to important churches and cathedrals.

The entries typically included two categories: prayers for the health and well-being *("o zdravii")* of the living members of the family, and prayers of salvation and penitence *("za upokoi")* for the deceased. In both cases, the names of family members are given so that they may be mentioned in the prayers. Unfortunately, the memorial book does not cite the specific language of the prayers, and only infrequently does it indicate the value of the family's offering. But the brief and uniform entries imply that the prayers were standard and formulaic. Nothing in the record suggests that the monks were specifically asked to seek the personal intercession of St. Catherine, and although women's names are listed as frequently as men's, there is nothing to suggest a special bond with female supplicants, as had taken place elsewhere in Europe in previous centuries. Still, the large number of entries, involving several dozen requests, indicates an elevated importance of the Sinai monastery for the seventeenth-century Muscovite elite.

The regency of Sofia saw the first systematic attempts to make the relationship of patronage between the Russian crown and the shrine permanent, an attempt that Kapterev interpreted as signifying Sofia's desire to be seen as the Orthodox tsaritsa of the Christian East.[73] Several years earlier, in 1667, the monastery's abbot and subsequent archimandrite, Ananias, had attended the Moscow Synod that formally condemned Nikon as part of the entourage of the archbishop of Sinai. This experience made him something of a known presence, and in 1682 Ananias headed a second delegation to Moscow. This embassy aimed to convince Sofia to extend the formal protection of the Romanov court to the monastery. He described a cloister that had become impoverished and found itself perpetually vulnerable to assault by local bandits; the cloister stood in dire need of Moscow's physical protection.[74] Ananias warned darkly that desperation could drive the monastery into the hands of "the Romans," who in every way possible were endeavoring to take over the monastery. Only with formal Russian patronage *("popechenie")* could the pope be kept at bay.

This dire account appears to have had as much to do with Ananias's own agenda, and the truly byzantine politics of the Orthodox church in the Holy Land, as it did with the material conditions or imminent perils to the monastery. Greek documents of the time, particularly those from the Jerusalem Patriarchate, revealed considerable irritation with Ananias's aggressive pursuit of Russian patronage, and they openly questioned whether relations with the local Egyptian population were perilous. Ananias apparently hoped to protect the monastery, not from imminent physical danger from the local Arab population, but from what he, representing the monastery's brethren, saw as the overbearing control of Jerusalem. He envisaged the Muscovite court as a protector that would leave the monastery more or less alone and would act as a political buffer against the patriarchal institutions of the Orthodox East.[75]

The gambit ultimately worked, and a serious inquiry was undertaken, apparently at Sofia's behest, one which included certification of the miraculous powers of the relics at Sinai. A manuscript of 1686 or 1688 by Archbishop Ioanniki of Sinai, entitled *A Description of Mount Sinai and a Treatise on the Relics of St. Catherine,* briefly delineated for the Muscovite court the history of her powers.[76] It included the following: "At the time when the false prophet Mohammed appeared in this world, the kings Hakimapril and Otakar [Melekhtakar] ruled in Egypt in [Mohammed's] name. Otakar's father was a Turk, but his mother was a Christian, and Otakar departed the Muslim faith and began preaching another faith, the *"truziiskaia"* [possibly Druze].[77] The followers of this faith believe in Christ and in the devil, and they possess idols. To this very day they dwell in high mountains in the land of Damascus."[78]

The account continues with a test of faith. Otakar's father brings him to Jerusalem in the care of the Orthodox patriarch, who advises him to turn to true Christianity, which he eventually does through the miraculous intervention of St. Catherine. The text then fast forwards to the reign of Aleksei Mikhailovich, who it asserts, had sent the ierodiakon Meletei to Sinai [one presumes this happened at the time of the tsar's vision in Ermolino], where he prayed to see her holy relics, "held behind three strong locks. The archbishop had one key, a priestess had the second, and an elder of the Cathedral the third."[79] His prayers answered, Meletei is permitted to witness the reliquary and he confirms her powers to the tsar, adding "even the western churches, the Franks and others, come here and pray and demonstrate a great reverence and they preach this throughout Italy."[80]

Confronted by such overwhelming evidence, Sofia relented. When Archimandrite Kirill of Sinai came to Moscow in 1687 with a petition signed by all the monks of Sinai, she agreed that Muscovy would become the official protector of the cloister of St. Catherine, and she issued a formal charter in February 1688 confirming her decision, as a consequence of which the Sinai monastery became known locally as "the Russian tsar's cloister."[81] To sanctify the decision in February 1689 the Muscovite court commissioned an imposing silver shrine for housing St. Catherine's relics, which its representatives presented to the monastery in 1691, in the name of the now disgraced Sofia, and the still reigning co-tsars, Ivan V, and Peter.[82] Simultaneously the co-rulers ordered a vessel made to house the relics of Alexander Nevskii, whose cult was to play a major role in the sanctification of St. Petersburg during Peter's reign.[83]

Recognizing what it had achieved, the Sinai monastery showered the Muscovite court with words of appreciation. In 1693, Kirill returned to Moscow to express his thanks in person. "This vessel constitutes an eighth wonder [of the world], which must now be added to the ancient ones," he proclaimed.[84] Coupled with his transparent display of sycophancy was Kirill's insistence that Moscow provide five thousand rubles a year to the Arab neighbors of the monastery, a small sum, he assured them, for protecting the site where Moses received the Commandments and where St. Catherine's relics had been delivered. He then sent separate letters to tsarevnas Natal'ia and Ekaterina Alekseevna in which he compared the former to Empress Theodosia and the latter to St. Catherine. Finally, he turned to his true pecuniary purpose, to secure additional precious stones and silver to adorn the saint's crown on the new shrine.[85]

In a series of clever, albeit reluctant, strokes these reciprocal gestures, however mercenary, affirmed the Russian crown's role as *the* powerful protector of Byzantine Christendom, its affinity to a site so holy that it was preached about all over Italy (i.e., its importance to all of Christendom), and its defense of Christianity against false prophets, specifically Islam. Not surprisingly, the implications of elevating Moscow, and in particular the Moscow Patriarchate, to the status of international protector of Orthodoxy left the other patriarchs, especially Dosifei of Jerusalem, decidedly uneasy. Dosifei wrote first to Ioakim, with whom he was not on good terms, and then to Ioakim's successor Adrian, to denounce the agreement as little more than a Muscovite grab for power and status. The monks at St. Catherine's, he insisted, were in fact living quite comfortably under the protection of the Egyptians, and they had no need for further support.[86]

A few years later the deteriorating position of the Orthodox population in Jerusalem compelled Dosifei to reverse field and endorse Russian protection, hoping thereby to encourage Peter to enter the war against the Ottoman Turks and subsequently to remain a combatant in spite of initial reversals.[87] Still, the decades of ambivalence on all sides reflected the sensitivities within Orthodoxy to Muscovy's commitment to Sinai. From Russia's perspective, protecting the St. Catherine Monastery amounted to an open-ended obligation with considerable and indeterminable risks, not the least of which was the potential to be drawn into armed conflicts of little strategic value. The decision to take on this role, therefore, constituted a political calculation in which the added prestige to the still young and insecure Romanov dynasty of protecting a particularly sacred site in the Holy Land, against Islam and Roman Catholicism alike, outweighed the pitfalls. From this perspective, Sofia's symbolic co-joining of St. Catherine's persona and holy relics with those of Alexander Nevskii, a native hero and homegrown warrior for Christ, further asserted the unity of ancient Russian heroism and the sanctity of universal Christendom. Through St. Catherine, the Romanov dynasty was renewing and even intensifying its claim to be the defender of the faith on Christendom's eastern flanks, the protector of seventeen centuries of Christian heritage, in particular in the eastern empire.

In this context of Russia as Christendom's eastern protector, it bears mention that the Mazurinskii Chronicle, composed in Moscow at some time during the 1680s, included brief accounts of the martyrdoms of far more early Byzantine saints, both male and female, than had been typical for Russian chronicles. The list included Evdokia (year 5660), Vera, Nadezhda, Liubov (5662), Khristiana (5700), Tatiana (5718), and several others. It added a new entry on the martyrdom and miracle of St. Catherine, "In the year 5804 [approximately 296 AD], the sainted martyr Catherine, during the reign of King Maxentius, was made to endure various torments, at the end of which she was beheaded. Instead of blood, milk flowed from her neck. And then angels bore her body to be buried on Mt. Sinai."[88] This heightened attention to Byzantine saintly women reflects the larger embrace of saints and the miraculous within official religiosity in the late seventeenth century. Paul Bushkovitch has described in detail a process in which the patriarchal church tried to curtail the proliferation of local miracle cults, a part of which involved elevating the cults of ancient saints as a substitute. Neither this nor any of the other relevant texts, it bears mentioning, made any allusions to the doctrine of the Third Rome or anything like it, notwithstanding the superficial affinity between protecting the Christian heritage of a fallen Byzantium and the claims of a new Rome, which according to the doctrine, would usher in the apocalypse, Christ's second coming, and the end of days.

Subsequent to this agreement, and for the next 230 years, the Sinai monastery emerged as a prime site for Russian religious pilgrimages to the Holy Land, and St. Catherine as an object of Russian-specific veneration. Several pilgrims have published moving accounts of their journeys, from which it is clear that the shrine of 1689 constituted a focal point that united national pride with the spiritual wonderment at having reached a special shrine. Some were overcome by its magnificence. Others spent days trying to decipher the Russian inscriptions and ponder their importance. Still others sought parallels back home, the most common being—once again—the reliquary of Alexander Nevskii in St. Petersburg.[89] Even those who did not necessarily linger at the St. Catherine Monastery made it a point to visit the many other shrines and chapels of St. Catherine scattered throughout the holy land.

In 1793 and 1794, for example, the monk Meletei traveled from his cloister in Sarov to Constantinople and Jerusalem, and he seemed to go out of his way to linger at St. Catherinian *sviatyni*. These include marking St. Catherine's Day in Constantinople, visiting a St. Catherine's church in Jerusalem, stopping at a St. Catherine's convent outside of Jerusalem, and, finally, spending the sixth week of Lent in 1794 in the monastery of St. Catherine.[90] The Moscow priest Ioann Luk'ianov received permission directly from the tsar to travel to the Holy Land in 1711 so that he might worship at the Holy Sepulcher. After many weeks of travel from Moscow to Kiev and then south, he arrived in Jerusalem and proceeded to connect virtually every footstep to events in the Old and New Testament (complete with marginal citations from Scripture) as well as to the first centuries of Christianity.[91] Among the sites he visited was St. Catherine's, to which he was summoned on her name day.[92] As a polemical counterpoint to these expressions of religious and historical wonder, Luk'ianov repeatedly decried the damage done to Christian sites by Turks, Tatars, and Arabs at nearly every town through which he passed. He therein directed the readers to recognize their own—and Russia's—oneness with the positive, moral, and godly antiquity of the Incarnation forever under siege from the Infidel.

Those pilgrims from the eighteenth through the twentieth centuries who did spend time at the Sinai monastery invariably made note of its connection to Muscovy, and they frequently conveyed their sense of awe at what they experienced there. After traveling on a camel through the desert in 1870, Archimandrite Antonin arrived at St. Catherine's, which he immediately recognized from pictures of it. Overwhelmed, he proclaimed, "O God of Sinai, God great and awesome! You indeed are our God, the one God of miracles!"[93] Later in his narrative Antonin went on for several pages marveling at the shrine of St. Catherine. "In spite of all the descriptions of the Sinai cathedral [which I had read], I could not have imagined it, especially [here] at the place of the miraculous epiphany."[94]

What is remarkable about this and other accounts, beyond the sheer power of the religious feeling that they convey, is their sense of having uncovered something simultaneously precious and distinctly Russian, nestled in the heart of the most sacred landmarks of the early church. Some visitors, of course, composed simple travel diaries, with lists and descriptions of towns and monuments. Others, on commission from the Russian Academy of Sciences or other scholarly bodies, spoke about specific artifacts and manuscripts.[95] A significant number, though, wrote as though their traversing through Jerusalem, Bethlehem, and Sinai was retracing and personalizing the geography of Scripture and early Christianity, as if for the first time.

When Grigorii Luk'ianov visited the monastery in November 1932 he described and dated the silver vessels with great precision, as if no one had done so previously. For some unknown reason the available descriptions at that time identified the vessels as gifts of Catherine II and Alexander II respectively. "From the first I doubted that the older of the two vessels dated from the late eighteenth century, the epoch of Catherine II. The elaborate Slavonic style of the inscriptions on five of its side medallions, the formalistic language and turn of phrases were more characteristic of an earlier time, the 17th century."[96] He then provided what he thought was the first complete rendering of the inscriptions on the medallions. These are etched in a condensed and angular paleography that, to be sure, is particularly difficult to decipher. And it may well be that the sign in front of them contained mis-attributions. Apparently unbeknownst to Luk'ianov, however, the inscriptions had been fully transcribed and dated as early as 1707 when the priest Andrei Ignat'ev and his brother Stefan accompanied Peter Andreevich Tolstoi on his embassy to Constantinople and the Holy Land. The trio spent several days at St. Catherine's during which time they copied out the inscriptions in full.[97] Subsequent visitors did the same, and a number of their accounts had come into print well before Luk'ianov's pilgrimage.[98] For them as for Luk'ianov, the coffin, ceremoniously inscribed on three sides in Russian, constituted a spiritual merging of two realms of their inner being: faith and national identity. In short, once formal patronage was confirmed, national identity and St. Catherine became co-joined in the experiences of Russian pilgrims to the Holy Land almost without their thinking about it.

As symbolism this was a noteworthy achievement for the Russian crown, both domestically and internationally, one that laid special claim to St. Catherine and her most sacred spaces as its own. Still, if officialdom meant with these acts to claim St. Catherine exclusively for itself, it had powerful competition at home. Within a few years of the formal consecration of the monastery in Ermolino, the *Life of the Boiaryna Morozova*, written probably in the early 1680s and portraying the great early female martyr of the Old Belief and one-time personal intimate of the ruling family, gave St. Catherine pride of place as a holy example toward which Morozova strived.

> Three days after the torture the tsar sent a musketeer commander to Feodora and spoke thus: "Righteous mother Feodosia Prokopievna! You are a second Catherine the martyr! I myself beseech you, listen to my advice. I want to restore you to your previous honor. . . . Righteous mother Feodosia Prokopievna! You are a second Catherine the martyr!"
>
> When Feodora saw and heard this, she said to the envoy: "What are you doing, man? Why are you bowing so much to me? Stop. Listen, so that I may begin to speak. I am not worthy of the words the sovereign spoke about me. I am a sinner and have not attained the virtue of Catherine, the great martyr."[99]

Inverting the official appropriation of St. Catherine, the work drew an implicit affinity with Morozova, herself a high-born, righteous, humble, but steadfast martyr to the faith. It is not known, of course, whether any such conversation ever occurred, or even whether Morozova linked herself and St. Catherine. Her biographer clearly did, however, and by extension so too did her household and the inner circle of early leaders of the Old Belief, from whose milieu the biographer likely came. A passage in the 1682 *Confession* of Deacon Ignatii of Solovetskii Monastery conveys a matter-of-factness that implies an uncomplicated acceptance of St. Catherine into the world view of the early Old Believers, one that made explicit the roles implied by the work on Morozova. As part of a lengthy condemnation of officialdom, Ignatii wrote, "Impious tormentors of earlier times, idol worshipers, were more merciful than you, as is shown in the sufferings of holy martyrs. In the suffering of the Christly martyr Catherine, Porphyrius the centurion brought the queen to the martyr at dark, and all the soldiers under his command believed in Christ, the true Light."[100]

By laying at least occasional claim to the Catherinian vita, the early Old Believer polemicists were extending its political meaning as far as they could stretch it. Aleksei Mikhailovich and his successors to the throne became latter-day Maxentiuses, and the Old Believers were thereby equivalent in their sacrifice to early Christian martyrs. The reference to the secretly baptized queen and centurions of Alexandria had a particularly ominous tone. As a member of the upper aristocracy, Morozova had maintained personal contact with the court and with the tsar himself well after she had fallen under a political cloud. Aleksei Mikhailovich's first wife, Mariia Il'inichna, had protected Morozova and her coterie until her own death in 1669, whereas the tsar's second wife, Natal'ia, had not. The anonymous musketeer of the Morozova tale becomes a second Porphyrius, the converted general, an ominous tone made explicit when Ignatii reminded his readers that Porphyrius brought all of his troops with him to the cause of the faith.

Ignatii's St. Catherine, then, raised the specter of sympathy for the Old Belief within the ruling family itself through the legacy of Mariia Il'inichna, and perhaps more widely within the tsar's own armed guards, the *streltsy*. To the survivors of the Solovki uprising this message implied that the earthly struggle was not yet lost. Perhaps in response, Abbot Nikon of the Krasnogorskii Monastery near Pinega, in the diocese of Archangel (the access point to the Solovki Islands), assembled fifteen books during the 1680s to win over the impressionable laity in the struggle against the teachings of the Old Belief. Most of these were sermons from the Greek church fathers against the heresies of their times. Others included *Skrizhal,* the *Book of Iosaaf and Varlaam,* and an extract from the *Menology* (Tsvetnik) *of the Life and Passion of St. Catherine,* the only saint's life so included.[101] Similarly, Ivan Meshcherinov, the newly appointed (1674) voevoda who crushed the Solovetskii uprising, had a manuscript service to St. Catherine, transcribed by a certain psalmist Senka, among the handful of books in his possession from his time in the far north.[102] It is not clear if he had purchased this manuscript for his own use or if he had confiscated it from the monastery's immense collection of fifteen hundred books and manuscripts, as he had many of the other books he held. Either way, the service was sufficiently important at that moment and place to merit specific transcription.[103]

All of this suggests that St. Catherine was recognized as a vital and strategic figure in the religious struggles of the latter seventeenth century, at least among court circles, serving men, and the upper clergy. More importantly, her entry into political discourse embodied very high stakes as a strategic and contested figure of female intellect, unassailable moral authority, and resistance,[104] a martyr now claimed on both sides of the new religious fault line.

5

Dimitrii Rostovskii and the Militant Bride of Christ

• This chapter focuses largely on the Catherinian theme in the writings of Dimitrii Savich Tuptalo (1651–1709), St. Dimitrii Rostovskii, who served as archbishop of Rostov during the last seven years of his life and achieved formal sanctification there in 1757. It pays particular attention to those writings he composed between the last two decades of the seventeenth century and the end of his life. During these decades the court cult of St. Catherine underwent subtle but important changes, both in content and in context. The changes in content brought into the foreground elements of the Catherinian vita, in particular the mystical marriage and the conversion of courtiers, that had been present but relatively muted in previous Russian texts and visuals. The contextual changes involved a coming-out of sorts, the evolution of the court cult from a familial and Kremlin-centered veneration into one that had a somewhat more public face and potentially wider reach than had been true in earlier decades. The agencies through which this occurred were the emergence of baroque styles at court and the marriage of saints' lives with movable type.

A remarkably prolific writer, Dimitrii authored at least two long texts about St. Catherine, the vita in his *Kniga zhitii sviatykh* (first published in Kiev in 1689) and a homily entitled "Pouchenie na pamiat' sviatyia Velikomuchenitsy Ekateriny," which was subsequently published in a posthumous multi-volume selection of his writings. He also appears to have revised a third text, the abbreviated vita account and name day service in the *Mineia sluzhebnaia* (Moscow, 1692).[1] Although it makes sense to inquire into these texts and Dimitrii's interest in this particular saint, it is equally important to understand that he was not alone in his interests. Rather he was one of several clerical—mostly Ukrainian—literati (Semen Polotskii, Karion Istomin, Epifanii Slavinetskii) who collectively gave rise to a modest literary celebration of St. Catherine at court during the latter decades of the seventeenth century, a celebration that was matched by the lavish official feast day celebration at the patriarchal court. Indeed, the menu for the patriarchal table for the 1698 celebration listed nearly thirty courses, including several fish stews, sturgeon, various meat pies and stews, veal, various types of caviar, cold dishes, cabbages, as well as a variety of hot fish dishes.[2]

Although mostly unpublished at the time, the literary texts seem to have circulated widely within the well-educated circles at court and among the ecclesiastical authorities. All were emblematic of the expressiveness of individual authors in and around centers of power. Given her elevated standing, St. Catherine figured prominently in several of them, primarily homiletics, but also some verse, a few inscriptions, and even performances in the early court theater. Semen Polotskii, for example, composed a sermon celebrating St. Catherine's name day, which was published in one of two posthumous collections of his homilies, *Vecheria dushevnaia* (which also included an image of Catherine, among several other saints, in the highly decorative ornamental page after the table of contents).[3] Although undated, Polotskii's collected sermons almost certainly were composed during his years in Moscow (1664 until his death in 1675), because they were written in a language that, the specialist literature agrees, was distinctly Muscovite rather than the western Rus' mix of Polish, Latin, and Russian of his earlier *virshi*.[4] In all likelihood, the St. Catherine homily was meant to honor Ekaterina Alekseevna—the tsar's daughter and the focus of the miraculous visitation in 1658—and by extension to pay homage to the tsar's religiosity.

Appropriately for an oration honoring a young tsarevna, the text celebrated female chastity, and it began with something of a spiritual taxonomy of the three states or roles *(sani)* for women: maiden, spouse, and widow. Polotskii organized his comments around a quote from Corinthians in which Paul admonished the Corinthians to abandon their excesses and to be pure in both body and spirit. He then briefly reviewed all three female states and quickly moved on to his main theme: those women, exalted by the church fathers, who maintained their maidenhood as adults after having been touched by an angel. The kingdom of heaven had selected ten such women, not earthly wives or widows, but maidens, one of whom was St. Catherine, the one true heavenly bride, the one whose humility ("ne imeia v sebe skvernago gordosti poroka") elevated her above all the others.[5] Consistent with the prescriptions of the *mineia obshchaia,* he remarked on her beauty, courage, and wisdom, and presented an abbreviated account of her ultimate martyrdom at the hands of Maxentius, the epitome of evil power.[6] For Polotskii, St. Catherine's chastity and mystical marriage were paramount, empowering her to become the paragon of the spiritual power of virgins in Christ to surmount earthly evil.

During the 1680s and 1690s, Karion Istomin also wrote a number of short verses on St. Catherine—this time dedicated mostly to Ekaterina Ioannovna, the daughter of Ivan V—and probably one or two name day sermons as well.[7] Although none have been published, S. N. Brailovskii's inventories of the manuscript codexes provide hints to their contents. Like Polotskii, Istomin dwelt on chastity and purity, and because these lines honored a young tsarevna, he spoke of good health as well. On November 24, 1693, for example, he composed a brief birthday homily in verse *("kratkoslovie stikhotvornoe")* on St. Catherine, wishing good health and long life to Ioann Alekseevich, his wife, and his two daughters.[8] The inscriptions, as described by Brailovskii, were intended for the holy gates of a cathedral "for a side room by the second window," and these too praised the virgin St. Catherine for her love of Christ and for her wisdom.[9] The inventory offers no details of the texts of the sermon(s) except the advice at the bottom, "Pray for one another, and then embrace" ("Molitesia drug za druga iako da istseleete").[10]

What is one to make of these particular works? In part they reflected the elevated visibility of the court cult of St. Catherine in the wake of the activities of the middle and later parts of the seventeenth century described previously, and her evolution into an unofficial patron saint of the Romanov women. St. Catherine's prominence had made her an attractive name day saint for the newborn girls of the Romanovs, and this association, in turn, attracted literary attention to her and thereby elevated the visibility of her cult at the tsarist court. A good illustration of this reciprocal process was the naming of one of Ivan V's daughters. Even though born on October 29, a full four weeks before St. Catherine's Day, and baptized on November 8, the family named her Catherine.[11] Had he so wished, Ivan could have chosen from several female saints whose vitae were recounted in the Russian collections of Saints' Lives—Zenobia (October 30), Matriona and Theoctista (November 9), Stephanida (November 11), Cecilia (November 22)—all of whose name days fell closer to the actual date of birth. If these proved unappealing, the Orthodox calendar also offered a much larger pantheon of saints whose days were listed on the calendar but without an accompanying vitae. These included the martyrs Juliana, Cyrenia (both November 1), Athanasia, Claudia, and Polactia (November 6), Karina (November 7), Alexandra (November 9) the Persian martyr Anna (November 20), the nuns Eustolia and Sosipatra (November 9), and the empress Theodora (November 14). The decision to pass over all these choices, venerable and obscure alike, suggests that St. Catherine was a deliberate choice, deemed more fitting for a tsarevna. And that choice in turn stimulated the production of these new St. Catherine texts.

Larger changes were afoot, however, in both culture and politics, and the cult of St. Catherine was but one aspect of them. This period marked the dawn of the Muscovite baroque in both the visual and verbal arts, an onset of elaborate poetic flourishes in which ornamentation, visual complexity, and rich stylistic virtuosity (some would say excess) brought in via Poland and Ukraine became something of the norm for Muscovite court and high church culture. The visual illustration for Polotskii's *Vecheria dushevnaia* is a prime example. This moment of transition also constitutes the accepted beginning of the individually authored Russian literature, much discussed in recent years by literary specialists, some of whom see it as the birth of the modern in Russian letters.[12] These early literati were educated clergy, almost to a man, and their subjects of choice tended to come from Scripture, religious celebrations, and panegyrics, often a combination of all three. What seemed to motivate the St. Catherine works was less the veneration of the saint and more the celebration of the ruling family, particularly via their name day saints. Thus, Istomin wrote other verses in 1689 in honor of the name day saints of Peter and his new bride, Evdokia Fedorovna, as well as a verse for Peter's mother, the tsaritsa Natal'ia Kirillovna, and his sister-in-law Parask'eva in 1692.[13] Several years earlier Polotskii himself had composed a lengthy series of epigrams honoring the name day saints of everyone in the tsar's immediate family.[14] Add to these the numerous panegyric verses to Sofia, Fedor Alekseevich, and virtually everyone else within the tsarist family, and it becomes evident that genre, family names, and poetic freedom played the primary roles in inspiring these texts, and that the attributes of the particular saint were of lesser importance.

By comparison to these rather brief works, it is the sheer volume and narrative force of Dimitrii's meditations on St. Catherine that stand out. Equally important, his vita of St. Catherine had the enormous advantages of print and of the official imprimatur of the clerical hierarchy in Moscow. The vita was a small piece of the first—and most carefully scrutinized—complete Slavonic menology set to type anywhere in Rus' and only the second complete menology ever produced in Rus'. Unlike almost all other St. Catherine texts in circulation (except for the truncated vitae in *prolog* and the service in *Mineia sluzhebnaia*), Dimitrii's was materially available in all the major repositories and thereby convenient to consult. His version was perfectly positioned to become the standard account for Russian Orthodoxy, which it did.

When the time came in the latter half of Peter's reign for clerical panegyrists to elaborate a new and more imperial St. Catherine cult, Dimitrii's writings, which in themselves contained few panegyrics, proved to be a fruitful and politically unassailable base upon which to construct the political hagiography. In part this was a matter of timing, the power of print, and sheer good fortune. Dimitrii had died in 1709, well after Catherine and Peter had been united, but a couple of years before Catherine was publicly elevated to the official position of consort and tsaritsa. His Catheriniana, consequently, could not be demeaned after the fact as apologia for cynical state power. Both during his life and posthumously, he had impeccable credentials within officialdom and within the Muscovite church establishment. He was one of the many vaunted Ukrainian bishops in service to the Russian church, and his links to the Ukrainian court in Kiev and Baturin ran deep. His father, Savva Grigor'evich Tuptalo, had been a *sotnik* (*hundred'sman,* or lieutenant of Cossack troops) for the Ukrainian hetman who had moved the family to Kiev in 1660. Dimitrii had thus grown up in the shadow of the hetman's court and was imbued with its outlook, as reflected, for example, in his early embrace of the cult of St. Barbara, whose local reliquary had become an important shrine as a female patron of Kiev.[15] Tonsured in 1668, he was notably bookish, and he cultivated strong links to the religious hierarchy in Kiev, the Moscow Patriarchate, and later the post-patriarchal authorities.[16] Unlike other prominent clerics in Muscovite service—Feofan Prokopovich, Stefan Iavorskii (a close friend), or Gavriil Buzhinskii—Dimitrii's association with the regime remained somewhat distant, both spatially and—except for his aggressive and highly visible posture against the Old Believers—from the exposition of its ideology. He corresponded with several members of the extended ruling family, including of course Peter, and had particularly close connections with the widow, Paraskeva Fedorovna, and the surviving daughters of Ivan V, Anna and Ekaterina. All three went to Rostov to attend his funeral in 1709, along with Iavorskii, who presided at the service and read the funeral oration.[17] Except for several visits, the longest being an eighteen-month hiatus recovering from an illness on his way to becoming the archbishop of Rostov, he spent relatively little time in Moscow, and even less at the Muscovite court. From that perspective he was a non-cosmopolitan. Nevertheless, he was a firm and even outspoken exponent of what might be termed pan-Russianness, the unity of the peoples of Rus', as opposed to any parochial or regional claims from among them for spiritual, political, or historical autonomy.

The clearest expressions of this view come from several historical works, both those he authored and those with which he openly associated his views, which link the history of Rus' to the broader sweep of world history, Christian and pagan. The most famous of these books is *Sinopsis, or a Brief Description of the Beginnings of the Slavic People,* a text attributed to Dimitrii's intellectual mentor, Innokentii Gizel', but which also is commonly included in a number of editions of Dimitrii's own writings, presumably because Dimitrii wrote his *Letopisets* as an addendum—albeit one that is far longer than the original work—to *Sinopsis,* thereby expressly linking his own name and reputation with it. *Sinopsis* was a well-known and widely circulated (five printings between 1674 and 1699[18]) celebration of a greater Russia by one of the most important Ukrainian hierarchs of the late seventeenth century. Unusual for his milieu, Gizel' was insistent that the preferred referent for the people and their language was the more inclusive "rossiisskii," rather than "russkii," so as to emphasize the unbroken connection of the Rus' synchronically (over geographic distance) and diachronically (over time, connecting the first baptism in Kiev with the Muscovite tsar and patriarchate). For example, when tracing their mythical origins from Japheth, the son of Noah,[19] Japheth's son Mosokh (or Meshech, Genesis 10:2), is deemed the forefather of all the Slavic peoples including the Muscovites, the "Slavenorossiiskie," Poles, Volynians, Czechs, Bulgarians, and others. Moscow's very name, one learns, is derived from Mosokh, and through this lineage "not only the Great nation of Moscow but indeed all of Rus', or Russia, derives its language."[20] The first princes of Kiev were also "Rossiiskie," and the celestial intercessor, the apostle Andrew was from the very origins of Rus' and forevermore the "Rossiiskii zastupnik" (intercessor for greater Russia).[21] In other words, Rus', by its heritage, history, language, land, and faith was one. Temporal separation, Dimitrii implied, could not undermine the unity of Rus', with "Great" Moscow as its center.

There is no doubt that Dimitrii embraced the insistence of Gizel' on a common history and religious heritage for Moscow and Ukraine. In addition to *Letopisets,* his homilies and vitae of sainted "Rus-ian" hierarchs typically referred to them as "Rossiiskie." Thus, a homily for Peter the Metropolitan identified him as "Mitropolit Vserossiiskii," "Mitropolit Moskovskii i vseia Rossii," and in one place "chosen through the good will and consent of all Russians (blagovoleniem i soglasnym vsekh Rossiianov izbraniem)."[22] Similarly, the homily to the Russian Saint Aleksei identified him as "Metropolitan of Moscow and all of Russia."[23]

A lengthy homage that Dimitrii composed in recognition of the first anniversary of the death of Gizel', entitled "The Pyramid or Column," resonated with encomia.[24] Organized around the theme of sacred memory, it began with an epigraph taken from two Old Testament sources valorizing bravery, wisdom, and defiance of unlawful power: 1 Maccabees 3:7 and Sirach (or Ecclesiasticus in the Latin text) 39:12-13. "His [Judah's] memory is blessed forever. The memory of him [Jesus Ben Sira] shall not depart away, and his name shall be in request from generation to generation, and the nations shall declare his holy wisdom, and the church shall shew forth his praise."[25] Such a man, Dimitrii says repeatedly, was Innokentii, whose words, goodness, and steadfastness in the face of his enemies ("in the warring that did such damage to Christian Ukraine") will make him immortal in the memories of humanity. This observation echoed the passages in Maccabees that immediately preceded the one he quoted: "And his enemies were driven away for fear of him, and the workers of iniquity were troubled. And salvation prospered in his hand. And he grieved many kings, and made Jacob glad with his works." Innokentii's pillars and pyramids were constructed not out of stone, iron, or marble, but of Solomonic wisdom and godliness. "For verily he was a singular pillar of God's church, and these words will be repeated among all the sons of Russia *(Rossiiskikh synov)* that Innokentii Gizel', the Archimandrite of the Caves Monastery, is a pillar and support of the church of God." Here we see the latter day Ben Sira, a student, pious scribe, and educator, who was willing to learn and pass along the wisdom of many nations (39:2-4), for whom the pursuit of holy wisdom was an end unto itself.

Such a conviction, championing the defender of the unity of faith between Great and Little Russia, served Dimitrii's career and reputation exceedingly well, in particular as he came to the attention of the authorities in Moscow. Like a number of other Ukrainian clerics, he had relied upon the patronage of the Kievan court and the left-bank Ukrainian hetman, initially Ivan Samoilovich and then after 1687 Ivan Mazepa, with whom he had corresponded and from whom he received material support and gifts of books. When Mazepa traveled to Moscow in 1689 he brought Dimitrii as a member of his entourage, the latter's first visit to the capital. During that initial stay the two were often together, and Mazepa intervened more than once on Dimitrii's behalf. In subsequent years Mazepa wrote to the Moscow patriarch, among others, in order to facilitate Dimitrii's access to needed texts, and even to smooth the waters for the publication of the second volume of *Chet'i minei*.[26] All of this took place many years before the fateful break with Moscow in 1708, of course, in pursuit of greater political autonomy for the hetmanate, and just prior to Peter's ascendancy as the single ruler. Still, Mazepa's betrayal of Peter set off tumultuous shock waves in both Kiev and St. Petersburg such that the Ukrainian clerics, especially those who had personal ties to the hetman and his court, were obliged to choose sides unambiguously. In that fraught environment Dimitrii's well-documented and long-standing pan-Russianism served him well and secured the continued reputation and eventual republication of his writings, even though the first Moscow or St. Petersburg edition of the menology did not appear until the 1750s.

Between 1702 and his death in 1709, Dimitrii found himself in Moscow on four separate occasions, the longest being more than a year (February 1702 to March 1703). Ill for much of that time, he nevertheless deepened his ties with some of the most important hierarchs in Moscow, including Istomin, Fedor Polikarpov, Stefan Iavorskii (then still archbishop of Riazan), and Ieromonk Feolog of the Chudov Monastery.[27] Dimitrii's major biographers agree that these experiences, although occurring rather late in his life, had a significant impact, both on Dimitrii's outlook and on his standing among the clerical literati. However firm had been his political allegiances to Moscow before this time, they were considerably strengthened over the last decade of his life, as he came to appreciate the intellectual maturity of its clerical elite and to turn to them for advice.

The first edition of *Chet'i minei* was published over a period of several years in Kiev, and the first volume (September through November) was completed in 1688, long before the attempt to create a public persona for Peter's future consort. All of this freed Dimitrii's writing in the eyes of churchmen from any overt association with a problematic secular modernity. Dimitrii died in 1709, two years before the initial valorization of Catherine after the battle of Pruth. Shortly thereafter figures in Rostov, and possibly Iavorskii himself, were considering Dimitrii for beatification, a status he received only decades later in 1757. Although not a political insider, Dimitrii was well respected at court, considered an educator, a systematizer, a militant foe of unsanctioned local practices, and an unmistakable champion of a Russo-centered church. He was a militant and highly visible opponent of the Old Belief, particularly active in his diocese, and he both preached and polemicized against Old Belief practices (both real and imagined), most famously in his tract *Rozysk o raskol'nicheskoi brynskoi vere* (An Investigation of the Schismatic Brynsk Faith), written in Rostov at the very end of his life and published in full for the first time in 1745.[28] At a critical moment in Peter's reforms Dimitrii publicly embraced the ban on beards, unlike Iavorskii for whom the ban was troubling, and maintained that those Old Ritualists who condemned the decree as heretical were confusing physical appearance with the substance of church dogma. This is how Novikov summed up Dimitrii's reputation in 1772: "This man of divine spirit possessed a sharp facility to reason and great learning, skilled in Slavonic, Latin, Greek, and Hebrew. He had a sagacious spirit, loved virtuous and honest people, assisted the poor, defended the helpless, and he had a remarkable inclination for scholarship. By disseminating the teachings of the Gospels, in both word and deed [he struggled] against the obstinate [religious] dissenters."[29]

A few decades later Metropolitan Evgenii Bolkhovitinov went even further in a lengthy passage on Dimitrii's life and writings:

> At the time there was still little education in the entire Russian nation, and in the Russian clergy for that matter. Dimitrii found this to be the case in Rostov, and for that reason he considered it his obligation to enlighten and to correct at the very outset the church teachers of his parsonage. He wrote and circulated to them two sets of instructions which delineated their responsibilities. . . .
>
> The name of this Pastor is praised not simply for his service to the literature of our Church, but for his high Christian virtues. In addition to his general patronage of his Parsonage, in addition to his many rare good qualities, he was particularly compassionate to the sick, the poor, the orphaned, and the defenseless, and on their behalf he employed all the assets of his personal property. This is why he left behind nothing other than a library. In his testament, written two years before his death, he stated that no property be sought for after his death, since, except for his books, he had not assembled any. . . . This will, on the order of the sovereign Peter the Great, was published in Moscow in 1717.[30]

Dimitrii's *zhitie* of St. Catherine was the lengthiest and most popularly written of all the Russian-language lives of St. Catherine, and it quickly became the standard version, widely circulated within Russian Orthodoxy even today, both at home and in the diaspora. The revised menology itself has a complicated history, and many of its particulars remain opaque. Peter Mohyla had initiated the revision in the 1640s, with the intention of returning to the Greek sources as best as possible. While several manuscript vitae were collected, and individual Slavonic vitae did get published in the typography of the Caves Monastery, Mohyla's group made little progress toward a complete new menology. After a hiatus of several years, the project revived under Gizel', who succeeded in assembling a large library of saints' lives. But the editorial work itself soon floundered, largely because of the inability to obtain a complete copy (of which there existed very few) of Makarii's *Menology* from Moscow, until Dimitrii revived it in 1684 at the behest of Patriarch Ioakim of Moscow. For this purpose Dimitrii moved from the Nikolo-Krutitskii Monastery in Baturin, Mazepa's headquarters where he had been living, to the Caves Monastery in Kiev, under the sponsorship of the monastery's archimandrite and an enthusiast for the initiative, Varlaam Iasinskii, where he would have greater access to the necessary sources.[31]

Although the new menology was intended as an authoritative account of the lives of saints important to Rus', and in that sense an updated version of Makarii's compendium, its actual relationship to Makarii's text remains far from clear. Some of the scholarship maintains that Makarii's version served as the primary template, reworked, but fundamentally true to its source. This was the conclusion drawn by I. A. Shliapkin based upon his analysis of the rough draft of Dimitrii's December volume, which in his view, maintained Makarii's organization and themes.[32] Others have contrasted the two texts more sharply, however, dismissing Makarii as a mere compiler, while praising Dimitrii as an author in his own right.[33] Dimitrii provided a very long list of sources from which he derived his material, many of them in Greek and Latin, of which Makarii's *Chet'i minei* was just one, and each hagiography included a notation of the basic sources from which it derived. From the perspective of Dimitrii himself, he was producing an original compilation, some of it from the works of others but recast in his own words.

The first volume, covering the months October to December, was completed perhaps as early as 1686 and was published by the Caves Monastery in 1689.[34] Three years later, in February 1692, Dimitrii was given a cell in the lavra to work on the menology full time. The next year he received a complete *Acta Sanctorum* from Gdansk, a gift from Mazepa, and this enabled him to work more easily from a wide assemblage of materials.[35] The three subsequent installments were published in 1695, 1700, and 1705, and a second printing, also from Kiev, appeared between 1711 and 1718.[36] Dimitrii, therefore, did not have access to the Bollandiste saints' lives when he published volume one. In any event the eighteen-volume Antwerp edition of *Acta Sanctorum* at that point ran only from January through May, which meant that Dimitrii could not have consulted it for his Life of St. Catherine.

As Dimitrii recounts in his diary *(diariush)* and as subsequent scholars have noted, final permission to publish the first volume did not come easily.[37] Moscow was understandably concerned about a massive editorial project that had been conceived, developed, and possibly even set in type entirely in Kiev, with almost no direct participation by Muscovite churchmen. In the past the autocephalous Ukrainian church would have been free to publish on its own, a privilege that had allowed the lavra's typography to become quite active. The political union with Moscow, however, obliged the lavra press to get Moscow's imprimatur before proceeding to final publication. In pursuit of this, Dimitrii and his many supporters employed every avenue of support, including direct contact with the patriarch.

The timing of its completion, coming as it did in the middle of the Eucharist controversy that pitted so-called Latinizers (associated in the minds of some Moscow authorities with the Ukrainian church) against Grecophiles, further complicated matters and delayed publication.[38] After a lengthy exchange of letters among the various parties, the Kievan authorities decided to publish the first volume in anticipation of receiving the patriarch's blessing. In the end they did receive that blessing but only after earning a sharp rebuke for having committed themselves to the physical production of the book without waiting to get permission first.[39] In order to avoid a rift, Dimitrii traveled with the new hetman to Moscow in the summer of 1689 to present a copy of the printed volume to the patriarch.

Once again the timing was serendipitous. When the company departed Kiev, Sofia was still the powerful regent. The group arrived on August 10, literally within days of Peter's coup against his half-sister and her forced acceptance of the veil. The delegation arranged audiences with Sofia and Ivan V on August 11, but initially failed to see Peter, who Dimitrii believed to be away on campaign but who in fact was on his way to Novodevichii Monastery to confront Sofia.[40] Dimitrii recounts that their group hovered in limbo for a full month while political events were being played out around them. The risk that they would become entangled in the political web or even worse deemed to be partisans of Sofia was considerable. Finally, Mazepa resolved to lead several members of the delegation (apparently including Dimitrii) directly to Peter, who was ensconced in Trinity-St. Sergius Monastery outside of Moscow along with Patriarch Ioakim, and to assure him of the delegation's loyalty. Ioakim interrogated them on their understanding of the Holy Gifts, and, satisfied with their responses, gave his blessing to Dimitrii to continue the project.

This early embrace of Peter and of Moscow's official position on the Eucharist were quickly put to the test. As described in his diary and carefully elaborated by A. A. Kruming, the first volume's title page went through three variants in 1689 corresponding to the ebb and flow of Moscow's politics.[41]

Initially dedicated to the three sovereigns ("To the thrice crowned Orthodox Power, our Great Sovereign Tsars and Grand Princes Ivan Alekseevich
and Peter Alekseevich, and the Great Sovereign Venerable Tsarevna and
Grand Princess Sofia Alekseevna."), the obverse of the title page also included some verses by Varlaam Iasinskii that were dedicated specifically to
Sofia. These had to be quickly rewritten to reflect Sofia's demise and Peter's
ascendancy. They were quickly replaced by a new dedication in which all
references to Sofia were excised. The revised title page added language that
articulated the subordination of the Caves Monastery to the Moscow patriarch, by referring to it as "stauropigial." One variant also included reference to the Constantinople patriarch ("and also, as it was from antiquity
[authorized by] the Most Holy Universal Patriarchs of Constantinople"),
while some copies did not include this language. Title pages and
colophons, so it would appear, constituted highly political texts for the
Muscovite court.

Although it added nothing radically new to what had long been the
standard components of St. Catherine's life, Dimitrii's text was no mere re-
working of Makarii's account. Indeed, Dimitrii may not have had ongoing
access to Makarii's text when he was preparing the work on the life of St.
Catherine. After a supplication to Samoilovich, the latter wrote to both his
friend V. V. Golitsyn and Patriarch Ioakim on Dimitrii's behalf, and the patriarch in response ordered the rare and very precious complete set of
Makarii's *Lives* sent from Dormition Cathedral in Moscow (the so-called
Uspenskii copy) to Dimitrii in Kiev, at some point in the mid-1680s, probably no earlier than the spring of 1686.[42] But Dimitrii was ordered to return the set to Moscow at the beginning of March 1688.[43] Unfortunately
the draft copy for November has not survived,[44] but Dimitrii's own notations in the published edition say that his primary references for the vita
were the *Saints' Lives* composed by the tenth-century Greek scholar St.
Simeon Metaphrastes (which he read in Latin translation),[45] and the St.
Catherine Life included in *Anfologion,* the compendium of 1660 discussed
previously. Metaphrastes's early vita is quite abbreviated, however, and it
was written long before many of the most enduring legends entered into
the St. Catherine hagiography. The more important and proximate source,
therefore, was *Anfologion,* a recently printed text that would have been
readily available to Dimitrii in any ecclesiastical library. According to
Derzhavin's exhaustive analysis, the St. Catherine vita was the only one
that Dimitrii extracted directly from *Anfologion* (in Aleksandr Derzhavin's
view the entire first part of the vita came directly from *Anfologion,* while
much of the second half was adapted from Metaphrastes). Derzhavin did
discern influences from *Anfologion* on other vitae (Aleksei the Man of God,
St. Theodore), but these were subtle and limited to specific details or
phrases.[46] One must assume, therefore, that the *Anfologion* text captured
the image of St. Catherine that Dimitrii wanted to convey.

In any case, Dimitrii's text had decidedly Greek—if in Latin translation

—rather than Muscovite, underpinnings. It followed a very different narrative trajectory from Makarii's, adding elements that Makarii had ignored or minimized, and it drew the reader to strikingly different biographic bases of her veneration. While Makarii began with a lengthy description of the impious practices of Maxentius's court, mentioning Catherine only several paragraphs later, Rostovskii introduced her in the first sentence. And although both texts lionized her high birth and cerebral accomplishments, Rostovskii chose to introduce her physical attributes and a recognizable personality at the outset.

> During the reign of the impious Emperor Maxentius, there lived in the city of Alexandria a maiden named Catherine, the daughter of Costus the former king. She was of royal lineage, remarkably beautiful and tall, and had reached the age of eighteen. She was revered for her wisdom and had studied to completion all the works of the Hellenes, and all the poets and philosophers of antiquity, for example Homer Virgil, Aristotle Plato, and others. Not only was she conversant with the works of the wise men of antiquity, but she had also studied the works of the most noteworthy physicians Asclepius, Hippocrates, and Galen. Moreover, she had studied all the dialects and rhetorical arts and knew many languages.[47]

Dimitrii's Catherine was multi-dimensional and far more passionate and lifelike than Makarii's. In Dimitrii's text, the multiplicity of Catherine's personal qualities, rather than her intellect alone, conveyed an unsurpassed attractiveness ("find me a youth who possesses the four things which I have [as you well know] in greater measure than all other maidens . . . a young man who is of noble lineage, healthy, handsome, and learned"). These qualities simultaneously marked her unavailability for mortal suitors ("Catherine's relatives said, 'Although the sons of emperors and great princes are highborn and wealthier than she, not one is as handsome or wise.'"). Physical beauty, vitality, and intellect, in other words, precluded marriage, and this circumstance provided the primary context through which Catherine began her journey to faith. Proud and independent, she preferred to remain a virgin rather than chance marrying a husband—any husband—unworthy of her remarkable qualities. All of this served as a prelude to Catherine's acceptance of Christ, an act that had taken place off stage and before the narration commenced in Makarii's account. Dimitrii employed this acceptance so as to highlight and even luxuriate upon the mystical marriage, a biographical element barely mentioned in Makarii's narrative and largely ignored in previous Muscovite hagiographies of the saint. But here, as in the *Anfologion* text on which it is based, the mystical marriage took center stage.

Catherine's mother, of course, wished her daughter to be wed, and in desperation she sent Catherine to a holy man (*chelovek sviati* in the original, and *muzh blagochestivyi i sviatoi* in the vernacular Russian), her spiritual advisor and a Christian, and he too noted her beauty and wisdom. This aged holy man *(starets)* counseled that he knew the ideal youth, a wondrous, rich and radiant Youth, but one without an earthly father (i.e., Christ), no small matter with dowries and bride prices to be negotiated. Catherine expressed her eagerness to meet this catch, and after a lengthy dialogue the wise man gave her an icon of Bogoroditsa and ordered Catherine to pray to her to intercede so that she be allowed to behold her Son. Catherine did as she was told, prayed, and then, like Aleksei Mikhailovich, Nikon, and others before them, she experienced a miraculous visitation while asleep. In the dream state she found herself gazing upon Mary, who held the Christ child in her arms. She then heard Mary command her son,

> "My Child, look upon Your slave Catherine, see how beautiful and virtuous she is."
>
> But the Christ child *(Bogomladenets)* responded, "No, this girl is completely dim and so unsightly that I cannot even look at her."
>
> At that point the Holy Bogoroditsa again said to the Lord, "Is this maiden not wiser than all the philosophers? Does she not exceed other maidens in her wealth and lineage?"
>
> But Christ responded to her, "Again I tell You, My Mother, that this maiden is stupid, poor and low born, and I shall not gaze upon her so long as she remains so impious."

After this, a long sidebar conversation took place in Catherine's dream, between Christ and an increasingly exasperated Mary. Christ was unrelenting and he ordered Mary to send Catherine back to the holy man for further counsel.

Catherine awoke and did as instructed. After recounting her dream she learned about Christian faith from the holy man, who then baptized her. Returning home, she again was visited in a dream, and this time the Christ child saw that she was transformed, and announced to his mother (without addressing Catherine directly) that the maiden was beautiful and worthy. Declaring his love for her, he said that he would take her as his bride. A ceremony was arranged and in the dream, Christ placed a wedding band on her right hand. Although her inner being was transformed, alive and filled with light, she remained chaste, as Christ paid homage to her virginity and declared the matrimony holy and physically unconsummated.

"'Lo [spoke Christ to Catherine], today I choose you to be My betrothed for all eternity. Take care to keep this trust inviolate, and promise yourself to no earthly bridegroom.' With this, He became invisible, and the vision came to an end." This scene of consummation hints vaguely at a bodily response, but it falls well short of the explicit carnality of, for example, Margery of Kempe, who described at length the physical sensations brought about by her mystical marriage: "When the maiden awoke, she saw on her right hand a wondrous ring and felt such joy and gladness that from that hour her heart was a prisoner of divine love. So great was the change which came upon her that she gave heed no more to worldly things, thinking only of her beloved Bridegroom day and night. For him alone did she long, and her thoughts were ever with Him, whether she was awake or asleep."[48]

Only after establishing the mystical marriage as the transformative moment did Dimitrii move on to the familiar accounts of Maxentius's court, the emperor's introduction to Catherine, and the fateful public disputations with the fifty philosophers. Here again Dimitrii dwelt on her visage, her "indescribable loveliness," that wounded Maxentius with its radiance and inspired wanton thoughts in him. In this account the defeat of the philosophers so enraged the emperor that he condemned them to death by fire. At this moment they saw the error of their pagan ideas and begged Catherine to pray to the one true God, her heavenly spouse, on their behalf that he might forgive them their sins and be acceptable for Baptism. Catherine counseled submission, saying that the fire would cleanse them of their sins and serve as their Baptism. So advised, they accepted their suffering joyously, and although consumed by the flames, their bodies remained whole, miraculously saved for burial by local Christians.

This brief exchange constitutes an important addendum, one that does not appear in Makarii's text or any of the other Russian ones so far as is known. For in this interchange it is the living Catherine, rather than the martyred saint, who was beseeched to play an intercessory role with heaven, and whose blessing affected a miraculous intervention, prior to the immolation of the philosophers, who themselves were thereby transformed into martyrs. This act of redemption underscored the towering hagiographic importance of the mystical marriage to Dimitrii's understanding of St. Catherine and the basis for her veneration.

Maxentius then returned his attention to Catherine, alternately threatening her and attempting to win her over. Here again Dimitrii's vita emphasized Catherine's carnality.

> "Lay aside your wiles, O Emperor, and cease to play the fox. I have already told you that I am a Christian and have betrothed myself to Christ. He alone is my Bridegroom, Guide, and the Adornment of my virginity. I prefer the robe of martyrdom to the imperial purple."
>
> "You compel me to dishonor you and to cover your fair body with many wounds even against my will," warned the Emperor.

The description of Catherine's martyrdom is particularly graphic on this score, detailing the lash marks left on her naked body, the pools of blood that flowed from her wounds, and the pain that the studded wheels would inflict. When the empress and General Porphyrius spoke up defiantly on Catherine's behalf, an enraged Maxentius commanded that his wife be placed against the edge of a crate so that her breasts were pressed down and then torn off prior to her being beheaded. At this point Maxentius had gone nearly mad with blood lust, but it is the purifying power of the blood that wins out: "Remember O Lord, that I am flesh and blood, and do not permit the cruel inquisitors to bring to light before Your dread judgment the sins I have committed in ignorance, but wash them in my blood. Make my body, wounded by torments and condemned to beheading, invisible to the eyes of Your enemies who persecute me." At that moment the executioner beheaded her and milk flowed from her neck ("I isteche ot iazvy mleko vmesto krove"), thus depriving the emperor in his thirst for more blood. And then a blessed angel (not the archangel as in Makarii's text) carries her off to Sinai.

Throughout the entire narrative one reads repeatedly of Catherine's high birth, her intellect, and her ability to defeat men at their own game. That she is fit to rule over them is made clear by her superior oratory and by the prominent mention of the cross in her hand and her crown *("venets"),* both as royal tiara and saintly halo.[49] The entry concludes with the troparion sung to her, which in a few lines repeats the themes of wisdom, martyrdom, and bride of Christ, from which she gains her crown.[50]

Precisely why Dimitrii chose this version to certify and then disseminate, rather than a more traditional Muscovite one, is not known. To some extent his prose reflected the language and emphases of his sources, but the florid and emotive prose that so many of his vitae displayed shows the unmistakable influence of the baroque. Page after page contains lurid descriptions of lust, desire, physical pain, and bodily mutilation. St. Zacharias's "blood was spilt upon the hardened floor,"[51] the martyr Cornelius was bound hand and foot and hanged upside down,[52] the martyr Lucia was nailed to the ground and had urine poured over her, St. Agatha of Palermo had her breasts torn away with iron claws, and so forth.[53] Several of his Lives, including those of other female martyrs, included lengthy flourishes, seemingly lifelike, personal and emotional encounters that tended to be far more affective in tone than those in previous collections, in particular Makarii's. Of course, the tropes for virgin martyrs had become narrative set pieces of saints' lives everywhere, but Dimitrii's lingering over their carnality and passions was very much a reflection of the literary trends that had begun to influence Muscovite court culture at this time.

Unlike Makarii, Dimitrii made frequent and poignant mention of a martyr's status as bride of Christ, and in most instances he gave that circumstance a prominent place in the telling of the life. To offer a few examples: as the emperor's soldiers dragged her off to be defiled, Theofila, one of the twenty thousand martyrs of Nicomedia wept, "Jesus, my love, my light, my breath, the Guardian of my chastity and my life, look down upon Thy bride! Make haste, O mine invisible Bridegroom, to come to my rescue. . . . Preserve Thy bride unsullied, O Bridegroom."[54] Justina of Antioch announced to a potential suitor, "My Bridegroom is Christ, Whom I serve"; the nun Paraskeva was a "beloved bride of Christ"; her namesake the Holy

Great Martyr Paraskeva had a "Bridegroom in heaven, Jesus Christ."[55]

Where Makarii tended to mute this element almost to the point of exclusion, Dimitrii interpolated dramatic declamations of this sort for a great many virgin martyrs and sainted nuns. Clearly, this general thematic shift goes a long way toward explaining the presence of such a drawn-out betrothal scene in the St. Catherine vita. But it does not perhaps explain it in full. For St. Catherine, the mystical marriage was a transformative experience, a liminal event in Victor Turner's sense, in some ways more dramatic even than her conversion. Although not singular, the liminality of the mystical marriage appears to have been specific to St. Catherine and perhaps one or two others in Dimitrii's compendium. St. Tatiana, by comparison, also underwent a mystical marriage, but Dimitrii passed over it briefly in just a few lines. "She was wounded by love for Christ, to Whom she betrothed herself, and labored for Him day and night in fasting and prayer. . . . On account of her exemplary life, she was ordained a deaconess, in which rank she served God like an angel in the body. Finally, the time came for Christ to crown His bride, deeming her worthy of martyrdom."[56]

Closer to St. Catherine was the virgin martyr Agnes, who was empowered by her betrothal to Christ, and able to resist earthly suitors. In Dimitrii's narrative she referred repeatedly and in deeply passionate language to her bridegroom Christ, who is "comely in beauty more than the sons of men, and His affections are incomparably sweet. . . . He has already pressed me to His chaste bosom; my flesh is even now joined to His. His blood is rouge upon my cheeks."[57] Significantly, St. Agnes did not engage the apparition of Christ as St. Catherine had in her dream. Her betrothal was constantly mentioned but not described in the text as an event in itself. St. Agnes repeatedly evoked Christ, prayed to and beseeched him. But Christ never appeared to her directly, and in this vita did not speak.

Some aspects of Dimitrii's vita of St. Agatha of Palermo followed a trajectory similar to St. Catherine's. A virgin martyr also of high birth, she steadfastly resisted the demands and seductions of the Roman general Quintianus, the commander of the legion of Sicily, and was remanded as a prisoner to the house of a wealthy noblewoman. Tempted with offers of jewelry, slaves, and carnal pleasure, she rejects them all and declares herself, in spite of her personal wealth and high standing, a slave of Christ. Tortured and mutilated for her defiance she is healed once (her severed breasts are made whole) by Christ's intercession, but is eventually tortured to death and ascends to heaven escorted by an angel. But nowhere in the text does Agatha deem herself a bride of Christ. Rather, he is her lord, and she his humble handmaiden, a metaphorical statement of social relationships in place of betrothal.[58]

In other words, within Dimitrii's work overall, there was a singularity to St. Catherine's mystical marriage that, when combined with her royal birth, high learning, and the bodily torment that he described so vividly, would have marked this vita as particularly noteworthy, at least among female saints. One cannot say precisely why Dimitrii invested so much in St. Catherine's mystical marriage, but it bears mention that these elements recurred elsewhere in late Muscovite discourse, both in his own subsequent writings and in other media, including iconography, ever more of which began to display St. Catherine in direct interaction with Christ, and in poses that gestured toward the mystical marriage.[59] An elaborate, if not very attractive, example of this thematic shift toward her personal link with Christ is a life icon of St. Catherine from the middle to the late part of the seventeenth century from the so-called Stroganov school.[60] Here St. Catherine is standing in profile in the foreground adorned in typical Byzantine style with her crown, and regally dressed in gold-trimmed robes. Her right hand is extended in the sign of the (three-fingered) cross and she is holding an unfolded scroll in her left. The scroll contains a prayer of intercession to St. Catherine and is being read by several simply dressed bearded men (perhaps the emperor's philosophers) and women kneeling at her feet and standing before her. In other scenes the icon displays her decapitation by an imperial guard, the archangel overseeing her ascent to heaven, her resting place in Sinai, and in the upper left corner, Christ, backed by the apostles and other heavenly figures, kneels down and extends a censer toward Catherine welcoming her into heaven.

It is unlikely that this particular icon was informed by Dimitrii's vita specifically, since the Stroganov school generally is associated with a slightly earlier period. But the elaborate, ornately drawn contents and prominently displayed three-fingered cross identify it as coming from the second half of the century. More likely, both reflected a common influence of baroque aesthetics and Byzantine Grecophilia, perhaps in this instance through the intercession of *Anfologion*.

Dimitrii amplified several of these themes in his revision of the *Mineia sluzhebnaia*, but with slightly different emphases. Unlike the basic *Menology*, still too expensive even in print for most churches to afford, the *sluzhebnaia* was designed for active use and was written explicitly for clergy, with directions on when and how to integrate the vita into the service for that day. Since several saints were recognized on any given day (in this case Catherine is bracketed with another lay martyr, St. Merkurii, and a second St. Merkurii of Smolensk), the narrative interweaves them and has more of a thematic character than the *Chet'i minei*. The text assumes a familiarity with the "facts" of her life, which it opts not to retell. But, what it lacked in literary narrative it made up for in functionality. Whatever the laity learned in church about St. Catherine almost certainly derived from the *sluzhebnaia*, rather than any other text.

Dimitrii here emphasized Catherine's cerebral qualities *(razum, premudrost', vsemudrost',* and *Bogomudrost'),* her virginity and youth (terms such as *devitsa, navyksha,* and *otrokovitsa* are used repeatedly). She is repeatedly invoked as an angel of Christ, his love, and his bride, who is possessed of divine beauty. Dimitrii calls her an example to all maidens who celebrate their chasteness in God's temple. One irmologion praises her for defending her faith in pharaoh's realm, entitling her to the martyr's staff *(zhezl),* cross, scepter, and crown. Another proclaims: "You are my fortress, O Lord, You are my strength, you are my God, You are my gladness," and declares thus that Catherine's suffering overcame the enemy.[61]

Dimitrii's other major text, the homily on St. Catherine's Day, is in some ways the most interesting. After all, he had no choice but to include St. Catherine in the menology, and given the furious pace at which he was generating text, one could surmise that he relied on *Anfologion* and Metaphrastes as much because of their ready accessibility as for any endorsement of their outlook. Certainly there is no indication from any contemporaneous work of his that suggests a special veneration of St. Catherine. On the contrary, his saintly patron, as he recorded repeatedly in his diary and demonstrated in his actions, was St. Barbara.[62] The only mention of St. Catherine in the diary, which otherwise was filled with references to numerous saints' days, was a brief notation from November 24, 1682, observing that the Bulgarian metropolitan, Melkhisedek, had visited the monastery and met with some of the brothers "on the Day of the Martyr St. Catherine."[63]

An icon of St. Catherine from the Church of the Intercession in Fili (1694)

Undated and without provenance in either the 1762 or the 1841 collections, there are some hints that Dimitrii composed the homily while in Rostov or perhaps during his stay in Moscow in 1706, possibly in honor of Tsarevna Ekaterina Ioannovna (even though she is not named in the sermon itself). First, a recent and seemingly complete checklist of his sermons written before 1700 does not include the St. Catherine one.[64] Second, the style of writing is consistent with the move away from rigid scholasticism, a shift that Dimitrii's foremost biographer, I. A. Shliapkin, associated with the sermons from the very end of his life.[65]

The text begins, customarily, with a troparion: "Jesus, Your angel Catherine calls unto You with a mighty voice: /I love You, my bewedded, and I humbly suffer for You, and lay myself down." It then takes the bride of Christ and arms her with the now familiar attributes of chastity, beauty, wisdom, love, and martyrdom, but above all with the cross. This time, however, the attributes were cast as weapons *("oruzhie")* of faith. Normally, he maintained, iconography represented holy virgins with an orb, a golden digit, or a sacred flower in their hand, but not the cross ("kresta zhenskomu polu v rutse ne daiut"). Archbishops, bishops, or other men of exalted rank might display the cross, but St. Catherine differs from other saintly women in that she is displayed bearing the cross in her right hand. It is this exceptionalism that provides the theme of his sermon: what does the cross signify when it is displayed in her hand?

For Dimitrii her cross represented many things: the banner of Orthodox faith protecting against the dishonest and unfaithful, as well as a symbol of her true faith, but also of the deeds she would perform in defense of that faith, specifically her martyrdom, which like the Biblical martyrs Aaron, Isaac, and Abel, allowed for her ascent into heaven. Catherine, Dimitrii preached, should be honored for her strength, bravery, manhood *(sily, khrabrstvo, muzhestvo),* the cross is her banner of knighthood *("krest znameniem est' kavalerstva"),* her weapon *("oruzhie")* with which she did mighty battle *("khrabrago voinstvovaniia")* against the devil. This passage expressed the counterpoint of gender and gender transformation quite vividly: the pure maiden become the mighty warrior. Catherine, "the beautiful maiden," "bride of Christ" was "a knight" possessed of "mighty bravery," whose "victory" was assured by the "insuperable weapon" she holds (i.e., her faith). Her divinely inspired wisdom—he terms her a thinking angel *("myslennaia agnitsa")*—also was a weapon with which, as he repeats several times over a number of pages, she defeated ungodly and worldly "Hellenic" wisdom and its philosophers, which devoid of faith can only serve the devil with their sophistic syllogisms, but within faith serves the cross. The cross, then, was "a scepter, a banner of the kingdom, yea the kingdom in heaven: for with the cross, with suffering, the heavenly kingdom is achieved." This is the meaning, says Dimitrii, of the cross in Catherine's hand: the weapon of "conquest over this world, the body, and the devil." It was the abnegation of the flesh, Christ's beloved bride's sacrifice, that her icon honors.

In the final section, Dimitrii compared St. Catherine to the zealous and warlike believer Judith in the Orthodox Old Testament, Maxentius to the Babylonian king Nebuchadnezzar.[66] Both women defeated all the forces of the world arrayed against them, and did so inside the very hearth of the ungodly. "And thus, just as in antiquity a single Jewish woman Judith brought the doctrine into the house of King Nebuchadnezzar, so too a single Christian maiden, St. Catherine, brought the doctrine into the house of the impious king Maxentius."[67] The cross of wisdom and manliness thus became, in Dimitrii's account, an instrument of love, love of God who gave his only begotten son on behalf of humanity, and love of Christ the Savior, her bridegroom. St. Catherine's own martyrdom, then, and its remembrance on her feast day, constituted an act of love for all who came after her, a deed for salvation.

The homily concluded thus: "We bow down to you, O beloved bride of Christ, holy martyr Catherine! With sincerity we kiss your honored icon, and the cross, held in your right hand. We lovingly celebrate your sacred memory: you reign along with Christ. Gaze upon us with mercy and send us the mercy of Christ the God, and in our striving for Him with your prayers may we receive salvation. Amen."[68]

With these final words Dimitrii summoned the full meaning of his dramatic interpolation of the bride of Christ. The learned maiden, martyr, debater, and brave Christian warrior now had an exalted place in heaven, second among women perhaps only to Bogomater. As his chosen bride, St. Catherine stood directly at Christ's side, and the cross that she alone among martyred women was entitled to bear signified, along with her crown, her celestial regality. St. Catherine reigned and those who bore her name or sought her intercession or supplication on one's behalf were but one step removed from supplication to Christ himself, or such was the implication of Dimitrii's writings. At the very outset of Peter's reign, then, the full complement of St. Catherine's attributes was now acknowledged in Russian Orthodoxy and available for anyone wishing to adapt them to political ends. Most of all, her name was now highly esteemed, a name day saint fit for a queen.

PART TWO

The Tsaritsa

6

The Order of St. Catherine

• By the end of the seventeenth century, and at the dawn of the protracted Northern War whose victorious end would mark the declaration of empire, Muscovite sacrality had generated an extensive inventory of Catherinian images, ideals, and consecrated sites. The happenings of the previous half century—Aleksei's miraculous visitation, the protectorate over Sinai, ceremonials at the *terem* chapel, the naming of tsarist offspring—as well as the new sermons, verses, and hagiographies dedicated to Catherine, had enabled these images to become common knowledge within elite circles, available for adaptation to new political purposes after Marta Skafronska was reborn as Ekaterina Alekseevna some time in 1703 or 1704. These now familiar roles included holy maiden; wise, quick-witted, and learned woman of purple; brave and faithful martyr to the faith; heavenly intercessor; and patron of the Romanov women; to which Dimitrii Rostovskii added the powerful figures of the knight-warrior of the cross and the dearly beloved and personally selected bride of Christ. How, then, were these deployed, in what combinations and in which settings, in the service of the Petrine state? Addressing this question requires turning attention away from St. Catherine per se and toward the carnal soon-to-be tsaritsa, in order to investigate how this rich and powerful medley of representations came to the service of the living Catherine, or at least her official persona, once her presence was officially acknowledged during the last dozen years or so of Peter's reign.

That Dimitrii's rendition of St. Catherine was known and revered at the Petrine court is unmistakable. For example, Peter's sister, Tsarevna Natal'ia Alekseevna, composed a play, untitled but commonly called "The Comedy of St. Catherine," that was performed, apparently several times, at her private theater. Relatively little is known about Natal'ia's private theater or its production of the St. Catherine play.[1] Established in Preobrazhenskoe in 1707, the theater moved to the new capital in 1711, where it remained until Natal'ia's death in 1716, and it was likely there that the drama was staged. The play itself is brief and unremarkable. It is lifted almost intact from a passage of the vita in Dimitrii's *Chet'i minei,* in which a wise man first apprises Catherine of the young Christ ("who has no earthly father") and of Mary Mother of God and the angels. The play contained only one speaking part, the *starets,* who pronounces three brief orations as Catherine stands silently on stage and at one point is handed an icon. The play ends with Catherine's baptism.

Peter is known to have attended performances at his sister's theater, and he very likely saw this one.[2] Writing in 1840, Prince Alexander Alexandrovich Shakhovskoi recounted a family legend implying that the play was produced frequently and in Peter's presence. The lore, passed down to him by his grandmother, maintained that his great-grandmother "Tatiana Ivanovna Arsen'eva, a boiarynia of tsarevna Sofia Alekseevna, had played the part of the martyr Catherine in the tragedy written by the tsarevna herself . . . and that Peter the Great, who was always in attendance at his sister's theatrical performances in the *terem,* nicknamed Tatiana Ivanovna 'the martyr Catherine with the big eyes.'"[3]

Although they almost certainly married privately in 1707, the available evidence suggests that Catherine's transformation from unacknowledged consort to official persona began only in 1711, in the hiatus between Peter's stunning victory over the Swedes at Poltava and the ominous new war declared against Russia by the Ottoman sultan. People already knew about her, of course, but only as a mistress *("liubovnitsa").* In a playful hint, perhaps at her impending emergence into the limelight, Peter in July 1710 named his two private yachts Catherine and Liubov,[4] a fact duly noted in the official record.[5] The campaign journal *(pokhodnyi zhurnal)* identifies March 7 (O.S.), 1711, as the date on which the tsar "publicly announced to all about the sovereign tsaritsa Ekaterina Alekseevna, that she is a true sovereign."[6] Thereafter, the journal, which had previously been silent about her existence, mentions her comings and goings regularly, identifying her as "the sovereign tsaritsa."

The vice admiral and aide to the Danish ambassador, Just Juel, who was present at the time and who understood Russian well, described a meeting of March 21 in which Peter assembled the tsaritsy and tsarevny to announce that in the future they should consider Catherine to be his lawful wife and the Russian tsaritsa. Peter worried about the upcoming campaign and wanted to guarantee that, in the event of his death, Catherine would be recognized as his lawful widow. He promised them that there would be an official wedding ceremony as soon as he had some free time.[7] Juel informs us that the women of the royal family immediately congratulated the couple and embraced the tsaritsa. Peter's premonitions proved well founded, and within a few months when he, the tsaritsa, and his army found themselves trapped at Pruth, Catherine's heroic actions, so the legend grew, literally saved Peter's head, and once the pair was out of danger, Peter moved quickly to institutionalize her persona as tsaritsa.

In a recent article, Ia. E. Vodarskii reviewed the entire history of the battle of Pruth, the sources that described it, and the tales that emerged from it.[8] One of the legends he seeks to debunk concerns famously brave and heroic Catherine's role as the one who ransomed her husband's safety when he was trapped by the vizier's forces. In reconstructing Peter's specific movements within the field camp, Vodarskii assigns primary responsibility to Peter's military advisors. He does not question Catherine's presence at Pruth or her participation in the discussions of options in the encampment, but he denies that her role was central. "Undoubtedly Catherine had a decided (and not insignificant) influence on Peter, but there is nothing to suggest that she had a head for matters of state."[9] Vodarskii admits, though, that his conclusion derives as much from common sense as from hard evidence. Later in the same article he questions whether, as Just Juel had maintained, Catherine was responsible for collecting the jewels that served as the bribe to the vizier, and here Vodarskii is on more solid ground. He points out that the bribe came in the form of Russian silver coins, rather than in gold or jewelry, and that Peter corresponded directly with his generals about this. No other eyewitnesses, Russian or foreign, mentioned the story about precious jewelry, even though they discuss the bribe openly.[10]

Be that as it may, there is no question that Catherine was a visible presence throughout the critical events at Pruth, and that her presence elevated her standing in the eyes of many, not the least of whom was Peter himself. It became the basis for her subsequent biographical glorification, and gave additional glitter to the formal betrothal of the two. The public wedding ceremony took place very shortly thereafter and word of her valor, recounted below, began to receive broad circulation.[11] Quick to seize the opportunity, the vice governor of St. Petersburg, Iakov Nikitich Rimskii-Korsakov, won the tsar's personal approval in 1713 to establish a church of St. Catherine on his estate in Krasnoe Selo, for which the Alexander Nevskii Monastery was instructed to provide an altar cloth *(antiminison)*.[12]

I. F. Zubov, The Konkliuziia (engraving) of the wedding banquet from Peter and Catherine's Official Wedding, 1712

At the end of 1713, Peter forged a highly public link between his bride and her name day saint by christening a new frontline ship as the *St. Catherine*.[13] Once christened, it played a prominent role in warfare, typically serving in the advance guard during battles at sea. The *St. Catherine* was no ordinary fighter ship. In a dispatch to Cardinal Dubois from November 5, 1721, Jean Campredon commented that the tsar had shown him the *St. Catherine,* which as Campredon described it, was embellished with magnificent carvings and sculptures. Peter, he related, intended to present the ship to the tsaritsa as a gift shortly thereafter.[14]

Acts such as these (and they were numerous) spoke as much about imperial aspirations as about Catherine herself: the representation of an early Byzantine saint on a vessel of the new navy, Peter's pride and joy, transparently suggested the link between his state and Christendom's first empire. The ideology of empire, formally proclaimed only in 1721, rested on multiple foundations, of course, religious and secular, familiar and imported. The imperial title embraced by Peter and his acolytes harkened back not just to Constantinople but to Rome and Egypt as well, all in an effort to establish a pedigree of greatness, a lineage conflating Russia with the power and civilization of antiquity.[15] Empire meant ruling over a large land populated by many peoples, a status that, with the incorporation of Siberia in the east and much of Ukraine in the west, Russia could de facto assert already in the mid-seventeenth century. To proclaim Russia a great state, however, Peter needed to articulate a transcendent greatness sanctifying and ennobling the act of rulership in the eyes of posterity and investing concrete meaning in the imposing metaphors of rulership that festooned his reign from its very onset.

A Medallion of St. Catherine from the Petrine era, post–1714

However glorious, the final defeat of Sweden and the Treaty of Nystadt of 1721 that formally inaugurated empire could not in themselves suffice. To prevail as the great power of northeastern Europe was historically momentous, but it did not exactly speak to the ages. On the contrary, it brought Russia more firmly into the preexisting fraternity of European crowned heads, certainly beneficial to Russia and momentous for European diplomacy, but little more. A more abiding greatness, one suitable for a realm that leapt across time to compare itself immodestly to ancient Rome and Egypt, obliged Peter to be a savior, a champion of something larger than his own realm, for which all of civilized humanity would be forever grateful. This moral imperative required not merely entering Europe on an equal footing in the Baltic northwest, but truly safeguarding the soul of Europe in the untamed steppe of the southeast, the imaginary boundary separating the faith of Christian Europe from the infidel Ottoman Turks, the barbarians who conquered Constantinople and who conveniently lay on the empire's southern flank. Thus, not just Russia and Orthodoxy, but all of Christendom fell, by such logic, under the empire's protection and remained in its debt.

This image was not new and Peter himself had employed it repeatedly before the proclamation of empire. As Michael Khodarkovsky has shown in his study of the steppe frontier, by the sixteenth century Russia and Spain "had risen as colossi to stand guard on Europe's eastern and western flanks against the world of Islam . . . the rulers in both Moscow and Toledo arrogated to themselves the notion of being protectors of all Christians."[16] The sixteenth-century siege of Kazan, the incursion into the northern Caucasus, the confrontations with the Persian shah, were explained repeatedly as defenses of Christianity and Christian peoples who had fallen under the yoke of the infidel.[17] In the seventeenth century this identification grew stronger still, if not as New Rome then as New Israel, the protector of all Orthodox peoples. The protectorate over the Sinai monastery constituted a particularly noteworthy piece of that policy, but as Kapterev showed long ago, there were many others.[18]

Like all ideological markers, this boundary proved remarkably adaptable when it suited the monarch's purpose. Thus the image of the infidel could shift northward in a twinkling, as when Feofan Prokopovich referred to Charles XII as the "Pharaoh of the North." Conversely, the seemingly iron curtain separating Christian Europe from the Ottomans could, when needed, miraculously disappear. When negotiations with the vizier were called for, Peter dropped the Christian/infidel divide, much as his forebears had done with numerous khans and mirzas, and spoke of the fraternity of European rulers, united by their faithfulness to God. So too did the many Islamic rulers in the region during their frequent pleas for Muscovite assistance against Islamic powers further south and east. Nevertheless, the presence of the Ottomans and all the layers of alterity that could be inscribed upon them at a moment's notice proved to be fundamental to the articulation of the new Russian Empire as a Christian realm that kept the infidel at bay.

Text and imagery of the Christian ruler abounded in the second half of Peter's reign, side by side of course with their seeming negation in the many carnivalesque rituals that he enjoyed. Many of these rituals, as Richard Wortman, Lindsey Hughes, and Ernst Zitser have effectively demonstrated, substantially departed from, or at least revised, seventeenth-century court practice, and in ways that contemporaries of sufficient age would have recognized immediately. Their interweaving of state and faith distinctively emphasized the preeminence of secular power, at least on this world. But faith, if not the institutional church per se, remained forever central to the narrative, and the neat separation of divine from secular was perhaps less obvious to Russians who bore contemporary witness than it has been to retrospective observers. In this context, the knightly Orders of St. Andrew, Alexander Nevskii, and St. Catherine that Peter established hold particular interest. All three, as well as the subsequent Orders of St. George (1769), St. Anne (1735)[19] and St. Vladimir (1782), were patterned after the knights of the crusades, even though none was sent off to fight or convert, and all explicitly, at times garishly, presented their inductees, honorific though they may be, as knights of the empire, champions of Christianity and the Europe that lay to their west.

The Order of Alexander Nevskii was by far the largest of the four, listing hundreds of inductees through the eighteenth century. Along with the Order of St. Andrew, it developed considerable prestige and visibility among guards' regiments and other elite servitors. Both followed a familiar European formula that combined the martial and the sacred, emphasizing Russia's standing as a Christian empire and theirs as symbolic warriors in Christ. The Order of St. Catherine had a different history, however. It enrolled relatively few members and none from the regiments. Indeed, alone of all the orders, it was designated to enroll only women. It had a clearly military—if non-martial—charge and religious function, that of ransoming Christian soldiers, in recognition of the tsaritsa Catherine's bravery at the battle of Pruth in 1711. An examination of this curious order, then, offers one glimpse into what might be termed the theory and practice of the feminine in the founding myths of Russian imperial discourse, as well as adding a new chapter in the court cult of St. Catherine. Since most of the eighteenth-century Russian crowned heads turned out to be women, this may also be a glimpse into some of the early threads of political mythology that would later be used to make female rule seem both natural and divinely inspired.

Peter had apparently grown enamored of western knightly orders, especially their ceremonies and regalia, during his Great Embassy, and it is thought that the idea for establishing Russian orders derived from that time. What he observed, of course, were rather pale vestiges of orders established during the Crusades and institutionalized throughout Europe during the Renaissance. In their prime the crusading orders presided over elaborate institutional networks replete with military organization, priories, churches, walled compounds, and immense private treasuries. By the late seventeenth century all of this existed largely as heritage, but it was the surviving honorifics, the large badges and sashes that members wore across their chests, insignias of bygone Christian military prowess, that inspired him. Accordingly, shortly after his return to Moscow (1698 or 1699), Peter created the Order of St. Andrew and made Prince Fedor Golovin its first cavalier (the second inductee, in 1700, was Mazepa, the hetman of Ukraine, an induction that was ritually undone by stripping an effigy of Mazepa of the insignias before a crowd in Moscow in 1709 and then dragging the effigy through the streets.).[20] At about the same time General Boris Sheremetev, a scion of one of the oldest aristocratic families and a close advisor to the tsar was made a knight of Malta, and he is described by contemporaries as wearing its insignias at important occasions of state.[21]

After Poltava, Peter's interest intensified and he commissioned a translation (published in 1710) of the 1692 survey of military orders and knights by the leading court engraver, Adriaan Schoonebeek.[22] Peter had at least one additional exposure to knightly orders in 1712, when the Polish king, Augustus II, made him a member of the Order of the White Eagle, which Augustus had established in 1705. In return, Peter made Augustus a member of the Order of St. Andrew, a ritual of reciprocity between two Christian crowned heads.[23]

Amidst the evidence for this growing curiosity about orders in general, one still can only speculate where Peter got the idea for an all-female order of cavaliers. Women had participated in the Crusading Orders and their successors, serving primarily in auxiliary roles, nonmilitary and subservient, and they typically wore habits or other monastic garb. Some orders did admit women, and a few were exclusive to them. One Pontifical Order, for example, the Order of the Golden Rose, had recently inscribed Queen Casimira of Poland into its ranks in honor of the Polish victory at Vienna.[24] Similarly, the Order of the Glorious St. Mary, founded in Bologna in the mid-thirteenth century and suppressed in the mid-sixteenth, granted women the titles of knighthood *(millitissa)*, as did the fifteenth-century Order of the House of Hornes, which enabled selected noblewomen to receive the title of *chevalière*.[25] Perhaps the closest precedent came from the twelfth-century Order of the Hatchet, founded by Raymond Berengarius, count of Barcelona. This exclusively female order granted knighthood to honor those who fought against the Moors for the liberation of Tortosa in Catalonia. Those so inscribed were granted extensive privileges and were given formal precedence over men in public assemblies.[26]

Whether Peter knew of these antecedents remains unknown. Schoonebeek's survey made no mention of female orders, and his account defined a knight *(kaval'er)* as one who provided service on horseback to the sovereign, a definition that ruled out women.[27] Schoonebeek did mention a previous order of St. Catherine ("of the hills of Sinai and Jerusalem"), founded according to conventional wisdom in 1063 and commanded to protect travelers in the Holy Land, specifically from marauding Turks.[28] But his account described it as a true military order consisting entirely of men.[29] A number of medieval English parishes had established so-called Guilds of St. Katherine, which enrolled both men and women.[30] These too had long since died out before the Great Embassy.

The founding statute of the Petrine Order of St. Catherine certainly gives no hint of precedence. First announced in a proclamation nominally penned by Catherine I and with an imprint date of December 1713, its formal existence dates from a proclamation issued on November 24, 1714, expressly designed to coincide with St. Catherine's Day and the name day of the tsaritsa.[31] The text begins with the observation that Peter and Catherine were in church on that day, and "when the Divine Liturgy had ended His Tsarist Majesty deigned to enter Her Tsarist Majesty into the newly established Knightly Order of the Holy Martyr Catherine, publicly (publichno) before everyone, for there was a large number of people in attendance."[32] In a less than subtle conflation, the living Catherine was publicly recognized as a defender of both faith and fatherland, like her "namesake and intercessor, the most blessed holy martyr Catherine," sacrificing worldly goods to the non-Christian vizier of the East so as to save the Christian ruler and his men. The medal, or star, that is cast for the members of the order contains a cross surrounded by a wheel and was inscribed, "For Love and Fatherland, meant to signify not merely Catherine's own bravery but also all previous acts of Christian liberation."[33] After her induction Catherine donned a ribbon and a badge with this insignia, which she wore at most ceremonial functions and which appears prominently in nearly every portrait of her.[34]

In a single gesture Peter had joined together his wife, his faith, and his own military virtue before God, the clergy, and the community of elite worshipers who attended the prayer service with him. His text, employing language reminiscent of Dimitrii Rostovskii's vita and sermon, intermingled language of sacred and personal authority, a prime example of the cooptation of sacred space for political ends that has drawn so much attention in current scholarship. Politics, in turn, served God and the pursuit of grace, a trademark of Peter's sense of the indivisibility of church and state, the reciprocity of God and nation.

What role, then, were female knights expected to fulfill in this panorama? The 1714 statute provides considerable insight into Peter's intentions, and since the document was issued in Catherine's name, it presumably conveys Peter's thoughts about her political place. It recounts at some length Catherine's activities at Pruth in July 1711, "Where Peter found himself surrounded by an incalculably large number of [Turks] those foes of the faith." Miraculously, the proclamation says, God intervened to save Peter, as he had been protecting Peter since his youth from untold thousands of dangers, blood, and warfare. Although this point went unmentioned in the text, readers could easily infer that God's agent, or one of his agents, in this act of salvation was Catherine, whose brave acts of ransom were constructed herein as divine intercession.[35]

Here for the first time in print was the formulation that would become fundamental to Catherine's public persona over the next dozen years, the living image of her name day saint. Just as St. Catherine had intervened spiritually in the fourth century by the grace of God, according to Dimitrii Rostovskii's account, to save the emperor's philosophers, his wife, his general Porphyrius and his palace guards, now her namesake intervened materially by the grace of God to save her spouse and his guards. In this way the miracle of Alexandria was reborn, this time on behalf of a righteous Christian king of Russia, but as before, against the ungodly designs of an emperor of the East, in this case the Ottoman sultan and his agent, the vizier.

When they had gained their freedom, the statute maintains, Catherine resolved to construct an eternal monument of this remarkable liberation, and thus she established the order "by the glory of Almighty God, and in honor of the most blessed holy martyr Catherine, my intercessor" to consist of "honest and God-fearing Ladies, both married and unmarried."[36] The linkage between the living Catherine and Christian heritage is made even more explicit with the explanation that the order memorializes not just the battle of Pruth "at which I was present and an eyewitness, but also as a monument to all other acts of [Christian] liberation which preceded it."[37] With this statement one sees many of the major elements of the saintly *zhitie* being inscribed on the tsaritsa: a queen surrounded by princesses so as to convey her newly royal blood; wisdom, selflessness, bravery, and great rhetorical power. A defender of the Christian faith, she was for the moment the single living embodiment of the cavalier in Christ whom Dimitrii had praised a couple of decades earlier, the echo of the miracle-working relics described in the 1686 memorandum to Sofia. Dropped, at least to this point, were explicit allusions to virginity, formal learning, and the bride of Christ. Some things, it would appear, just could not be easily invented even in the highly performative world of Petrine intertextuality. But they too would emerge in subsequent years.

The rules of membership specified that there be one leader *("Pervenstvuiushchaia Persona")*, who would be the order's sovereign, "and as many Ladies of the great cross as there are princesses of Tsarist blood, also 12 other Ladies of the great cross, and 94 Lady Knights *(Damy kavalerstvennye)*, all of noble birth."[38] The twelve ladies presumably signified both the apostles and the twelve jewels that were said to adorn St. Catherine's crown. The referent for the number ninety-four is unknown, however. The fact that all members had to derive from the nobility valorizes the Petrine sense of heraldry, that is, nobility as an undifferentiated category of exalted birth rather than one defined by Muscovite gradations or precedence. By the same token, the emphasis on princesses of the blood, who stood just below the sovereign lady in status and who were to be inscribed into the order as soon as they were born without any particular ceremony, suggests that Peter was not so heedless of royal bloodlines as some scholars have suggested.[39] By placing Catherine at the head he was in essence inscribing her into the imaginary community of the blood, over whose female members she now stood as *"Gospozha ordena."*

The document left no doubt that final authority derived from still higher and distinctly patriarchal sources, however, namely God and Peter, Catherine's sovereign lords, rather than from consanguinity. "I [Catherine] preside over this order under the protection of the Tsar, My Sovereign. I request this honor as a sign of the fervid love and deep respect in which I hold Him."[40] Endowed by the Father(s) with authority, she was free to exercise it unilaterally, as in article 8: "I reserve to Myself alone, and to the others who succeed me *(Posledovatel'nitsy)* the honor of Grand Sovereign Lady of the Order."[41] The sovereign lady alone chose the other members and she alone had the power to expel members. This articulation of a revered female authority presiding independently in the name of physically absent male sources of authority is particularly noteworthy because it anticipates by more than a decade the formulation used to legitimate the reign of Catherine I after Peter.

If the leader proved indisposed, responsibility would pass to the first princess of the blood, entitled to be called *Velikaia Namestnitsa,* but with certain limitations on her authority.[42] The *namestnitsa* acted on behalf of the *gospozha* (sovereign lady), but she could not add or subtract members. The order had a secretary-treasurer, not necessarily a princess, who would maintain the membership list and a roster of possible new enrollees. She also was obliged to maintain the crosses that were returned to the order through the death or expulsion of a cavalier. Finally, the order was to have two official emissaries *("khodaki")* who would apprise the ladies of the day and time to be at court, and of the services required of them.[43]

How would these ladies serve? The statute prescribed five specific obligations plus some general responsibilities for all of them: to thank God every day for the merciful liberation of the tsar; to pray to God every day to care for the tsar, to protect him and his family; to recite the Lord's Prayer three times every Sunday in honor of the Holy Trinity; to strive as much as possible to banish anything untrue to the faith; and to liberate through ransom one Christian held by barbarians.[44] Every lady was constrained to obey the tsar and not to do or think anything offensive regarding him. This promise was sworn by an oath on the Gospels in the presence of the lady sovereign and officials of the clergy. Violating this oath would lead to banishment from the order.

These regulations reflected the valorization of hierarchy, office, service, fidelity, and nobility typically associated with the masculine or service side of elite life in Russia, specifically the service state and the future Table of Ranks. The insignias and symbolic attire, as well as the specific delineation of responsibilities among the officers, are reminiscent of such future fraternities as the Freemasons and the post-Napoleonic Union of Salvation, albeit without the secrecy, inner circles, ritual fetishes, and inflated sense of entitlement. Under the protection of God and tsar, the order became a feminized and entirely symbolic state within a state, an unplanned dress rehearsal, perhaps, for female rule. But here is where ritual and real, blood-and-guts politics parted company. The order had no political standing, no voice in the service state, and its membership held no privilege in the company of important men.

Upon induction Catherine I became the order's first patroness, her first public identification as intercessor. In a theme that was to be repeated several times over the next decade, Peter commended Catherine for her bravery at Pruth, specifically for her willingness to collect all the jewelry on hand so as to bribe the Grand Vizier of Turkey and thereby enable Peter and his troops to escape from Ottoman encirclement.[45] By itself, ransom was neither new nor particularly noteworthy in diplomacy. Russia had had a long and chronic history of ransoming its own—Christian—prisoners held captive by non-Christian states, especially by Tatar khanates. Prior to its capitulation to Muscovy, the khanate of Kazan in 1551 was said to hold over 100,000 Russian prisoners, who depended upon the ability of the tsar and wealthy magnates to buy their freedom in ransom.[46] In this and previous cases the Orthodox church was enlisted to help pay for the ransoming of Christian souls, largely by raising money from monasteries. On the one hand, ransom was a righteous obligation both of Orthodoxy and of the state treasury in the face of infidels in arms. On the other hand, it was costly, so much so that *Stoglav* devoted a chapter to the issue in the mid-sixteenth century.[47] The council emphasized that ransoming Christians was a duty, virtually a commandment. Quoting Enoch: "Do not suffer for [the loss of] gold and silver when it is for the sake of a brother, but redeem him. Do so again and again as if it were directly from God."

In this instance, however, the ransoming agency was a woman, and by the terms of the order's charter, the act of Christian ransom would henceforth be deemed feminine. By transposing the spiritual imperative from the church and the faithful in general directly to the women of the Order of St. Catherine, the statute was recognizing the living Catherine as a defender of both faith and fatherland, sacrificing worldly goods to the non-Christian vizier of the East so as to save the Christian ruler and his men. In recognition, the medal, or star, that was cast for the members of the order contains a cross, surrounded by a wheel (the "Catherine's wheel"), and is inscribed "For Love and Fatherland."[48] After her induction Catherine donned a sash with this insignia which she wore at most ceremonial functions.

The testimony of foreigners, many of whom had only the barest grasp of Russian, demonstrates that even they understood that the new order had symbolic importance at court, even if they were not entirely certain what that importance was. For example, Peter Bruce, a British officer in the Petrine armed forces recounts that "the Czar . . . instituted the order of St. Catherine in honour of the czarina to perpetuate the memory of that love and fidelity which she manifested toward him in his distressed situation reduced and surrounded by the Turks on the bank of the Pruth. . . . The empress had the liberty of bestowing it on such of her own sex as she thought proper, and appeared in it herself for the first time at the festival of St. Andrew this year."[49] Subsequent eighteenth-century historians, including Voltaire, I. I. Golikov, and G.-F. Muller, took similar note of it.[50] Little wonder, since Peter wasted no time in making the sash and star of the new order standard fare in official portraiture.

A 1715 engraving by A. F. Zubov, for example, entitled *Presvetlomu tsarskomu bogom sopriazhennomu soiuzu* shows Peter arriving on a ship, while on shore Catherine and their daughters await him. The star of St. Catherine radiates so boldly on her torso that it appears to extend beyond her body.[51] A 1717 Zubov engraving of Catherine was dedicated explicitly to the order and her name day.[52] In it Catherine stands next to Peter and her children at the exact center of the effigy in the middle of a very busy picture, surrounded by centurions, cherubs, muses and citizens, with what appears to be Moscow in the background. Above them, in the heavens are the archangel, other angels, and a ray of light emanating from the sun, with the letters of Jesus' kingship, INRI, in the center. Below is a lengthy text extolling Catherine and the name day.[53] Most subsequent portraits, medals, and coinage depicting Catherine also displayed the regalia of the order. Thus a 1727 silver ruble shows a profile of Catherine wearing the sash of the order, a pose that was reproduced with the visages of subsequent empresses on silver coinage throughout the century.[54] Similar portraiture could be found on the three-ruble coin, and the four-poltina coin.[55]

Like so much of Russian history, the subsequent evolution of the Order of St. Catherine, at least through the reign of Paul, bore faint resemblance to the prescriptions of its founding charter. For example, the order never did enroll the intended number of members, and through 1796 there were only seventy-six inductees, not more than a few dozen at any one time.[56] Between its founding and Peter's death in January 1725, Catherine remained the order's only member, and aside from fashioning a ceremonial sash, robe, and medallion, the Petrine order engaged in no public activity, no acts of ransom. Even the gender barrier quickly fell when Catherine inducted Prince Alexander Menshikov in 1726. Still, there is little doubt that Catherine exploited the order and her name day to rouse the capital to celebrate her name. Court records for November 22, 1725, reveal that Catherine decreed November 24 be celebrated both as her name day and as the day of her order, and she instructed that vats of wine and beer should be set forth for the general populace around the Winter Palace, and that the guards regiments should distribute wine to the soldiers.[57] Toward this worthy end the palace chancellery distributed fifty vats of wine and twenty vats of beer.

There is no record of the St. Catherine Order ever convening formally in the eighteenth century, keeping accounts, or of individual members executing their obligations of ransoming Christian prisoners, notwithstanding the multiple Russo-Ottoman wars and skirmishes with the non-Christian inhabitants of the eastern steppe. At some point the order's members began the practice of gathering annually to celebrate St. Catherine's Day with a mass and a feast, but this event seems to have been largely ceremonial. Only at the very end of the century, shortly after Paul I reaffirmed its charter, did the order establish an identity independent of court formalities, first by founding a school for girls of the nobility in 1797 in the Tauride Palace and some time later a charity hospital.[58] Also at about this time all of the knightly orders gained a permanent presence in the Moscow Kremlin, with each receiving a special hall in Bol'shoi dvorets. The St. Catherine Hall, which today is a reception room in the residential complex of the Russian president, had earlier been the throne room of the tsaritsy and was redesigned to become a public space and site for official functions of the order. In St. Petersburg the order received its own church, across from the Tauride Palace, thereby following the example of the existing male orders, both regimental and honorific.[59] Shortly thereafter a second school and church were opened in Moscow in a house that had originally been built for A. V. Saltykov in 1777 and was immediately purchased by the empress as a veterans' home.[60] From this point onward the Russian St. Catherine took on less of an imperial cloak and came increasingly to resemble the St. Catherine of Renaissance Europe: healer, protector of vulnerable women (especially those in childbirth), spiritual intercessor for those in personal need.

In the absence of formal transcripts, one must turn to alternative sources to reconstruct the uses to which specific monarchs put the order, including the roster of eighteenth-century inductees and an assortment of visual and testamentary evidence from memoirs, letters, and foreigners' accounts. Catherine I, for example, appointed eight new members of the order, all of whom were either Romanov women and thus potential rivals (her daughters Anna and Elizaveta; Peter's three nieces, Ekaterina, Anna, and Praskov'ia Ioannovna; and Grand Duchess Natal'ia Alekseevna, sister of the future Peter II) or were crucial personal and political supporters (Alexander and Dar'ia Menshikov). Peter II continued in this vein, appointing three additional Menshikovs, including "Oberhofmeisterina" Varvara Mikhailovna Arsen'eva, Dar'ia's sister, and the wife of the voevoda of Iakutsk, who would have become Peter II's aunt had he lived.[61] He also appointed Princess Ekaterina Alekseevna Dolgorukova, daughter of Supreme Privy Councillor Aleksei Dolgorukov and the betrothed of the young emperor. Most of these early inductees were soon dropped from the ranks of cavaliers with the fall of Menshikov in 1730. Thus membership in the order—and being subsequently stripped of it—appears initially to have been a way of rewarding and cultivating personal and familial loyalty (and thereby stabilizing the dynasty) by affording public honors to wives and daughters of important men at court, or in Menshikov's case, men themselves.

Symbolic politics did not come cheaply. A decree of July 26, 1727, ordered the palace chancellery to give six thousand rubles to a certain Litman to purchase diamonds for three inductees.[62] This was quite a sum of money at a time the treasury was severely short of funds in the wake of Peter the Great's endless wars. A further demonstration of the extravagance of this expense is the fact that three years later the treasury was too strapped for cash to be able to afford the necessary jewels for the coronation tiara of Empress Anna. Instead, several were removed from the tiara of Catherine I, thereby explaining why, to this day, Catherine's crown is missing several of its precious stones.[63]

The strategy of political sisterhood, employing the order to cement matrilineal ties to other crowned heads, continued throughout the century, but the nationalities of the members shifted to the west, as ever more German princesses and duchesses were inscribed during the reigns of Anna, Elizabeth, and Catherine II. Not surprisingly, under Anna the celebration of things Catherinian diminished. For example St. Catherine's Day was dropped as a state holiday in favor of the day of St. Anna the Prophetess, and the tsarevna inducted only four new members to the order, all of whom were German, including the daughter of the duke of Mecklenburg, the wife of the king of Poland and viscount of Saxony, the duchess of Saxony-Mecklenburg, and the duchess of Kurland and wife of her advisor Johann Bühren (Biron). Only one, the duchess of Kurland, even resided in Russia. Gestures such as these, which simply ignored families at court in favor of Germanic solidarity, help to explain why Anna generated such resentment against the exaggerated sway of Bironovshchina. Little wonder, as well, that the duchess of Kurland was stripped of her membership with the fall of Bühren and his party in the middle of Ivan VI's reign (she was reinstated by Catherine the Great in 1762).

Elizabeth maintained this preference for German princesses and duchesses (eleven out of thirteen inducted, including the future Catherine II and her mother upon their arrival in Russia in 1744), but in contrast to Anna, she was inclined to honor unmarried women (eleven out of thirteen), whether widowed or never married, rather than the spouses of favored men. The only currently married women inducted during Elizabeth's reign were Princess Anastasiia Ivanovna (Trubetskaia), the wife of the recently retired General Field Marshal of the Russian forces, Prince Ludwig Wilhelm of Hesse, and Maria Elizabeth August, the wife of the viscount of Pfaltz. Of course, all the women owed their standing to birth and were thus inextricably linked to the male-centered world of dynastic politics. Still, Elizabeth's penchant for the unmarried is noteworthy and one suspects that it reflected a desire to valorize the standing of women, like herself, who maintained a political presence, officially chaste and without the benefit of a spouse, much in the spirit of the virginal—if espoused—St. Catherine. This over-representation of maidens and widows may also have been a subtle reinforcement of the virgin empress myth, the bond with Bogomater' on which she, like her English namesake, occasionally relied. Was it mere coincidence that five of her inductees were named Maria? From a dynastic perspective, these inductions constituted a ritual of empire par excellence, extending from the God-given authority to rule her own realm to the man-made (Peter-built) authority of the order's overseer to command women from the smaller Baltic states, a *prima inter pares* among several other European and Christian female crowned heads. As the imperial protector of Christendom's eastern flank, she now presided as the knightly matron over her grateful Christian sisters.

Catherine II's memoir contains a colorful description of her own unceremonious induction into the order on February 10, 1744. She and her mother had arrived the previous day in Moscow and were taken to the Golovin Palace, where the empress stayed when she was in Moscow. "The Empress emerged from her toilet exceptionally done up. She had on a brown dress adorned in silver all of which was covered in diamonds, that is on the head, neck, and bust. . . . Count Aleksei Grigor'evich Razumovskii followed behind her. He was one of the most attractive men I had ever seen. He carried the insignia of the order of St. Catherine on a large golden tray. I was a little nearer to the door than my mother was. The Empress inducted me into the order of St. Catherine, and then she did the same to my mother. At the conclusion she kissed each of us. Countess Vorontsova pinned the star on my mother, and Cholokova on me."[64]

This hurried scene, confirmed by an entry in her mother's diary,[65] lacked pomp and ceremony, but it did faithfully reproduce the spirit of the statute as regards those princesses whose membership came as a birthright. And it constituted an important rite of passage in the eyes of Empress Elizabeth. Catherine was on the verge of becoming a princess of tsarist blood, and the induction was sufficiently urgent to Elizabeth that it took place even before Catherine and her mother had laid eyes on her soon-to-be husband, Grand Duke Peter, and four and a half months before she pronounced the Symbols of Faith and took her new Orthodox name of Ekaterina Alekseevna.[66] Induction thus bound the mother and daughter from Zerbst to Elizabeth's realm, a ritual of sorority that simultaneously welcomed them as "princesses of the blood," and placed them formally under Elizabeth.

Peter III's brief reign saw six new inductees, again mostly German or personal favorites of the emperor (including Countess Elisaveta Romanovna Vorontsova, who was promptly dropped from the rolls shortly after Catherine II ascended the throne). Once Catherine II took over, the order reestablished its affinity for courtiers and clan networks. Her thirty-nine nominees included many women supporters, the first of whom were Ekaterina Dashkova, Ekaterina Razumovskaia, and, once again, the duchess of Kurland, now recently restored from exile. Dashkova's induction came even before Catherine's official coronation, and the inductee wore her regalia when Catherine was crowned in the Dormition Cathedral in Moscow. Its prominence was described by one of Dashkova's biographers, "The Orlovs had the ordering of the ceremonies on this occasion, and as precedence depended on military rank they saw to it that Dashkova took a subordinate place in the proceedings. Her Order of St. Catherine, *though a coveted and distinguished honour* [italics added], conferred no precedence."[67]

The list of Catherinian inductees also restored some balance between Russians and Germans, alternating between one set and the other, between relatives abroad and allies and royals at home. Thus, between 1764 and 1774 only German ladies were inscribed, then for the rest of Catherine's reign the balance tipped toward Russians, especially women of the ruling family, and those, like the future Empress Mariia Fedorovna and her mother, who married into the Romanov line. Presumably Catherine was using the order to reinforce the position of Paul as her designated successor, since Paul's daughters, wife, and mother-in-law all were inscribed.

Paul himself took the order rather seriously. On the day of his coronation he issued three decrees that collectively were intended to change the tone of monarchy as it had been practiced by his mother. The first *ukaz* put into law the new rule of succession, establishing the heredity principle as paramount and all but assuring that no female ruler would ever again mount the Russian throne. The second decree announced Paul's famous three-day-a-week limit on *barshchina*, a controversial if ultimately ineffective intervention into landlord-serf relations. It is the third decree that is interesting here, however. In it Paul reviewed the six knightly orders currently active (St Anne, St. Catherine, St. Andrew, St. Alexander Nevskii, St. George, and St. Vladimir). The first four received his imprimatur and approval for continued subsidy. The latter two, each established by his mother, were denied support, even though in both cases royal patronage was restored somewhat later.[68] To underscore his regard for the Order of St. Catherine he inducted several new members on the day of his coronation. Shortly thereafter he decreed that all the grand duchesses of the realm were to be inducted.[69]

This degree of imperial attentiveness would seem to confirm Dashkova's understanding that the order was "coveted and distinguished," at court, a view further underscored by the many portraits of empresses and ladies at court displaying the sash and insignia with great prominence. At the celebration of the Treaty of Nystadt, Catherine is described as having changed gowns frequently, but throughout she wore a diamond-studded sword and her regalia of the order.[70] Almost every secular painting of Catherine I after 1714 gives the order's sash and star an almost larger than life visibility. For example, G. S. Musikiisskii's miniature "Family Portrait of Peter I," painted in 1720, placed Catherine in the center of the frame, with Peter on one side and the three offspring on the other. One's eye is drawn immediately, first to Catherine, and then to the prominent sash and insignia that crossed her torso. An untitled portrait of Catherine alone, identified by the *Granat* encyclopedia as belonging to the Rumiantsev Museum made the sash and insignia so central that one can easily read the words on the insignia.[71] Portraits of Catherine II, including one taken of her in mourning dress after the death of Empress Elizabeth, her mother, and other prominent ladies also displayed the signs of the order.[72]

Interestingly, Elizabeth, Peter III, Catherine II, and even Paul used membership in the Order of St. Catherine as a mechanism for honoring the kin of Petrine *ptentsy*,[73] as if to perform a ritual renewal of the Petrine covenant. Among those so chosen were the granddaughter of Shafirov, Countess Anna Alekseevna Matiushkina (1797); the niece of Catherine I, Countess Anna Karlovna Vorontsova [nee Skavronska] (1762); another Skavronska, Countess Mariia Nikolaevna, who had married the cousin of Elizaveta Petrovna (1797); the second wife of Dmitrii Kantemir, Anastasiia Ivanovna, (1741); and the daughter of Andrei Matveev, Mariia Andreevna Rumiantsova (1775).[74] This repeated gesture constituted an ongoing perpetual renewal of the veneration of Peter the Great as progenitor of the dynasty as it had come to exist in the eighteenth century, a perpetual reminder that the women of the order traced their lineage to Peter and in this way belonged to him.

By Elizabeth's reign the members of the order had become a visible presence during official gatherings to which women were invited, identifiable by the stars, ribbons, and gowns that they alone could wear. The founding charter prescribed that the ladies of the order "wear a cross on their dress, on the left side by their heart, from which would hang a white ribbon, on which would be written in gold letters 'For Love and Fatherland.'"[75] Portraits of the day show the empresses wearing the insignias and regalia of the order, a further indication of its visibility. Even the more abbreviated *mesiatsoslovy* of the late eighteenth and early nineteenth centuries, which listed far fewer saints and holidays than earlier ones, continued to identify November 24 as an important day honoring both St. Catherine and the order.[76] In addition to special prayer services and sermons, celebrations included fireworks, balls, and banquets, particularly during the reigns of the two Catherines, both of whom had been re-baptized into Orthodoxy in her name. Friedrich Bergholz, for example, provided lengthy descriptions of the celebrations of Catherine's name day during the early 1720s, an event that may have rivaled the St. Andrew's Day martial celebration on Palace Square. "On the name day of her majesty the empress there was the usual celebration accompanied at the end of the divine liturgy by a firing of the cannons in the fortress. In the evening there was a grand feast at the winter palace, in the new hall of knights, which concluded with an excellent display of fireworks."[77]

At these moments the ladies of the order took center stage, and their appearance was of sufficient moment that Elizabeth, Catherine II, and

Paul each issued instructions concerning their dress. The founding statute itself designated the following insignia: a white cross in the hand of St. Catherine, signifying her purity, against a field of royal purple. In the center there would be a smaller cross, arrayed with rays of light symbolizing the light of the Gospels. Between the crosses were to be the letters *DSFR,* for *Domine salvum fac Regem* (God save the Tsar), as enunciated in Psalm 19 (Psalm 20 in the modern Bible). God and tsar; cross and the state; Latin and Russian; the body of Christ, the body of the realm, the female body of the knight, all were co-joined. Every lady of the order was expected to wear the cross on a ribbon, next to her heart, with the motto written in gold lettering.[78] Special dolls were fashioned of wood and ceramics to show ladies in the dress of the order, smooth silver brocade with green velvet trim and trains of varying length reflecting the standing of the specific person in the order.[79]

The uniform prescribed a velvet hat with a large turned-up brim. Each hat displayed the badge of the order, with a section of the "Catherine wheel" done in silver and a gold feather. Even among the highly decorative society women of the capital, this attire stood boldly out as the only uniform specific to women in public life. Catherine II herself wore the complete uniform at many occasions, as did Mariia Fedorovna after her. At other events of state she wore very prominently her star of the order, festooned with diamonds, gold and red enamel, the Catherine wheel, and the order's motto.[80]

Beyond marking the individual's membership in an exclusive body that conferred considerable status, what did knightly ornaments convey at the Russian court? Contemporaries clearly noticed them, but what meaning did they attribute to them? First and foremost, the insignias conveyed Russia's oneness with Europe. Irrespective of the name of the order or its mission, badges and sashes inscribed on the body of the member were their unifying element. If one were to place an eighteenth-century portrait of a Russian cavalier side-by-side with one of an English or Italian cavalier, one would be struck by their similarity. Status in Russia was thus recognizable and familiar in every European court. But the orders were just as surely Russian in that they were named after long revered and familiar saints within Orthodoxy. To wear the regalia, then, gave one the very special and highly public honor of inscribing onto one's person the symmetry of Europe and Russia, the Christian empire against the non-Christian east, the unity of opposites against all odds: national self and other, state and faith, elite and popular, old and new. That this symbolism of symmetry under Christ was perceived as desirable and natural goes some distance toward explaining why the imperial project thrived so heartily in the eighteenth century.

If one examines the advent of Catherine/St. Catherine in the founding of the order in 1714 against the backdrop of Peter's repeated self-association with the early Christian empire, one begins to understand how these two myths could subsequently intertwine and eventually provide a faith-based rationale for the tsaritsa's public emergence. Fourth-century Christendom, especially the reign of Constantine, was a foundational moment for Russian Orthodoxy, well described in numerous texts that circulated in Muscovy. It provided a fundamental and constantly invoked link between Russian rulership and godly kingship, since the Laurentian Chronicle proclaimed Prince Vladimir "the new Constantine [himself, the new King David] of mighty Rome who baptized himself and his subjects."[81] Already in the 1690s, leading clerics were employing this tool as a way of situating Peter as a Christian monarch fighting against the unbelieving vizier. Most frequently this identification with Christian empire exploited the image of Constantine the Great and his conquest of Maxentius, that is, the king who had Catherine put to death. For example, the widely discussed pamphlet on triumphal processions, entitled "Preslavnoe torzhestvo svoboditelia Livonii" (Triumphal Processional of the Liberator of Livonia), by the prefect of the Moscow Academy, Iosif Turoboiskii, proclaimed that within Christianity such gates were part of the political world and not sacred space "as in the time when King Constantine [built gates] in Rome after having defeated Maxentius."[82]

Turoboiskii termed Peter "a rock," thus echoing "the rock of faith" of St. Peter in the Gospel of St. Matthew. Peter himself employed this Byzantine precedent several times, and even had it inscribed on the triumphal gates of Moscow after the second Azov campaign. On the gates is written, "vozvrat s pobedy tsaria Konstantina" and elsewhere "pobeda tsaria Konstantina nad nechistivym tsarem Maksentiem Rimskim."[83] Subsequently the Constantine precedent was also used by Feofan Prokopovich, Feofilakt Lopatinskii, and Gavriil Buzhinskii. Peter was the new Constantine— whom Orthodoxy deemed equal to the apostles, champion of the faith in and against the East. Catherine was his warrior-bride, the new St. Catherine (Constantine's approximate contemporary), whose courage and wits safeguarded the eastern flanks of the Christian world. Peter's founding myths of empire from this time forward included a discreetly feminine, if decidedly subordinate, narrative, as the official story of Pruth now joined that of Poltava and the other valiant tales (both faith-centered and classical) to mark the monarchy's inexorable and heroic advance. Through this myth, and its institutional expression in the Order of St. Catherine, the evolving myth of the tsaritsa could be elaborated more fully, and in ways that would enable Catherine to be something more—and something different—than the royal intercessor or holy womb of a Muscovite tsaritsa. She was a cavalier of the cross, an emergent female counterpart to Alexander Nevskii, by whose wits and bravery the realm had been saved. The elaboration of this myth, and its place in imperial ideology had yet to receive a full elaboration, but that would be the work of the court panegyrists of the last decade of Peter's reign.

7

The Saint's Living Image

• The Order of St. Catherine notwithstanding, most representations of the living Catherine between 1714 and the declaration of empire in 1721 fell within the accepted and familiar bounds of a Muscovite tsaritsa. She was the traditional loyal helpmate, *"zemnaia mati"* (earthly mother), who stayed out of politics, at least for the formal record. Frederic de Bassewitz's admiring view, dating back to 1713, had been that Catherine contributed to the realm by easing Peter's melancholies, a personal intervention that he termed "magical" and "miraculous."[1] As late as 1721, Campredon assured his court that "she has no influence on affairs of state, in which she never interferes. All her concerns are dedicated to maintaining the Tsar's love, to steer him away from drinking too much and his other debauches."[2] This comfortable and unchallenging characterization would remain central to her persona right up until the eve of her coronation, at which point even foreign envoys began to take her more seriously.

Here and there one sees traces of an expanded and even innovative public persona, but these generally are set well within the established Muscovite role of helpmate and intercessor until the latter years of Peter's reign.[3] In addition to engaging the tsar on behalf of his subjects, she now augmented that role by intervening with the realm on behalf of the sovereign. She appeared, for example, in several issues of *Vedomosti,* Russia's first quasi-newspaper, accompanying Peter, and sometimes representing him in his absence. The issue of August 8, 1719, announced that the tsaritsa had received word from Peter of a successful incursion in Sweden, not far from Stockholm, for which she instructed Stefan Iavorskii to order a service of thanksgiving in all the churches.[4] Again on August 30, *Vedomosti* informed its readers that Peter had sent a letter to Catherine regarding successful military affairs on the island of Lammeland.[5] This identity of Catherine as the official helpmate and blessed intercessor was so firmly established that it traveled abroad with Peter and Catherine during the second Great Embassy in 1717. Some brief verses by Johann Jacob Klermondt and a sermon by a Lutheran minister, Caspar Diedrich Van Daie, included extensive paeans to Catherine.[6]

The year 1719 also marked the emergence of a Catherinian persona in Petrine legislation, in particular laws on state service that prescribed an oath of office. Prior to this time she had received occasional mention, as in the legislation establishing the Order of St. Catherine or decrees establishing her annual budget from state accounts (a whopping 200,000 rubles in 1714).[7] As Peter institutionalized his reforms in his latter years through wave after wave of monumental legislation, Catherine's presence in these laws became regular, systematic, and more governmentally entrenched. For example, a Senate decree of 1723 established a separate chancellery for Catherine's patrimonial lands, under the direction of state secretary Leontii Artsybashev, who was commanded to send regular reports to Her Majesty.[8]

The instructions to those serving in regional governments and provinces, issued in January 1719, included a new clause that soon became standard in the relevant legislation, requiring the commissioners to swear before God to be "Faithful, honest, and law-abiding servants of His Tsarist Majesty, Her Majesty the Lady Tsaritsa, and their heirs."[9] Similar language recurred in the Regulations for the Commerce College (March 1719), this time requiring members of the college to be "loyal, honest, and good people and servants" of the tsar, tsaritsa, and their heirs.[10]

Insisting that the oath of service include obedience to the tsaritsa was something new for Russian legislation, suggesting that the office and person of the tsaritsa were expanding in undefined ways beyond those of helpmate and intercessor. As the new oaths of office were formalized, several moved away from the anonymous language of "tsaritsa" and began to call upon servitors' loyalty not just to the title but to Catherine by name, thus making manifest Peter's intention to direct this inscription of public respect explicitly to his flesh-and-blood spouse. In October 1719, the oath administered to the secretary *("d"iak")* of the College of Serf Affairs *(Kollegiia Krepostnykh del)* demanded loyalty to Peter, his lawful heirs, Catherine, and to all the powers and authority of His Majesty's sovereignty *("Samoderzhavstvo").*[11] Similar language was used in the oaths included in the General'nyi Reglament, the Instruction to the Zemskii D"iak, the Regulations for Town Magistrates, the Spiritual Regulations, and the instructions sent to the Governor of Astrakhan.[12] Sometimes the oaths referred to Catherine as Peter's spouse, but all emphasized that the servitor was swearing allegiance to Catherine, individually and separately, and to unnamed heirs, as much as to Peter.

A comparable oath was composed for the Kamer College in December 1719, but with some subtle changes that demonstrate the attentiveness paid to the wording of these oaths as well as the concerns that weighed on Peter's mind barely a year after the disinheritance of Aleksei Petrovich.

> I, the person named below, do promise that I wish to and must honor my natural and true Tsar and Lord, the All-radiant, Almighty Tsar and Lord, the Lord Tsar Peter the First and Sovereign of All Russia. . . . And after him all the lawful heirs of His Tsarist Majesty, and in particular The Most Radiant Heir the Grand Lord Tsarevich Peter Petrovich, and all the Heirs who may follow, and the succeeding Godchildren who, as the Tsarist Majesty so deigns, have been specified and will in future be specified, will be deemed worthy of receiving the throne.
>
> That I wish to be a loyal, honest, and obedient servant and subject of His Tsarist Majesty and Her Majesty the Lady Tsaritsa and the Most Radiant Heirs.[13]

The abbreviated elevation of Tsarevich Peter Petrovich, cut short by his death in childhood, reveals the depth of Peter's worries about succession. By insisting on this form of loyalty before God, he was endeavoring to secure the realm, the new institutions, and the continued power of his current immediate family should they survive him. Clearly, the hope in 1719 was that the young Peter would be the heir, with the corollary that Catherine could fulfill the role of regent if circumstances required until he reached adulthood. In order to pave the way for this outcome Catherine needed to command *public* loyalty then and there, while Peter was still alive and well. For reasons of state her name had to become a commonplace in basic legislation, it needed to be uttered by all who desired to serve the tsar, and her persona needed to develop a more visible presence so as to make her potential regency seem both natural and divinely planned.

Against this backdrop of political exigency, Catherine's name day saint loomed ever larger. In 1717, several new published texts extolled St. Catherine and transparently linked the tsaritsa to her. The first was Feofan Prokopovich's long and impassioned name day sermon on "St. Catherine the Great Martyr, the Name Sake of the Good Sovereign Lady Catherine, the All-Russian Tsaritsa."[14] Initially orated at the Trinity Church in St. Petersburg and published the next month in a run of three hundred copies, the sermon echoed many of the themes and images prescribed for martyred women in the *Mineia obshchaia*. It contrasted the hypocritical corporeal love of the minions of the Persian emperor Darius with the true love of the holy martyr, a godly and selfless love that, in Feofan's words, is embodied by "the other Catherine," the tsaritsa, who shares her divinely inspired wisdom *("bogomudraia"):* "The female sex is by nature soft and gentle. And in this instance it is not just the female sex [to whom we refer] but a maiden, noble, beautiful, abundant in wealth and glory and much natural goodness. And she was in the spring of her youth, a time when life is sweet."[15]

Once again, the proof of this love lay in her accompanying Peter and showing bravery on his forays abroad. Feofan then mentioned the new order. "We cannot pass over in silence this most wonderful affair of yours, o divinely wise monarch, by which your love for God and for the one near you [i.e., Peter] is honored. . . . That is, the newly established glorious title of cavalier which is granted to you, in the name of your name day saint the martyr Catherine and with a title adorned by the intercession of God."[16]

A second proclamation was a "Greeting from the Saint Petersburg Typography to the Great Sovereign, All-Russian Tsaritsa most noble Grand Princess Ekaterina Alekseevna on her name day," the ceremonial text that accompanied Ivan Zubov's 1717 *konkliuziia*. It offered prayers to the tsaritsa and praise for her incalculable bravery *("bezmernoe muzhestvo")* at Pruth. The text wished her joy, peacefulness, and good health, and it congratulated her for being the only member of the Order of St. Catherine.[17] This theme echoed a *konkliuziia* by Zubov and Pikart of two years earlier celebrating the victories of Peter's navy. Although filled with celebratory and celestial images, its foreground displayed Peter on the bow of a ship, Catherine on land awaiting him. Catherine stood in front of a temple, and at her side stood St. Catherine. Catherine and St. Catherine secured the land, Peter ruled the seas, while above the heavens rejoiced.[18]

Through proclamations such as these, the persona of Catherine/St. Catherine had become a public and blessed fact, with godly wisdom now as much an attribute of the tsaritsa as it was the holy martyr. In their mutual honor a church of St. Catherine was constructed in Kalinkina, near Ekaterinhof, and consecrated on May 18 (Catherine's birthday), 1721.[19] These texts and sites redundantly underscored the now familiar tropes unifying feminine love with female manliness, faith and Christian martyrdom with military victory over a real-life opponent from the east, political power and a crucial intervention in affairs of state, and most importantly crown and halo. They also demonstrate the transformation in celebrating St. Catherine's day once the court had moved to the new capital. Formerly, the homage paid by the living Romanov women to the dead was paid within the walls of the Kremlin, as symbolized by the midnight processional of the cross from the St. Catherine Church to the St. Catherine side chapel at Voznesenskii Convent. Sermons may have been preached, but these remained unpublished in their day, and they functioned as fundamentally private exchanges between the prelate and the ruling family. The move to St. Petersburg precluded a processional to the graves of female ancestors, and its place—at least on November 24—was taken, first, by the publicly orated (and frequently published) sermon, and, then, by lavish fireworks.

All of this reflected not just the valorization of St. Catherine but also the increasing use of tsarist name day celebrations as a medium for highly public political ceremonials. These events have attracted little more than passing interest, but during the last several years of Peter's reign they had evolved from the religious—admittedly lavish at times—feasts and fasts they had been in Muscovy into highly charged, and not very subtle, spectacles, at which attendance was obligatory. Name days had the distinct advantages of being recurring events on the Christian calendar and of being familiar. Every baptized subject had a name day, and the celebration of the tsar's name day could at one level express an intimate link every year between ruler and ruled, by reminding everyone that the tsar too was incarnate and a Christian. As already seen, the nation had been celebrating special masses on princely and tsarist name days for several generations, since long before the Romanov dynasty, so the repetition was nothing new. Keeping in mind the axiom that rituals of authority constituted repeated acts of public reassurance, ways of making the exercise of power both seem natural (in the sense of being a regular element of cyclical time) and consistent with the mysteries of faith, name day spectacles proved an ideal vehicle. Giving them broad public exposure through visual and printed media, as was Peter's métier, allowed them to become nationwide statements of a celestial affirmation of Peter's reign, the affinity of rulers and saints (and of course the clergy's essential role in conveying to the laity God's view of the reign and articulating its spiritual rectitude).

A July 1719 issue of *Vedomosti* devoted nearly all twelve of its pages to a description of the religious festival of Saints Peter and Paul on June 29, which was also Peter's name day. It recounted the vespers service at the Trinity Cathedral in Petersburg officiated by Stefan Iavorskii and attended by Catherine, members of the Senate, and many others of both sexes. It included a lengthy summary of Iavorskii's sermon, complete with biblical citations, on the theme (found in John 21) of walking in the footsteps of Christ. In an analogy that would prove to be central to the elevation of Catherine to rule, he put forth the proposition that just as Peter the Supreme Apostle (Petr Verkhovnik Apostol'skii) followed Christ's path, so too does Russia's supreme Peter (Petr Verkhovnik Vserossiiskii). Repeatedly conflating the two Peters as Verkhovniki, Iavorskii explained that they followed Christ's path on land, on water, at war, as a good shepherd, seeking out the fallen lambs, and in obedience. The post-church celebrations—cannon fire, singing, trumpets blaring, fountains alit, the ever-present fireworks—were duly noted, as was a naval ceremony in Peter's honor at Hangut.[20]

Two of Stefan Iavorskii's published sermons, and several unpublished ones, were devoted to St. Catherine's Day. Both of the published homilies are undated but some clues in the sermons suggest that one was penned early in Peter's reign and the other some time later, probably between the time of Peter's coronation as emperor and Catherine's as empress. Interpreting Iavorskii's sermons is particularly vexing, in part because of the absence of dates and settings, but also because the published volumes, containing twenty-nine *slova,* constitute only a fraction of the author's homiletic output, said to number over two hundred by Ilarion Chistovich, the only scholar to date who has examined the manuscripts in detail.[21] Nevertheless, there do exist these two published texts, and they provide at least a partial glimpse into Iavorskii's thoughts.

Comparing the two homilies, separated in time by just a few years, reveals the changing face of St. Catherine within the expanse of Peter's reign. Each reprises the miracle of the mystical marriage to Christ and the superiority of godly wisdom over pagan philosophy, and even over the conventional wisdom of the day. They counterpose the power of a single divinely inspired virgin and the impotence of fifty—male—pagan philosophers, the one true God over the many false ones.[22] But whereas the first, possibly a name day service for Princess Ekaterina Alekseevna or Ekaterina Ioannovna, makes no mention of the ruling family, the second directs these themes to the glory of Peter and Catherine.[23] Early in the sermon Iavorskii speaks of how the image of St. Catherine stands as "our conscience, our light which will always burn bright and unextinguished."[24] He then returns to this theme several pages later around the person of the tsaritsa: "The Russian State reveres you, as through your merciful intercessions it has [gained] its very own inheritor *(naslednitsu)* of your virtues, the great tsaritsa, the most pious sovereign lady of the great tsar. [She is] the living image of you and your virtues, truly bearing in her own person your inextinguishable light in her soul."[25] To this he added that Peter, the true father of the Russian fatherland, had chosen Catherine to be his wife and the tsaritsa and that she is there with her spouse, the Russian emperor.[26] One did not need to be a cleric to hear the loud echo of the bride of Christ in this pronouncement.

Gavriil Buzhinskii, the powerful archimandrite of the Trinity-St. Sergius Monastery and a Petrine stalwart among the clergy, added his voice to the hagiography by orating at least three name day sermons for Catherine before the ruling family and other leading personages (1718, 1720, 1720).[27] Although he, too, stressed the theme of God-inspired wisdom (Solomon was frequently invoked), Buzhinskii's sermons were more Christological than Feofan's, less focused on the two Catherines and more on the worship and teachings of Christ. In this context, the bride-of-Christ theme regained the prominence that Dimitrii had afforded it, but since Buzhinskii's sermons had a living referent in attendance and Dimitrii's did not, Buzhinskii's interpretation was rather different. Where Dimitrii dwelled on the miraculous betrothal and wedding ceremony itself, Buzhinskii stressed the familial implications of the heavenly marriage (a term he used repeatedly). This was the name day of the mother of the fatherland,[28] the ruler's spouse, helpmate, and protector. St. Catherine, thus, fulfilled what Buzhinskii termed the "domestic" *(ekonomicheskii chin)* place as defined by God, caring for husbands, wives, all family members, orphans, and servants.[29] She followed in the footsteps of Esther and Sarah, good wives to blessed kings. She was humble, loving, worshipful, and submissive, honest, beautiful, pure. In these qualities she outdid even the ten great maidens described by Chrysostom.[30] And she was strong.

Like Iavorskii, Buzhinskii described the tsaritsa as "the living image" *(obraz)* of the holy martyr. "One sees in her wisdom that very divine wisdom possessed of St. Catherine," the same mercy, kindness, humility, and piety.[31] She was an example to young men and women. Like her namesake, the tsaritsa lived her life according to the dictates of their common teacher, the holy church. Peter the Great, he tells the reader in 1721, chose for himself a spouse who carries out the words of Ecclesiastes: "the husband of a good wife is blessed, and his days are enriched."[32] Now she, like Peter, is "revered in all of Europe," all to the benefit of Russia.

Buzhinskii made special mention of the Order of St. Catherine as well, and it was in this context that he broached the tsaritsa's *muzhestvo*. For him the experience at Pruth carried two lessons. First, it demonstrated Catherine's wifely devotion to those nearest to her, and it was to honor this trait that the Order of St. Catherine was emblazoned into eternal memory.[33] But Pruth also demonstrated the power of faith, the necessity of struggling as much as possible against the enemies of the faith, of freeing Christians from the oppression of barbarians, and even of ransoming them with one's own money if need be.[34] "O the fruits of Christianity! O the deeds of youth! O, the love of the one who is like an angel! We speak here of our Tsaritsa's goodness, that she carried out those measures by her own labors that were difficult and seemingly impossible."

Much more than Feofan, then, Buzhinskii deemed it essential to proclaim in the presence of the tsar and the court the primacy of faith over secularity, or as he put it the priority of *"dukhovnyi chin"* (spiritual sphere) over *"politicheskii"* (political) or *"grazhdanskii"* (secular) *"chin."*[35] His homilies thus embedded the Petrine veneration of Catherine/St. Catherine within the Holy Spirit, the struggle against the devil, and the authority of the archbishops. The pagan learning of the ancient Greeks, military victory, and the striving toward Europe all had their place, all could constitute good works, but only in the service of the Holy Spirit. Otherwise they became ungodly, destined to perdition in a struggle that Buzhinskii deemed "entirely unequal," between divine wisdom and artful human reason. If Peter found this message disagreeable, he never said so.

Further momentum to the veneration of St. Catherine, if any was needed after those overpowering sermons, came in a decree of 1721 fixing certain days as major state holidays, a roster that included Catherine's name day. Henceforth November 24 would occasion a series of new public celebrations in addition to the name day service, a practice that Catherine continued after Peter's death. Peter's final years saw a flurry of decrees and protocols on imperial name days, indicating both Peter's attempt to elevate the public individuality of members of the ruling family, and a desire by both church and ruler to make certain that these public celebrations would have faith at their core. Name days, the days of one's angel, were to be celebrated rather than actual birthdays.[36] Bishops were instructed to make certain that all the churches in their dioceses conformed, and to send reports not only of the church services, but also of names of missing congregants.[37] The non-Russian cohorts at court soon got the message and produced their own texts of homage, including a 1721 panegyric in German by Efraim Ferchmin in honor of the name day of the realm's "Landesmutter."[38]

After Catherine's coronation in 1724, a similar wave of decrees went out regarding mandatory attendance of prayer services on May 7, the anniversary of the coronation.[39] In addition to making certain that all Orthodox subjects paid respects to the imperial family within a consecrated place, these decrees had an explicit element of social control. Along with the newly mandated confessional lists *(ispovednye knigi),* counting heads in church was a way of determining who was missing, and who thereby might be a potential religious schismatic.[40]

Still, Catherine was a major beneficiary of this particular merger of faith and raison d'état, and she now regularly received calls and notes of congratulations on her name day, as did her favorites.[41] Even those close to her at court, including Menshikov, seem to have treated November 24 as a propitious time to approach her with a request for personal intervention.[42] As already seen, virtually every leading cleric produced lengthy homilies for the name day,[43] congregants in churches and monasteries sang prayers to her, and Peter arranged lavish banquets, concerts, and fireworks displays.

To a certain extent, these celebrations had the good fortune of harkening to their pre-Petrine precedents, as if to maintain the myth of unbroken lineage while simultaneously propagating the myth of the new imperial female warrior in Christ. Celebrated throughout the late sixteenth and seventeenth centuries, St. Catherine's Day had become a major feast day during the 1690s, almost certainly in homage to Peter's niece and half-sister. Thus, in 1698, Patriarch Adrian authorized a St. Catherine's Day feast that included numerous courses of fish, caviar, meat pies, stews, roast, and other delicacies. Special additional requisitions were ordered for the monastic clergy on duty, priests, sacristans, choir members, household servants, and twelve selected paupers, thereby linking the feast day with the Last Supper, as would be fitting for a bride of Christ.[44] In the last seven years of Peter's reign, however, these celebrations grew far more lavish, more public, and more statist, albeit still firmly embedded within the theme of the martyr to the faith.

Bergholz, considerably more useful in narrating what he saw rather than what was being said, has left behind lengthy descriptions of these celebrations in diary entries for every year from 1721 to 1725. In 1721, the festivities started at 6:00 in the morning with an hour-and-a-half orchestral concert, followed by a parade, a feast, and fireworks. The merriment did not end, he relates, until 1:30 in the morning![45] The next year Bergholz had relocated to Moscow along with the entire court. Since both Peter and Catherine were away on the Persian campaign, the celebration, overseen by Menshikov, was slightly tamer—it began at ten o'clock—and politically less important. The duke of Holstein had to be bribed by his wife in order to get him to the service, but he did go, as did all the notables then present in Moscow. They proceeded to the Dormition Cathedral for a service and sermon by the archbishop of Novgorod, none of which Bergholz understood because, so he confesses repeatedly in his diary, he did not know Russian and had no familiarity with Russian religious ritual.[46] He does note that, at the end of the service, the archbishop held up a silver cross brought to him on a silver tray by two deacons, that the archbishop blessed all those present with the cross, and that all the congregants went up to the altar to kiss the cross. Everyone then repaired to the Senate, where the remaining foreign dignitaries had gathered, after which there was a very large banquet (an oenophile par excellence, Bergholz was adept at recalling the various wines he drank).

November 24 was now established in everyone's mind as a regular major holiday, and by 1724, Bergholz had become rather more blasé about the whole affair.

> November 24. On the name day of her majesty the empress the usual cele-
> bration took place, accompanied, at the end of the liturgy, by a procession to
> the fortress. In the evening, in the emperor's winter palace, in a new hall of
> cavaliers (Kavalerskii zal), there was a great feast, followed by a magnificent
> fireworks, which was presented over the ice [presumably on the Neva] and
> which was lit by the figure of an angel from a rocket fired from the hall. . . .
> In the space between the two pyramids there burned the letters: V. C. I. R.,
> i.e., Vivat Catharina Imperatrix Russorum.[47]

The official campaign journal observed in addition that the evening fireworks included a display of Venus in a long carriage borne by swans, with the inscription "Joyous harmony."[48] This display left little to the imagination: Catherine, soon to be crowned, was extolled as both Venus and martyr with Latin letters projected between the most recognizable symbols of ancient Egypt available in St. Petersburg, the pyramids, and with rockets fired into the heavens from the new hall of knights in the shape of an angel. At that moment one could have justifiably inquired precisely where St. Catherine ended and where Ekaterina Alekseevna began. Lest there be any doubt that all of this was thoroughly political and had little to do with personal sentiment, one needs to recall that only eight days previously Catherine's disgraced lover, William Mons, had been publicly beheaded for graft at the order of Peter and the Senate.[49]

But what of the religious side of the name day, particularly the liturgy that Bergholz did not even pretend to understand? Peter left no doubt that he expected the clergy to celebrate Catherine's name day, as well as his own, with a service and prayers of thanksgiving *(Ekteniia)* to her health. In October 1723, he ordered the Synod to compose three new hymns and a song of praise *(slavnik)* for St. Catherine post haste, a task that the Synod assigned to the bishop of Astrakhan, Lavrentii.[50] Those clerics who failed to do so, even rural ones, if they were discovered, got into serious trouble. In 1722, for example, Mitrofan Arkhipov, a village priest from the Novgorod diocese, was investigated by the Secret Chancellery for his alleged refusal to celebrate a mass in honor of Catherine's name day.[51] The sacristan of the church claimed that Mitrofan had even prevented him from conducting the service, a statement that two parishioners later corroborated.[52] It subsequently emerged that Mitrofan was a drunken and quarrelsome sort and that he had grumbled once too often about Catherine's name day, claiming that Catherine was not an empress but a mistress, and hence not deserving of a service. In the end Mitrofan was stripped of his vows, defrocked, and sent into forced labor.

At least five similar cases reached the Secret Chancery during the early and mid-1720s, a clear indication that churches and monasteries were under careful scrutiny to make certain they celebrated the name day.[53] Regimental and military clergy came under the same scrutiny, so that Major Avram Bukhol't of Schlusselburg Fortress reported disapprovingly to the Alexander Nevskii Monastery on November 26, 1719, that two days earlier the priest Vasilii had celebrated the tsaritsa's name day with the usual prayers to the health of the tsaritsa. Instead of singing as should be done in a cathedral, however, he had them sing "as they would in a small, parish [church]."[54]

The Synod's official *mesiatsoslov* for 1725 elevated St. Catherine's Day even further by granting it the status of a major religious feast day. Unlike previous religious calendars, this one included a section that had been ordered by the Synod, entitled, "Celebrations, holidays, and victory days that are to be celebrated annually." It listed eighteen dates, mostly celebrating important military victories and dates of selected members of the ruling family. Thus, of the eighteen, four celebrated the empress: February 19, her anniversary; April 5, her birthday; May 7, the day of her coronation; and November 24, her name day.[55] By the end of Peter's reign icons and visual images of St. Catherine were being sold, apparently widely, on the open market.[56] One assumes, therefore, that the celebration was widespread and that church attendance was particularly high on November 24.

Iconography-as-commodity became an important element in the use of visual media to convey the unity of the saint and her living image. One particularly vivid example, dating from October 11, 1721, represents this conflation in all of its myriad facets, and before an audience that would not fail to understand. The icon, one of three originally housed in the Alexander Nevskii Lavra, measuring approximately sixteen inches by thirteen, presents St. Catherine in a regal gown, as ever wearing a crown, and with the spiked wheel and sword and sheath in front to her right. Behind her and descending from the heavens in a familiar pose are the Mother of God holding and presenting the Christ child, who in turn reaches out to St. Catherine's hand with a wreath and ring. This image signifies the mystical marriage as the central fact of her persona, just as Rostovskii's vita had done, and the heavenly source of her divine wisdom.

The faces of cherubs encircle mother and Christ child, and in the background looms a town by the sea, seemingly on an island. Unnamed, the town, lying on a hill and with a river emptying into an estuary, very possibly is meant to represent St. Petersburg as the New Jerusalem (and the Neva as the new Jordan), a trope that was becoming increasingly popular during the last decades of Peter's reign. Gavriil Buhinskii, for one, had employed New Jerusalem in a sermon he had orated a few years earlier in praise of St. Petersburg and its founder. Echoing a phrase in praise of Mary that was known to everyone from the Easter service, he pronounced, "Shine, shine, New Jerusalem! God's glory illuminating thee." Before the eyes of the viewer stood a bold visual argument for the new capital as consecrated space, the transposition of New Jerusalem from the Moscow Kremlin to the Gulf of Finland. As Grigorii Kaganov has remarked, "For Peter I and his contemporaries, only one city existed that was filled with the divine presence. . . . Petersburg, it turned out, was being compared to Jerusalem on the mount, the city temple, which was considered the heavenly prefiguration of all earthly Christian cities."[57]

Consider for a moment the possible meanings of this particular imagery. Like so much that had preceded it in the previous two decades and that would follow it over the next several years, it articulated a dynamic and reciprocal relationship of authority between secular power and the tsar, on one hand, and the kingdom of heaven and salvation, on the other. Petersburg was here incorporating one of the most powerful symbols of *sviataia Rus'*, New Jerusalem, as a buttress to the emerging ideology of empire. The flourishing of cultural history in recent years has made political gestures of this sort, most notably the Kremlin's celebration of Palm Sunday, better known and more accessible to modern eyes, and they reflect very clearly what Viktor Zhivov and others have seen as the state's appropriation and redeployment of symbols of sacralization on behalf of its modernizing and secularizing agendas. But this was only half of the equation. In adopting church symbols so openly and aggressively, the Petrine state was acknowledging the continued centrality of faith, granting to the church and sacred images the authority to explain transpositions and make them safe in the eyes of God, and thus consistent with grace. In this way the post-patriarchal church emerged with its independence greatly reduced, but with its public identity as the single body empowered to declare to the faithful that the tsar's actions were pleasing to God in a sense reconfirmed by the state itself.

Although crowded with a dizzying assemblage of politically important details, this 1721 icon situated St. Catherine in the center, as the focus of attention. Looking vaguely oriental, she is adorned with a bride's crown and wedding dress, symbolizing both her marriage to Christ and, by implication, to the church. She stands in front of what appears to be a canopy bed, in anticipation perhaps of lying together with her beloved, and she holds one book (but no cross), while on the table next to her sit four others. The lettering on the books, barely discernible, identifies them as prominent Petrine school texts: one is *Arifmetika,* Leontii Magnitskii's compendious 1703 guide to mathematics, and another is *Ritorika,* a guide to spoken and written language written in Latin by Stefan Iavorskii and later translated into Russian by Fedor Polikarpov. The book in her hand is open to a page that reveals the words *"premudrost'"* and *"razumnykh otvetov,"* (divine wisdom and well-reasoned answers), a reference to her conquest of the pagan philosophers in verbal combat. At the foot of the table stands an orblike object, a compass or other measuring instrument.

Among the educated clergy the Rhetoric constituted a particularly evocative and contested talisman for knowledge. As Lidia Sazonova has argued, the Rhetoric had come to be the primary signifier of practical knowledge since the outset of the Russian baroque. For the court clerics and poets of the latter decades of the seventeenth century who had lobbied so hard—and successfully—to establish an academy in Moscow, the valorization of the Rhetoric was a badge of pride, emblematic of cultural progress.[58] Conversely, religious traditionalists, including Avvakum, had denounced the Rhetoric as "superficial wisdom," unrelated and even antithetical to the *premudrost'* of Holy Mysteries, Holy Communion, and God's will. This icon, then, put St. Catherine on the same side as those in the church (and in officialdom, of course) for whom divine and human knowledge were intimately and inextricably linked. Simultaneously it embedded the tsaritsa within the sacraments of the church as they had come to be understood by Polotskii, Medvedev, and those who succeeded them.

Much like the St. Catherine vita, the 1721 icon endeavored to bring together the two meanings of enlightenment, at once both secular and miraculous, then current in Russian writing: secular, in the form of language, arithmetic, and instruments of science, and divine in the presence of St. Catherine, the celestial embodiment of miraculous intervention and miraculous bride of Christ. This celebration of the miraculous had been a principle theme of reform in the late seventeenth-century church, a centerpiece of the unity of enlightenment and holy mysteries encouraged by Polotskii and others. Miracles, mediated by homiletic guidance, could teach even the simplest of folk about God's presence and powers.[59]

Although there is no relevant documentation, the guiding hands of Peter and his closest archbishop, Feofan, seem to be at work because of the prominent place given to objects of science and practical knowledge. Similar images had appeared in various book illustrations and secular representations, and no one would have had any difficulty in getting the point. More interesting, though, is the affinity between the icon and Feofan's outlook, especially his numerous declarations on the relationship between the miraculous and the profane. His treatise on unbelief *("afeizm ili bezbozhie")* offered a spirited defense of miracles, and the need for faith in their reality, as a precondition for a proper grasp of worldly wisdom.[60] Atheists, by which he meant pre-Christian Athenian philosophers and their latter-day enthusiasts, would be skeptical of miracles and demand rational and physical proof. In the end they would never believe because they rejected the very possibility of holy mysteries. But those who accepted the true faith, embraced the miraculous unhesitatingly, and the testimony about past miracles contained in the Old Testament (and confirmed in the New) could then put profane knowledge to good and proper use, much like the triumphant St. Catherine.[61]

This line of reasoning remained relatively consistent throughout Feofan's clerical life, recurring as late as 1730 in his essay on Solomon and the Song of Songs.[62] In all times and under all circumstances (read here, Peter's Russia), the divine words of Scripture stood superior and anterior to all man-made learning, and without it human knowledge would lead to harm. Against the backdrop of the church's institutional subordination to the state, to which Feofan of course had given a resounding endorsement, the primacy of faith needed to be reasserted as a reminder both to the clergy of their irreducible role as shepherds of souls and to the men of state that there was something beyond this world.

The 1721 St. Catherine icon reproduced this relationship through its vertical design. True, the image was filled in the foreground with the fetish objects of science. But St. Catherine stood above them, and heaven soared above her, populated not by wise men and books, but by Christ, the Mother of God, and cherubs.

Perhaps the most noteworthy features of this icon are the visages of the Christ child and St. Catherine. The former bears a strong resemblance to childhood portraits of Peter, in particular an earlier icon from the late seventeenth century, in which Peter and his half brothers Ivan and Fedor are represented as the three magi.[63] St. Catherine's appearance and household objects (canopy bed, side table, and pillow) seem vaguely exotic, almost Persian or Turkish in style, as if to convey her Alexandrian roots. The face seems equally stylized, and it is unlike other visages of St. Catherine from its time. It reminds one of the secular portraiture of the day, and it bears a strong likeness to generic portraits of the tsaritsa. If that was the intent, then the mystical marriage was being openly conflated with the marriage of Peter (now as Christ figure) and Catherine, with Peter's mother, Natal'ia Kirillovna one assumes, standing in as Mother of God. If so, this troika transposed living figures onto sacred ones in a particularly transparent tableau, in the process bringing St. Catherine and her living image even closer.

There would have been nothing sacrilegious about including the faces of living persons in an icon, as the Stoglav Council of 1550 had resolved this issue long before. Ivan IV had convened the council not long after the

158

Icon of St. Catherine and the Mystical Marriage from the Alexander Nevskii Monastery, 1721

G. S. Musikiiskii, An engraved portrait of the tsarist family, 1717, with Peter, Catherine, and the tsarevnas Anna, Elizabeth, and Natal'ia Petrovna, and a young boy, probably Peter Alekseevich, the future Peter II (1727–1730)

An allegorical engraving from the 1690s of the adoration of the Magi, showing the co-tsars Peter and Ivan V, along with the young tsarevich Aleksei Petrovich, as the magi. Note the resemblance to the visage of the infant Jesus in the 1721 icon of St. Catherine.

calamitous Kremlin fire of June 1547 had destroyed many of the sacred images in the Kremlin's cathedrals.[64] As the council deliberated the reconstruction—along with many other issues of doctrine and liturgy—it confronted the question of whether it was acceptable to paint the images of living figures on icons in the form of figures in prayer before the presence of God and Mother of God.[65] This was part of a larger inquiry into the proper approach to icon painting in general, at that moment quite an urgent matter as the readornment of the Kremlin cathedrals was underway. The council warned against allowing a role for individual imagination and innovation, and it insisted that painters follow "ancient models" that followed the teachings of Church fathers. Thus, in depictions of the Holy Trinity only the inscription "Holy Trinity" was to be used. God the father could not be portrayed because only "Christ our God has been portrayed in the flesh."[66] To the question of living people, the council responded in the affirmative, remarking that ancient icons had depicted not just individual tsars, clergy, and tsaritsy, but even ordinary people from all walks of life. As Jack Kollmann has remarked, "it [was] permissible to portray laymen and living persons in icons because of the precedent in Greek and Russian examples of 'The Exaltation of the Cross,' 'The Intercession of [The Mother of God],' and 'The Last Judgment.'"[67] The "Intercession" (Pokrov), for example, showed the apostle Andrew praying before the Mother of God in the presence of a large number of people.[68]

With this ruling in hand, painters from Makarii's workshop in the 1550s were able to produce a new icon, the "Church Militant"—which many specialists maintain depicted the living tsar, Ivan IV—at the head of columns of saints, both Greek and Russian, and being crowned by the Mother of God and Michael the Archangel. As more than one commentator has noted, this use of a living ruler was itself something new, an innovation cloaked, like so many of Peter's reforms a century and a half later, in the discourse of repetition or skilled copying and the mantel of Byzantine antiquity and precedence. Although the post-Nikonian councils of 1666–1667 subsequently overturned several of the Stoglav's judgments on rituals and liturgy, the ruling on icons remained in force. The scholarship has observed that Russian iconography to that point had not superimposed the visages of living rulers on the images of saints, but that barrier too would fall in the late sixteenth century with an image of Vasilii Ivanovich as St. Varlaam, in monk's garb and with a nimbus, standing next to St. Basil the Great.[69]

A number of seventeenth-century icons also presented tsars as saintly images, so that, while hardly commonplace, these representations had achieved acceptability well before the 1721 icon of St. Catherine. It is even possible that this was not the first St. Catherine icon with the visage of a living figure, since a 1694 icon from the Church of the Intercession in Fili shows a radiant and almost naturalistic St. Catherine believed by some to bear the face of one of the Naryshkin women.[70] What does seem new (at least no antecedents could be found among recorded icons) was the representation of a *living tsaritsa* in this manner. Catherine and St. Catherine, saint and living image, were here visually inseparable, joined in a regal pose and possessed of grace, personal wisdom, and courage triumphant. Their mastery of all knowledge, via the sword, wheel, and book, serves a faith that is at once practical (rhetoric, arithmetic, compass) and religious (Mother of God, Christ, angels, and saints). The image permits no division between salvation and utility, empire and heaven. Pagan knowledge was now fully domesticated, sacralized and made subservient to Christ, Mother of God, and the state. The midwife for this unbroken chain, the embodiment of the perfect union of heaven and the Russian Empire was, at least on this day and in this icon, Catherine/St. Catherine.

Related images appeared almost simultaneously, once again on some of the first structures of Alexander Nevskii Monastery, a coincidence that suggests a good deal of forethought in placing St. Catherine at the very heart of the sacralization of the new capital. Founded in 1710 on the putative site where Prince Alexander defeated the Swedes in 1240, it stood for several years as St. Petersburg's only monastery, and, along with the Cathedral of Saints Peter and Paul, its most sacred ground. The monastery, and later the seminary, lavra, and academy that joined it on its site, consecrated one of the founding myths of the new capital and empire, and it installed St. Alexander Nevskii, alongside Saints Peter, Aleksei, and Andrew, as a patron saint of the city.

The political cult of Nevskii had begun well before Peter, as reflected in several of the fifteen manuscript variants of Nevskii's vita from the sixteenth and seventeenth centuries that intermingled his military heroism and his piety after taking monastic vows.[71] In 1630, Patriarch Filaret dedicated a cathedral in Nevskii's honor adjacent to Tainitskii Gate in Moscow, and both tsars Mikhail and Aleksei participated in cross processionals on the honoree's name day, November 23.[72] As seen, Nevskii's elevation continued from early in Peter's reign, with the decrees of the 1690s commissioning the silver casket and commanding that the saint's day be given special veneration. The *pokhodnyi zhurnal* recounts that in July 1710, Peter surveyed the land on which the new monastery in the name of the Holy Trinity and St. Alexander Nevskii would reside. Then, "in the presence of the ministers and the nobility", Archimandrite Feodosii placed a cross consecrating the site.[73] Feofan Prokopovich had orated a special sermon in Nevskii's honor in 1718, shortly after actual construction had begun, one that emphasized the saint's place as Peter's forebear.[74] To this point, however, the textual celebration had a relatively muted profile, as reflected in the sermon's small press run of well under one hundred copies.[75] Then, in 1722, matters changed. A memorandum from Campredon to Cardinal Dubois, dated February 9, 1722, mentioned that the tsar intended to establish the knightly order of Alexander Nevskii, to be patterned after the French Ordre de S. Louis.[76] Shortly thereafter, Peter decreed that the prayers and hymns honoring St. Alexander be revised to reflect his new visage, and that these be printed and widely circulated.

The formal decision to move the saint's remains came in late May 1723, and in June, Archbishop Feodosii, who was then the archimandrite of the monastery, alerted the Synod that Peter wanted the remains to be buried on the monastery's grounds. Unearthing saintly remains for reasons other than to verify miracles, which in Alexander's case had occurred in 1380, was not unknown, but it was uncommon and apparently ritually unsettling. Even after the rigorous purges of unsanctioned celebrations carried out by successive heads of the Russian church, dating back at least to Metropolitan Joseph, the veneration of saintly relics often remained a distinctly local affair, marked by well-defined cross processionals and visitation of religiously significant sites. Thus, moving them long distances away from local rites of veneration would have unsettled matters still further. But there was no choice, as the emperor had resolved to embrace the saint on behalf of the entire imperial project. The Synod was then confronted with the need to organize the event in conformity with precedent and consistent with Peter's wishes.

Orthodoxy offered a number of well-known antecedents from antiquity, including the transposition of Chrysostom's relics during the reign of Theodosius the Younger from Comana to Constantinople, as well as those of Boris and Gleb, of Ignatius, and of Feodosii, the first native-born metropolitan of Kiev.[77] All of these were described in the available sources, including chronicles, saints' lives, and the *paterik* of the Caves Monastery in Kiev, and all were familiar to the clerical hierarchy.[78] The most recent precedent, and the one chosen as the template for reburying Nevskii, had taken place in 1652 when, at the behest of the tsar, Patriarch Joseph had ordered the then archimandrite Nikon to oversee the transposition of the miracle-working remains of St. Filipp, the metropolitan during the reign of Ivan IV, from Solovetskii Monastery to the Dormition Cathedral in Moscow.

In many respects the reference to St. Filipp made sense, especially because it had taken place relatively recently and was widely known within the clergy, as witnessed by the 150 manuscript copies of his vita produced during the seventeenth century. Nevertheless, transposing Filipp's remains had been politically delicate.[79] Venerated both as a martyr and as a Muscovite patriotic symbol, hagiographies typically linked him with St. Peter the Metropolitan, St. Aleksei, and St. Ion as symbols of Moscow's greatness and holiness. Filipp's martyrdom, though, had come at the hands of Ivan IV, and while Aleksei Mikhailovich wished to amend this maltreatment by returning the saint's remains to the capital, he did not want to dishonor the memory of the late tsar. Dimitrii Rostovskii had appended a very brief discussion of Filipp in the entry in the *Chet'i minei* for January 9, and his language left little doubt as to what had transpired. "Saint Philip was unjustly stripped of rank and publicly vilified in the Cathedral of the Dormition in Moscow by false witness. Then he was . . . driven out of the church, put in a sled, further reviled, beaten with brooms, and dragged off to the Otroch Monastery in Tver. The holy hierarch . . . was finally suffocated with a pillow by one of the Tsar's counselors."[80] It was important, therefore, to orchestrate the event carefully, and to engage the nation and clerical elite as fully as possible.

The official account detailed how the tsar prayed, and then chose to move St. Filipp—on the advice of the patriarch, the entire cathedral clergy, the boyars, chancellery officials, nobles, and the nation at large. A letter of September 3, 1653, from Aleksei to Prince Nikita Ivanovich Odoevskii used the transposition of Chrysostom's relics as the tsar's precedent. He explained that "God has granted us, the great sovereign, the great sun *(velikogo solntsa),*" a metaphorical reference to Christ. He had granted to the ancient Emperor Theodosius the return of the relics of a radiant *("presvetlogo")* sun Chrysostom. In this way God had granted Tsar Aleksei to return the relics of "the radiant sun Metropolitan Filipp of Moscow and Miracle Worker of All Rus'," "a new Peter and second Paul the Preacher," "a second Chrysostom."[81] The precedent, therefore, was simultaneously rooted in church practice and commanded by God to Aleksei through the Incarnation of Christ.

Nikon's responsibility included ameliorating the monks and populace of Solovki, arranging transportation on land and water, preparing the new resting place, and organizing the all-important greeting party once the relics neared the city gates. By all accounts, these tasks were accomplished with considerable finesse. As Filipp's remains approached the Kremlin, the tsar went out to meet them, accompanied by several church hierarchs and bearing the cross and numerous icons. "With heart-felt joy" he kissed the relics, and then accompanied them to the cathedral. "Untold numbers of people" attended the return and reburial, weeping and praying in thanksgiving. For three days and nights the coffin lay on display in the cathedral, and for three days and nights the faithful streamed in to bear witness and to receive blessing from the saint.[82]

Establishing this specific precedent was essential to embedding the transposition of Nevskii's remains within sacred tradition, and thereby maintaining the myth of full consistency with the precepts of faith, without which the propagandistic value of the transposition would have been severely compromised. It enabled the Synod to accede to Peter's wish with a clear conscience, and Feodosii was ordered to work with the Senate on the specifics of security and cost sharing.[83] These details included construction of a special silver reliquary and elaborate arrangements for transporting the remains undisturbed and safe from the risk of fire. In accordance with the script written for St. Filipp, the Synod demanded that a guard consisting of high-ranking clergy, a lay official "comparable in status to a boyar," and armed dragoons accompany the relics, and that they send regular reports along the way.[84]

From a political perspective, however, St. Filipp was a complicated choice to interpose into church-state relations during Peter's latter years. Scholars have not been of one mind as to Filipp's dispute with Groznyi, and they have offered few insights into the understandings that seventeenth-century church officials who presided over Filipp's rehabilitation had of those events. As Paul Bushkovitch points out, the vita of Filipp valorized him for defending the church against the incursions of state and tsar.[85] "Its author, a monk of one of Russia's three most important monasteries, thought that the Church was to be consulted on important secular policy decisions, that it had the right to act contrary to the will of the monarch, and that Ivan and his *Oprichniki* had committed an evil and sinful act not only in executing Filipp but in refusing to listen to his reproaches."[86] If nothing else, Filipp had come to symbolize the legitimate voice of the church in the face of the abusive exercise of tsarist power, and his rehabilitation a century later could easily be interpreted as a godly tsar righting the wrong of an ungodly one. The return of the spiritually repressed, if you will: this surely was the implication of Aleksei Mikhailovich's references to Chrysostom, a saintly church father who had famously run afoul of secular power and suffered exile because of it.

Less than three years after the establishment of the Synod, a reform that was controversial and had been criticized by more than one prominent ecclesiastical authority,[87] this reading of the transposition of Filipp, suggesting an inevitable redemption and return of the righteous, would have been particularly worrisome. Perhaps this is why Feofan chose it as a model, so as to subtly reassure the upper clergy of his own commitment to the primacy of faith. Perhaps for that very reason, Peter intervened directly into the refashioning of the cult of St. Alexander. On June 15, 1724, he commanded that the saint be represented, both visually and in his vita, only as a prince, a ruler, and a military hero, rather than use the monk's garb used more typically in previous icons (since he had taken monastic vows and spent his last few years in a monastery).[88] To underscore this transition the tsar simultaneously decreed a new Order of St. Alexander, honoring the prince for his patriotic valor in defense of Christian Rus'.[89] Peter also shifted St. Alexander's feast day from November 23, the date of his death, to August 30, the date on which his remains arrived in St. Petersburg, and, more importantly, the anniversary of the Treaty of Nystadt.[90] The thirteenth-century victory over the Swedes was now united with the eighteenth-century one, Alexander with Peter. Peter wanted Alexander's vita to reflect these revisions, and he ordered that the text of the *prolog* change accordingly, adding a passage on the transposition of the remains.[91] Within two years Gavriil Buzhinskii had composed a new August 30 service of thanksgiving to St. Alexander, one that linked him explicitly with the Swedish peace treaty. By 1726, it had gone through seven printings totaling nearly twelve thousand copies.[92]

As befit his name and political stature, Alexander Menshikov had become something of a patron to the monastery, and Peter gave him special responsibility to oversee transporting the saint's remains from Vladimir, but with instructions that he remain out of sight as the bier proceeded. An elaborate route was mapped out so as to maximize public exposure in towns and along major roadways. Huge throngs were reported in town after town. On the evening of August 17, the procession arrived at Krasnoe selo, on the outskirts of Moscow, where it remained until the next morning. Throughout the night waves of people came to view the ark, and when the bells of Moscow rang the next morning, these people accompanied the ark in a massive processional of the cross. The assembly proceeded to the precise spot, outside the church of St. Basil the Caesarian, where the remains of St. Filipp had been met in 1652, at which point the participants joined in a mass of thanksgiving before accompanying the ark to the Kremlin.[93] From Moscow the ark made its way to St. Petersburg, met at each stopping point by large groups of worshipers.

Both Bergholz and Bassewitz have left eyewitness descriptions of the event. Once in the capital, the bier was loaded onto a river barge to traverse the final mile to the monastery, with the banks of the Neva packed with onlookers. At five o'clock in the morning the residents of the capital were awakened by cannon fire—the prearranged signal to make their way out of the city (at this point the monastery was not considered a part of St. Petersburg proper)—toward the monastery.[94] Bassewitz recalled that "thousands of priests, monks, and worshipers" met the procession at every stopping point.[95] At ten o'clock there was another round of cannon fire to announce the arrival of the barge housing the saint's remains. A flotilla of richly ornamented boats then proceeded up the river, led by Peter's famous *botik* bearing the Russian flag and followed by the barge and the imperial yacht, the *Princess Elizabeth*.[96] Standing on deck were the emperor and the imperial family, and other parts of the flotilla housed the notables currently in the capital.[97]

As they approached the monastery, all the ships gave another cannon salute, at which time Peter came on shore to meet the barge as it was being offloaded. Peter then returned to the yacht and hoisted the imperial flag as an honor to the "returning" saint. The clergy, attired in their finest vestments, awaited the entire party by the gates of the monastery, and they conducted the officers on board to bring the casket to the chapel, where it would remain until the cathedral—Alexander's final resting place—had been completed. Peter stood with the clerical choir, and as the relics were being moved, the bells in the city rang continuously. The large crowd of onlookers, Bergholz noted, repeatedly crossed themselves and bowed down before the saint. Many wept openly, both common people and noblewomen, but a few stood aside and laughed at this reaction, seemingly bemused at the behavior of what Bergholz termed, "the blind and stupid crowd."[98] A more evocative contrast of earthly skepticism and otherworldly reverence could scarcely be imagined. Interestingly, however, Peter was among those who crossed themselves and bowed, and Catherine joined the train behind the reliquary as it approached its temporary site. At this point the cannons gave off yet another salute and the clergy conducted a liturgy, including a sermon by Feodosii, after which the imperial family returned to its boats. That evening the city was lit by a fireworks display.

The ceremony continued through the next day. Peter, the family, and other Russian dignitaries returned to the monastery for a feast—with the women moved to a separate chamber. There was a performance of choir singing and a guided tour of the monastery, and then at four o'clock the entire imperial family plus its attendants went to pay respects at the grave of the deceased widowed tsaritsa, presumably the wife of Ivan V. At that point the party returned to St. Petersburg, first to the fortress and then to Menshikov's palace, where Peter congratulated his old friend on his new name day. Once again that evening the city was alight.[99]

Before returning to St. Catherine, it is helpful to consider the various meanings ascribed to this ceremony by contemporaries and subsequent scholarship. Both Michael Cherniavsky and James Cracraft have argued, in Cherniavsky's words, "that the saint prince was put to work not for the salvation of Russian souls but for the glory of the imperial state and its new capital, St. Petersburg."[100] Recently, Irina Chudinova has offered a more nuanced, but essentially identical, version. In speaking of the entire eighteenth century, she maintains that, "the Alexander Nevskii monastery becomes a key point of the structure of church and state, not only for the Petersburg socium but for the entire empire. Its place in semiotic space stood at the very pinnacle of hierarchical authority."[101]

This reading of the ceremony and Nevskii's reinvention is surely defensible, but perhaps one-sided. As already noted, the statist appropriation of the Nevskii cult was not new. Nor was the link with the men of the Romanov family. It is true that the new *prolog* vita dwelled almost entirely on the theme of a national prince, and it linked his veneration explicitly to the victories over the Swedes, to the exclusion of the monastic *(prepodobnyi)* element that had been basic in the earlier manuscripts. Buzhinskii's fuller text, however, drew a more multi-faceted picture, one that spoke of Nevskii's piety, his prayerfulness, and his adoration of Mary. He presented Nevskii simultaneously as a national hero and Christian exemplar, perhaps a subtle effort by Buzhinskii to describe the ideal of a Christian monarch in the new imperial reality in which Russia found itself.[102]

Bassewitz, who witnessed the entire set of events in August 1724, interpreted their meaning very much in the reciprocal and multi-dimensional vein of Buzhinskii's text. In his view, this gesture, "honoring the memory of a saint who had served both God and his nation with such distinction, cleared the Emperor from the suspicion that he intended to completely destroy the faithful respect *(poklonenie)* which the Greek [i.e., Orthodox] Church afforded to its patrons in heaven. The Nevskii Monastery had become a comfortable place of worship for the imperial family."[103] Bergholz's picture of the banks of the Neva teeming with onlookers, simple folk and boyars alike crossing and prostrating themselves, and old women weeping uncontrollably, suggests that most of those in attendance, including perhaps Peter and Catherine, experienced an overpowering religious feeling beyond a simple imperial patriotism. Rather, it may well have been the ceremony's multiple and powerful meanings that palpably overwhelmed those in attendance, what might be characterized as the simultaneity of holiness and national glory, the reciprocity of the saint's relics honoring the empire and the emperor embracing a particularly sacred and ancient symbol of Russian religiosity, much as Bassewitz maintained. Even if Peter was merely going through the motions, so as to replicate in full view his father's behavior at the ark of St. Filipp and thereby appropriate the ceremony for his own purpose rather than leave its meaning ambiguous, the moment revealed his understanding of the irreducible place of faith and religious precedent in political life. Exploiting the faith to validate the state meant, here and elsewhere, that the state was validating faith as the ultimate agency of legitimation. For most eyewitnesses as well, faith and salvation remained at the heart of the experience, not in contradistinction to state power but in symbiotic—if unequal—partnership with it, the very reconciliation that Bassewitz had perceived.

Coming as it did in 1724, and overseen so closely by Peter, the transfer of Alexander Nevskii's relics was virtually assured of providing St. Catherine a visible role, in this case within the walls of the monastery that bore that saint's name. In the monks' newly constructed private quarters, the *monastyrskii korpus* (long since destroyed and redesigned), along the wall facing the upper cells there stood a painted image of Christ on the cross with the Mother of God and various prophets standing in front. Next to it was an image of Mother of God and child extending their hands to St. Catherine, the traditional representation of the mystical marriage, and a related picture of mother and child and Joseph.[104] A stone iconostasis stood on either side of the holy gates of the monastery's upper church. St. Catherine was depicted on the left side of the doors next to Archangel Michael. On the right side were images of St. Alexander Nevskii and Archangel Raphael.[105]

These images did not superimpose the visage of the empress (or, if they did, the descriptive texts do not say so), but they hardly needed to. Here was the tsaritsa's angel granted pride of place in newly consecrated space precisely when the empress herself was gaining an individual presence in political iconography and when Nevskii was being enshrined as the patron saint of St. Petersburg. In what arguably was one of the two most sacred locations of the new capital (along with the Cathedral of Saints Peter and Paul), St. Catherine gazed prominently upon the congregants and upon the newly transferred relics of one of Russia's greatest patriotic saints, in the place some thought was the very ground on which he had defeated the Swedes in the thirteenth century. Elevated above almost all saintly figures, outside of the holy family and the prophets, her images reminded the brethren daily, when they emerged from their cells and when they went to pray, of her special link with Christ and Mother of God. St. Catherine was, at last, Russia's own great saintly female martyr, placed in a central locale on the same level with Alexander Nevskii, and in his own house. As if these images were not sufficient for situating the empress in saintly and divine company, one of the monastery's monks, Aleksei Savast'ianov, recalled that the empress had presented to Feodosii a diamond-encrusted *panagiia*, designed by the court jewel smith Samson Larionov, with the crucifixion on one face and Catherine I on the other.[106]

Although St. Catherine and St. Alexander had been previously co-joined in the 1690s with the construction of silver ossuaries for each, the physical proximity and visual parity reflected in the iconography of the monastery represented a transposition, of sorts, of the patron saint of the Romanov women from the old capital to the new. Soon the new chapel in the Summer Palace also came to be called the St. Catherine chapel, and the new empress prayed there frequently. Throughout the rest of the century, St. Petersburg came to house numerous churches, private chapels, and iconic images of St. Catherine, thereby reinforcing her status as an imperial and politically powerful female saint. She also remained intertwined with Alexander Nevskii and with Peter and Paul. This type of iconographic pronouncement was soon replicated in other important institutions, including the cathedral of Peter and Paul in St. Petersburg, where St. Catherine occupied a prominent place on the original iconostasis, situated on the south side in an upper tier with the archangel Gabriel, Christ, Mary, St. Peter, and—right next to St. Catherine—Alexander Nevskii.[107]

The Novodevich'ii Convent in Moscow also became a site for St. Catherine. Founded in 1525, this monastery had close ties to the ruling family from its outset. Three of Peter's sisters (Sofia, Catherine, and Evdokia) were buried in its cemetery, as was Evdokia Fedorovna, the sister of the first Romanov tsar, Mikhail Fedorovich. Much of the most precious ornamentation in the main cathedral and chapels had been gifts of the ruling family, honoring the family saints of the Romanovs.[108] The fateful negotiations of 1682 that established Sofia as regent were held here, and it was here that Sofia took her vows after losing the power struggle in 1689. Peter's first wife, Evdokia, also had taken the veil, as a nun at Novodevich'ii, even though she was kept locked away in Schlusselburg Fortress until 1727, when her grandson, Peter II, ordered that she be allowed to live her remaining years at the convent.

All of this meant that Novodevich'ii was a well-established site for political gestures, as it would remain throughout the imperial period. The Petrine iconographic gesture took the form of a redesign of the main cathedral, the most public consecrated space in the monastery. Here, over the northern doorway was now painted the so-called Coronation of the Mother of God. Standing before her in prayer were the apostle Peter and St. Catherine.[109] As the official description explained, this scene memorialized the spirit of Peter and the coronation of Catherine, and both now gazed down upon the images of saints associated with previous members of the ruling family (Aleksei the Man of God, the Saints Feodor, Anna, Mary the Egyptian, Evdokia, Martha, Sofia, and Tat'iana) as well as the many precious arks and reliquaries that stood below in the cathedral.[110]

At the moment of Catherine's coronation, therefore, the sacralization of the tsaritsa's image had become widespread, literally plastered on the walls of consecrated spaces in the old capital and the new. To imagine the saint was to envisage the tsaritsa, who now was graced with her own redeemer, an expressly feminine pathway to the kingdom of heaven.

8

The Archbishop and the Empress

THE CORONATION OF 1724

• Against the backdrop of an intensive and largely faith-centered Catherinian discourse during the previous dozen years, one can now return to the coronation of 1724. Peter had settled on a coronation ceremony perhaps as early as 1722, and the mint had gone so far as to print special coronation coins stamped with the date of May 1723.[1] This decision to afford the consort a coronation can only be termed extraordinary in the fullest and most literal sense of the term. For one thing, the ceremony had no obvious practical consequence. Officially married since 1712, Catherine had long since been received formally and openly as the consort, "the Lady, Her Majesty, the Tsaritsa." A decade of intensive and publicly performed adulation of the tsaritsa as the living image of St. Catherine had already transformed the consort into a persona of considerable presence. The coronation, however rigidly prescribed, in no way altered her public authority or endowed her with any added sovereignty.

Imperatritsa

Catherine had inherited the right to be called "imperatritsa" from the moment Peter became emperor in 1721, and private and official documents alike referred to her as such.

For example, a letter of April 4, 1723, from the tsaritsa Praskov'ia Fedorovna, widow of Ivan V, began, "My dearest lady, dear sister-in-law and mother, Empress Ekaterina Alekseevna" (Gosudarynia moia milostivaia, dorogaia nevestushka i matushka Imperatritsa Ekaterina Alekseevna).[2]

As was always the case with official nomenclature, none of this had been left to chance or individual preference. The joint decree from the Senate and Synod of October 22, 1721, that announced Peter's new imperial title informed that the tsaritsa would be referred to henceforth as "Her Majesty the Empress," and that the princesses would be greeted as "Their Imperial Highnesses, the Princesses."[3] Two months later the Senate issued a more detailed decree on the imperial titles of the empress, grand princesses, and children of the imperial family, thus making it absolutely clear that the new title extended to all of them.[4] Over the next year a series of decrees set down the proper forms to be used in oaths of office and allegiance and prayers of thanksgiving, which collectively guaranteed that the title "empress" would become as commonplace in public speech as it would in official documents.[5] Failure to employ it would be a glaring omission, a serious offense against crown and the church. In short, Catherine had become the empress in all the relevant contexts in 1721 and without requiring an act of coronation.

I. F. Zubov, The Coronation of Catherine, 1724

G. S. Musikiiskii, Portrait of Catherine as Empress, 1724

Even more perplexing was the fact that the coronation of a sitting consort had virtually no precedent in Russia, and what little history it did
have—namely, the ad hoc coronation(s) of Marina Mniszek, the Polish
wife of both the first and second False Dmitrii—constituted the epitome of
illegitimacy in the Russian imagination. Everyone at court knew about
Marina's coronations, but no one endowed those events with any legality
or legitimacy as precendents. Quite the opposite, they constituted in public memory the very negation of the divine order, an assault on the nation
never again to be emulated. The official record and chronicle accounts
condemned them as ungodly usurpations, the literal theft of sovereignty
and crown by a common brigand and his Polish wife, a Catholic to boot.[6]
Even resident foreigners recognized the transgressive quality of these coronations. Jacques Margeret, for example, observed, "it is not the custom of
this country to crown the wives of emperors or grand dukes. Dmitrii was
the first."[7] Those who privately dismissed Catherine as another illegal,
non-Russian, and un-Orthodox usurper from the Baltics would have had
little difficulty in making the connection. Clearly, no one in authority
wanted to arouse those sorts of sentiments.

Peter's decree of November 15, 1723, endeavored to explain both the
doctrinal foundation and the political import of the act of coronation.

Whereas it is widely known that in all Christian states it had been the custom for potentates to crown their spouses, and not just at the present moment but this also occurred several times in antiquity among the Orthodox Greek emperors. Specifically, Emperor Basil crowned his spouse Zinovia, Emperor Justinian crowned his spouse Liupitsiia, Emperor Heraclius crowned his spouse Martinia, Emperor Leo the Wise crowned his spouse Maria. And others did so as well, about whom there is no space here or useful purpose to recount.

And whereas it is widely known that in the preceding twenty-one years of war We have encountered such heavy burdens, including the fear of death itself to Our own person, on behalf of Our fatherland, and with God's help We have brought these to a close such that Russia has never before seen so honorable and profitable a peace. And in all these matters just described where Russia gained such unwonted glory Our beloved spouse, the Lady Empress Catherine was a great helper, and not just here but also in many times of battle, notwithstanding her feminine weakness, by the force of her will she stood with us, and assisted wherever possible in the battle of Pruth against the Turks [in which our forces numbered 22,000 and the Turkish side had 270,000]. She understood the severe disadvantage in which we found ourselves, and, in a masculine rather than a feminine manner *(kak muzheski, a ne zhenski),* she declared it perilous not just for the army but for the entire state. Let it be known that by the authority *(samovlastiiu)* granted by God, We intend to honor Our spouse for her labors, if God permits, an act that We shall carry out this coming winter in Moscow. We apprise all Our loyal subjects of this, Our intention, to which We, in Our Imperial mercy, have arrived and are irreversibly so inclined.[8]

Here Peter himself employed the ascription of "empress" ("Our beloved spouse, the Lady Empress Catherine") a full half year before the formal coronation. The glorious victory over Sweden, and Catherine's remarkable heroism at Pruth had so moved Peter that he resolved to place his spouse on a footing equal to that of the empresses of Christian Rome. The precedent came not from immediate history, but once again from Russia's heritage of Christian empire, or so the decree asserted. Peter, like his father and forefathers the reigning and living image of Constantine, was making his spouse the official equal of the consorts of the earlier Orthodox Christian emperors. The martial themes are thus manifest in this decree, but Christian empire, Byzantine traditions, the grace of God, and holy womanhood and queenship (martyr and intercessor) stand out as well, especially against the backdrop of the previous decade's propaganda. All the properties of Catherine/St. Catherine are extant: the devoted bride that Buzhinskii valorized, as well as the clearheaded and manlike warrior for Christ and fatherland that figured prominently in the name day celebrations homilies, and the Order of St. Catherine. Now, however, these attributes had been so effectively and repeatedly transposed from St. Catherine to Tsaritsa Catherine that the former could go unmentioned. St. Catherine became the ubiquitous proverbial unseen presence, as Peter and his clerical panegyrists endeavored to sever the iconic umbilical cord that had heretofore bound the tsaritsa to the saint who defined her. For the first time she was being presented on her own, as the self-standing embodiment of all the political virtues inscribed onto the feminine, the heir to Byzantine womanhood but not merely its living image.

Before proceeding to the coronation itself, one might reflect on Peter's possible motives for decreeing it in the first place. No doubt he did want to honor Catherine for her years as a devoted consort, as he proclaimed in the decree. As politics, however, that explanation reduces the coronation to little more than whimsy. And "whimsy" is not a term usually associated with the adult Peter, and certainly not with such a carefully planned and symbolically fundamental event as a coronation. Some have accepted Feofan Prokopovich's ex post facto contention that the coronation was the prelude to Peter's naming Catherine as his successor, which he now had the right to do. But, as Isabel de Madariaga has surmised, this seems unlikely.[9] If Peter had made up his mind, nothing prevented him from saying so publicly at the time in order to avoid a destabilizing interregnum. Or, if not at the time, why not announce it or commit it to paper some time thereafter? Recognizing that his health was failing, Peter struggled in his last years to consolidate or institutionalize the many changes that he had generated. About that there is no disagreement. Why, then, not resolve the succession openly if he had determined in his own mind who the heir would be? If he had confided his decision to Prokopovich, as Prokopovich suggested in 1725, surely it would have been prudent to amend *Pravda voli monarshei,* by this time widely disseminated throughout the realm, so as to include the monarch's widow in the archbishop's very short list of imaginable categories for legitimate female rule. This, too, seems never to have been considered.

An additional hint that the coronation did not anticipate the eventuality of female rule emerges from the precedents (or, to be more precise, faux precedents) that the 1723 decree cited. Several scholars have taken note of the resort to Byzantium as part of a larger strategy for explaining the new imperial title overall.[10] As it happens, however, almost everything that this particular decree said about Byzantine precedent was inaccurate, much of it fantastic. Heraclius's consort (his second wife) was indeed Martina, but the other references are to one degree or another erroneous. Justinian's wife was the empress Theodora, Leo the Wise's—four—consorts were named Eudoxia and Zoe/Sofia, and none of the Basils (or any other Byzantine emperor) had a Zenobia as a consort (although Basil I's consort *was* named Maria). The only Zenobia to be found in the relevant sources was the second-century warrior Queen Zenobia (or Xenobia) of Palmyra, a decidedly non-Christian and pre-Byzantine personage. Liupitsia was almost certainly a reference to Lupicina, the consort of Justinian's uncle, Justin, and the *ukaz* may have confused Leo III, who was married to a Maria, with Leo the Wise, who was not.[11]

Without a great deal of archival work the sources for or reasons behind these wild misstatements remain opaque. Still, some hypotheses are more plausible than others. Whoever the antecedents were meant to be, almost all were obscure figures in Byzantine history, none became saints, and their names appeared briefly if at all in the relevant Russian texts of the day. Hardly anyone outside the most well-educated clergy would have heard of them. More importantly, none—so far as one can determine from the mangled historical references—ever ruled independently after the death of their spouse, even though both Lupicina and Martina wielded considerable political influence as consorts.

Had Peter wished to find—or invent—antecedents who ultimately reigned on their own from among the Byzantine empresses, as a way of signaling his intentions without stating them overtly, he easily could have chosen from among several very prominent figures (Theodora, Theodosia, and others), any one of whom would have been instantly recognizable to clergy and courtiers with even a passing knowledge of church history. But either he or someone under his direction decided on minor Augustas, mentioned only briefly in the available histories. In other words, composing this *ukaz* required forethought and some work.

An equally vexing question involves the insistence that all these imperial consorts underwent coronations. Although the standard Greek sources list several empresses who *did* receive formal coronations, they give no clear indication one way or the other whether Lupicina or Martina, the two consorts whose identities can be verified, had done so, other than to say in passing that the crown signifying "Augusta" adorned them. Neither do Russian chronicles or the *khronograf* published recently by Tvorogov.[12] If one very generously assumes that the decree meant to refer to one of the Zoias to whom Leo the Wise had been married, the reference to an actual coronation is somewhat more direct, at least in some Slavic translations of Greek texts. The *chronograph* of Theofanes, for example, says explicitly that Leo crowned Zoia, and his palace priest blessed her.[13] Once again, to have chosen such dubious and obscure referents seems strange when better known and less ambiguous ones were readily available.

Lupicina and Martina were curious choices in other ways as well. What is known about the former comes almost entirely from Procopius, "[Justin] was married to a woman called Lupicina, a foreign slave who had previously been purchased by another man and had become his concubine. But in the evening of her days she became joint ruler with Justin of the Roman Empire."[14] Her name, which derived from the Greek words for she-wolf and prostitute, was deemed unseemly by the standard-bearers of etiquette at the Byzantine court, and it was changed to the more respectable Euphemia, the name by which she was known in almost all of the relevant sources available in St. Petersburg at the time.[15] Yet the 1723 *ukaz* chose to refer to her by her slave name, Lupicina, an appellation that would have caused the educated clerical hierarchy to raise their collective eyebrows even if no one else understood the reference. Martina, a free and well-born woman, was the second wife of Heraclius (his first wife had been named Eudoxia, another coincidence), but the fact that she was Heraclius's niece, his sister's daughter, made the marriage controversial. Many at the time deemed it incestuous, despite the patriarch's blessing, and in direct contravention of the rules regarding marriage set down by Constantine the Great.[16] That all of this was known in Muscovite manuscripts, if only to a select few, is beyond question. For example, the chronicle of Constantine Manasses, a copy of which Arsenii Sukhanov had brought with him among the many texts he carried from Mount Athos to Moscow and had translated during Nikon's patriarchate, wrote scathingly about Martina and the marriage, openly declaring it to be illegal and adulterous.[17]

At this point one must resist the temptation to read particular or hidden meanings into these allusions. The archival record shows that Peter drafted the original text of the coronation decree in his own hand, but the pathways by which these particular antecedents found their way into the published decree cannot be determined with any finality. Peter's first draft did not list any Byzantine empresses, but it did note that they should be added in *("vpisat'")*, an instruction that was subsequently circled by someone, possibly an aide.[18] One might assume, therefore, that he left it to others to come up with the names, but if so, to whom and with what instructions is simply not known. It is unlikely that Peter knew about such minor figures on his own, but it is not impossible. The inventory of his library shows that it included a codex containing, inter alia, passages from *chronographs,* and both the chronicles of Malalas and Amartola. The library also included the works of Procopius and a number of other texts in which the relevant material could have been uncovered.[19] The published inventory does not indicate who had access to these books or what marginalia they left behind. But the fact that the books were there means that Peter had the means to conduct his own research. The apparent carelessness with the historical record also points to Peter, since it is difficult to imagine a clergyman familiar with early Byzantium making so many basic mistakes (here the confusion of Justin with Justinian is especially glaring). Likewise, one can scarcely imagine an aide being so cavalier or brazen as to present the emperor with such a roster of errors, knowing full well that someone else might be summoned to check the references.

A subsequent draft of the *ukaz,* this one penned by a scribe, went to Peter for his approval, and by then the names of the Byzantine empresses had been added. This version included a phrase that Peter crossed out: "a ceremony that is also observed in our own times in all neighboring Christian states, as is well known" (ponezhe to i v nyneshnikh nashikh vremenakh vo vsekh okrestnykh khristianskikh gosudarstvakh kak vsem izvestno chinittsa).[20] Obviously, Peter cared about the particular wording, and the excision of the oblique reference to contemporary practice elsewhere in Europe—which could have provided several examples—underscores his determination to emphasize the backdrop of "Holy Rome" above all else. But this is where the paper trail grows cold.

In the end, the striking coincidences between the lives of Lupicina and Martina and the lurid tales that circulated about Catherine's own origins and wedding must for the time being remain just that, coincidences. Still, their obscurity and absence of independent authority seem to be more than happenstance, especially in light of Peter's interventions in the final wording. All of this lends support to the idea that Peter himself oversaw the process and was in search of antecedents of a particular type, to the decided exclusion of powerful and independent consorts or empresses who ruled on their own. In other words, he was not employing this manifesto to set the stage for eventual female rule.

A more promising explanation for Catherine's coronation begins with the same premise, that Peter's failing health and the unresolved succession framed the central political contexts, but it shifts the focus away from the still unbroached (at least textually) possibility of Catherine's rule and toward the widely rumored possibility of regency, in which Catherine would serve as regent for a young male heir, Peter's grandson, Peter Alekseevich. Having a young male heir rule under the guidance of a female regent was a familiar—if not the most desirable—pragmatic solution at the Russian court in the absence of a suitable adult male heir. Ivan IV, Ivan V, and Peter himself had coexisted with female regents, as would the ill-fated Ivan VI from 1740 to 1741. Female regency fit comfortably within the Marian role of intercessor to the anointed male that tsaritsy had long fulfilled. It also corresponded to the position of almost all of the powerful Augustas at the Byzantine court, with the single exception of Irene. In A. A. Vasiliev's words, "Since the time of the founding of the Empire wives of emperors had borne the title of 'Augusta,' and in case of the minority of their sons, had fulfilled the functions of imperial power, but always in the name of their sons. . . . Theodora . . . had occupied an exceptional position of influence upon political affairs. But Theodora's political influence depended entirely on the will of her husband, and the other women had all ruled in the name of a son or a brother."[21] Thus, no new doctrine was required, no arcane search for precedents or ritual legerdemain. The choice of a regent, however, had wide repercussions at court, affecting not just the designee but members of her clan and those aligned with them.

Russell Martin's research into royal weddings has shown that the political stakes ran high and competition was concomitantly cutthroat whenever a bride was to be brought into the ruling family and her relatives installed in positions of prominence in Moscow.[22] These events unavoidably produced winners and losers (those who were installed and those forced to vacate). But, limited as they were by the mortality of the flesh, winning and losing the bridal wars were never fixed in perpetuity. Memories were long, clans were large, tenacious, and interconnected, hope sprung eternal, and revenge was sweet. When the ruler had had more than one wife either through death or divorce, as had become the norm at least since Ivan IV, the conflicts between the present and former bridal clans could grow particularly acrimonious. Peter's own childhood offered a textbook example of such acrimony. The clans of his father Aleksei's two wives, the Naryshkins and Miloslavskiis, had split court allegiances, especially after Aleksei's death in 1676, and in the struggle for influence the clans contributed to pitting Aleksei's offspring against one another. Both clans were also deeply complicit in the subsequent bloodshed of the 1680s, and it was only with great difficulty and after several turbulent years that the Naryshkins, and with them Peter, prevailed. Peter knew that, in the absence of a clear signal, a similar or even more fraught scene could easily recur after his own death, involving his first wife's clan, the Lopukhins, opposed by whatever party might close ranks around Catherine and her own motley clan, the hastily ennobled Skavronskiis. This time, however, the stakes would have been greater and the risks to the entire apparatus of reform more perilous.

Evdokia was still alive, apparently ambitious, and widely thought to have the sympathy of her grandson, not to mention those who saw her as a living link to the imagined anti-Petrine traditionalism associated variously with Sofia, Ivan V, and Tsarevich Aleksei Petrovich. Such fears came ominously close to realization when the young Peter actually did ascend the throne in 1727. One of his first acts was to free his grandmother, after twenty-seven years of confinement, and to restore her clan at court, an unmistakable gesture of respect toward his disgraced and deceased father, and disrespect toward his grandfather and step-grandmother.[23] Rather than return to court herself, Evdokia Fedorovna chose to enter Novodevich'ii Convent in Moscow, where she was given the cell previously occupied by Peter the Great's sister and namesake of his just-deceased spouse, Ekaterina Alekseevna.[24] Substitutions such as this one leave little doubt as to the intended meaning.

Shortly thereafter, in July 1727, the Supreme Privy Council formally annulled the manifesto of February 1718 that had removed the late Aleksei Petrovich from the line of succession, an even bolder gesture rejecting his grandfather's legacy in favor of his father and the Lopukhin clan. So sensitive was this issue of clan rivalries that Anna Ioannovna reinstated the manifesto in December 1731.[25] From the perspective of the early 1720s, the specter of Evdokia returning as regent, however unlikely, would have been deeply ominous for the Petrine court, a threat incarnate to turn the clock back, renew the Lopukhin and Miloslavskii alliance, and unseat an entire cohort of Petrine loyalists. These two families could claim lineage, tradition, aristocracy, and a direct blood tie to the younger Peter. By comparison, Catherine could claim no pedigree, not even Russian blood. Prior to her coronation there existed no ceremonial investiture of a formal claim on her behalf to post-Petrine authority other than the wedding of 1712. A struggle over the regency would have been even worse, almost certainly involving physical disorder and with no guarantees as to the outcome.

And yet, had Peter announced an intention to name his grandson as heir and Catherine as regent for Peter Alekseevich, momentum toward a Lopukhin revival, nominally based on the superior matrilineal blood connection to the new ruler, would have been almost unavoidable. The decision to crown Catherine as empress without mentioning the succession forestalled this outcome, or at least countered it. It palpably elevated her to a status, merited through individual accomplishments and her marriage to him, unparalleled by any other female in the realm, past or present. It also announced Peter's unmistakable decision to cast the empire's immediate future with her and those who surrounded her, irrespective of matrilineal blood lines. To put it crudely, an imperial crown trumped any claim that the former tsaritsa Evdokia's supporters might make.

If this line of speculation corresponds to what Peter was thinking at the time, it helps to demystify one of the most widely mentioned elements of the coronation: Peter's choosing to place the crown personally on Catherine's head rather than have the archbishop do it, as had been the case with previous—male—coronations. It has been argued that the decision to have Peter place the crown on Catherine's head constituted a sharp break with tradition. In this view, the gesture demonstrated a new sense of monarchic charisma in which the tsar replaced the head of the church as the vicar of Christ *("mestnik Bozhii")* within Russian Orthodoxy, who could thereby pass on God's blessing and anointment directly, without the intervention of clergy.[26] Some have seen this change as a gesture of secularization, in that it continued the shift of authority from mother church to the body of the monarch. Others argue just the opposite, that the act reasserted the divine origins and sacral basis of monarchic legitimacy. Both of these constitute plausible arguments, consistent with the gestures so far as they are understood. One might suggest, then, that the meaning of this deed is irresolvably ambiguous, and likely deliberately so.

One should note that the prescriptions and choreographic scripts prepared in advance of the coronation expressed the matter differently, and no less plausibly, by focusing as ever on the necessity of precedence within Christendom. Sensitive to the absence of a recognized Russian precedent for crowning a female head, the pre-coronation investigations examined coronation rituals elsewhere. Although the 1721 decree proclaiming Peter emperor and father of the fatherland traced its lineage back to the Roman emperor Maximilian, the specific explanation for having Peter crown Catherine derived from the dual coronations of several Byzantine rulers in which the patriarch crowned the emperor and the emperor, in turn, crowned the empress. Constantine Porphyrogenitus's *Book of Ceremonies* states that, in coronations of the "Augusta," the patriarch was to bless the crown, and then the emperor was to take it from him and place it personally on his spouse's head.[27] The official *Opisanie* notes that this is precisely what transpired in 1724.

In the *Book of Ceremonies*, passing the crown from the head of the church to the hands of the emperor did not imply a gesture of independent monarchic charisma. Rather, in dual coronations (Justin and Euphemia, Justinian and Theodora), the clerical coronation of the emperor was seen as spiritually covering both heads. The emperor was, thus, extending the blessing that he had received to his consort, and enabling the empress to be cojoined with him under the one blessing. If the empress alone were being crowned, the patriarch's blessing of the crown had the same effect. By adopting a Byzantine rationale, the coronation's choreographers deftly left the troublesome issue of monarchic charisma ambiguous. Transposing these tenth-century prescripts to Russia could imply that the archbishop—and not the tsar—was, in this time and place, Christ's vicar. The ritual had the additional advantage of avoiding any unwanted conflation with the ceremony performed at the Mniszek coronation, which also happened to take place in May, on the 8th (18th), 1606. In the account contained in Stanislav Nemoevskii's diary, the patriarch on that occasion took the crown from two notables, blessed it, and then personally placed it on Marina's head.[28] At such a highly charged moment in 1724, the critical juncture during an unprecedented ceremony for which the articulation of precedent was paramount, it was more prudent to genuflect toward Byzantium than to follow a path whose formal symmetry with the coronation of tsars might be misinterpreted as a gesture toward the False Dmitrii.

One can only guess whether those at worship in Dormition Cathedral on that day found Peter's actions reassuringly embedded in ancient Orthodox—if not exactly Russian—tradition or radically innovative. Under the circumstances, however, the Byzantine example fit as well as any other. At the very least, it created a space allowing for a clerically more traditional reading of the crowning itself, a comfort, perhaps, to more than a few. Keeping in mind that the coronation was cast as a liturgical event in consecrated space visually surrounded by saints and angels; that those crowding into Dormition Cathedral gazed throughout upon a large fresco of the Last Judgment; that Peter's placing the crown on Catherine's head was preceded and followed by prayer and priestly invocations; that Catherine spent much of the ceremony on her knees in prayer; and that the elaborate ritual of *pomazanie* was fundamental and defining, it is hard to imagine that those in attendance could lose sight of the centrality of faith to the ritual, or of the divine legitimation that it conveyed.

This surely was the Synod's priority, and its preparatory instructions emphasized prayer and employed signposts from the liturgy as if endeavoring to make the coronation appear more familiar to the clergy involved. "Just before the day of coronation all Cathedrals, monasteries and parish churches will conduct a special vespers service. . . . On the day of the coronation an early Cathedral bell will toll, and then . . . as usual there will be an entrance with the cross in which the assembled bishops and ecclesiasts will pray for the health of His Majesty and the Empress."[29] Frederic de Bassewitz, whose command of Russian was excellent, recognized this interweaving of liturgy and state power, and he saw Feofan and Feodosii as playing a fundamental role in the proceedings.[30] Even the liturgically inattentive Bergholz knew that the coronation required blessing Catherine in the holy mysteries, and thus necessitated a lengthy fast on her part.[31] Like the rest of the diplomatic corps he was confined to the cathedral balcony and could not hear very well. But he understood that it was preeminently a service, that holy unction was fundamental to it, and that the clergy played the major role[32].

Peter also understood the religious centrality of the coronation, or at least conceded the necessity of respecting that reading, a point not lost on disgruntled clergy distressed by the wholesale acquiescence of the ecclesiastical authorities, including perhaps Archbishop Feodosii of Novgorod, who as the most senior archbishop presided over the coronation.[33] After the death of Patriarch Adrian, Peter had gotten into the habit of writing to the patriarch of Constantinople from time to time, particularly when he wanted his troops to be granted dispensations from fasting. When he sought and received the patriarch's blessing for the coronation, he was being entirely consistent. The blessing arrived in a letter on June 25, 1724, and both Peter and Catherine wrote in response that September. Peter thanked Patriarch Cyrus for his warm greetings and prayers on behalf of the empress, "our beloved spouse." He beseeched the patriarch to continue praying for them. Catherine's letter to her "father in Christ" expresses similar sentiments, and it adds, "We especially thank you for your heartfelt paternal congratulations on the coronation, with which, by God's grace, his imperial majesty, my sovereign spouse has seen fit to honor me." She too asked the patriarch to continue to pray for them.[34]

The Homily

Against this backdrop Feofan's long-winded—it lasted an hour and a half—oration takes on a different and particularly cloudy aura. When compared to his other *slova* and those of contemporary Petrine-era clerics, its singularity stands out, in some ways transgressively, relative to the conventions that had come to regulate clerical speech in consecrated spaces since Semen Polotskii's day. First of all, it did not fit the structural traditions of a homily, notwithstanding its location in a major liturgical service. Contrary to other published sermons of the day, which invariably began with a biblical citation, the text of this sermon contained not a single quote or marginal notation from Scripture, with only one rather cryptic reference to biblical antecedents, and no glosses on the holy mysteries. Although God was frequently and thunderously invoked, the sermon made but one fleeting reference to the Holy Spirit, and no other mention of Christ or the cross.[35] Indeed, it did not even employ the word 'Christian.'

These absences are particularly glaring when one confronts the written text. As Riccardo Picchio has famously noted, biblical citations and marginalia had long functioned as signifiers in hagiographic texts—thematic clues, as he terms them, to the spiritual message of the work.[36] It was the reader's, or listener's, task to follow these clues in order to establish the semantic connection between the Bible and the "higher meaning" of the hagiography.[37] This rhetorical principle transferred seamlessly from saints' lives to original Russian sermons, orations that from their advent in the 1670s provided extensive scriptural citations. Yet, this sermon, in most respects hagiography par excellence, offered no biblical signifiers, no guides that would have allowed an audience to place the archbishop's words into a scriptural setting and thereby derive its meaning. In their place it offered a unique mixture of lavish encomia to Catherine herself, mythology and history, Christian identity and pagan allegory.

Cognizant that the ceremony had no acceptable precedents in Russia, Feofan sought, as did Peter's decree of the previous year, to reassure the assembled that female coronations had a worthy history, but one that required explanation. Earlier queens, he remarked, had been crowned on far less merit than Catherine. Ignoring the specific foremothers cited by Peter, Feofan referred instead to the Book of Esther, one of the most familiar female figures in Russian sermons, and the subject of the most famous play performed at the court theater in Preobrazhenskoe during the 1670s. "Artaxerkes" [Xerxes], he said, "had wished to crown Astinia [Vashti] merely for her beauty, but decided against it because of her sense of pride. For beauty alone this same monarch did crown Esther, her piety being unknown and unimportant to him. Still another received a crown by the worth of her blood alone."[38] In other words, Esther exhibited many virtues but these did not bear upon her coronation.

He continued with a brief review of practices elsewhere in Europe— Spain, Portugal, Sweden, England, Poland, Denmark, and other states— and concluded that none could claim a coronation of this sort. He provided no details, failing even to name any of the several crowned European queens of recent vintage. But he nevertheless concluded that European practice did not apply to Catherine, who he observed quite accurately, was being crowned not for her bloodlines or family alliances, but for her personal qualities, not for the frivolity of beauty alone, but for her strength of character, fortitude at Pruth, as well as her beauty.

Feofan then turned to distant history—or what he termed history—as his fundamental referent, to queens, crowned by their spouses, whose coronations had truly reflected their merit. Eschewing the obscure antecedents of Peter's manifesto, he put forth instead a motley array of famous women of history and mythology, most of whose names would have been familiar to those listening to him.

> We may note that a not insignificant number of glorious wives in history have either received a royal crown or have been worthy of it. Such examples as Semiramis of Babylon, Tamira [Tomyris] of Scythia, Pentheselia the Amazon, Helena, Pulcheria, and Eudoxia the Roman Empresses. And should there

not be an equal degree of praise for our Russian Catherine? . . . I do not pro-
pose equating the above named heroines to Catherine, however. Each of
them deserves praise in her own way . . . : Semiramis is to be praised for her
bravery, but dishonored for killing her husband. We praise Tomyris for her
courage, but not for wisdom. The radiant Amazons for their deeds in war, but
they are darkened by their uncommon lack of humility. . . . Helena's zealotry
in her faith, the singular chastity of Pulcheria, the singular wisdom of Eudoxia. And thus for these other monarchs we justifiably offer honor to their
praise-worthy queens, but not unqualified praise. You then, o Russia, shall
you not bear witness to God's coronation of your own Empress, who when
compared to the others, is possessed of all of their gifts? Are you not pleased
to see in her a humble piety before God, an unwavering love and faithfulness
to her husband and Sovereign, a tireless concern for her daughters and
nieces, her grandson, and the entire [ruling] family, charity for the poor,
mercy for the weak and fallen, maternal caring for all her subjects?[39]

On the surface all of this fit together quite well. Catherine was following in the footsteps of frequently cited and praiseworthy crowned female
heads of antiquity, but she outshone all of them, standing virtually alone
in history and mythology by the totality of attributes that justified her
coronation by God and Peter and before the Russian people. If these lumi-
nous queens could be crowned for lesser accomplishments, surely Catherine deserved coronation. Feofan had employed this rhetorical device in a
number of earlier panegyrics, especially in declaiming that Peter exceeded
even the most vaunted names in the pantheon of glory. The famous sermon on the victory at Poltava, an oration that profoundly shaped Feofan's
future path as a leading Petrine acolyte, compared Peter favorably to Samson, Heraclius, and Domitian.[40] Many of those in the cathedral knew the
Poltava text (or knew of it), and the familiarity of the trope might well
have reassured them that the archbishop would be traversing well-trod
rhetorical ground. Now, perhaps, they could relax.

The coronation sermon went on to enumerate the human qualities of
Catherine: heroism, fortitude, good will, the perfect harmony of her feminine caring and masculine courage, repeating again and again how personally worthy she was of this coronation. St. Catherine, who had been
neither earthly queen nor wife—at least not in the traditional sense,
would have been a poor fit for such an argument (although she was not
entirely absent from the coronation). But in fact the oration had already
gone off in an uncharted direction. The substitution of the personal for
the sacred, and history (or quasi-history) for Scripture, passing over in silence the predecessors Peter had mentioned as well as more recently
crowned Christian queens, and substituting for them an intermingling of
mythological, pagan, biblical, and sacred female figures from early Byzantium (Semiramis, Tomyris, Pentheselia, with Queen Esther and Helena,
and Pulcheria and Eudoxia, the Christian Roman empresses) was, like the

coronation itself, without precedent in Russian homiletics. By eschewing scriptural signifiers in favor of allegorical and historical ones, Feofan seemed to be inviting the assembled to return to these man-made sources to derive his meaning, just as they had been expected to do for nonliturgical panegyrics or for court theatrical productions.

Wortman points out that "Prokopovich's analogies from legend and world history removed [Catherine], like Peter, from the Russian past and placed her in a universal context."[41] The St. Catherine *lik* (living image) had accomplished this already, however, in extensive and very public displays. Comparing Russian rulers to ancient Byzantine forebears, real or imagined, was hardly an act of displacement, moreover, having been practiced since the earliest Russian chronicles and sermons had compared Vladimir to Constantine. In his *Sermon on Law and Grace,* for example, the eleventh-century Metropolitan Ilarion of Kiev referred to Vladimir as the "likeness of Constantine the Great. . . . He and his mother Helen transported the Cross from Jerusalem—from the city of Constantine—and established it throughout all your land, and so you affirmed and confirmed the faith. And as you were the likeness of him, so God granted you to partake with him in like honor and glory and in heaven because of the devotion you showed in life."[42] As recently as the Church Synod of 1666–1667, which had sanctified Nikon's reform of the liturgy and church ritual, Aleksei Mikhailovich was praised formally as "a second Constantine, a true disseminator of Orthodoxy and faithful servant of Christ."[43] Semen Polotskii took up this theme shortly thereafter in his homily on the day of St. Vladimir, in which he turned praise for the saint into a panegyric of Aleksei Mikhailovich.[44] As a literary device, this mechanism would not have removed Catherine from the Russian past so much as embedding her in it, by establishing a matrilineal link to Constantine, however fleeting, (and by extension, to David and Abraham) analogous to the entirely familiar patrilineal one.

But if either transposition or lineage were Feofan's intentions, he chose an obscure way of conveying them. His own explanation of reassurance, that only in combination did the attributes of these earlier crowned women equal Catherine's, does not go very far since the passage in question made almost no connection between the bravery, piety, zealotry, chastity, and military prowess with which the earlier heroines were endowed and the faithfulness, charity, humility, and maternal tenderness ascribed to the empress in the very same paragraph. Feofan devoted most of his sermon (when not praising Peter) to extolling Catherine's devotion to Peter, both in battle and in domestic companionship, in ways that had little to do with the way he characterized Semiramis and others. Reading the text closely, one is drawn to the decidedly unreassuring conclusion that Feofan could find no equivalent precedents at all to Catherine's coronation, not in Europe, antiquity, Scripture, or myth. How, then, was the deed to be understood? More precisely, what associations might the names have evoked to Feofan's audience(s), beyond the abbreviated comments of the sermon?

With the partial exception of Tomyris,[45] all had been widely represented in Russian book culture for centuries, primarily but not exclusively through the many manuscript redactions of khronografs and the popular translations of the work of Guido delle Colonne (or de Columnis), namely his thirteenth-century *Historia destructionis Troiae,*[46] large sections of which had been recopied numerous times during the sixteenth and seventeenth centuries and then published three times during Peter's reign (1709, 1712, 1717).[47] Virgil, Homer, Herodotus, and basic church history would have provided additional background for these references.

Feofan himself knew these texts well, and he referred to them at length in his theological tracts, particularly those written in Latin after his return to Kiev from his studies in Rome. An essay on reliquaries, for example, included a long section entitled "Narratio Heroditi de Sepultura Aegyptorium" that, as its name implies, summarized Herodotus's description of Egyptian burial practices. This same essay also included learned references to Virgil, Homer, Ovid, Xenophon, and Plutarch.[48] Most of his other theological writings included similar references.

The Russian texts characterized all the pagan queens as beautiful, brave, and politically significant. Semiramis, for example, distinguished herself at the mythical battle of Bactia. Shortly thereafter she married King Ninus, who was transfixed by her beauty and courage, and then she succeeded him upon his death. Tomyris—identified by Herodotus and most subsequent texts as a Massagetai rather than a Scythian—led her forces in the 530s BCE against the Persian king Cyrus, taking personal revenge by beheading him in the decisive battle.[49] She was extolled by Asthinia (Vashti) in *Artakserkovo deistvo* for her glory and courage.[50] This image also corresponds to her persona in European allegory generally, in which she was commonly bracketed with the biblical Judith as a strong and beautiful warrior ready to go to battle to defend a political order she deemed just.[51] Similarly, Pentheselia the Amazon was praised for her skill in weaponry and for her bravery in fighting to liberate Troy.

This valorization of martial qualities, of course, would have been Feofan's most transparent and didactic point, the temporal context of Picchio's "double code" and the meaning most likely derived by those in attendance who knew the popular lore. Catherine was the embodiment of all the strong and fearless women of history and myth. To the educated clergy and laity in attendance who knew the texts, however, the immediate message would have been ambiguous, first, because Feofan's characterizations did not neatly correspond with current conventions, and, second, because most of these identity figures had manifested a dark side to their personae. Semiramis, at the time considered as much a mythological figure as a historic one, was noted for her physical charms and sexual excess. Prominent in her legend were the curious tales that she had been the daughter of the fish goddess Atargates, raised by a dove, and that prior to marrying Ninus she had been wed to Memnon, one of Ninus's generals. In light of the rumors about Catherine's previous marriage to a Swedish officer, what was one to make of that? Spoken at a time when rumors about her affair with the soon to be executed William Mons were widespread, this analogy may have been biographically more accurate than the St. Catherine persona, but it hardly suited a newly anointed mother of the fatherland.

One version that circulated in Muscovy related that, shortly after presenting Semiramis with the crown, Ninus chose to let her rule for five days, during which time she had Ninus killed.[52] After a long and successful reign she delivered the realm to her son and then disappeared. What were the implicit lessons here? Dante, whose work Feofan knew from his time in Rome even if many of the congregants did not, had consigned Semiramis to the second circle of hell because "She was corrupted so by lechery that she made license lawful in her realm, to take away the blame she had incurred."[53]

Pentheselia, too, was the daughter of pagan gods, Orithia and Ares, and in her noted battle she inadvertently killed her sister (some versions say she killed an allied Amazon queen). Her beauty was said to seduce men, including Achilles, and her name meant "compelling men to mourn." Chapter 37 in Colonne's *Trojan History*, entitled "The Death of Pentheselia, Queen of the Amazons," characterized her as "noble and warrior-like." Pentheselia personally engaged in hand-to-hand combat, killing thousands. In the end, though, she was killed in the battle to recapture Troy, and her demise proved so painful that neither the Amazons nor the Trojans had the heart to continue on the field of battle.

Tomyris, who was linked to righteousness and bloodshed in virtually all the relevant texts,[54] saw her son Spargapises drugged and taken prisoner by the Persians, as a result of which he took his own life. More alarmingly, she presided over a people noted by Herodotus for their bizarre sexual customs. "Although each man marries a wife, they all make their wives available for anyone else to have intercourse with. In Greece this is said to be a Scythian custom, but it is Massagetan, not Scythian."[55] Evidence of late Muscovite familiarity with this lore comes from Andrei Lyzlov's *Scythian History* (1692), an unrelenting historical diatribe against the Mongols and the Tatar yoke. Lyzlov himself was neither a highly placed court poet nor a learned cleric. A member of the service gentry, he had spent many years in the military, participating in the Crimea and other campaigns. In 1682 he accompanied Sofia on her fateful visit to the Trinity-St. Sergius Monastery, which established her status as informal regent. With the benefit of Sofia's patronage he spent much of the 1680s collecting materials from the Patriarchal Library and composing his work on the Scythians. Written against the backdrop of the wars of the 1680s, *Scythian History* is generally seen as an ideological defense of the newly established Christian Holy League (Muscovy, Austria, Poland, and Venice) against the Ottomans and the Crimean khanate.[56]

Purporting to show that the Mongols (and by extension the Crimeans and perhaps the Ottomans) descended from the ancient warlike peoples of the southeast, Scythians and Amazons, Lyzlov included both Pentheselia and Tomyris among these militaristic and uncivilized ancestors. Basing his account of them on Homer, Virgil, and Herodotus, he characterized both women as fearless and heroic in their battles against male generals and, in Tomyris's case, drenched in the blood of Cyrus.[57] Russian texts had regularly cast Cyrus as a positive figure, a good king whose practices Feofan himself had only two years previous extolled when explaining the precedent for allowing the sitting monarch to choose a successor.[58] Yet here was Cyrus's slayer, "drenched in blood"[59] from his beheading, being mentioned as an identity figure of sorts for the newly crowned empress.

A few years later, do note, Tomyris's bravery was deployed in an entirely positive and patriotic manner on an early Russian triumphal gate, as described by Iosif Turoboiskii, the influential prefect of the Slavonic Academy in Moscow, in a 1704 treatise. "On the left side [of the back face of the gates] stands Tomirisa, the fearless Scythian queen. . . . Tomirisa is the emblem of the Russian power courageously defeating the Swedish forces and liberating Ingermanland from them."[60] Thus, her negative image was not entirely determined, even though most of the imagery was decidedly unflattering.

Semiramis, too, garnered occasional praise. In his book, *The Chronicle*, a compilation of narratives of human history from creation though the birth of Jesus, Dimitrii Rostovskii wrote at length about her reign. In his telling, the beautiful Semiramis at first appeared admirable, and Dimitrii employed language strikingly reminiscent of the St. Catherine vitae. Like St. Catherine, Semiramis possessed a mind and a spirit that were decidedly wise, rational, brave, and masculine ("ne zhenskim razumom," "muzhestvennoiu svoeiu khrabrostiiu," "ne zhenska ouma i serdtsa, no pache muzhestvenneisha,"), her obscure background and problematic marital history notwithstanding. After the death of Ninus, she ruled in her son's name, often dressed in men's attire and on horseback, true to her warrior spirit. She graced Babylon with grand buildings, magnificent walls, wondrous gardens, and flourishing orchards, but in the end, Dimitrii concluded, her personal sinfulness overshadowed her virtues. Enamored of her many lovers, she became the embodiment of lawlessness and wanton violence. In Dimitrii's balance sheet, Semiramis' reign of forty-two years constituted a study in extreme contradiction. Begun with good, her life ended in evil; possessed of wisdom, she behaved mindlessly; initially joined in wedlock, she ended up as an adulteress. For all of her accomplishments, it was the downward trajectory, the dishonor of her later life that seems to have lingered in memory.[61]

In sum, each of Feofan's women of mythology and pagan history had contradictory, if perpetually hyperbolic, reputations in Russian book culture. Although heroic and fearless, each was associated with massive carnage and family tragedy (the violent death of a sister, a son, and the murder of a husband) affecting the political fate of their peoples. All had been complicit in sexual depravity, either as predators or by presiding over the predations of others. Feofan alluded briefly to the violence, even the regicide, as if to direct the attendees to remember those traits too. Sexual excess, however, which marked Catherine's own reputation every bit as much as those of the antecedents named in the homily, was treated by Feofan with a deafening and unmistakable silence, familiar to all who knew the literary texts but with no spoken trace in the homily itself. More strikingly, he contradicted all extant accounts by distilling these complex and multi-faceted figures and making them one dimensional, embodiments of only a single positive quality, and for most a single negative one.

The godly women fared little better. I. M. Kudriavtsev's exhaustive study of *Artakserkovo deistvo* has demonstrated that the Book of Esther circulated widely in the Muscovite court and higher clergy, particularly during the later seventeenth century, and that it was subject to numerous literary adaptations and homiletic commentary, particularly during Pentecost.[62] Karion Istomin, Semen Polotskii, and other Muscovite court poets wrote about Esther, as did Dimitrii Rostovskii.[63] Almost all of these glosses told the story rather differently than Feofan did, and they took considerable license with the biblical narrative. The play, which Kudriavtsev maintained was a parable on the virtue of strong women and the relative attributes of men and women, painted Vashti in a positive and sympathetic light, and maintained that Xerxes offered her the crown not for beauty, as she had thought, but out of love. Her refusal to accept it, born of pride, was thus a tragedy, and too late did she realize the nobility of her husband's offer.[64] Esther, although frightened and conveying her sense of unworthiness for the crown, comes to recognize that it honored not merely her exceeding beauty but Xerxes' love and respect as well. Xerxes' advisors assure her that she is indeed worthy, and that she is blessed by heaven.[65]

Feofan's comments bypassed this more nuanced reading, even though he might plausibly have appropriated it to establish Catherine's heritage and the rightfulness of her supplanting of the tsaritsa Evdokia. Instead, his comments reverted to the more one-dimensional version of the Old Testament coronation text, in which the themes of vanity and beauty are paramount. Although he did not identify this with marginalia, as would normally have been done, Feofan was referring specifically and rather narrowly to Esther 2:17, "Now the king was attracted to Esther more than to any of the other women, and she won his favor and approval more than any of the other virgins. So he set a royal crown on her head and made her queen instead of Vashti. And the king gave a great banquet, Esther's banquet, for all the nobles and officials. He proclaimed a holiday throughout the provinces and distributed gifts with royal liberality."[66]

The almost dismissive reference to Empress Helena, granting her grudging respect for her religious zeal alone and deeming her only a fraction of the heroine that Catherine was, must have sounded gratingly discordant. The mother of Constantine the Great, Helena was among the most deeply revered Byzantine female saints throughout Orthodoxy. Doctrinally equivalent to the apostles, Helena was the namesake of numerous churches and cathedrals in the Christian east. Tradition had credited her with discovering the Holy Sepulcher and the true cross during a pilgrimage to Jerusalem in 324 when she was seventy-five years old, an accomplishment for which she was anointed the apostolic mother of the church.[67] All of this was recorded extensively in Slavonic texts, exalted in numerous homilies, and well known to those assembled in the Dormition Cathedral.[68] The symbolism of the true cross permeated Orthodox worship, and it resonated profoundly in the representation of St. Catherine, ubiquitously shown holding the true cross in her right hand, the image so powerfully explored in Dimitrii Rostovskii's writings just a couple of decades earlier. As Thyrêt has shown, the reign of Aleksei Mikhailovich had employed the veneration of the cross as a central visual element in representing the piety of the tsaritsa Mariia Il'inichna and of portraying Aleksei himself as the new Constantine.[69]

Within panegyrics, Helena's identity had been inextricably linked for centuries with Constantine's, and if Peter was the second Constantine, as he was often declared to be, then it would have been appropriate to sketch Catherine, hyperbolically perhaps, in the image of St. Helena rather than superior to her. Numerous other queens, beginning with the Byzantine Eudoxia (377–404) and her daughter Pulcheria (399–453), had openly aspired to be "the new Helena," and to have applied this title to Catherine would have constituted high praise, fully consistent with the priestly hagiographies of Russian crowned heads. But such was not Feofan's choice.

Although unmentioned in Peter's 1723 decree, Eudoxia and Pulcheria were revered throughout Orthodoxy as heroines and saints from early Christian Byzantium, crowned as wives of Roman emperors, and remembered as powerful women in their own right. Pulcheria (whose very name conveyed physical beauty to those who knew some Latin) became co-empress with her brother, Theodosius, at the death of their father, Arcadius, and according to most accounts, she later ruled independently, although not in her own name. She took a vow of chastity, the act that Feofan chose to praise, for which she earned wide acclaim throughout Orthodoxy. But the standard account did not ascribe the veneration of Pulcheria to virginity alone.[70] Rather, her chastity, matched by her wisdom, were seen as a source of political purification, as in the 1687 inscription by Sil'vestr Medvedev that praised her intelligence ("Pul'kheriia takovym umom bo smysliashchi.")[71] Once crowned, she established a monastic atmosphere at court, although she subsequently married one of her generals, Marcian of Thrace, who became emperor himself (450–457). Another version that circulated in Russia, from the *Chronicle of John Malalas,* claimed that Theodosius had named Marcian as his successor, and that the assembled nobles then duly elected Marcian. It was his choice, according to Malalas, to marry Pulcheria, "a maiden of fifty-four."[72] In either scenario she ended the patrilineal dynastic line of her family, an unhappy outcome in the Slavic texts.

Eudoxia, whom Feofan extolled for her wisdom, was well known in the histories of the Eastern Church, in part for her piety but also as the power behind the throne of her weak husband, Arcadius. She had arranged for the downfall of the king's trusted friend and her own former ally, Eutropius—whom Chrysostom himself had criticized in two well-known sermons—even though Eutropius had introduced her to Arcadius and had arranged their marriage. She was described as jealous of Chrysostom's influence with her husband and with the people of Constantinople. Chrysostom had chastised the public adoration that Eudoxia had received and had delivered a sermon criticizing as near idolatry the crowd's adulation at the unveiling of a statue to her. In his eyes, she was another Jezebel.[73] In response, Eudoxia had Chrysostom publicly denounced by other churchmen, in particular by his aide, Bishop Severian of Gabala, and then famously had him exiled from his patriarchate in 404.

Subsequent church commentaries, including many that were written or translated into Slavonic, reminded the learned faithful of this damnable behavior again and again, especially during the 1650s and 1660s, when the multiple church synods and the schism escalated ecclesiastical discourse to new heights of hyperbole. Paul of Aleppo, admittedly no friend of the ancient Greeks, described Eudoxia, as well as the collectivity of Byzantine empresses, in particularly unflattering terms. "How could it be otherwise, when the Empresses were such as Eudoxia, who struck Chrysostom on the face, and, borne away by violence of her passion, committed acts in the Church of God which the worshippers of idols in their time refrained from doing; and such as other Empresses, who intrigued against their husbands and murdered them, and taking others to their bed, made them Emperors, as the modern day histories of the Grecian empire describe? Would to God no memorial existed of their infamies."[74]

None of these details, unspoken on that day but nevertheless familiar to anyone with even a general knowledge of church history, could have brought much comfort or clarity to the well-read congregants, including Peter and most of the clergy. All these antecedents were marked by duplicity, treachery, unfaithfulness, and radically conflicting images of female sexuality. What, for example, would Peter have thought about even mentioning Empress Eudoxia, in history a crafty manipulator of men and yet the namesake of many past princesses and tsaritsy, including his grandmother and several other Romanov women, and most sensitively his first wife, still apparently esteemed by many? Just a few years earlier, in 1718, rumors had been rife that Evdokia continued to dress in the garb of a queen rather than that of a nun; that she had refused to pray for Catherine; and that she was anxiously awaiting Peter's death so as to return to power with her son, Aleksei. The accounts had placed Bishop

Dosifei of Rostov, who had prophesied Evdokia's return to power, at the center of these tales, and they warned that many clergy dearly hoped that such an event would come to pass.[75] Even if untrue or exaggerated, everyone had heard the rumors, and the name Evdokia, previously one of the most popular female names and name day saints for the ruling family, had been little mentioned in the intervening few years, except with sharp opprobrium.

What might the unlettered Menshikov or his confederates have thought if someone clued them in to the fate of Eutropius at the hands of Eudoxia (or the mention of an empress who had married Marcian, a leading general)? What did it mean to the assembled clergy when the archbishop compared the newly crowned empress with one who had exiled Chrysostom, the revered church father, or to one who ruled with her brother, when Catherine's own brother had only recently been found and installed in the capital? And why, in 1724, should Catherine have been associated with women who ruled first through their husbands and then on their own, typically with unhappy consequences? Pulcheria's ascendancy, for example, marked the end of the male line of the Theodosian dynasty of Spanish descent, and the ascendancy of an Illyrian dynasty whose home base was the Balkans. Most confounding of all, if one pondered it, what could the multiple and contradictory scenarios of rulership after the deaths of the kings possibly imply for a realm without a declared heir and whose own emperor was known to be in declining health? True, Catherine possessed all of their virtues, Feofan said, and none of their faults, but why mention most of them at all, in particular in a way that seemed to challenge openly the most rigid conventions of Russian homiletics? Why not employ safer or less ambiguous precedents—Olga, for example—who were well known and subjects of long-standing veneration?

To some extent the facts of Byzantine dynastic history limited Feofan's options. Although there had been many Augustas, most, like Catherine, came from non-noble backgrounds, and quite a few had ambiguous biographies. Frankly, Feofan would have been hard pressed to find one who was both well known and without political or personal blemishes. Empress Theodora, for example, was the daughter of a bear keeper and had started working in the theater at a young age, achieving fame, apparently, for a strip tease that she performed, entitled "Leda and the Swan." If Procopius is to be believed, Theodora too was sexually voracious, had a daughter out of wedlock, and engaged in prostitution.[76] Similarly, Irene (empress from 797 to 802), the consort of Leo IV, had been an orphan (albeit from a reasonably prominent clan) when married to Leo at a young age. But neither Theodora nor Irene had the biographical stains that, in the cases of Eudoxia and Pulcheria, came uncomfortably close to Catherine's apparently dark past and current alliances. As empresses, both had largely positive reputations. Theodora was known in all the Greek histories for her good works, such as banning prostitution, fining and arresting the brothel keepers, and freeing the prostitutes from slavery.[77] Several Greek chronographs described her heroic role in suppressing the Nika revolt, decisively intervening on behalf of Justinian when he appeared surrounded on all sides by armed enemies supporting the pretender to the throne, Hypatios.[78] Surely this could have been likened without problem to Catherine's own bravery at Pruth.

Empress Irene famously reversed the ban on icon worship, thus rendering her problematic for the generally iconoclastic Petrine court. Still, her career could have served Feofan as an example of a long and successful regency (780–797) on behalf of her son Constantine, who was crowned as co-emperor by his father and who succeeded him in 780.[79] In this capacity Irene protected the authority of her son and held off spirited challenges from other members of the imperial line. All of this was well known to Feofan, who could have easily and appropriately alluded to it in the sermon. But he did not, perhaps because Irene, alone among Byzantine empresses, came to rule independently (797–802) and entirely in her own name, as basileus rather than augusta.[80]

Unraveling the Homily

Whatever his reasoning, Feofan's choices of Byzantine antecedents could not have been random or haphazard, not in a sermon at such a momentous occasion. In the absence of textual transparency, we are obliged to search for still more layers of meaning beyond the dual code, ones that would have been discernible by elements of his high-powered audience. Peter and his more senior associates would have known that several of those named had been applied in recent memory to other women of the Muscovite court. The unspoken link between Empress Eudoxia and the tsaritsa Evdokia would have been transparent to all, but both Mariia Il'inichna and Sofia Alekseevna had been compared to Pulcheria (in Sofia's case many times), and Sofia had also been compared to Semiramis.

Paisius Ligarides, the Greek archbishop of Gaza and a man every bit as notorious and as central to Russia's church-state politics as Arsenius the Greek, told the following anecdote in his history of the church council of 1666, which formally condemned Nikon, concerning prayers for the women of the tsar's family:

> It was the new year's day of this new year 1667 from the Incarnation; and the emperor Alexis Michaelovich thought that he ought to observe the Roman custom. Wherefore he sent for the two partriarchs privately, as if that they might give their blessing to the most religious lady the Augusta Maria, and her eldest son the hossoudar Alexis Alexievich, and the sisters and daughters of the emperor, with all his house. . . . May the Most High be pleased to subject to your rightly-dividing feet all the barbarous nations scattered over many lands, and now unbelieving; that the people who sit in darkness . . . may see the great light of the knowledge of God. . . .

Then the patriarch, turning to the empress, addressed her thus: "Many daughters have wrought mighty things . . . but thou hast exceeded all, as we may now say with the wise Solomon, O most serene Christian empress, Lady Augusta, Maria Ilichna, new blessed Helena, and *beauteous Pulcheria* [italics added]. The Lord has chosen thee out of so many women to be more honourable than them all." . . . "Blessed in truth is thy womb, which has given us four princesses, that we may bless and sanctify thee, that their empire may increase perpetually even to the very ends of the universe."[81]

This minor interchange, replete with celebrations of a January new year in 1667 and references to the sacred womb and to the tsar's evangelical and imperial mission among non-Christian peoples, lends itself to multiple interpretations. Ligarides had been something less than forthright in his public life. While studying in Rome he had converted to Roman Catholicism, and in the ensuing decades he repeatedly switched allegiances between Rome and Constantinople, awkward facts that he kept hidden from his Russian hosts until confronted by his past in the midst of the interrogation of Nikon. But he had stood by the tsar's side throughout much of the 1660s, acting as the primary interrogator of the former patriarch and frequently serving as the tsar's personal interpreter of the Greek and Latin proceedings.[82] The focus here, though, is on the tsaritsa, and on the identification with Helena and Pulcheria, who are themselves exalted far more than in Feofan's text, in a body of prayer largely devoted to celebrating Russia as a Christian empire. Of equal note is the panegyric content of the prayer, especially its elevation of Maria to beatific heights of Christian queenship, much as Feofan did for Catherine, but stopping well short of raising her above her forebears, a barrier that Feofan ignored.

Sil'vestr Medvedev's previously cited inscription of 1687, for example, was dedicated to a portrait of Sofia, and Pulcheria's wisdom anticipated Sophia's own. In the lines preceding this one, Medvedev also compared her to Semiramis and Elizabeth I of Great Britain.[83] In his *Sozertsanie kratkoe* he repeated this image, likening Sofia's courage during the Khovanshchina to Pulcheria's, emphasizing the latter's philosophical nature, her virginity, and her steadfast support of her brother during turbulent and violent times.[84] Karion Istomin employed much the same image in several of his writings, suggesting that, like Pulcheria, Sofia was the embodiment of divine wisdom, because she understood that without wisdom and learning one could not know God or achieve salvation.[85]

Although well established, the identification of Sofia with Pulcheria was not uniformly positive, and those, like Andrei Medvedev, who held Sofia responsible for the bloodshed of 1682 insisted that she reproduced Pulcheria's dark side. "In her thirst for power the tsarevna revealed an untamed desire for great personal honor [to reign] through her brother [Ivan], the aforenamed tsarevich . . . as if she were following the ancient example of the Greek Emperor of the East, Theodosius the Younger, whose sister, the

Princess Pulcheria, ruled autocratically in his name more than the king him-self, about which the history of the Greek Empire recounts quite precisely."[86] Finally, Natal'ia Kirillovna had been known at court as "the Muscovite Es-ther," and the popularity of the story of Esther at the court of Aleksei Mikhailovich was meant, in large measure, to be an homage to her.[87]

All of these familial associations would have been immediately appar-ent to Peter and many other senior figures at court. Heard in this way, the sermon would have served to situate Catherine within and elevate her above prominent Romanov women, both living and of recent memory, and to convey through codes of indirection why she was receiving the crown when they had not. The uncrowned Sofia/Pulcheria was thus a vir-gin (at least officially) and by implication was not the paragon of wisdom and bravery of panegyric poetry. The less said about her the better. The displaced Eudoxia/Evdokia may have been wise, but her example of scheming behind the scenes and plotting against the fathers of the church disqualified her from coronation.

If this type of dynastic history through metaphor was one of Feofan's messages, why muddy the waters with the pagans? To understand just how transgressive and discordant these antecedents must have seemed, and how at odds they were with Feofan's stated views on the place of pa-gans, one needs to revisit Turoboiskii's fundamental distinction between consecrated and public space, and his elaborations in subsequent treatises on the distinction between the public space of triumphal processions and arches, which allowed for pagan allegory, and the sanctified space of the church (the true *khram*), which permitted only sacred images, a distinction subsequently echoed in Buzhinskii's sermons. Peter had initiated the prac-tice of triumphal gates upon his return from the Azov campaign of 1696, when he had forewarned Andrei Vinius while still on route that he wanted to be greeted by a triumphal gate when he arrived in Moscow.[88] Almost immediately this instruction set off discussion within the church regard-ing the intermingling of religious figures and the mythological imagery of Hercules and Mars that were associated with military victory. In contrast to fireworks displays, which literally dispersed before one's eyes, carved images implied permanence, as reflected in the contemporaneous bas re-liefs of the apostles done in Moscow by Stepan Ivanov Polubes. Placing images of the divine and the mythological side by side risked public con-fusion and sacrilege.[89] To avoid this problem, the initial triumphal arches were defined explicitly as temporary structures, wooden decorations to be dismantled after a short time. In 1709, Peter had other gates deco-rated in an equally transient manner, for example, with scenery and cos-tumes taken from the old Preobrazhenskoe theater of Pastor Georgi.[90] The worry remained, however, and Turoboiskii's treatise was meant to re-solve it by emphasizing the palpable antinomy of consecrated and un-consecrated spaces, churches and boulevards. More broadly, it consti-tuted an early statement of what would become a major theme of the

THE ARCHBISHOP AND THE EMPRESS · 195

eighteenth-century church regarding the physical sanctity of the church, whether cathedral or parish, and the determination to exclude nonreligious activities from it.

Turoboiskii was not the first churchman of his era to insist upon this distinction. At least three sermons written during the late 1660s and early 1670s, two by Semen Polotskii and the other by an anonymous author, insisted that the church building was the house of God. It was, in Cathy Potter's words, "sacred space, sharply delineated from the secular space outside the church. . . . Reverent worshipful attention must be accorded to the former, not to the latter.[91] At the time the clerics were more concerned with establishing decorum within the church and expelling the business of the workaday world from it. But the overall implications were much the same: different rules governed sacred and profane spaces, and behaviors and gestures that might be permitted on the outside were not tolerable within.

This separation appears, on the evidence, to have extended from the visual to the spoken image, if not as a formal proscription at least as a general practice for church orations. The proliferation of homiletics during the late seventeenth and early eighteenth century produced literally hundreds of original sermons, many more of which were preached than were subsequently published. Yet only a handful of those for which there exists a paper trail included allegorical or mythological imagery (with the glaring exception of two sermons by Stefan Iavorskii), even though the authors of these sermons employed such imagery freely in verse and in panegyrics intended for non-consecrated spaces.[92] Feofan himself followed this principle fairly rigorously in his previous church sermons, at least in those published in the eighteenth-century four-volume collection and the slightly different selection of 1961. In these he made quite a few references to Mars, the widely employed symbol of war, when speaking of Peter's military prowess. The association between Peter and Mars had been very popular, and one persistent rumor even claimed that the planet Mars had been unusually bright on the night of Peter's conception, thought to have been in August 1671.[93] But the sermons mentioned Mars only in passing and metaphorically, never dwelling on Mars with the type of elaboration employed in Catherine's coronation sermon. Typically Feofan referred to Peter's Mars-like strength or bravery, as in the 1709 *slovo* celebrating the victory at Poltava.[94] A sermon commemorating Peter's birthday spoke of how the sovereign bought freedom not with the merchant's silver but with the iron of a Mars ("ne srebom kupecheskim no marsovym zhelezom").[95] Feofan employed the same metaphor in the coronation ceremony, when in describing Catherine's bravery at Pruth, he spoke of the "Mars-like thundering *(Marsovykh gromakh)* in the turbulent seas."[96] Lest anyone be confused by these brief references, Feofan cleared the air in a Petrine name day sermon orated at the Trinity Cathedral in St. Petersburg in 1726. "And if a Roman lad of ancient times, blinded by pagan superstition, were to appear among us he would believe that [Peter] had in truth been born of

Mars."[97] *But he would be wrong.* Peter and the people of Christ, insisted Feofan, defeated the Turks, not the pagan gods of superstition. Echoing the language of the coronation, he said that Peter exceeded Xerxes, Alexander, and Caesar in his accomplishments, for which Peter had achieved his place with Christ in heaven.[98]

This type of fleeting and carefully disempowering statement typified references to pagan gods in Russian homiletics before and during Peter's day. For example, a sermon by Stefan Iavorskii, entitled "Kolesnitsa torzhestvennaia" (The Wheel [or Cycle] of Celebration) celebrated a victory over Sweden shortly before the end of the Northern War. In it Iavorskii employed the term "Mars," by now the ubiquitous symbol of military prowess, no fewer than eight times, but only as an adjective that gave no place for supernatural authority: "Mars-like harvest of victory," "lion of Mars," "Mars-like spirit," "Mars-like iron," "music unto Mars."[99] A 1720 sermon celebrating the victories of the Russian navy made similar use of Hercules, to whom Feofan briefly referred in three separate sermons, consigning him to legend, the product of "a Greek tale" *(povest' ellinskaia).*[100] Tantalus was similarly reduced to "a certain Tantalus from poetic fables."[101] Thus, pagan and allegorical imagery were used here to reinforce Christian belief, to reassert the religious sanctification of Peter's persona and rule, power like that of the mythical Mars, but in the service of Christ.

Such concerns loomed large in Feofan's understanding of pastoral responsibility. His didactic works dwelled repeatedly on the proper order of knowledge, the primacy of the sacred over the mortal—of which classical allegory was one particularly seductive part. His 1730 essay on the Song of Songs, for example, apparently the product of a dialogue with V. N. Tatishchev, insisted that even Solomon's vaunted wisdom could not have produced the psalms without the intervention of the Holy Spirit.[102] Similarly, his essay on atheism cautioned against being seduced by the philosophies of the ancient Athenians or by modern skeptical philosophers, especially Spinoza, whom he saw for some reason as being inherently atheistic.[103] The skeptics refused to believe in the miraculous, whereas Christian piety recognized it as Divine interventions, as happened with Moses, Daniel in the lions' den, and in many passages of the New Testament.[104] The divine word of Scripture, Feofan concluded, was the source of all true wisdom, and remained forever superior to all other writing, however artful.

Feofan devoted an equal degree of attention to language and to modes of communication, taking care that the laity would understand the message correctly. His noted catechistic primer, *Pervoe uchenie otrokom* (A Student's First Lesson), eschewed literary flourishes in favor of simple phrases that would make the Ten Commandments, around which the lessons were organized, clear to even the most unlettered of congregants. A lesser-known, but highly telling work, entitled *Things and Matters about which a Spiritual Teacher Should Instruct a Christian People, Including General Ones for*

Everyone and Others for Specific Individuals, amounted to a formulaic guide-book of proper homiletics, emphasizing yet again the primacy of God.[105] The first section, on the general audience, listed twenty maxims for preaching, the first of which was "On God, that is, in opposition to athe-ists, or the godless."[106] Each subsequent point reemphasized this message, the unity of God's work, its presence in all things, the truth of Christian confession versus the sinful nature of humanity leading to eternal torment in hell, but for the mercy of God's forgiveness, as revealed in Scripture. The second section, for specifically targeted audiences, delineated sixteen themes of sin and virtue that could be the topic of sermons. These, too, were framed around the love and fear of God, but they focused primarily on categories of virtue as against those of sin and sinners (thieves, law-breakers, drunkenness, simony, hypocrisy).[107]

So concerned was Feofan—and, for that matter, the entire ecclesiastical establishment—not to mislead the laity, even by inadvertence, that he in-serted disclaimers into translations that made extensive reference to pagan and allegorical figures, even when Peter himself had ordered the works be published. When, at Peter's behest, Feofan arranged for a translation of Apollodore's encyclopedia of pagan gods, *An Athenian Grammar* (Moscow, 1725), Feofan had the translator, Aleksei Barsov, include a special intro-duction "to the curious reader" that explained that these gods were not real, and that the tales contained therein were not actual history. In a sec-ond introduction, Feofan himself explained that the emperor had ex-pressed an interest in the book in 1724 and wanted it published "out of an honest curiosity" about the tales of these pagan gods and where they origi-nated. To forestall any misunderstanding, the book, published in a run of only three hundred copies, included an appendix of Christian writings, supposedly at Peter's insistence, so as to make manifest to an impressionis-tic readership the difference between pagan superstition and true, sacred Christian history.[108] Apollodore's roster of potentially misleading pagan gods, notably, included both Pentheselia and Tomyris.[109]

The only apparent exception to this practice of excluding or demystify-ing pagan allegory among published sermons came from another homily penned by Iavorskii, coincidentally the first of his printed homilies to commemorate St. Catherine's Day, likely in honor of the tsarevna Ekate-rina Ioannovna. Here he spoke at length of pagan gods, albeit to reveal their limitations and unworthiness.

> The god Mercury is revealed as a thief. Jupiter conducts himself outside the law. Saturn himself devoured his own children. Pluto entranced Pros-erpine [his wife], and for this reason there was anger and disorder between them. Neptune wished to destroy Troy, but Apollo saved it. While Venus has your kindness, Pallas is unmerciful. Whichever of them reigns in the rivers does not possess the mountains. Whoever rules the forests does not reign in the lakes.[110]

One cannot compare this sort of supernatural wisdom of a given era *(pre-mudrost' veka)* with the wisdom of God. The [pagan] philosophers put forward these dishonest and false gods. But this is what [St.] Catherine says: the most natural idea fortifies a human being, that your God is himself the one true God. There is none greater than He, none more powerful. But you [philosophers] have so many gods, some of whom have great quality, some lesser.[111]

In other words, these pagan objects of worship are unnatural, inhuman, and contrary to the true strivings of humanity. They are false and ungodly, the very antithesis of identity figures for Christians, and by extension Christian rulers. Unfortunately, the sermon is undated, and nothing in it affixes it to a specific year or site, although presumably it was written well before the emergence of the persona of Catherine/St. Catherine. But its narrative echoes closely the concerns of Turoboiskii, even if in so doing it brought the names of pagan gods into a name day service. Iavorskii, like Feofan in 1709 and 1726, seemed intent on using the pulpit to make it unmistakably clear that the vivid images that adorned the triumphal gates were artistic, imaginary, and one uttered their names in church only to reveal their impotence, their absence of supernatural authority.

Zhivov and Boris Uspenskii have suggested that these specific references were characteristic rhetorical devices of the Ukrainian clerics who entered Russia at the time, a new way of expressing the political legitimacy of the ruler. Where before pagan images had been unclean and incommensurate with Russian Christianity, now they were being domesticated, a sacralized paganism that, in the eighteenth century, became a part of the sacralization of the monarchy.[112] They argue that the very act of linking paganism explicitly with idol worship, as Feofan and others had done, was new and in some sense western. The evidence presented here is largely consistent with that interpretation, but it suggests a less straightforward shift. The link between pagan gods and idol worship had been present—in the Catherinian vita if not elsewhere—centuries before the migration of Ukrainian clerics. Conversely, the pre-Petrine and Petrine *homiletic* discourses of idolatry continued to honor many of the old proscriptions and even elevated them to a new level of didacticism. The militant defense of sanctified space most assuredly arose amidst a state-sponsored cultural transformation, but its exponents, like Feofan and Buzhinskii, struggled to domesticate those forces of cultural change even as they endeavored to implement them as the state's clerical midwives.

Only through God, Feofan repeatedly proclaimed, could something so bold as this coronation be sanctioned and understood. God and Peter the Great.[113] Precedent, history, myth, even Scripture failed at this moment, the sermon seemed to be saying. As he had written in *Pravda voli monarshei*, it was not for mankind to challenge the monarch's will, even if his will violated religious convention and the archbishop's own sensibilities. God alone would judge, not the people, the church, or the vicar of

Christ. This had been the message all along, inscribed even on the memorial coins thrown to the people. One face showed an altar with the imperial crown on a pillow placed upon it. Around the circumference was the inscription "From God and Emperor."[114] By omission Feofan's oration essentially removed the church, the Trinity, the cross, and the clergy from the chain of explanation or responsibility. "The heart of the tsar is in the hands of God" (serdtse Tsarevo po rutse Bozhii), he concluded.[115] "Blessed are you, high family of the monarchy! This is your light, your joy, a glory of your very own making" (Vash se svet, vasha radost', vasha slava svoistvenneishaia).[116] What forms of thanksgiving, he asked, could Russia offer in return? In awe, he concluded, "We do not have the words." And with this last rhetorical surrender to incomprehension the sermon ended abruptly. No final prayer, not even an "amen."

Feofan and the Test of Faith

The unavoidable question arises at this point as to whether Feofan was conveying a personal ambivalence in 1724, carefully enveloped perhaps in codes that only the clergy could see, or even disapproval, at Catherine's coronation. Once Peter died, of course, Feofan made his peace with what was now a fait accompli, and if the official account is to be believed, he became a prime mover in Catherine's ascendancy to ruler. But the sermon flagrantly violated so many conventions and opened itself to so many competing and still accessible levels of meaning that the ambivalence must surely have been intended. So, what, in the last analysis, was Feofan trying to say?

Subsequent coronation sermons, including Feofan's own homilies for Peter II and Anna Ioannovna, reverted to the accepted format, organized around scriptural text and keyed to scriptural marginalia, with little or no recourse to myth. But Feofan's final few homilies in praise of Catherine reflected some of the eccentricities of the 1724 coronation, if considerably muted. On May 7, 1726, for example, Feofan orated a sermon of remembrance at the Holy Trinity Church in St. Petersburg in honor of the second anniversary of Catherine's coronation.[117] This lengthy oration, nominally in honor of the empress, mentioned Catherine exactly twice, both times as the creation of her deceased spouse, Peter, whose name garnered repeated and lavish praise. In contrast to the coronation *slovo*, here Feofan adopted the accepted format of a homily, and it was replete with biblical references and allusions to Christ, the cross, the prophets, and the apostles. Gone were the echoes of pagan and mythological women, with a single exception in which Feofan proclaimed that a [queen's] crown such as Catherine's was present "not just in the pagan histories of antiquity, but also in the sacred books of the Old Testament."[118] The entire homily reprised the message of obedience to God's will. Only God, through Peter, could have delivered one such as Catherine to Russia. As in 1724, Feofan pronounced "the heart of the tsar is in the hands of God," and he repeated this phrase several times, as if to reinforce the impression that Catherine's reign could be understood as the work of God and Peter the Great, and in no other way.[119]

It is in this last phraseology, one could argue, that may be found the essence of Feofan's unease with the circumstances, what might be called the test of his own faith and the theological reconciliation that he attempts between his unshakable loyalty to Peter and his deep-seeded religious convictions, if for no other reason than to convince himself of the rectitude of his public affirmations of actions (Catherine's coronation and then female rule) about which he was unenthusiastic. When Anna Ioannovna acceded to the throne in 1730, Feofan composed a brief but hyperbolic proclamation of nationwide joy and thanksgiving. But his sermon at her coronation in April 1731 was completely devoid of praise—or even any mention—of the new empress. The text contained no expressions of joy at her selection, and more tellingly, it made no effort to connect her to the legacy of Peter the Great, whose name was nowhere to be found in the text.[120] This may have been a strategic decision on Feofan's part, since at that moment he could not know Anna's attitude to Peter's legacy. Still, the absence is striking. A second coronation day oration by Feofan offering public thanksgiving of all the ranks was slightly more generous. In wishing Anna a long life, Feofan compared her briefly to her name day saint, Anna the Prophet. Married at fourteen and widowed at twenty-one, the prophet Anna lived the rest of her very long life as a widow. She is mentioned in the Gospel of Luke as having been entrusted, at the age of seventy-two, with raising the three-year-old virgin Mary until Mary's betrothal to Joseph. She was present at the temple when Mary and Joseph presented the baby Jesus. Feofan expressed the sentiment that the years of widowhood that had been their shared misfortune[121] was evidence that by God's mercy she would emulate her saint not just in name, but in deed ("Upodobil zhe Bog tebe ne imianem tokmo, no i delom tezoimenitoi tvoei Sviatoi Anne Prorochitse; mozhet bo mnogobednoe vdovstvo tvoe soravnitisia vdovstvennomu eia mnogo letiiu, a kak onoiu, tak i s toboiu byl milostivyi Gospod").[122]

This not quite scriptural passage echoed the identification of a living crowned head with a name day saint that had been fundamental to the construction of the Catherinian persona, and it brought the pasage directly into the service of legitimizing female rule. However, it failed to offer personal praise of Anna—an astonishing omission for a panegyric oration—or to endow her with the virtues of her angel. The speech conveys restraint and faint regard, language that in its own way appears even more conditional than the sermon of 1724, which for all its perversity, nevertheless attributed to Catherine the mighty strength of women warriors and the wisdom of female saints. This tone also contrasts markedly with the textual euphoria over the adolescent and little known Peter II's ascen-

sion in 1727, a "new Peter," the grandson of the great emperor. It is difficult, then, to avoid the inference that Feofan had significant reservations
about female coronations and rule, or about the first two instances of it,
neither of which was anticipated in *Pravda voli monarshei*.

Ultimately one cannot read Feofan's mind, and he left behind no private correspondence or diary to explain what motivated him to speak as
he did on this day in 1724. One can only guess how the assembled re-
acted, given their near total silence in the historical record. No one spoke
of it afterward, so far as the written record reveals, except for Bergholz,
who had no idea of its contents. A memoir attributed to Villebois, a
Frenchman serving in the Russian *gardes de marine* at the time, was published only in the mid-nineteenth century. It briefly paraphrased Feofan's
sermon without mentioning the archbishop, and even referred to Semiramis and Tomyris. But that was it. If Feofan's words contained a single
overarching message, it was profoundly religious and directed at the assembled clergy and pious laity, a thundering and fearsome invocation of
an unmediated faith, perhaps his own, a faith beyond human reason or
understanding, in God the Father as the redeemer. Without that, nothing
in Russian experience or in the institutions of the church could succeed in
making sense of Catherine's coronation; nothing could reconcile it with
any doctrine prior to Feofan's *Pravda*.

In this context, it is worth noting that the sermon was omitted from the
official *Opisanie*, other than the brief mention that a *slovo Bozhii* had been
delivered. Unlike Feofan's other major or panegyric sermons, it was not
published as a separate edition, neither in Peter's day nor thereafter. It has
appeared in print only once, in a four-volume edition of Feofan's sermons
and speeches published in the 1760s by the Infantry Corps of Cadets. This
latter piece of publishing history is more consequential than it may seem.
Peter had become interested in the written legacy of his reign during his
later years, and one part of that legacy consisted of sermons, hundreds of
which had been orated during his political lifetime. Deciding which ones
would achieve immortality through print was not easy, and the court engaged the Synod in extended discussion concerning the assemblage and
publication of sermons. Peter wanted to be kept informed of the process
and to be told well in advance which sermons were to appear in print.[123]

Unfortunately, the other sermons of thanksgiving delivered in various
cathedrals in honor of Catherine's coronation have not survived, even
though at least one, by Archimandrite Gedeon, had been approved for
publication.[124] Whether the tone was unique to this single text or emblematic of the event itself cannot be judged. The only other recorded performance for Catherine's coronation was a play, and not a very complex
one at that, and it offers little guidance. Entitled *Fama Rossiae*, this drama
transposed the now firmly established tropes of female bravery and piety
into an allegorical fantasy. It was performed at the Moscow hospital on
May 18, 1724, a mere eleven days after the coronation.[125] The hospital had

been the sight of several public performances during the previous two years, and the *pokhodnyi zhurnal* confirms that Peter and Catherine were in attendance on that day.[126] Located at a site that was both public and unconsecrated, these performances, like those in Natal'ia Alekseevna's theater, had freer reign to blend allegory and faith, and this particular play took full advantage.

Fama Rossiae was authored by a surgery student named Zhurovskii, and it bore the hallmarks typical of the scholastic dramas penned by students at the Moscow Academy during this time, from whose advanced classes Zhurovskii had almost certainly been recruited.[127] Written in Russian, with Latin inscriptions, the play consisted of a pre-prologue, a prologue, and two brief acts constructed around dialogues among the Virtues, including Pallas (Wisdom/Mudrost'), Sapientia (Holy Wisdom/Premudrost'), Fortitudo (Bravery/ Muzhestvo), Victoria, and several others. Each of these virtues corresponded to a figure at court, with the title of Virtus Rossiae being reserved for Catherine herself. For Zhurovskii, as for Peter's ecclesiastical panegyrists, Russia's glory *(fama)* was manifested in military success, in victories at Poltava, Derbent, and elsewhere.[128] Following Peter's own reasoning, the prologue located Catherine's virtue, and thus the justification for her coronation, martially, in her courageous contributions to those victories ("DOBRODETEL' ROSSIISKUIU za muzhestvo i khrabryi podvig ot Rossii koronovannu byti"). The second act, an allegorical representation of the actual coronation, included brief soliloquies by Piety (Blagochestie) and Love (Cupido) that praised Catherine for her faith, goodness, and love.[129] Although the evil forces of Envy, Pride, Rage, and Fury scorned and mocked the coronation, they were decisively countered by Truth and Divine Wisdom, who pointed out the justice and rightness of the coronation. Who or what the malefactors may have represented is anyone's guess.

In the final scene, the road is festooned with flowers, as Russia's Victory, mounted on lions in triumph, expresses thanks to Virtus/ Dobrodetel'/ Catherine and approval of the sight of her with the crown. Virtus, in turn, offered her gratitude to Russia, repeating the unity of victory, courage, and piety. She then bids all the Virtues to labor no more on that day, but to return to their separate quarters.[130] And here the play ends.

Even then, perplexity over the meaning of the coronation did not end. St. Catherine aside, how might the emperor's subjects have understood the event? Discretion and the risk of an accusation of *slovo i delo* (crimes against the name or deeds of the sovereign) constrained most voices to silence,[131] but here and there isolated expressions of disgruntlement did reach the central authorities, specifically the Preobrazhenskii prikaz and the Tainaia kantseliariia. One very curious case from 1726 involved several monastic peasants, convicted as brigands and incarcerated in a labor colony. Two of them, Andrei Labutin and Semen Vasil'ev, accused a third, Iakov Spiridov, of spreading insulting rumors about the empress.[132] Spiridov, so they claimed, had deemed Catherine's coronation illegal because, for the previous three years (i.e., since Peter himself had been crowned as emperor), she had lived with him "in sin and without the crown [of marriage]" *(bludno bez ventsa)*.[133] Insisting that he had been present in Moscow during the coronation and had heard "unseemly talk" *(nepristoinye slova)* in the streets of Moscow, Spiridov termed the empress a foreigner who had no right to the crown. In pursuing its investigation, the Preobrazhenskii prikaz was troubled that no one other than the two complainants had heard Spiridov utter the seditious phrase "in sin and without the crown."[134] They could confirm that there had been widespread expectations within the penal colony of a general amnesty in the wake of the coronation, and this had not happened.[135] Thus, the entire episode may have emerged out of the general disappointment of the inmates instead of a particular concern over female authority. Nevertheless, the Preobrazhenskii prikaz recommended harsh punishment, and in November 1728 Spiridov was duly executed.

Disingenuous or not, the link that the inmates drew between their dashed expectations and the rituals of a distant high politics vividly underscores just how consequential these seemingly arcane and remote rituals could be among the populace, and how uncontrollable their reactions could be. One can only marvel at Spiridov's reasoning wherein he superimposed the old and familiar denunciation of Catherine (that she was a *bludnitsa*) on the act of coronation. Somehow, in his imagination the imperial crown and wedding crown had become one and the same, the wedding of 1712 notwithstanding. Having cohabited with Peter and without the imperial crown, she was and would always be a mere mistress, and no after-the-fact ceremony in Moscow could change that fundamental reality in his way of reasoning. Far from reinforcing her stature, this free-floating and ill-defined coronation might well have conveyed Catherine's vulnerability and—for Spiridov—her immutable illegitimacy. Russian precedent, familiarity, and met expectations, it would appear, could still matter greatly in popular imagination, notwithstanding the archbishop's messages to the contrary.

As a postscript, lest one imagine that St. Catherine was absent from this quixotic but apparently foundational moment, mention should be made of two further episodes in the coronation. The first took place as part of the Kremlin rituals when Catherine and a large entourage of guards and clergy went on a processional from the cathedrals to Voznesenskii Convent to pay homage to the graves of the ancestors *("poklonenie roditel'skim grobam")*.[136] This was a new element for Russian coronations, intended largely as a gesture that brought Catherine together with the many past women of Muscovy's ruling families who were buried there, her political ancestors as it were. More subtly, perhaps, the processional also retraced the route of the Kremlin's St. Catherine's Day processional of the cross that a generation or two earlier had tied the chapel saint with the buried princely women. The *terem* chapel of St. Catherine had long since lost its special identity (replaced to some extent by the St. Catherine chapel in the Summer Palace). But the reclamation of this pathway of the cross, this time on behalf of the imperial rather than the celestial Catherine, and the revival of its gesture of ancestral respect, echoed the meaning of the earlier ritual. Both meanings conveyed a reconnection, however fanciful, to the Muscovite past and in their own way suggested continuity.

The second episode is recounted by Bassewitz, who recollected that the day after the coronation itself, Catherine sat on the throne accepting the well-wishes of the notables and others who were allowed in. The day concluded with a magnificent fireworks display, prominent in which were representations of St. Catherine and the Order of St. Catherine.[137] This open-air presentation, visible in the sky to countless more people than had witnessed the coronation itself or had heard Feofan's sermon, and which was commented on by several foreign guests, announced to the nation who was being crowned, and why. In a display that seems to have anticipated the name day fireworks later on in that year, the pyrotechnics projected into the heavens not Semiramis or Tomyris, but St. Catherine, the empress's one true patron saint, the single sacred identity figure who, after all the words and deeds of the previous days, reigned once again triumphant over all other challengers, just as she had done in antiquity at the court of Maxentius.

9

Sacralizing Female Rule

• On January 28, 1725, Peter the Great died, attended up to the very end by Catherine. As retold in numerous histories, he had languished in bed for several days, afflicted perhaps with pneumonia after having waded into the frigid waters in the village of Lakhta in early November to help free a boat that had run aground. By then he was suffering from other painful ailments and had stopped concealing his declining health.[1]

Hardly a surprise (he had made final confession nearly a week before he died), Peter's passing nevertheless caused considerable shock, in particular among the remnants of his inner circle, the embodiments of his reforms and those with the most to lose if they were undone. The very survival of these reforms, as well as the future of the still fragile Petrine order, depended on a quick and reasonably peaceful succession, which would need to be manufactured without any template or accepted precedence. By the terms of the new rules the monarch alone would choose his successor. But Peter had not done so, at least not in any formal sense, and prior to his death no one had made so bold as to claim to know his intention, if in fact he had one. The questions these insiders faced were, first, who was the best choice and, second, how to announce the resolution to make it conform to the law and public sensibilities.

A. G. Ovsov, Portrait of Catherine as Ruling Empress, 1726

The First Female Monarch

No first-person accounts exist (other than the assorted ex post facto rumors and official versions) that might reveal something of the negotiations and conflicts that led to the choice of Catherine as heir, the first crowned female ruler in Russian history. It may be that in the weeks or days leading up to Peter's death the most prominent loyalists had caucused and resolved the matter privately. Equally plausible is the scenario described later in Feofan's official account that suggested the consensus was reached quickly, but only after Peter died. In any case, the list of choices was short, and none would have been especially appealing. The limitations had been made painfully clear already in 1721, in the formulation of prayers of thanksgiving prescribed by the Synod for the now imperial family.

> O, for our Most Pious Lord Peter the Great, All-Russian Emperor and Sovereign, and our Most Pious Great Lady Empress Ekaterina Alekseevna, and Gracious Ladies Tsesarevnas and Gracious Tsaritsa and Grand Duchess Paraskeva Fedorovna.
>
> And for the Gracious Grand Duke Peter Alekseevich and Gracious Tsarevnas and Grand Duchesses, and for their entire Household and for all of them do we pray, O Lord.[2]

Over the intervening three years the list had gotten shorter still. Other than Catherine, there were Peter's daughters and grandson, Peter Alekseevich, whose elevation carried the real risk of returning his grandmother Evdokia and her anti-Petrine associates to positions of influence. Otherwise, no male candidates loomed on the horizon. Neither of the two sons from Peter's marriage with Catherine had survived beyond early childhood. His half brother Ivan, long since deceased, had two daughters, Anna and Ekaterina, and his sisters had not produced any available sons. And then there was Evdokia herself. In a practical sense, Peter's men had only two choices: anointing Peter Alekseevich with Catherine as regent or accepting some form of female rule.

In the end they chose Catherine, presumably as the safest and least disruptive option, and the one that afforded Peter's men their best chance of holding on to their collective authority. How, then, were they to present to the empire this new turn, this apparent rupture of the unbroken chain of patrilineal authority traced retrospectively again and again through Aleksei Mikhailovich, Vladimir, Constantine, David, and ultimately to God the father? How were the self-conscious constituent audiences, especially the court, the guards' regiments, and especially the clergy, none of whom had been prepared for this change, meant to understand it?

If the previous discussion of the St. Catherine cult has shown the centrality of faith to Petrine political culture, and its importance for the adulation of Catherine as a figure of legitimacy and power, it does not quite get one to female rule. The available evidence, analyzed in the previous chapter, gives no reason to imagine that Peter saw the valorization of his spouse, including the coronation, as a prelude to her succession. Indeed, her iconography in the years preceding Peter's death emphasized ever more her spousal and intercessory role, Buzhinskii's vision of the helpmate Christian warrior. The one possible exception, via the coronation sermon, would have been to link Catherine's ascent to the doctrine of the unchallengeable if mysterious hand of God and will of Peter. This, however, would have been a perilously thin reed on which to balance the inauguration of female rule, and the surviving Petrine *ptentsy* certainly knew it.

But by 1724, Catherine did have a highly visible, carefully constructed, and formally revered persona of her own and clearly distinct from (if largely inclusive of) those represented in the idealized Muscovite tsaritsa. This persona exalted her individual accomplishments and masculine capabilities, rather than those of her spousal position per se. The decision to elevate Catherine from consort to ruler demanded a deft and immediate adjustment of the persona that brought to the fore her heavenly links, both as the living image of St. Catherine and, with Peter now dead, as the metaphorical transposition of the bride of Christ onto the throne of St. Petersburg.

The formal justifications of female rule, its theoretical possibility and subsequent necessity, came in two works by Feofan, the *Pravda voli monarshei* of 1722, which famously explained and defended Peter's new law of succession, and the *Brief Account of the Death of Peter the Great,* which recorded the official version of Peter's final days and Catherine's succession.[3] Feofan devoted most of the *Pravda* to systematically dismantling the principle of primogeniture in the succession in favor of the unfettered will of the reigning monarch. "Now if we have understood thus, we understand beyond a doubt and must unreservedly acknowledge, that every sovereign, in all his other deeds as in that which is our present subject, namely the appointment of the heir to the throne, is absolutely free to act as he chooses."[4] "It must be understood, however, that when the jurists say that the supreme power called *majesty* is not subject to any other power, they mean any human power, for it is subject to God's power, and it must obey the laws of God, both those which he has written in [human] hearts and those which he has handed down in the Decalogue . . . it is subject to God's law only in the sense that it is answerable for transgressing it to God's judgment alone, and not to man's."[5]

Feofan here offered the clearest polemical expression of the irreducible fatherhood of God, echoed in the coronation sermon two years later, and the obligation of all earthly beings, including the monarch, to obey his immutable laws and submit to his eternal judgment. The political constitution that elevated the ruler above all man-made laws and institutions that might mediate between himself and God, what some have termed the emperor's charisma,[6] was both just and feasible, explained the archbishop, because of the irreducibility of grace and the inevitability of the day of judgment. Hardly original, to be sure, and not explicitly Orthodox, but the argument was incomprehensible outside of a cosmology that placed the desire for eternal salvation at the center of all earthly endeavor.

Still, Feofan's political imagination was far from revolutionary, in that he assumed in *Pravda* that the heir would almost always come from among the monarch's sons. In those rare and exceptional cases when "a monarch should be so unfortunate in his sons that he could not see even one fit and able to rule, then, before God, to whom he is accountable for his stewardship, he must seek out a fit and virtuous stranger and appoint [that person] as his successor."[7] In 1722, when Peter had no sons living from whom to choose, this reference to "a fit and virtuous stranger" must have sent minds racing.

What, then, of the current situation, when most of the likely candidates appeared to be women? The text allowed for the theoretical possibility of female rule, and in language that reflected Russia's current dilemma. "These considerations concerning a monarch's sons should also be understood to apply, in the absence of sons, to his daughters (where female rule is not excluded, as in France), and to his brothers and other immediate members of his family if the monarch dies intestate."[8] This careful phraseology ("in the absence of sons," "daughters," "brothers," "other members of the immediate family") hardly constituted a ringing endorsement of *any* variant of female rule, except perhaps for France. True, it did not explicitly exclude wives, sisters, or nieces, but it made no effort to include them either. Implicitly the phrase "other members of the immediate family" appeared to rule out distant relatives or individuals utterly unrelated to the monarch. The language implied that the heir would in almost all imaginable cases be male, which turned out not to be the case just three years later. Everyone at court, as well as the entire foreign diplomatic corps, knew whose names would be on the short list, but the *Pravda* formulation offered only the vaguest directions of how the looming dilemma of Peter's later years might play out in the absence of an obvious heir.

In earlier writings, well before the new decree on succession had come into being, Feofan had expressed himself differently, and he had dwelled on the desirability of an inherited crown, with the heir coming from the immediate family. The monarch's freedom to choose notwithstanding, more than one of Feofan's orations had connected God's will, a well-ordered state, and orderly transitions with the royal bloodline. The most vivid example comes from the thanksgiving homily at the birth of Peter Petrovich, the first male issue of the tsaritsa Catherine, in 1715. As was his wont, Feofan anchored his hosannas to the new tsarevich in history, arguing for the virtue of an inherited throne over a chosen, or elected one. Monarchy, he insisted somewhat artfully, had almost always functioned as an act of inheritance within a single family. The ancient Assyrian state was that way from the time of Nimrod. So too were the ancient lands of Medea and Persia. God imposed the same order on Israel, and even the ancient Egyptian pharaohs accepted this rule. Spain, France ("Gallia"), England, Denmark, Sweden and other strong European states followed the same rule. Even in Africa (Tunis, Ethiopia) and Asia (India, China, Japan), inherited monarchy was the rule. The only exception to this rule of inherited monarchy was Poland, "and we should not envy them that *(da i ne v zavist'!)*."[9]

An inherited throne allowed the sovereign to concern himself with the general well-being *("o dobre obshchem")* of the entire realm, just as he would in his own household. But in most monarchies where the ruler is selected, factions tend to form that struggle against each other for the throne at the expense of the common good. The interregnum is the most dangerous moment in these states, Feofan warns, a time when the risk of a general conflagration becomes palpable, especially when the claims and power of the rivals is more or less equal. Russian history since the Time of Troubles had assuredly confirmed him in this view. To its good fortune, he wrote at that time, Russia has an inherited monarchy and, thus a new son, a second heir, was at hand. "And so we observe, you who hear me, what joy we receive, having received from God a royal son: Russia shall maintain its well-being through the inheritance of the scepter of monarchy, and may this good fortune be long lasting."[10]

The biblical passages that Feofan selected to verify what otherwise had been essentially a statement of pragmatic and secular politics came from three Psalms, namely, 71:11, 98:3, and 78:65,66 (70, 97, and 77 in the Slavonic Old Testament), which he stitched together in a single paragraph, all of it dealing with establishing the house of David as the rulers of Israel. The first of these psalms, alluding to the despair of the Rus' at the death of Vladimir the Great lest his ruling house come to an end, proclaimed, "They say, 'God has forsaken him [David]; pursue him and seize him, for no one will rescue him.'" The second, interposed by Feofan as a rejoinder to the first, reassured, "He [the Lord] has remembered his love and his faithfulness to the house of Israel." (The Russian text adds "and his mercy to Jacob" after "his love"). The third amplified further, "Then the Lord awoke as from sleep, as a man wakes from the stupor of wine. He beat back his enemies; he put them to everlasting shame."[11] Once again, biblical kingship linked the house of David with the house of Vladimir, and then both with the house of Romanov, the new Israel. And just as God had chosen Jacob's line, from which David descended, to inherit Israel's throne, so too he chose the Romanov line, from which Peter, the latter-day David, descended to establish Russia's imperial inherited line. As Psalm 78 continued,

> 70 He chose David his servant
>   and took him from the sheep pens;
> 71 from tending the sheep he brought him
>   to be the shepherd of his people Jacob,
>   of Israel his inheritance.

72   And David shepherded them with integrity of heart;
      with skillful hands he led them.[12]

God's love and mercy brought this to pass both then and now, Feofan
declaimed. It was God's plan (at least in 1715) and Russia's good fortune
that this inheritance of the house of Romanov would continue, ideally
from father to son.

As Feofan would soon learn, such good fortune proved to be fleeting.
Aleksei was disgraced and eliminated from succession in 1718 and Peter
Petrovich died the next year. Feofan was nothing if not adaptable, however. Hence, the *Pravda*. When Peter did die, the remote hypothetical scenarios raised in the *Pravda* became urgent reality. Feofan and Menshikov,
according to most accounts, were rumored to have played the critical role
in orchestrating Catherine's succession in the immediate aftermath of Peter's death; to a lesser extent Peter Tolstoi, Bassewitz (in reconciling
Iaguzhinskii with Menshikov, his erstwhile rival), and the admiral
Apraksin also participated. Campredon's memorandum, for example, emphasized Menshikov's role in winning over the guards' regiments to
Catherine's side during Peter's last days, and thus forestalling the risk of
civil war.[13] Once the emperor had expired, he claimed, the regiments
proved their loyalty by declaring that they would cut off the heads of anyone who opposed granting complete sovereignty to the empress.[14]

For the sake of legitimacy, however, and for what under the circumstances passed for legality, the intentions of the deceased emperor were
paramount. Feofan's own version, in the *Brief Account,* addressed this matter head on. On January 27, with Peter's death seemingly imminent, the
Synod and Senate resolved to convene as soon as the tsar expired. The entire Senate and four members of the Synod held an all-night vigil at the
Winter Palace, along with several members of the nobility. The talk, Feofan writes, was all about the succession.[15] One group insisted that the
scepter could only go to the empress, since she had been so recently
crowned. Others demurred, pointing out that elsewhere the coronation of
a queen did not automatically convey the right to rule, a proposition that
was fully consistent with everything that Feofan had written and preached
on the subject up until this time.

At that very moment an unnamed person recalled that Peter had expressed his intentions just prior to the Persian campaign, that he had
specifically told four of his ministers and two persons from the Synod
[here also unnamed] that he was crowning his spouse, "a custom which
previously did not exist in Russia," so that the throne would not be left
without a successor. With this choice, the empire would be spared the risk
of disorders and troubles inherent in an interregnum. The unnamed herald, Feofan explained, carried the day—as well he should have—and all
present agreed that the empress should inherit the Russian throne. A public declaration was immediately composed, and the assembled party went

to convey the news to the empress, who was still sitting tearfully in the room with Peter's dead body. The supplicants then asked the empress to accept the mantle of rulership, "which God and her spouse had placed upon her." Tearful in time-honored and virtually obligatory fashion, Catherine initially refused but then relented and agreed to become the sovereign head of state, Russia's first formally chosen female ruler, until her death in May 1727.

This version of the succession, however much it may have sanitized the turbulence going on behind closed doors at the Winter Palace, immediately became gospel. Quickly published in both St. Petersburg and Moscow in large but not massive editions, Feofan's text held true to the twin principles of kingly discretion and the will of God as the only sources of supernatural authority left available. Catherine would now rule as sovereign because this was what Peter intended and what God had ordained. In what passed for legality under the circumstances that was all that mattered. Everyone in authority recognized, however, that much more would be needed than a mere pamphlet before the legal fact of female rule, especially the rule of this particular female, became natural. God's will, however mysterious, had to be displayed in every manner possible, and insisted upon as often as possible, if the non-noble, non-Russian, non-male Catherine, still deemed an incestuous mistress and usurper of the rightful place of the living Evdokia in some quarters, the widow of the anti-Christ in others, were to reign as *pomazanitsa* (the anointed one) with at least a semblance of legitimacy. Lest there be any doubt about this plan of action, or about the urgency of generating clerical support for the official line, the relevant agencies grew particularly vigilant about offenses to the now reigning empress. Thus, in October 1725, the Preobrazhenskii prikaz investigated a report concerning several clergy from Menshikov's estate in the Nizhnii Novgorod region who made knowing claims about how long Catherine would reign.[16] Under pain of death, two clergy, Stefan Fedorov and Ivan Mikhailov, acknowledged hearing that Catherine would remain on the throne either five years or three years—the accounts varied—and that this rumor had originated in the local cathedral.[17] Interrogated further, they claimed to have been drunk when they heard the rumor and when they repeated it (entirely plausible, of course, but this was also a well-rehearsed exculpatory line in Russian history). Hence they could provide no further details or names.[18] The file ended in January 1727 with no indication of the action taken.

If not quite rising in imagination to pretender myths—Peter the Great was indeed dead—stories such as this one, or the rumor discussed in the last chapter of a general emancipation of labor-camp inmates, demonstrated how fluid popular understanding of Catherine's authority could be in the months after her accession, or how quickly the vacuum caused by a paucity of broadly accepted readings of female authority could be filled by locally invented ones. Once again, therefore, Gavriil Buzhinskii provided the spiritual message that enabled the transition to present the illusion of seamlessness. In a remarkable sermon preached on the first anniversary of Peter's death, Buzhinskii harkened to a theme made common in the panegyrics of 1725: the emperor's two bodies, the body natural and the body politic.[19] Peter was dead in the flesh, his body lay in the sarcophagus, and yet he remained alive in the deeds and structures he left behind. This premise, so fundamental to Christian kingship since the late Middle Ages, especially in Britain, was less familiar in Russia, where the older dualism of God in heaven and tsar on earth had prevailed, side by side with the allegorical reincarnation (the living Constantine, and others) of sacred kingship. Nevertheless, the idea that the political body of Peter lived on through his good works reverberated in Russian churches and academies throughout the eighteenth century, and beyond. (In a sermon of 1770, Archbishop Platon put it even more boldly, declaiming that Peter was resurrected *["on voskres"]*).[20] In the presence of the empress who was adorned with both the crown and the St. Catherine's cross, he intoned, "Peter the Great is alive: I am the resurrection and the life . . . and whoever believes in me will live forever. This knowledge should be a salve to your heart's wound, Russia,"[21] for Peter was "forevermore our guide and teacher."[22]

Peter, Buzhinskii continued, left behind his wife, Catherine, through whom he lived on as well. His spirit had ascended to Christ in heaven, but his bride, the bride of the now celestial Peter, remains on earth. Here, finally, the ruling empress Catherine was transformed metaphorically into the bride of Christ, adorned on earth like her angel with her queenly crown, her husband in heaven. Much like the 1721 icon in the Nevskii Monastery, the mystical marriage of Christ and St. Catherine was reproduced as the union of Catherine and Peter. The living Catherine now ruled, however briefly, as the chosen both of Peter and Christ, the complete incarnation of St. Catherine—save perhaps the virginity.

Catherine's entourage, including the empress herself, embraced this identity with the regal angel wholeheartedly. On June 15, 1725, she ordered a second bulwark to be built by the harbor, to be named after St. Catherine.[23] On August 7, she dedicated the private church at the Summer Palace to St. Catherine and, as the daily entries of the *kamerfur'er* confirm, she made it a point to attend liturgy there quite often.[24] In March of the next year she gave a portrait of St. Catherine, apparently painted by Peter himself, to the Lithuanian hetman Sapego.[25] Lockets also were made of Catherine in the pose of St. Catherine. A medallion *(panagiia)* of her reign in the form of a crown includes a picture of the empress in the pose of St. Catherine. These medallions symbolized the rank of a bishop, but they had been worn by members of the tsarist family since the sixteenth century. They were thus emblems of the mythical continuity of Russian rulership under God and the church, Catherine's sacred bond with holy Rus'.[26]

The state of official mourning obliged Catherine to celebrate her name day in a subdued manner in 1725, primarily with a service and a sermon by Lopatinskii, even though the court diary did note that the homes in St. Petersburg remained illuminated throughout the evening.[27] Her name day that year also was chosen for the official opening of the Academy of Sciences, with St. Catherine's blessing replacing that of the pagan gods, so the official proclamation explained, who had adorned the academy of ancient Rome.[28] At the banquet that evening the academy's president, Blumentrost, toasted the empress and recognized her as the academy's patron. The next year the name day was celebrated lavishly over a two-day period, with a mixture of church services, parades, feasts, dancing, and fireworks.[29] Greetings came from all corners of the empire, and with little of the mournfulness of the previous year.[30] Recognizing the political dimension of the St. Catherine persona, several individuals and parishes petitioned to construct St. Catherine churches and chapels on their land. The French envoy commented in his report that the entire month preceding had been taken up with preparations for the festivities.[31] In 1726, at least this event outshone every other public festivity in the capital, a clear indication of the political importance the empress's entourage placed on her saint.

In February 1727, a landlord requested, and received, permission to add a stone chapel of St. Catherine onto a church on his land in the village of Elmanovo (Glinskii stan, Vereiskii uezd).[32] In June 1727, the Synod approved a petition to build a St. Catherine's church in Pereiaslavl-Zaleskii in eternal memory of the recently deceased empress.[33] A Georgian church of St. Catherine was begun in October 1725 in Derbent, the locale of Peter's most recent battle against Persia, a Muslim power and the place where he allegedly spoke of his intention to have Catherine succeed him.[34] Noble families also grew enamored of the name Catherine for their daughters. The memoirs of Prince Iakov Petrovich Shakhovskoi, for example, described the scene at the home of his patron Ivan Golovkin on November 24, 1741, in which a number of the women present, including Golovkin's own daughter Catherine, had gathered to celebrate their common name day.[35]

There was also some effort to construct a direct female parallel to princely resurrection, as in a well-known 1725 engraving by Aleksei Zubov commissioned by the Synod in which Catherine is surrounded by fifty-six Russian rulers (all of them men) from Riurik to Peter. The inscription, which spoke of Catherine's loyalty to Peter's legacy, included the phrase, "Russia's second Ol'ga, the worthy descendent of a great monarch."[36] But for whatever reason, this imagery of a second Ol'ga appeared infrequently. And only once, one should note for the record, did she reprise Amazonia, and then as a fleeting gesture enacted outside of consecrated space or ceremony.[37] In the end Catherine's heavenly blessings, the only bases upon which sacral legitimacy could possibly rest, were cast almost entirely as her saint's living image and as the chosen one of her heavenly spouse, the first mother of the fatherland. Thus, on July 10, 1725, Catherine, dressed in her cloak of mourning, attended a service of thanksgiving at the capital's Trinity Church to celebrate the anniversary of Peter's liberation at Pruth, the iconic foundational moment of Catherine's special designation by Peter. At the first anniversary of Peter's death, as one more of the multiple ritual enactments of her selection as the spouse of a heavenly tsar, she attended a memorial service at the Church of Peter and Paul and two days later marked the end of official mourning with a service at the Church of St. Catherine.[38] In this way Catherine I became, in turn, both the model and the bodily vessel through which the divine sanction of female rule would be ritually reaffirmed over the rest of the century. A model, in that subsequent female rulers went to considerable lengths to publicize their own name day saints, and themselves as living images, often at the expense of the name day saints of their predecessors. A vessel, in that hers was the sacred womb that produced Elizabeth and in that through Catherine's precedence Sophie of Zerbst was rechristened as the new Ekaterina Alekseevna, a second Catherine for the new Peter. It was thus fitting that Catherine chose the closing of the liturgy for Elizabeth's name day as the moment to inscribe her in the Order of St. Catherine, thereby making her daughter (and her daughter's angel) the second woman of the royal family to become a Knight of Ransom and guardian of Christian empire.[39]

The Daughter of Catherine I

A recent scholar of the Elizabethan court has contended that "Peter's daughter had been preparing herself for November 25, 1741, carefully and persistently for more than ten years."[40] Ten years may be an exaggeration, but the larger point is certainly true: Elizabeth's ascension to the throne had been carefully planned and well choreographed. On the evening of November 24, 1741, Tsarevna Elizaveta Petrovna attended a St. Catherine's Day mass, knowing full well that, as she knelt in prayer to her late mother's angel, a coup was taking place that would bring her to the throne on the following day. Shortly after eleven o'clock, seven grenadiers came to inform her that the coup was under way.[41] Years earlier Empress Anna had dropped St. Catherine's Day from the calendar of official state holidays in favor of the day of Anna the Prophetess (December 9), her own saint.[42] (She had downgraded, but did not eliminate entirely, the newly transposed day of Alexander Nevskii, another celestial symbol of Peter's Russia, or perhaps more to the point, Peter's branch of the Romanov succession.) Empress Anna also had made the Order of St. Catherine less visible, preferring instead to celebrate the Polish Order of the White Eagle, which she associated with her late husband, who had been an inductee.[43] November 24 nevertheless remained a noteworthy feast day on the church calendar, and Elizabeth, openly pious and respectful of her mother, celebrated it regularly during the 1730s.

Elizabeth, of course, was renowned before 1741 for patronizing church institutions very extensively, and she relied heavily on religious imagery to establish her political identity.[44] Iconography of St. Elizabeth abounded during her twenty-year reign, in particular in the capital. The iconostasis of the Church of the Savior dedicated in 1737 depicted Christ and Alexander

Nevskii together on the right side, and Mary and St. Elizabeth on the left.[45] A decade later, on September 2, 1747, the new Church of Saints Zachariah and Elizabeth was consecrated in honor of the empress's name day saint.[46] Then in September 1756, the empress dedicated yet another church of this name on Voskresenskii Prospect.[47] Each of these gestures—and there were many others associating St. Elizabeth simultaneously with the Holy Family and with Nevskii (whose holiday was elaborately reinstated in 1743)—reproduced in great and visible detail the symbolic politics of Catherine I.[48]

Elizabeth sought to derive her legitimacy in large part from her mother's testament. Although it is rarely mentioned in the literature, she went to considerable lengths throughout her reign to reassert the matrilineal link and to honor her mother's memory. Her very first manifesto of November 25 emphasized her blood link *("blizost' po krovi")* to Peter the Great *and* Catherine I, as did the sermon of thanksgiving for her enthronement delivered by Dmitrii Sechenov.[49] A homily orated on Elizabeth's name day in 1742 by Archbishop Arsenii Matveevich, the zealous and irascible defender of Orthodoxy against its "enemies and plunderers" real or imagined, in the presence of the empress and her newly named heir, the young Peter, praised her for pursuing her faith through good deeds. It went on at some length about biblical prophets, remarking that while every prophet's father had been a prophet himself, this was not true of most of their mothers. The exception was John the Baptist, both of whose parents (conveniently, Saints Elizabeth and Zachariah[50]) achieved recognition as prophets. "And we observe a comparable example in you [Empress]. For you are a monarch [born] of monarchs, an empress from emperors."[51] This was quite a family romance that Matveevich had painted: the virgin queen, an echo of the Mother of God, affiliated simultaneously with John the Baptist and, through her name day saint, John the Baptist's mother!

Matveevich was not alone in combining the living image of St. Elizabeth with family metaphors from the early church so as to exalt a ruler whom the upper clergy fervently believed to be its ardent supporter. Elizabeth's coronation sermon, composed by Archbishop Amvrosii of Novgorod, went to great lengths to associate the new monarch with all manner of figures from the birth of Christianity. Christ himself had chosen Elizabeth for the throne as God's instrument to protect the realm from false teachings, as the apostles had preached and the female martyrs had exemplified in their lives. In the spirit of the living image, Amvrosii spoke of how the Virgin Mother of God had from time to time visited the home of Zachariah and Elizabeth, congratulating them on the birth of John. And now, through the blessing of the son (a reference to Jesus, John the Baptist, or both), Russia had received its own Elizabeth onto the throne of her parents, whose spirit lived on within her. If Peter I was a second Solomon, Elizabeth was the new Judith. "We see in her chaste *(devicheskoi)* spirit God's long-term design, we see an indomitable bravery *(muzhestvo),* a heroic heart, a high divine wisdom, a fearless strength (khrabrost'), a love and mercy for the fatherland without artifice."[52] Although Amvrosii never mentioned Catherine I or St. Catherine directly, he did reprise a theme that had been central to the legitimation of Catherine's reign by reminding the congregants that the Orthodox Church was the bride of Christ ("nevesta khristova tserkov' pravoslavnaia"), so as to reveal the divine foreshadowing of Elizabeth's ascent to power. But in a transparent echo of Matthew 16:18, Amvrosii declared that the Petrine rock on which the throne rested was Peter's beloved daughter ("kamennoe Petra Velikogo osnovanie, to est' Dshcher' Ego vseliubezneishuiu").

Even in rough paraphrase, the literary license of these two sermons is apparent. Formally, however, the orations followed the scholastic model of Bible-centered commentary. Within a few years this would begin to change as a number of leading court preachers began to experiment with language and thematic structure. Departing from Church Slavonic (or Latin) and the scholastic formulae upon which Russian sermons had relied since Semen Polotskii's day, some Elizabethan hierarchs began to preach and write in Russian and to experiment with literary flourishes designed to win the approval of the increasingly Europeanized noble congregants. As Viktor Zhivov has pointed out, these modifications are associated largely with Archimandrite Gedeon Krinovskii (1730–1763) of the Trinity-St. Sergius Monastery, who "strove to attract his listeners' attention not so much by moral pathos as by sensitivity to the tastes of his upper-class audience."[53] This newly found attentiveness to the sensibilities of audience differed markedly from Feofan's preoccupation with the many layers of prescription of just a few years previous. Determined to reach the ears of even the least attentive laity, Feofan kept the surface language relatively straightforward. Gedeon, by contrast, introduced literary references and stories into his homilies, as much to amuse his audience and to hold their attention as to edify them.

The leading panegyrists, including Elizabeth's preferred preachers, Amvrosii Iushkevich (1690–1745), the bishop of Vologda; Arsenii Matseevich (1709–1780), metropolitan of Rostov; and Dmitrii Sechenov (1709–1767), metropolitan of Novgorod, witnessed these changes and some endeavored to adapt to them.[54] In so doing they sustained the Catherinian theme by anointing Elizabeth the daughter of Peter the Great (as is invariably noted) and of Catherine I (words that the scholarship almost always leaves out).[55] Three weeks after the coup, a sermon by Amvrosii stated "with a great diligence Peter obtained [his achievements]; and in all these matters Catherine was also present and similarly achieved."[56] Kirill, the archimandrite of Zaikonospasskii Monastery reiterated this theme: "The Lord gave her a brave/manly (muzhestvennoe) heart, the spirit of Peter, the courage of Judith. . . . Do you know, children, who I am? And whose daughter I am? My magnanimous parents, Peter the Great and Catherine toiled, commanded rectitude, created a magnificent treasure with their mighty labors [italics added]."[57]

A printed description of a 1742 fireworks display in honor of the future Peter III refers to him as "the worthy grandson of His Imperial Majesty, Peter the Great, and the Empress Catherine."[58] A panegyric on Elizabeth's birthday, December 18, 1741, praised Elizabeth for recognizing and abjuring the vanity of striving for greatness without the handiwork of God. "Who could have harbored any doubts that she, this most worthy daughter of Peter the Great and the praiseworthy Empress Catherine, in her ascent to the throne [occupied by] these glorious parents, would be endowed by nature both with the heroic bravery of her great father and the magnanimous virtues of her mother?"[59] This same birthday, celebrated literally days after the coup, included a massive display of fireworks whose centerpiece was a great fire wheel, a universally recognized symbol of the Catherine/St. Catherine persona.[60] The event had other visual displays of the new empress flanked by both her parents.

Sechenov, who at the time was serving on a commission to convert Muslims and pagans in Nizhnii Novgorod and Kazan, orated a sermon on March 25, 1742, extolling Elizabeth for reviving the pious zeal of her mother, Catherine, who had converted to Orthodoxy when asked to by her spouse ("Ekaterina, sobliudi pravoslavnuiu veru").[61] One month later, at the coronation service in the Kremlin, Amvrosii articulated what would be an abiding religious trope of Elizabeth's reign: the piety of the virgin. "We see in her chaste soul (v dushe devicheskoi) the marvelous work of God. We see indomitable bravery (muzhestvo), a heroic heart, exalted divine wisdom, fearless courage (khrabrost'), and love and an alloyed mercifulness toward the fatherland."[62]

A verse celebrating the treaty with Sweden in 1743 continued this theme of dual parentage. Praising Elizabeth as the securer of peace ("utverzhditel'nitsa mira"), the paean marvels at her success in securing victory so quickly and explicitly harkens back to the time of Catherine, calling Elizabeth "the daughter of heroes and glorious monarchs."[63] Here and in numerous other texts, the lineage of the original comes from both her parents, a fact that would have been obvious long ago had the practice of cutting off the quotes just before her mother was named not been adopted.

The formal proclamation of ascendancy published three days after Sechenov's sermon explained that Elizabeth's right to rule derived from a clause in Catherine's testament allegedly prescribing that, if Peter II were to die childless, he should be succeeded by Elizabeth, assuming of course that Peter II predeceased her.[64] As Anisimov has shown, however, the testament said no such thing, and instead delineated a different order of preference, albeit one that accepted female rule. Upon the death of Peter II the throne would pass to Anna Petrovna, Elizabeth's sister, and Anna Petrovna's heirs. Only if Anna Petrovna died childless, the testament prescribed, would Elizabeth become empress.[65] Once again the vaunted right of the monarch's will was being honored in the breach, yet nominally confirmed in the official record.

Still, the clause asserting Anna's precedence did establish the distinct possibility, if not desirablility, that female rule would recur, perhaps indefinitely.

> 8. If the Grand Duke [Peter II] were to expire without heirs, then Tsesarevna Anna Petrovna and her descendents would succeed him. After her, Tsesarevna Elizabeth and her descendents, and then the Grand Duchess and her descendents. However, heirs of the male sex take precedence over those of the female sex, and under no circumstances shall anyone occupy the Russian throne who does not follow Greek [Orthodox] Law or who holds another crown.[66]

Perhaps because of this documentary sleight of hand, Elizabeth went to considerable lengths to return the memory of her mother to public consciousness and to official memorialization. At stake, after all, was the ascendancy not just of the Petrine line of the family, but also of the Catherinian branch of that line, of which she was the offspring, as against the branch of Evdokia, which had produced the second Peter. These images of devotion and filial piety competed with and complemented a much wider assortment of media and visual representations of female power than had been the case in her mother's day. As the court records show, the pious and officially unwed Elizabeth was more than willing to be represented as pagan or mythological goddesses in secular art, balls, and public spectacles. But public piety occupied a very prominent place in her persona, and a central affirmation of that piety was the blessing of her mother's angel, whose name day now served the added role of initiating the annual celebration of Elizabeth's rise to power, each celebration now reinforcing the other.

The feast day of St. Catherine returned to state calendars, and Elizabeth is recorded as having observed it regularly with a mass and court ceremony, feasts and balls well into the night.[67] As if to carve the date permanently into the state calendar, November 24 was further inscribed as the annual day of the St. Catherine Order.[68] When her future daughter-in-law, Sophie, converted to Orthodoxy shortly after her arrival on Russian soil in 1744, Elizabeth gave her the name of Ekaterina Alekseevna in memory of her mother. This act, rich in symbolic possibilities, ritually reincarnated the first Catherine so that Sophie could wed the new Peter, a reconstitution of the marriage that had generated both the empire and Elizabeth herself. Lacking an official husband or legitimate offspring, she ritually reproduced her own progenitors instead, thereby symbolically reenacting the virgin birth. It was this unity of husband and wife, imperator and imperatritsa, Peter and Catherine, from which Elizabeth repeatedly drew her own heritage and her fitness to rule, and which she restaged in the marriage of her nephew, the new Peter, to the newly renamed Catherine. Perhaps aware of this iconic link between the intercessor saint and the living empress, the Swedish Lutheran congregation in St. Petersburg received permission to construct a stone church

S. I. Poliakov, Portrait of St. Catherine, 1759

of St. Catherine on Malaia Koniushenaia almost immediately after the arrival of the heir's new bride, the second Catherine.[69]

To explore in full the rich and multivalent Elizabethan imagery of the triumphant virgin daughter and the metaphoric rebirth of the celestial parents deserves a separate study unto itself, far more than even the most patient of readers is prepared to endure at this point. Instead, let this section conclude with just a single visual example of the revived cult, an icon of St. Catherine painted by the court artist Stepan Ivanovich Poliakov in 1759.[70] An inscription on the icon reveals that the scene was painted on the commission of Princess Elena Vasil'evna Dolgorukaia in memory of her daughter Catherine. Standing erect with sword in her left hand and sheath in her right, the saint wears both the corona of heaven and the crown of royalty. As the archangel observes her from heaven, two cherubs place the wedding wreath on her head. To one side is a prayer to St. Catherine on behalf of the empress. It calls upon the holy martyr—brave, beautiful, wise, virginal—to employ her mercy to pray for the empress and to intercede on her behalf in the kingdom of heaven so that Elizabeth too may use bravery, piety, and wisdom to protect Russia from its enemies and to pass on to her successor *(naslednik)* [i.e., the reborn Peter] the same heavenly blessings through the ages.

The Second Catherine

When she took power in mid-1762, Catherine II was under considerable pressure to legitimate her right to rule. Like Catherine I, Anna, and Elizabeth, she had come to the throne in the midst of a political crisis and without the necessary imprimatur from her predecessor, as mandated by Peter the Great's law of succession. The nuptial contract between Catherine and Peter stipulated that Catherine could become the heir only if Peter died childless, a circumstance that technically was obviated by the birth of the proclaimed heir, the future Paul I.[71] Like Catherine I and all the subsequent consorts, she was a non-Russian and convert to Orthodoxy who gained the crown from a deceased husband, and like Anna and Elizabeth, she was elevated to power on the backs of powerful court factions, whether they be the demands of the *generalitet* or a coup orchestrated by armed elite regiments. However, Catherine II was in other respects unique among them. She had been brought to Russia specifically to be the consort of the heir to the throne. By contrast, Elizabeth had never married, at least officially; Anna had been sent to Kurland to be consort to a foreign duke, but had spent most of her life as a widow; and Catherine I was a helpmate and informal consort for years before her official marriage. Catherine II, like all the others (including the female regents Anna Leopoldovna and before her Sofia Alekseevna and Elena Glinskaia) ruled without the presence of an official consort, an unstated but seemingly absolute requirement to remain a female ruler in Russia. Women in power could have lovers and perhaps even secret husbands, as is often surmised for both Elizabeth and Catherine II. But they could not have a male consort, and non-Romanov potential heir, sitting beside them, given the unruly politics of eighteenth-century Russian succession. The second Catherine followed a singular route to official spouselessness, however. Alone among the female rulers, she came to the throne as the willing beneficiary of a coup that first unseated, and then murdered, her own husband, the reigning emperor, Peter III. Of all the irregular paths to the eighteenth-century imperial throne, complicity in the regicide of one's husband had, until 1762, not been one of them.

Unlike her predecessors, Catherine II had the advantage of multiple female precedents, as a result of which she was less obliged than the other reigning women to articulate the right of female rule per se around the pantheon of female saints. Instead she was compelled to convey *her own* right to rule, which she did throughout her reign by means of an array of proclamations, ritual displays, portraits, and public ceremonies. Yet even she, by far the most secularist of Russia's female monarchs, turned repeatedly to St. Catherine and to the larger lineage of female piety—including the chastity myth—to establish her standing as an Orthodox ruler. During her reign the capital saw several new St. Catherine churches appear, including a Catholic (begun in July 1763 and dedicated in 1783) and an Armenian (dedicated in 1779) cathedral located side by side on Nevskii Prospekt, both of which remain in operation.[72] The former is also the burial place of Catherine's early lover and late Polish king, August Poniatowski.[73] A St. Catherine's church (begun under Elizabeth) was consecrated on August 4, 1764, at the newly opened Monastery of the New Virgin in Smolnyi. A year later Catherine dedicated the church of Saints Elizabeth and Zachariah at Smolnyi in homage to the deceased empress.[74] The chapel at the Academy of Arts opened in the same year, and it too was (and remains) dedicated to St. Catherine.[75] So also was a wooden church of 1764 opened on Panteleimonovskaia Street, next to the capital's church of St. Panteleimon.[76] The Trinity Church of the Kabardinskii Regiment on Vasil'evskii Island was renamed after St. Catherine in the 1760s.[77]

Many older churches throughout the empire also took to building altars and side chapels *(prideli)* of St. Catherine at this time. In the Moscow and St. Petersburg dioceses alone there were several new St. Catherine side chapels dating from the later eighteenth century, many of them in important sanctuaries. These included St. Isaac's Cathedral in Petersburg, which installed matching chapels of St. Catherine and Alexander Nevskii;[78] a side chapel in the Peter and Paul Cathedral;[79] and the church of the Second Corps of Cadets (the Alexander Nevskii Church), which added a St. Catherine chapel in 1762.[80] In Moscow, the list of St. Catherine *prideli* was even longer, including the Church of Nicholas the Wonderworker, the Convent of St. George, the Church of St. Dmitrii, a church of the Savior, a church of Saints Kira and John, and quite a few more.[81] Other noteworthy St. Catherine churches and chapels opened at the homes and estates of prominent individuals of the chief of gendarmes; the estate of Count Alexander Romanovich Vorontsov, the president of the Commerce College; the Moscow household church of Ivan Betskoi; the Moscow home of A. V. Saltykov; the Tambov Convent of the Transfiguration.[82]

Catherine ordered two thrones installed at the Peter and Paul Cathedral, one in the name of the apostles Peter and Paul and a second, constructed in 1773, for St. Catherine. Subsequent to this, the cathedral celebrated processionals of the cross on both of the relevant festival days, June 29 and November 24.[83] Although most of her vast portraiture was decidedly secular, the empress remained mindful of the visual element of the Catherine/St. Catherine persona. The most outstanding example of this came with the remodeling of the Dormition Cathedral in Vladimir between 1768 and 1774. Catherine instructed the College of Economy to budget 14,000 rubles for the work and to order a new iconostasis for the cathedral. The lower row of the iconostasis included an icon of St. Catherine across from where Catherine the Great had stood to pray when in the cathedral. By some accounts the visage on the icon was of Catherine the Great herself.[84]

Catherine also wasted no time in reinstating her saint's day on the official calendar, and court records show that the capital celebrated it regularly, even in those years when the empress was absent.[85] But, as the descriptions show, the central locus of the celebration (or at least of its official recordings) had moved gradually but decisively away from the portentous consecrated space of cathedral, service, and sermon to the more light-hearted public realm of feasts, performances, and *potekhi* (amusements). The official court diary of 1763 recorded that the empress celebrated her name day in Tsarskoe selo, beginning with a parade at eleven o'clock in the morning. An hour later the new empress emerged in the regalia of the Order of St. Catherine to greet those assembled. They proceeded to the church for a mass, after which the empress was honored with a 101-gun salute. She then dined with her company (including the ladies of her order) and received a 51-cannon salute. Tsarevich Paul then received his own 31-cannon salute. In the evening she and her party repaired to the Amber Room for cards, songs, and violins. She had a late supper with twenty-eight cavaliers and ladies of the court.[86] Similar celebrations took place at court in subsequent years.

With the flourishing of print during the 1770s and 1780s this annual spectacle took on a second life as published news. The official newspapers, *Sanktpeterburgskiia vedomosti* and *Moskovskiia vedomosti,* published descriptions of the festivities for these state holidays, and the articles leave no doubt that St. Catherine's Day was, once again, a very major event. The November 28, 1777, issue of *Sanktpeterburgskiia vedomosti* informed its readers that the celebration began at eleven in the morning, when dignitaries of both sexes assembled at court along with representatives of the nobility. At noon they were joined on the nearby parade grounds by the diplomatic corps. At 12:30, the empress emerged, adorned with the regalia of the Order of St. Catherine, and was led in by her courtiers and the cavaliers of her order. All then attended a liturgy at the court church, with Archbishop Gavriil Petrov presiding. At this point the assembled celebrants returned to the Winter Palace for a formal ball.[87] Correspondents from Riga and Kaluga reported in subsequent issues that they too had celebrated the empress's name day. In Riga the local dignitaries celebrated with a dinner and a performance of two French comedies, "Niania" and "Zalog," at the home of the vice governor. The Kaluga remembrance was decidedly more spiritual, with a morning service in the cathedral and a midday dinner. Kaluga's authorities also chose the occasion to announce the opening of a new school.[88] These celebrations revived the link between St. Catherine and Alexander Nevskii, in part by inviting the first four classes of the Order of Alexander Nevskii to participate in St. Catherine's Day celebrations, often side by side with the Order of St. Catherine.[89] In return, the empress celebrated with them on August 30, typically by walking in the processional of the cross (as had Elizabeth), at which moments she often wore the insignia of the Order of St. Catherine.

For the first time, a separate printing of the St. Catherine service appeared in 1765.[90] St. Catherine's Day sermons also reappeared, albeit with considerably less at stake ideologically than before. Thus, two name day sermons by Arsenii Vereshchagin (1779 and 1794), at the time the bishop of Tver, praise Catherine the Great as "God's anointed one", and St. Catherine as an example of "true faith and a great soul." But neither of these contains the language of the living image, instead using the occasions to praise godliness in general. Catherine the Great is the light of the fatherland and a source of divinely inspired glorious deeds, but nothing more.[91] Similarly, Arsenii's sermon at the dedication of the Church of St. Catherine at the Second Corps of Cadets in 1804 (by which time the new law of succession had all but precluded female rule in the future), lavished praise on Peter the Great, Catherine the Great, and Alexander I, but made almost no mention of St. Catherine.[92] An unpublished name day sermon of 1784,[93] orated in the empress's presence, returned for its theme to one of the biblical texts most commonly associated with St. Catherine, the parable of the ten virgins in Matthew 25: "At that time the kingdom of heaven will be like ten virgins who took their lamps and went out to meet the bridegroom. Five of them were foolish and five were wise. The foolish ones took their lamps but did not take any oil with them. The wise, however, took oil in their jars along with their lamps."[94] It too eschewed the political language of the living image in favor of a disquisition on true enlightenment and reason, the value of experience, and the necessity of placing one's fate in the hands of God.[95] The empress was referred to only once, as *"monarkhinia,"* whose crown represented her love of humanity, wisdom, and godliness. All these attributes were consistent with the St. Catherine persona, but the sermon did not connect the two. Finally, Bishop Amvrosii Serebrennikov of Olonetsk (later, archbishop of Ekaterinoslav and member of the Imperial Russian Academy) published a name day service in 1786 that made no mention whatsoever of the empress or the saint. For him, this was an occasion to praise Orthodoxy as the embodiment of true faith and love, and to extol its superiority over Roman Catholicism.[96] Other clerics known to have published name day sermons in the empress's presence included Gavriil, the important archbishop of Novgorod (1777).[97]

None of these Catherinian sermons bore the immense ideological weight of the name day sermons for earlier female rulers. This de-emphasis of the living image reflected, in part, the broader changes in Russian homiletics that had begun in midcentury. Although still organized around biblical exegesis, the sermons downplayed biblical history and precedent and dwelled instead on the relevance of Scripture to the here and now, as guides for living a Christian life. This, of course, was what the newly emergent court literati demanded, but the disconnection between saint (barely mentioned in any of the name day sermons of this era) and living image in what were essentially panegyrics is still striking. As an unmistakable turn toward secularization, it reflected a shift in the meaning of the female monarch's name day. Rather than constituting an annual—and apparently essential—reassertion of the special divine sanction of female rule, as it had for much of the century, the name celebrations of Catherine II's reign seemingly took that sanction for granted. So commonplace had female rule become, so well known were its prescriptive foundations within the court and educated society, that the necessity of regularly and thunderously restating them from the pulpit became moot. Breaking with tradition, both Catherine and the Synod permitted lay literati to celebrate the day. Several of Catherine's name day texts, in fact, were neither clerically authored nor orated on consecrated space, a jarring shift toward *obshchestvo* (educated lay society) and further evidence of how normalized female rule had become, and how it no longer required the intense reaffirmation of the saint's living image. Thus, in both 1762 and 1783, Dmitrii Anichkov, a student and later instructor of mathematics, made a public speech at Moscow University in honor of the empress's name day.[98] On November 28, 1775, the distinguished jurist, Semen Desnitskii, delivered a public speech of national thanksgiving for Catherine's name day.[99] And, in 1783 Khariton Chebotarev, a professor of rhetoric and history, published a name day *slovo* of sorts that had been delivered on November 25 the previous year at a public gathering *("publichnoe sobranie")* dedicating a new wing at Moscow University.[100] This secularization of name day celebrations was part of a broader convergence of homiletic and lay writing, reflecting perhaps the participation of educated clergy in the broader streams of Russian intellectual life and the desire of these clergy to reach educated parishioners by adapting their rhetorical and narrative practices. In that case the orated text became something of a performance, even a presentation of the literary self, and as such was—in the Russian twilight of female rule—worlds removed from the strict separations of sacred and worldly speech and space of Iosif Turoboiskii in 1703 and his clerical successors.

Epilogue

• Over the preceding chapters this book has put forth the following overarching propositions relating to the intersection of religion, gender, and politics in early modern Russia. First of all, it has—I hope—demonstrated that St. Catherine of Alexandria, present in Russian Orthodoxy from the earliest surviving church texts, emerged as a venerated cult figure within the Muscovite court during the early sixteenth century and that her cult grew in visibility and importance among the ruling elites from that time forward. This cult drew from the same sources as did the St. Catherine cults in western Christendom, but it developed a preeminently statist focus when compared to most of the rest of Christian Europe. In the place of household cults, local pilgrimage sites, and personal intercession for young women, Russia's St. Catherine came to be defined, above all, by her regal place in the heavenly kingdom, the brave manliness of her faith and martyrdom in the face of bodily pain, her intellect, and, only belatedly, by the mystical marriage. These attributes put St. Catherine to the service of the ruling families and endowed her with a particular role as a patron saint for the Romanov women, around which an accretion of commemorative and ritual acts and consecrated sites evolved over the course of the seventeenth century.

This study has proposed further that the cult of St. Catherine provided an inventory of sacred and august images and identities that proved fundamental to the emergence of Catherine I as a public persona while a consort, as a political persona once she became empress in 1721, and ultimately as a crowned monarch at the end of January 1725. When it came time to reinvent Marta Skavronska as Ekaterina Alekseevna and subsequently to prepare the ground for her as a new tsaritsa, the name "Ekaterina" had developed a clear association with the Romanov family, and its association with St. Catherine was universally understood within the political and clerical elite. From 1711 onward, the panegyric and visual association between the tsaritsa and her name day saint became ever more intimate, reaching an apotheosis during the early 1720s in which the saint and the living image became almost indistinguishable. It is upon this foundation that the sacralization and naturalization of female rule came to rest once it became a political necessity in January 1725.

The book has maintained throughout that the discourses and gestures upon which the public representations of Catherine I were constructed depended preeminently and repeatedly upon the articulation of precedence, both Byzantine and Muscovite, and that these discourses and gestures were almost invariably faith-centered. Again and again, previous justifications, prior experience, earlier practices and rulings were brought to the foreground as explanations for Peter's own practice. They functioned as tropes and gestures to be sure, with no small measure of imagination and disingenuity, but also as didactic explanations, especially when their defense was put in the hands of the learned intellectual clerics who offered their services to the tsar. The Petrine use and invention of precedence were themselves based on precedents deeply embedded in Russian culture, rhetorical strategies for making troublesome decisions seem normal, jarring discontinuities seem primordial and divinely sanctioned. Peter and his inner circle saw fit to deploy precedence, what might be termed a discourse of continuity, alongside their more celebrated displays of innovation, renewal, modernity, and anti-tradition from the 1690s until Peter drew his final breath. Ultimately, therefore, the political culture of the Petrine era, for all of its breathtaking transformations, cannot be completely grasped without recognizing this dynamic.

In many instances, however, the pursuit of precedence entailed much more than political strategy alone, or at least involved multivalent gestures intended to address the conflicting and layered concerns of more than one audience. The transposition of the remains of Alexander Nevskii provides a prime example of this multiplicity of gestures, his ambiguous reinvention as a warrior-saint taking place simultaneously with his identification in the milieu of the Orthodox hierarchy with the decidedly anti-statist martyr, Filipp. Other examples, more central to the argument of this book, were the decree of 1723 on Catherine's coronation and Feofan Prokopovich's coronation homily of the following year, the latter seemingly intent on addressing the concerns of multiple constituencies by way of an intertextual layering that only someone with Feofan's learning and rhetorical sophistication could have accomplished.

This insistence on the relevance of the historical past leads to some important observations, which I hope have emerged from the book. First, the issue of Petrine continuity and discontinuity is even more complex than we had believed, and the place of Muscovy more relevant to his reign. Secondly, political ideology, in particular regarding the rights and legitimacies of rulers, was constructed by faith-centered arguments and symbolism, even when this ideology employed secular political philosophies. Others have made this same point recently, especially Boris Uspenskii and Viktor Zhivov. But it cannot be stressed enough. Before, during, and after Peter's reign, legitimation was inseparable from *pomazanie*. The mysteries of God's will, grace, and Judgment Day permeated the texts, including the laws, and they constituted explanations of last resort when all else failed. This means that the corpus of sermons (not merely their panegyric sound bites) and liturgical events stood at the core of political culture and therefore need to be taken somewhat more seriously than they have been as sources for understanding ideology in the first generations of the Russian Empire.

The centrality of faith-centered discourse raises the question of audiences: to whom were these words and gestures addressed? That the pursuit of audiences was preeminently a political issue should by now be manifest. I have argued in this book that audiences were multiple and varied, and that certain texts, primarily the sermons, were directed at several audiences simultaneously. Even if the motives behind the addresses were cynical, or as seems highly probable, were driven more by political exigency than by prayer, the fact remains that everyone recognized the urgency of making such presentations and the necessity of first putting forth a claim of legitimacy and, second, of basing that legitimacy on these specific arguments rather than on some others. Clearly, someone or some groups were paying attention, and those audiences had to be mollified, if not thoroughly contented.

Prominent among such groups were the well-entrenched noble families, the newly prominent men of Peter's court, and the elite guards' regiments who were rapidly coalescing as a self-conscious collective force. From an ideological perspective, however, the most critical audience came not from the lay elites but from the ecclesiastical authorities themselves, the very spiritual gatekeepers who had to perform the rituals on behalf of the monarch and in the presence of the courtiers acknowledging the specific individual's right to rule. Even if, following the dictates of *Pravda voli monarshei,* the monarch answered to God, directly and exclusively, it remained the distinct role of the church to intercede between ruler and God, to act as the agent of heaven at the moment of anointing. If no one else understood the complex fabric of Feofan's sermons, these authorities surely did. And, if they could not be persuaded, or at least compelled, to preach the divine sanction of the new order, the succession and perhaps the empire itself were in trouble, for these priests alone were empowered to explain divine sanction to the Orthodox laity. Hence the importance of homilies addressed to Russia's elites, and of sacred oaths, revised liturgies, and narrated saints' lives addressed to everyone else. These were the verbal media through which female rule was interposed and made sacred against the backdrop of Christian kingship.

One final question that deserves at least brief mention here is the matter of timing. Is it significant that female rule came to pass in Russia during the eighteenth century, in the wake of Sofia's regency and then Peter's reign? Can one say that Russia was in some sense more ready for a female monarch in 1725 than it would have been earlier? Was the fact of Sofia's regency, in the face of all the furiously hostile ex post facto commentary, sufficient in itself to introduce the possibility of a female on the throne into the *mentalité* of Russia's elites? Did the endless assaults on tradition, the release of the Romanov women from the supposedly cloistered life of the *terem,* the obligatory female presence at Peter's *assamblei* and other court spectacles, the move away from Moscow's Kremlin to St. Petersburg's open spaces enable female rule to appear less transgressive among the clergy and serving families than it would have in earlier eras? More boldly, did the Petrine era make female rule not merely imaginable, but necessary, as Richard Wortman has suggested, since no male could hope to be a second Peter or to successfully defend his heritage?[1]

These possibilities continue to be intriguing, and in some of their elements compelling, even if almost impossible to subject to any hypothesis testing. Surely, the high visibility of women at the new court in St. Petersburg had an effect on the more public side of sociability and the perception of women within it, although how this might have related to the engendering of power and legitimacy is far from clear. More telling, I suspect, were the panegyrics and public declamations in which the praise of specific women, first among them Catherine, had no small role. In the last analysis then, it was the preachers themselves, through the didacticism and imagery of their own speech acts inside the church and printed texts elsewhere, who prepared the soil for making female rule imaginable to the Petrine and post-Petrine elites.

Notes

Abbreviations

AAE   *Akty arkheograficheskoi ekspeditsii*

Chteniia   *Chteniia v Imperatorskom obshchestve istorii i drevnostei rossiiskikh*

DRV   *Drevniaia rossiiskaia vivliofika*

PSPR   *Polnoe sobranie postanovlenii i rasporiazhenii po vedomstvu pravoslavnogo ispovedaniia rossiiskoi imperii* (St. Petersburg, 1872–1876)

PSRL   *Polnoe sobranie russkikh letopisei*

PSZ   *Polnoe sobranie zakonov rossiiskoi imperii*

RGADA   Rossiiskii Gosudarstvennyi Arkhiv Drevnikh Aktov (Moscow)

RGIA   Rossiiskii Gosudarstvennyi Istoricheskii Arkhiv (St. Petersburg)

RIB   *Russkaia istoricheskaia biblioteka*

SIRIO   *Sbornik Imperatorskogo russkogo istoricheskogo obshchestva*

SK   *Svodnyi katalog russkoi knigi grazhdanskoi pechati XVIII v., 1725–1800*

TODRL   *Trudy Otdeleniia drevnerusskoi literatury*

ZMNP   *Zhurnal Ministerstva narodnogo prosveshcheniia*

1—The Problem of Female Rule

1. Brenda Meehan-Waters, "Catherine the Great and the Problem of Female Rule," *Russian Review,* vol. 34, no. 3 (July 1975), p. 306.

2. Isolde Thyrêt, *Between God and Tsar: Religious Symbolism and the Royal Women of Muscovite Russia* (DeKalb: Northern Illinois University Press, 2001).

3. The single Russian precedent, of which everyone was aware but that no one accepted or acknowledged, was the coronation of the Polish wife of False Dmitrii, Marina Iur'evna Mniszek, on May 8, 1606. A. P. Bogdanov, *Moskovskaia publitsistika poslednei chetverti XVII veka* (Moscow: RAN, 2001), p. 23.

4. Catherine, in principle, should not have had to undergo a second baptism since the Russian church had formally accepted the Greek position on this matter in the fateful synods of the 1650s and 1660s. First expressed in a patriarchal epistle of 1593, the instruction ordered the Russian church to repudiate the terms of the 1551 Stoglav Church Council requiring those who converted from Catholicism to Russian Orthodoxy to have an Orthodox baptism. The view in the rest of the Orthodox world

had been that a previous Christian baptism was acceptable, and the instruction made the modification of Russian practice a condition of granting Russia its own patriarchate. Largely ignored until Nikon's time, this regulation appears to have been rigorously enforced thereafter.

5. Reinhard Wittram, *Peter I, Czar und Kaiser. Zur Geschichte Peters des Grossen in seiner Zeit* (Göttingen: Vandenhoecken & Ruprecht, 1964), p. 271. S. M. Solov'ev, *Istoriia Rossii s drevneishikh vremen*, vol. 16 (St. Petersburg: Tovarishchestvo "Obshchestvennaia Pol'za," 1913), pp. 54–56; Théophile Hallez-Claparède, comte de Villebois, *Mémoires secrets pour servir a l'histoire de la cour de Russie sous les règnes de Pierre-le-Grand et de Catherine Ire, d'après les manuscripts originaux du sieur de Villebois, chef d'Escadre et Aide-de-Camp de S. M. le Czar Pierre I* (Paris: E, Dentu, 1853), pp. 68–97.

6. A. A. Kizevetter, "Ekaterina I," in *Entsiklopedicheskii slovar'* [Granat], vol. 19 (Moscow, n. d.), p. 618; Paul Bushkovitch, *Peter the Great: The Struggle for Power, 1671–1725* (Cambridge: Cambridge University Press, 2001), p. 237; Makarii, *Istoriia russkoi tserkvi*, vol. 10 (St. Petersburg: Tipografiia R. Golike, 1881), pp. 46–54.

7. An official wedding ceremony and formal *brakosochetanie* took place in February 1712, of course, but it was commonly assumed that Peter had secretly wed Catherine some years earlier, probably in 1707. To this day, however, no documentation confirming the earlier ceremony has been uncovered. I. I. Golikov, *Deianiia Petra Velikogo, mudrogo preobrazovatelia Rossii*, vol. 4 (Moscow, 1788), pp. 67–68. *Pis'ma i bumagi imperatora Petra Velikogo*, vol. 12, *January–June 1712* (Moscow: Universitetskaia Tipografiia, 1975), pp. 83 and 361.

8. Cited in Jack V. Haney, *From Italy to Muscovy: The Life and Works of Maxim the Greek* (Munich: Wilhelm Fink Verlag, 1973), p. 53.

9. P. S. Smirnov, "Vzgliad raskola na perezhivaemoe vremia v pervoi chetverti XVIII veka," *Khristianskoe chtenie*, vol. 229 (1909), pt. 1, pp. 685–86. Solov'ev, *Istoriia Rossii*, vol. 16, p. 55. According to Solov'ev, however, she was known as Katerina Vasil'evskaia within Menshikov's milieu prior to adopting the patronymic "Alekseevna." Solov'ev perplexingly cites Patrick Gordon's diary as the source for his version of Catherine's conversion, including the tale that Aleksei Petrovich became her godfather [his note reads Patrick Gordon, *The History of Peter the Great*, vol. 2, p. 258]. Solov'ev presumably was referring to the full and unpublished six-volume diary, but even so, Gordon died in 1699, a full four years before the earliest dating of Catherine's conversion, and at least three years before anyone at court knew of her. Aleksei Petrovich's letters to his father, dating as far back as 1703, make no reference to Catherine at all until February 1709, and at that time the tsarevich called her merely "Katerina Alekseevna," with no indication of a specific Christian or familial relation. Only in 1713, after the official wedding between Peter and Catherine, did Aleksei choose to refer to her as "matushka." *Pis'ma tsarevicha Alekseia Petrovicha k ego roditeliu gosudariu Petru Velikomu, gosudaryne Ekaterine Alekseevne, i kabinet-sekretariu Makarevu* (Odessa: Gorodskaia Tipografiia, 1849), pp. 56, 65–66.

10. In 1711, when the official marriage was still a rumor, the diplomatic corps in Moscow was already wondering what would happen if Peter married his mistress, and whether they would be obliged to call her "Your Majesty." See Just Juel, *Zapiski Iusta Iulia, datskogo poslannika pri Petre Velikom (1709–11)* (Moscow: Universitetskaia Tipografiia, 1899), pp. 373–74. The claim that she was merely a mistress proved to be by far the most frequent theme in the allegations of *lèse majesté* investigated by the Preobrazhenskii prikaz involving denunciations of Catherine during her lifetime and immediately thereafter. See, for example RGADA *f.* 7, *op.* 1, *d.* 135, regarding a 1722 case in which a monk was defrocked for saying that Catherine was not a tsaritsa, but a *"preliubovnitsa."*

11. *Zapiski Iusta Iulia*, pp. 124–25. Juel claimed to have heard this account in Narva, from local residents "who had known her well and who were familiar with all the details"; Villebois, *Mémoires secrètes*, p. 76; Olga E. Glagoleva, "The Illegitimate Chil-

dren of the Russian Nobility in Law and Practice, 1700–1860," *Kritika* 6, no. 3 (Summer 2005), p. 479.

12. The coronation act of 1724, appropriately, did not include the term "*samoderzhitsa.*" But after Peter's death, when she was acclaimed as empress, "*samoderzhitsa*" came to be included in all oaths, official documents, and governmental memoranda.

13. A. V. Gavrilov, *Ocherki istorii St. Peterburgskoi sinodal'noi tipografii* (St. Petersburg, 1911), p. 25.

14. Richard S. Wortman, *Scenarios of Power: Myth and Ceremony in Russian Monarchy,* vol. 1 (Princeton: Princeton University Press, 1995), pp. 73–75. Wortman's other discussions of the iconography of Catherine also emphasize the secularity, the link with warriors, Minerva, Semiramis, et al. See also, Isabel de Madariaga, "Tsar into Emperor: The Title of Peter the Great," *Politics and Culture in Eighteenth-Century Russia* (London: Longman, 1998), p. 37. Viktor Zhivov and Boris Uspenskii's "Tsar i Bog" offers a more multidimensional reading of these same rituals. V. M. Zhivov and B. A. Uspenskii, "Tsar' i Bog. Semioticheskie aspekty sakralizatsii monarkha v Rossii," in *Iazyki kul'tury i problemy perevodimosti,* ed. B. A. Uspenskii (Moscow: Nauka, 1987), pp. 47–153.

15. These are described in M. I. Pyliaev, *Staryi Peterburg* (St. Petersburg: Izdatel'stvo Suvorina, 1889).

16. RGIA, *f.* 796, *op.* 58, no. 43, p. 23.

17. V. G. Druzhinin, *Pisaniia russkikh staroobraidtsev. Perechen' spiskov sostavlennyi po pechatnym opisaniiam rukopisnykh sobranii* (St. Petersburg: Tipografiia Aleksandrova, 1912), pp. 396–97, ms. No. 537.

18. RGADA, *f.* 9, *op.* 6, *d.* 38; A similar case arose in February 1725 on word that the bishop of Astrakhan had not yet administered the oath to all his clergy. *Opisanie dokumentov i del khraniashchikhsia v arkhive sviateishago pravitel'stvuiushchago sinoda,* vol. 5 (1725 g.) (St. Petersburg: Sinodal'naia Tipografiia, 1897), pp. 79–86.

19. Both letters can be found in *Opisanie dokumentov i del . . . sinoda,* vol. 7 (1727), pp. 1–4.

20. V. M. Zhivov, "Kul'turnye reformy v sisteme preobrazovanii Petra I," in *Iz istorii russkoi kul'tury,* vol. 3, *XVII–nachalo XVIII veka,* ed. A. D. Koshelev (Moscow: Shkola iazyki russkoi kul'tury, 1996), pp. 533, 540 ff.

21. "Iz sochineniia kodina ob obriadakh konstantinopl'skago dvora i chinakh velikoi tserkvi," *Chteniia* (1883), bk. 1, pp. 9–10.

22. *Opisanie koronatsii eia Velichestva Imperatritsy Ekateriny Alekseevny* (St. Petersburg, 1724). The actual service begins on p. 34 of the *Opisanie.* The exact prayer of acceptance was "Gospodi Bozhi nash, Tsariu tsarstvuiushchikh i Gospod gospodstvuiushchikh, izhe cherez Samuila proroka izbravyi raba Tvoego Davida i pomazavyi ego vo tsari nad liudem Tvoim Izraelem!" I. Tokmakov, *Istoricheskoe opisanie vsekh koronatsii rossiiskikh tsarei, imperatorov i imperatrits* (Moscow, 1896), pp. 70–71.

23. Michael S. Flier, "Court Ceremony in an Age of Reform: Patriarch Nikon and the Palm Sunday Ritual," in *Religion and Culture in Early Modern Russia and Ukraine,* ed. Samuel H. Baron and Nancy Shields (DeKalb: Northern Illinois University Press, 1997), p. 75.

24. Zhivov has provided considerable evidence demonstrating that Peter's contemporaries saw a clear and essential distinction between pagan allegory and Christian antiquity, and they endeavored with considerable effectiveness to confine them to separate spaces with separate meanings. "Kul'turnye reformy," pp. 541–47.

25. The texts of these orations appear not to have survived, but the detailed descriptions of the coronations of Aleksei, Fedor, Ivan, and Peter all make reference to a patriarchal *slovo.* "Perechen' iz chinovnoi knigi o venchanii na tsarstvo tsaria Alekseia Mikhailovicha s ukazaniem otmen, sdelannykh pri koronatsii tsarei Ivana i Petra Alekseevichei," p. 95. "Patriarkh tvoril Tsariu slovo uchitel'noe," and "Perechen' iz chinovnoi knigi o venchanii na gosudarstvo tsaria Feodora Alekseevicha," p. 103: "A potom tvoril Sviateishii Patriarkh pouchenie Velikomu Gosudariu i blagoslovil Velikogo Gosudaria krestom." Both are published in *Chteniia* (1883) bk. 1.

26. On anointing tsars into the mysteries of faith see B. A. Uspenskii, *Tsar' i imperator. Pomazanie na tsarstvo i semantika monarshikh titulov* (Moscow: Iazyki russkoi kul'tury, 2000), pp. 27–29. Uspenskii limits himself to male rulers, however, and does not discuss the implications of female monarchy for the meaning of anointing.

27. Roy Strong, *Splendour at Court: Renaissance Spectacle and Illusion* (London: Weidenfeld and Nicolson, 1973), p. 24.

28. The textual basis of the tree of Jesse is in the Old Testament, Ruth 4:16–22.

29. This famous icon has been reproduced in many collections, most notably by D. A. Rovinskii. See also Frank Kaempfer, *Das russische Herrscherbild von der Anfaengen bis zu Peter dem Grossen* (Recklinghausen: Verlag Aurel Bongers Recklinghausen, 1978), opposite p. 223. Other depictions of the tree of male authority from this time can be found in a 1682 *Sinodik* and several other sources.

30. See Thyrêt's discussion in *Between God and Tsar*, pp. 70–79.

31. The mode of reasoning was quite simple, and it required merely that the reigning monarch be made the living image of at least one forebear in the unbroken chain of kingship. Thus, calling Peter the new Vladimir reminded the listeners that Vladimir had been the new Constantine, and that Constantine had been the new David.

32. Jacques Margeret, *The Russian Empire and Grand Duchy of Muscovy. A Seventeenth-Century French Account,* trans. and ed. Chester S. L. Dunning (Pittsburgh: University of Pittsburgh Press, 1983), pp. 14–15.

33. Strong, *Splendour at Court,* p. 76.

34. Viktor Zhivov has made this point repeatedly. See also A. S. Eleonskaia, "Skazanie o kreshchenii Rusi v literaturnykh obrabotkakh XVII–nachala XVIII veka," *Germenevtika drevnerusskoi literatury,* vol. 8 (1995), pp. 36–41.

35. *The Nikonian Chronicle,* vol. 5, ed. Serge A. Zenkovsky (Princeton: Darwin Press, 1989), p. 124.

36. Zhivov and Uspenskii, "Tsar' i Bog," pp. 51–54.

37. Ibid., pp. 60–61.

38. Thyrêt, *Between God and Tsar,* pp. 139–69; Lindsey Hughes, *Sophia, Regent of Russia, 1657–1704* (New Haven: Yale University Press, 1990), especially pp. 102–4, 142–44, 224.

39. Thyrêt, *Between God and Tsar,* p. 163.

40. Semen Polotskii, *Virshi* (Minsk: Mastatskaia literatura, 1990), pp. 297ff.

41. S. N. Brailovskii, "Odin iz pestrykh XVII-go stoletiia," *Zapiski Imperatorskoi Akademii nauk po istoriko-filologicheskomu otdeleniiu,* vol. 5 (1902), p. 179 and elsewhere in the volume. A. P. Bogdanov and V. I. Buganov, eds., *Pamiatniki obshchestvenno-politicheskoi mysli v Rossii kontsa XVII veka. Literaturnye panegiriki* (Moscow: Akademiia nauk, 1983), pp. 210, 211, passim.

42. Thyrêt, *Between God and Tsar,* pp. 47–79.

43. "Na koronatsiiu Ekateriny I," in *Pamiatniki literatury drevnei Rusi, XVII vek,* ed. V. P. Grebeniuk (Moscow: Nauka, 1979), vol. 3, pp. 339–40.

44. "Koronatsionnye zhetony i medali XVIII veka," *Chteniia Imperatorskogo Obshchestva istorii i drevnostei rossiiskikh* (hereafter *Chteniia*) (1883), bk. 1, pp. 154–55; I. Tokmakov, *Istoricheskoe opisanie vsekh koronatsii rossiiskikh tsarei, imperatorov i imperatrits* (Moscow, 1896), p. 71. Bergholz's description of the coronation has Menshikov tossing the coins. See F. V. Berkhgol'ts, *Dnevnik kamer-iunkera F. V. Berkhgol'tsa vedennyi im v Rossii v tsarstvovanie Petra Velikogo s 1721-go po 1725-i god,* pt. 4, 1724–1725 (Moscow, 1903), p. 40.

45. A. M. Panchenko, "Russkaia kul'tura v kanun petrovskikh reform," in *Iz istorii russkoi kul'tury,* vol. 3, *XVII–nachalo XVIII veka,* ed. A. D. Koshelev (Moscow: Shkola iazyki russkoi kul'tury, 1996) p. 63.

46. Elizabeth Kristofovich Zelensky, "Monarchic Imagery in the Reign of Sof'ia Alekseevna," paper presented at the meeting of the American Association for the Advancement of Slavic Studies (1993).

47. Thyrêt, *Between God and Tsar,* pp. 144–47.

48. A. I. Nikol'skii, "Sofiia Premudrost' Bozhiia," *Vestnik arkheologii i istorii,* vol. 17 (1906), pp. 76–79.

49. Writing in 1872, D. A. Rovinskii claims that some of the portraits survived only in a couple of copies. Rovinskii, "Slovar' russkikh gravirovannykh portretov," in *Zapiski Imperatorskoi Akademii nauk,* vol. 21 (appendix), p. x; M. A. Alekseeva, "Portret tsarevny Sof'i gravera Tarasevicha," *Pamiatniki kul'tury. Novye otkrytiia* vol. 2 (1975), p. 240.

50. The often violent factional struggles of the 1680s have been retold many times, most recently by Bushkovitch, *Peter the Great,* 125–69.

51. Hughes, *Sophia, Regent of Russia,* pp. 242–61.

52. Nikol'skii, "Sofiia Predmudrost' Bozhiia," p. 78.

53. M. I. Lileev, "Opisanie rukopisei khraniashchikhsia v biblioteke chernigovskoi dukhovnoi akademii," *Pamiatniki drevnei pis'mennosti,* vol. 6 (1880), pp. 220–21.

54. Ernest A. Zitser, *The Transfigured Kingdom: Sacred Parody and Charismatic Authority at the Court of Peter the Great* (Ithaca: Cornell University Press, 2004), p. 29.

55. Ibid., p. 41.

56. My thanks to Christian Raffensberger for providing me with this information, thus clarifying why I had been unable to find any trace of the marriage in the chronicles. His research indicates that the attribution of such a marriage appears only in the seventeenth century in connection with the claim that the relics in the Kievan monastery were those of St. Barbara. See Alexander Kazhdan, "Rus'-Byzantine Princely Marriages in the Eleventh and Twelfth Centuries," *Harvard Ukrainian Studies* 12–13 (1988–1989), p. 419.

57. According to Aleksei Popov's study of East Slavic akathysts, there were several manuscript akathysts for St. Barbara as well as early printed ones. In 1639, Archimandrite Iosaf Krokovskii of the Caves Monastery in Kiev composed a new St. Barbara akathyst, and it was republished in 1691, 1698, 1706 (a variant), and 1712. It was included in dozens of published texts over the next two centuries even though the Synod insisted early on that the church typography in Kiev cease publishing the akathyst and vita without receiving prior permission from St. Petersburg. Aleksei Popov, *Pravoslavnye russkie akafisty* (Kazan: Imperatorskii universitet, 1903), pp. 33, 95–104.

58. Irina is described as being dressed in tsarist attire, carefully ornamented, her hands held in supplicatory prayer, and with a crown *("korona")* on her head. A. I. Uspenskii, *Piat' vnov' otkrytykh ikon kisti Simona Ushakova* (Moscow: I. Efimov, 1901), pp. 2–3. The icon includes all of the offspring of Aleksei Mikhailovich through Tatiana, thus dating it before the birth of Ivan Mikhailovich in 1664).

59. This is not to suggest that birthdays were entirely ignored. Seventeenth-century documents occasionally record quite lavish birthday celebrations. Nicholaas Witsen, who served in the Dutch embassy in Moscow during the mid–1660s describes at some length what he termed "the great holiday" celebrating the birthday of Tsarevich, and presumptive heir at the time, Aleksei Alekseevich. His diary affixed this celebration to February 22 (N. S.) but Russian sources list February 5 (O. S.) as the tsarevich's birthday, a discrepancy of a few days, but still several days before the day of his name day saint, Aleksei the Metropolitan on February 12 (O.S.). Bells rang day and night, and a major religious festival was held on an open square (presumably Red Square), followed by a large banquet at which the tsar himself served. Nikolaas Vitsen, *Puteshestvie v Moskoviiu, 1664–1665. Dnevnik.* (St. Petersburg: Symposium, 1996), pp. 118–20. On the birthdays of the ruling family see V. N. Tatishchev, *Istoriia Rossiiskaia,* vol. 7 (Moscow: Nauka, 1968), p. 171.

60. *Istoricheskoe opisanie moskovskogo novodevich'ego monastyria* (Moscow: Tipografiia Snegireva, 1885), pp. 49–54.

61. Uspenskii, *Piat' vnov' otkrytykh ikon kisti Simona Ushakova,* p. 2.

62. Berngard Tanner, *Opisanie puteshestviia pol'skago posol'stva v Moskvu v 1678 godu.* (Moscow: Universitetskaia Tipografiia, 1891), p. 74.

63. Ibid., pp. 74–75.

64. On the periodic investigations of rumors surrounding Evdokia see, inter alia, Evgenii Anisimov, *Dyba i knut. Politicheskii sysk i russkoe obshchestvo v XVIII veke* (Moscow: Novoe russkoe obozrenie, 1999), pp. 51–52.

65. Russell Edward Martin, "Dynastic Marriage in Muscovy, 1500–1729." (Ph.D. diss., Harvard University, 1996), p. 69.

66. The circumstances of Marta's conversion and name change remain elusive. It is widely thought that she accepted Orthodoxy at Peter's suggestion long before they were officially wed, but this is not certain. The choice of "Ekaterina" as her new name probably came with her conversion, while the reason for selecting it can only be imagined. Alexander Menshikov, by then Peter's favorite, is mentioned as playing some sort of role as well, and there is no doubt that a personal closeness developed between Catherine and Menshikov, who in the earliest surviving letters referred to Catherine occasionally as "my sister-in-law" *(moia nevestka)*. Menshikov's name day saint, Alexander Nevskii, was at the time celebrated on November 23 (changed to August 30 in 1724 by Peter), i.e., the day before St. Catherine's Day on the Russian calendar. The very next day, November 25, was the day of St. Peter, martyr and bishop of Alexandria at the time of St. Catherine (he served between 300 and 311). The apostle Peter was the tsar's name day saint, but Peter was occasionally linked to his Alexandrian namesake. One is tempted to imagine (nothing more) that the invention of Catherine was thus concocted by Peter and Menshikov to fit her in between the two as the replacement for both Evdokia and Peter's former mistress, Anna Mons. This imagined arrangement between the favorite and the tsar would have conveyed the joint indebtedness of Peter and Catherine (of Alexandria) to Menshikov. Equally seductive (and equally lacking in documentation) is the possibility that Peter was honoring Marta with a fond remembrance of an earlier dalliance involving the English actress Letitia Cross with whom he was rumored to have had an affair. During his stay in London in 1698, so the tale goes, Peter attended the theater, saw "Mrs. Cross" perform, and arranged to meet and then romance her. The best-known portrait of her, by Sir Godfrey Kellner, was in the pose of St. Catherine. This same Kellner also painted a portrait of Peter in 1698, so Peter may well have known of the portrait of Mrs. Cross. Or not. Cross (Anthony, that is) has reviewed the documents and has found no contemporary evidence that Peter and Mrs. Cross ever met, though the rumors of their liaison started circulating well before Peter's death. The Kellner portraits are reproduced on the page facing p. 136. According to most secondary accounts, Catherine adopted the patronymic "Alekseevna" because Tsarevich Aleksei Petrovich served as her godfather in the ceremony. But as with everything else connected to this episode, there exists no documentary paper trail to substantiate such an explanation. Sigizmund Librovich, *Petr Velikii i zhenshchiny* (Iaroslavl, Severnyi rabochii 1991), pp. 18–19; Juel, *Zapiski Iusta Iulia*, p. 124; Jean Rousset de Missy, *Mémoires du règne de Catherine Impératrice et Souveraine de toute la Russie* (The Hague: Rousset, 1728), pp. 12–14, 604–13. Joseph Viteau, *Passions de saints Ecaterine et Pierre d'Alexandrie, Barbara et Anysia* (Paris: Librairie Emile Bouillion, 1897), p. 68; Anthony Cross, "The Old Man from Cambridge, Mrs. Cross, and Other Anglo-Petrine Matters of Due Weight and Substance," in *Peter the Great and the West: New Perspectives,* ed. Lindsey Hughes (London: Palgrave, 2001), pp. 5–10. For further flights of fancy, although none less plausible than the ones that are scattered in some of the nineteenth-century scholarship, one may wish to peruse Phil Stong, *Marta of Muscovy: The Fabulous Life of Russia's First Empress* (Garden City, New York: Doubleday, Doran & Company, 1945).

67. Konstantin Nikol'skii, *Posobie k izucheniiu ustava bogosluzheniia pravoslavnoi tserkvi* (St. Petersburg: Sinodal'naia Tipografiia, 1907), p. 104. An English translation was published in London in 1899, based upon an 1862 Moscow *mineia obshchaia*. The editor of the English edition surmised from the language that the *obshchaia* was translated from Greek originals, although he acknowledged that no such originals had been uncovered. *The General Menaion, or The Book of Services Common to the Festivals of Our Lord Jesus Christ of the Holy Virgin and of the Different Orders of Saints,* trans. Professor N.

Orloff. (London: J. Davy & Sons, 1899), preface (no pagination). I have used this old, and somewhat archaic, translation for the selections given in the text, occasionally adding the Russian wording in parentheses where it seems useful. Having examined several—but by no means all—redactions of the *obshchaia*, both manuscript and printed, I found that the prescriptive language remained virtually identical from one edition to the next, and one century to the next, so that the formulations found in the English translation conform to those in the Slavonic texts I examined, covering the period between the sixteenth and the twentieth centuries.

68. There are no *minei obshchie* listed in the 1984 catalogue of Slavo-Russian manuscripts, eleventh to thirteenth centuries. Several other relevant studies describe it as a commonplace of manuscript book culture, however, certainly from the fourteenth century onward. See S. O. Schmidt et al., eds., *Svodnyi katalog slaviano-russkikh rukopis-nykh knig khraniashchikhsia v SSSR XI–XIII vv.* (Moscow: Nauka, 1984); A. I. Rogov, "Minei (spravka)," in *Metodicheskoe posobie po opisaniiu slaviano-russkikh rukopisei dlia Svodnogo kataloga rukopisei khraniashchikhsia v SSSR*, vol. 1 (Moscow: Arkheografich-eskaia komissiia, 1973), p. 299.

69. RGIA, *f*. 796, *op*. 58, no. 23 pp. 1–12.

70. Nikol'skii, *Posobie*, p. 104.

71. *The General Menaion*, p. 141.

72. See *Mineia obshchaia* (Moscow: Sinodal'naia tipografiia, 1790), pp. 105–16.

73. The texts comes from the 1899 English translation, pp. 203 and 209.

74. Caroline Walker Bynum, "Women's Stories, Women's Symbols: A Critique of Victor Turner's Theory of Liminality," in *Fragmentation and Redemption: Essays on Gender and the Human Body in Medieval Religion* (New York: Zone Books, 1992), p. 38.

75. Caroline Walker Bynum, *Jesus as Mother: Studies in the Spirituality of the High Middle Ages* (Berkeley: University of California Press, 1982), p. 136.

76. *The General Menaion*, pp. 223–25.

77. Ibid., p. 243.

78. Ibid.

79. Ibid., pp. 243–44.

80. Ibid., p. 246.

2—Vitae

1. Alban Butler, *Butler's Lives of the Saints* (Collegeville, Minn.: Liturgical Press, 1995), p. 420; S. Baring-Gould, *The Lives of the Saints* (Edinburgh: John Grant, 1914), p. 541.

2. René Coursault, *Sainte Catherine d'Alexandrie. Le myth et la tradition* (Paris: Editions Maison Neuve et Larose, 1984), p. 108.

3. Pere Hippolyte Delehaye, *The Legends of the Saints* (New York: Fordham University Press, 1962), p. 181. For a summary and mild criticism of this skepticism see Jane Tibbetts Schulenberg, "Saints' Lives As a Source for the History of Women, 500–1100," in *Medieval Women and the Sources of Medieval History*, ed. Joel T. Rosenthal (Athens, GA: University of Georgia Press, 1990), pp. 285–309. The writings of Peter Brown among others have brought saints' lives back into historical discourse, not so much as biography but as rich representations of cultural norms and expectations, tropes and topoi, of the elites of the times in which they were penned and in which the cults gained popularity. Peter Brown, *The Cult of Saints: Its Rise and Function in Latin Christianity* (Chicago: University of Chicago Press, 1981), p. 56ff; Raymond Van Dam, *Saints and Their Miracles in Late Antique Gaul* (Princeton: Princeton University Press, 1993), pp. 4–7.

4. Delehaye, *Legends of the Saints*, pp. 38–39.

5. See, as one of many such examples, V. S. Kolesnikova, *Russkie pravoslavnye prazdniki* (Moscow: Kron-press, 1996), pp. 299–301.

6. Eusebius, *The History of the Church from Christ to Constantine*, trans. G. A. Williamson (London: Penguin, 1989), p. 276.

7. Ibid., pp. 276–77.

8. Ibid., p. 272.

9. Coursault, *Sainte Catherine d'Alexandrie*, p. 7.

10. Ibid., pp. 38–39.

11. Katherine J. Lewis, *The Cult of St. Katherine of Alexandria in Late Medieval England* (Woodbridge: The Boydell Press, 2000), p. 47; Bruce A. Beatie, "Saint Katherine of Alexandria: Traditional Themes and the Development of a Medieval German Hagiographic Narrative," *Speculum* 52, no. 4 (October 1977), p. 788.

12. Lewis, *Cult of St. Katherine*, p. 47.

13. Eugen Einenkel (ed.), *The Life of Saint Katherine from the Royal MS. 17a xxvi with its Latin Original from the Cotton MS. Caligula A viii* (London: N. Trubner and Co., 1894), p. viii.

14. On the Codex Palatinus, see Joseph Viteau, *Passions des saints Ecaterine et Pierre d'Alexandrie, Barbara, et Anysia* (Paris: Librairie Emile Bouillion, 1897), pp. 4–23.

15. Coursault, *Sainte Catherine d'Alexandrie*, pp. 64–65; Lewis, *Cult of St. Katherine*, pp. 63–66; Beatie, "Saint Katherine of Alexandria," pp. 790–799.

16. *Acta Sanctorum Quotquot Toto Orbe Coluntur Vel a Catholicis Scriptoribus Celebratur . . . Propylius* (Brussels: Victor Palme, 1940), pp. 543–44.

17. Jacobus de Voragine, *The Golden Legend of Jacobus de Voragine* (New York: Arno Press, 1969), pp. 708–16.

18. John Capgrave, *The Life of St. Catherine of Alexandria* (London: Kegan, Paul, Trench, Trübner & Co., 1893).

19. Ibid., p. xxiii, 19–22. Capgrave's account of Athanasios and his relation to Catherine begins on line 127 of the prologue ("There was a clerk with this same Kateryne Whose name we clepe in Latyne Athanas"). The fanciful explanation of how this manuscript came to fall into Capgrave's possession begins with the tale of a certain Arrek, who translated the piece into an obscure Latin (line 173 of the prologue), and continues with the manuscript's eventual journey to England and there into Capgrave's hands. Not surprisingly, although the attribution of Athanasios dates back to the Codex Palatinus, no Greek or Latin manuscript corresponding to Capgrave's account has ever been found. Unlike the life of St. Catherine, the existence of St. Athanasios is well documented and extensively described in contemporary sources. As the second patriarch of Alexandria he was central to the religious life of fourth-century Alexandria, especially in the prosecution of Arianism. See Timothy D. Barnes, *Athanasius and Constantius: Theology and Politics in the Constantinian Empire* (Cambridge, MA.: Harvard University Press, 1993), pp. 1–9.

20. Antonina Harbus, *Helena of Britain in Medieval Legend* (Cambridge: D. S. Brewer, 2002), pp. 117–18. It is widely believed that Constantine the elder and Helena landed and stayed in Yorkshire as part of an early effort to convert the British tribes then living under the authority of Rome.

21. Delehaye, *Legends of the Saints*, p. 18.

22. Lewis, *Cult of St. Katherine*, p. 45.

23. Delehaye, *Legends of the Saints*, p. 18; Lewis, *Cult of St. Katherine*, p. 45.

24. Shifting and confusing Byzantine emperors was a commonplace among the relevant saintly vitae throughout Christendom. In the Welsh *Mabinogion*, for example, the life of St. Helena conflated Maximus and Maxentius.), Harbus, p. 59.

25. Viteau, *Passions*, pp. 6–10.

26. Voragine, *Golden Legend*, p. 710.

27. Voragine, Ibid., p. 711.

28. Lewis, *Cult of St. Katherine*, p. 47; Coursault, *Sainte Catherine d'Alexandrie*, p. 66.

29. Jill Kamil, *The Monastery of Saint Catherine in Sinai* (Cairo: American University of Cairo Press, 1991), pp. 18–21; Coursault, *Sainte Catherine d'Alexandrie*, pp. 29–30.

30. N. F. Kapterev, "Russkaia blagotvoritel'nost' Sinaiskoi obiteli v XVI–XVIII stoletiiakh," *Chteniia v obshchestve liubitelei dukhovnogo prosveshcheniia* vol. 2 (October/November 1881), pp. 345–425.

31. Moshe Altbauer and Horace G. Lunt, eds., *An Early Slavonic Psalter from Rus'*; vol. 1, *Photo Reproduction* (Cambridge, MA: Harvard Ukrainian Research Institute, 1978).

32. Lewis, "Pilgrimage and the Cult of St. Katherine," pp. 37–47.

33. Tracy R. Sands, "The Saint as Symbol: The Cult of St. Katherine of Alexandria among Medieval Swedish High Aristocracy," in *St Katherine of Alexandria. Texts and Contexts in Western Medieval Europe*, ed. Jacqueline Jenkins and Katherine J. Lewis (Turnbout Belgium: Brepols, 2003), p. 95.

34. Lewis, "Pilgrimage and the Cult of St Katherine," p. 47. See also Julie Hassel, *Choosing Not to Marry: Women and Autonomy in the Katherine Group* (New York: Routledge, 2002).

35. Christine Walsh, "The Role of the Normans in the Development of the Cult of St Katherine," in *St Katherine of Alexandria*, ed. Jenkins and Lewis, p. 26.

36. Ibid., p. 27.

37. During this time the percentage of saints who were women grew significantly, at least in western Christendom, from about 10 percent in the eleventh century to 29 percent in the mid-fifteenth. Moreover, as Bynum reported, "there were more female than male *lay* saints in the period between 1215 and 1500." Bynum, *Jesus as Mother*, p. 137.

38. Lewis, *Cult of St. Katherine*, p. 107.

39. Elements of this myth may date from an earlier time, as Coursault has found references to a "Passio Ecaterinae virginis dei" from the mid-ninth century. But the narrative of a specific mystical marriage of the virgin Catherine to Jesus appears to have originated later. Coursault, *Sainte Catherine d'Alexandrie*, p. 67.

40. Voragine, *Golden Legend*, p. 713.

41. Lewis, *Cult of St. Katherine*, p. 1.

42. Karen A. Winstead, *Virgin Martyrs: Legends of Sainthood in Late Medieval England* (Ithaca: Cornell University Press, 1997), pp. 147–55.

43. Ibid., p. 14.

44. Ibid., pp. 5–14.

45. Ibid., p. 3.

46. Caroline Walker Bynum, "Women's Stories, Women's Symbols: A Critique of Victor Turner's Theory of Liminality," *Fragmentation and Redemption: Essays on Gender and the Human Body in Medieval Religion* (New York: Zone Books, 1992), pp. 38–41.

47. The arguments in this paragraph are drawn largely from Winstead, *Virgin Martyrs*, pp. 36–37.

48. See for example, Mary Laven, *Virgins of Venice: Broken Vows and Cloistered Lives in the Renaissance Convent* (New York: Viking, 2002), p. 249.

49. *The Travels of Sir John Mandeville*, trans. and with intro. C. W. R. D. Moseley. (Middlesex, UK: Penguin Books, 1983), pp. 70–71.

50. *The Trial of Jean D'Arc*, trans. W. P. Barrett (New York: Gotham House, 1932), p. 59.

51. Ibid., p. 61.

52. Ibid., p. 65.

53. Ibid., p. 91. Additional references to St. Catherine as intercessor and messenger from God to Joan are on pp. 58, 60, 65, 75, 97, 101, 106–7, 113.

54. *The Book of Margery Kempe*, trans. John Skinner (New York: Doubleday, 1998), p. 70.

55. *The Letters of St. Catherine of Siena*, vol. 1, trans. and with intro. Suzanne Noffice (Binghampton, NY: Medieval and Renaissance Texts and Studies, 1988), Letter 31, p. 110. See also Igino Giordani, *Saint Catherine of Siena—Doctor of the Church* (Boston: St. Paul Editions, 1975), pp. 17–18.

56. E. Ann Matter, "The Personal and the Paradigm: The Book of Maria Domitilla Galluzzi," in *The Crannied Wall: Women, Religion, and the Arts in Early Modern Europe*, ed. Craig E. Monson (Ann Arbor: University of Michigan Press, 1992), p. 89.

57. Lance G. Lazar, "'E faucibus daemonis': Daughters of Prostitutes, the First Jesuits, and the Compagnia delle Vergini Misrabili di Santa Caterina della Rosa," in *Confraternities and the Visual Arts in Renaissance Italy,* ed. Barbara A. Wisch and Dane Cohl Ahl (Cambridge: Cambridge University Press, 2000), pp. 259–262.

58. Louise Smith Bross, "She is among all virgins the queen . . . so worthy a patron . . . for maidens to copy": Livio Agresti, Cardinal Federico Cesi, and the Compagnia delle Vergini Miserabili di Santa Caterina della Rosa," in *Confraternities and the Visual Arts,* ed. Wisch and Ahl, p. 287.

59. P. L. Travers, *Mary Poppins Comes Back* (New York: Harcourt, Brace and World, 1963), p. 217. My thanks to Julia Monk for providing me with this reference.

60. Capgrave, *Life of St. Catherine of Alexandria,* p. 56.

61. Ibid., pp. 58–62, 192ff.

62. Lewis, *Cult of St. Katherine,* p. 66.

63. Gordon Kipling, ed., *The Receyt of the Ladie Katheryne* (Oxford: Oxford University Press, 1990), bk. 2, pp. 13–14.

64. O. V. Loseva, *Russkie mesiatsoslovy XI–XIV vekov* (Moscow: Pamiatniki istoricheskoi mysli, 2001), pp. 122 and 211.

65. V. Jagic, *Menaea Septembris, Octobris, Novembris. Sluzhebnye minei za sentiabr', oktiabr', noiabr' v tserkovno-slavianskom perevode po russkim rukopisiam 1095–1097 gg.* (St. Petersburg: Tipografiia Akademii nauk, 1886), pp. 446–61: "Sviatogo Klimenta papy rimskago. I sviatago Petra Episkopa Aleksandr'skago. I sviatyia muchenitsa Ekateriny."

66. Jagic's notes indicate that the typographical copy of the *mineia sluzhebnaia* did not include the prayers to St. Catherine, although they did have the services to Saints Clement and Peter.

67. Jagic, *Menea,* p. 457.

68. Ibid., p. 457 and elsewhere.

69. Ibid., p. 448.

70. Ibid., p. 446, 460. "Premoudryia dobryia muchenitsa Ekateriny ver'no, gosudarevy v''zyvaiushche slava ti, prosveshchaia serdtsa chelovecha slava ti, poch'tyi do vliuiu v strakh, toia milostvami, Khristos Bozhe, spasi dusha nasha."

71. Ibid., p. 459, 460.

72. Ibid., p. 458, 460.

73. A. V. Gorskii and K. I. Nevostruev, *Opisanie slavianskikh rukopisei moskovskoi sinodal'noi biblioteki,* vol. 3, pt. 2, *Knigi bogosluzhebye* (Moscow: Sinodal'naia Tipografiia, 1917), p. 26, 319, 353. See also S. O. Shmidt, ed., *Svodnyi katalog slaviano-russkikh rukopisnykh knig khraniashchikhsia v SSSR XI–XIII vv.* (Moscow: Nauka, 1984). The Shmidt catalogue lists all the early manuscripts that were held in Soviet repositories in the 1980s, according to which the earliest *prologi* for the first half of the year (September to February) date from the very end of the twelfth century (no. 162). It lists six *prologi* that include November for the thirteenth century (nos. 177, 293, 377, 378, 379, 469). Unfortunately it does not indicate which saints' days are included. However, an article on the *prolog* by N. I. Bubnov, published in a methodological volume that preceded the catalogue by a decade, provides at least a partial—if slightly opaque—listing of the saints included in the first two manuscript redactions. Bubnov's list does not show St. Catherine, but it is impossible to determine whether his roster is exhaustive. N. Iu. Bubnov, "Slaviano-russkie prologi," in *Metodicheskoe posobie po opisaniiu slaviano-russkikh rukopisei dlia Svodnogo kataloga rukopisei khraniashchikhsia v SSSR,* vol. 1 (Moscow: Akademiia nauk, 1973), pp. 286–89. In still another work, Bubnov describes 3 thirteenth-century *prologi* of which partial manuscripts survive. All 3 are missing most of November, and none includes St. Catherine for the November dates that it does show. N. Iu. Bubnov et al., eds., *Pergamennye rukopisi biblioteki Akademii nauk SSSR* (Leningrad: Nauka, 1976), pp. 49–57.

74. Loseva lists one manuscript with St. Catherine for the first half of the eleventh century, 2 for the late twelfth century, 6 for the thirteenth century, 12 for the

fourteenth century, and 4 for the early fifteenth century. Loseva., *Russkie mesiatsoslovy,* pp. 122–26, 209–11.

75. Through the fifteenth century Russian texts listed her name day variously as November 24, 25, or 26, and sometimes November 20. Of the manuscripts listed in Loseva, 8 celebrated her on November 24, 14 on November 25, and 5 on November 26. Loseva, *Russkie mesiatsoslovy,* pp. 209–11.

76. In "Slaviano-russkie prologi," Bubnov does not list a vita for St. Catherine for either redaction, but his lists are not all-inclusive. See also N. Petrov, *O proiskhozhdenii i sostave slaviano-russkago Prologa (inozemnye istochniki)* (Kiev: Tipografiia Ermeeva, 1875), especially chap. 3, "Otnoshenie slavianorusskago Prologa tem i drugim istochnikam," which discusses the *Menologium* at some length. Detailed descriptions of the twelfth-century manuscripts are in I. Kuprianov, *Obozrenie pergamennykh rukopisei novgorodskoi sofiiskoi biblioteki* (St. Petersburg: Akademiia nauk, 1857), p. 25, and Andrei I. Khludov, *Opisanie rukopisei i katalog knig tserkovnoi pechati* (Moscow: Sinodal'naia tipografiia, 1872), pp. 374–76.

77. *Freski Spasa-Nereditsy* (Leningrad: Gos. Russkii Muzei, 1925), no. 65, chertezh 2.

78. *Novgorod Icons of the Twelfth–Seventeenth Century* (Oxford: Phaidon, Leningrad: Aurora, 1980), plates 6 and 7, commentary on p. 279.

79. Ibid., plate 17, commentary on p. 282.

80. *The 'Paterik' of the Kievan Caves Monastery,* trans. Muriel Heppell (Cambridge, MA: Harvard University Press, 1989), p. 111 n. 317.

81. L. V. Stoliarova, *Drevnerusskie nadpisi XI–XIV vekov na pergamennykh kodeksakh* (Moscow: Nauka, 1998), p. 148

82. As cited in V. A. Meniailo, "Agiologiia Velikomuchenitsy Ekateriny na Rusi v XI–XVII vekakh," *Iskusstvo khristianskogo mira. Sbornik statei,* vol. 4 (2000), p. 94.

83. My thanks to Viktor Zhivov for the references to the early manuscript *prologi.* Every manuscript *mineia sluzhebnaia* for November that I consulted, either directly or through a detailed printed description, included the St. Catherine service. See, for example, the *mineia sluzhebnaia* for *noiabr'* from the late fifteenth or early sixteenth century, housed in the manuscript division of Moscow State University library. Microfilm available in the collection *Drevneishie slaviano-russkie rukopisi XIII–rubezha XV/XVI vv. Nauchnaia biblioteka MGU* (New York: Norman Ross Publishing, 1998).

84. *Novgorodskie letopisi, PSRL,* vol. 3, (St. Petersburg: Arkheograficheskaia kommissiia, 1841), p. 70.

85. See *Ioann Zlatoust v drevnerusskoi i iuzhnoslavianskoi pis'mennosti XI–XVI vekov. Katalog gomilii,* ed. E. E. (Evgeniia Eduardovna) Granstrem, O. V. Tvorogov, and A. Valevichius (St. Petersburg, 1998), entry 45 (p. 26): "Slovo velikoi muchenitse Ekaterine." The attribution derives from Makarii's *Great Menology,* but as the editors themselves point out in the introductory essay, many of the works attributed in translation to Chrysostom were written either by other Church fathers or by Russian aphorists.

86. *Letopisets ellinskii i rimskii,* ed. O. V. Tvorogov (St. Petersburg: Dmitrii Bulanin, 1999).

87. *Kondakarii v grecheskom podlinnike XII–XIII v. po rukopisi moskovskoi sinodal'noi biblioteki No. 437 s drevneishim slavianskim perevodom kondakov i ikosov kakie est' v perevode* (Moscow: Tipografiia Kudriavtsevoi, 1879), pp. 242–43.

88. Gorskii and Nevostruev, *Opisanie slavianskikh rukopisei,* vol. 3, pt. 2, p. 319.

89. *Kondakarii v grecheskom podlinnike,* p. 77.

90. Gorskii and Nevostruev, *Opisanie slavianskikh rukopisei,* vol. 3, pt. 2, pp. 293–98.

91. Ibid., p. 564.

92. *Opisanie slavianskikh rukopisei biblioteki sviato-troitskoi sergievoi lavry* (Moscow: G. Riss, 1878), nos. 264, 266, 268, 269, 272, 274, 316, 319, 320, 641, 645, 648, 653, 670, 682, 683, 751, 754, 771, 778, 779, 786, as well as several other menologies for November that probably include vitae of St. Catherine.

93. Ibid., no. 771.

94. Ibid., no. 285. "Ashche kto molitvu siiu prochitaet na vsiak den', izbavlen budet vechnyia muki."

95. The testament is published in *Kolonial'naia politika moskovskogo gosudarstva v Iakutii XVII v.* (Leningrad: Nauka, 1936), pp. 145–46. My thanks to Daniel Kaiser for bringing this testament to my attention.

96. "Postroenie chasovni v derevne Zarubina," in *Predaniia russkogo severa,* ed. N. A. Krinichnaia (St. Petersburg: Nauka, 1991), pp. 43–44. The legend originally appeared in 1901 in the journal *Etnograficheskoe obozrenie,* and was reprinted a year later in *Vologdskiie eparkhial'nye vedomosti.*

97. The 1963 catalogue of the Tretiakov Gallery's Old Russian art collection includes about 25 icons with St. Catherine, the majority dating from the late sixteenth and seventeenth centuries. Inventories of cathedrals around Rus' typically include at least one pre-Petrine image of St. Catherine. A recent catalogue also identifies a female image in a fourteenth-century Pskov fresco as possibly being St. Catherine. The sixteenth-century identification, from a triptych found in a church near Archangel, is more certain. V. I. Antonova and N. E. Mneva, eds., *Katalog drevnerusskoi zhivopisi,* vol. 1 (Moscow: Iskusstvo, 1963), pp. 30ff.; *Opisi imushchestva novgorodskogo sofiiskogo sobora XVIII–nachala XIX v.* (Moscow: Akademiia nauk, 1988), pp. 66, 85. Yuri Piatnitsky et al., eds., *Sinai, Byzantium, Russia: Orthodox Art from the Sixth to the Twentieth Century* (London: St. Catherine Foundation, 2000), pp. 215–16.

98. Antonova and Mneva, *Katalog drevnerusskoi zhivopisi,* vol. 1, p. 97, no. 30.

99. Ibid., p. 141. See also a fifteenth-century icon of St. Nicholas from the Rostov-Suzdal school and another one from Vologda, included in the work by Antonova and Mneva, *Katalog drevnenrusskoi zhivopisi,* pp. 221, 367, in which St. Catherine is one of the surrounding saints.

100. *Byzantium: Faith and Power, 1261–1557,* ed. Helen C. Evans (New Haven: Yale University Press, 2004), plate 46.

101. N. N. Pomerantsev and S. I. Maslenitsyn, eds., *Russkaia derevinnaia skul'ptura* (Moscow: Izobrazitel'noe iskusstvo, 1994), nos. 212, 213; O. M. Vlasova, ed., *Permskaia derevinnaia skul'ptura* (Perm: Permskoe knizhnoe izdatel'stvo, 1985), p. 50.

102. See, for example, Antonova and Mneva, *Katalog drevnerusskoi zhivopisi,* vol. 1, p. 259.

103. Antonova and Mneva, *Katalog drevnerusskoi zhivopisi,* vol. 2, no. 86, p. 139.

104. *Drevne russkoe shit'e,* N. A. Maiasova (Moscow: Iskusstvo, 1971), plates 22 and 23; also in *Opisi novgorodskogo sofiiskogo sobora,* ed. E. A. Gordienko and G. K. Markina (Moscow: Akademiia nauk, 1968), p. 85.

105. "Gospodi, bozhe moi, uslyshi mia, eliko ashche tebe sia moliu. Ashche kto vospomianet imia moe Ekaterinu pri iskhode dusha ego, privodi ego mirom."

106. See, for example, the eighteenth-century icon listed in "Russkii svodnyi ikonopisnyi podlinnik XVIII v.," *Vestnik obshchestva drevne-russkogo iskusstva pri moskovskom publichnom muzee* (1876), nos. 11–12, p. 67.

107. Antonova and Mneva, *Katalog drevnerusskoi rukopisi,* vol. 2, no. 443 (p. 79). Similar icons of the sixteenth and seventeenth centuries are no. 361 (p. 23); no. 411 (p. 62); no. 651 (p. 231), and in *Sinai: Byzantium and Russia,* no. S31, p. 217. No. 411 is identified as coming from the Moscow school in the first quarter of the sixteenth century.

108. Antonova and Mneva, *Katalog drevnerusskoi rukopisi,* vol. 2, no. 372, pp. 29–30.

109. Ibid., no. 504, pp. 114–15. The catalogue includes several other icons like this from the sixteenth century.

110. Meniailo, "Agiologiia," p. 96.

111. "Otryvok iz letopisi o vremenakh tsaria Ioanna Vasil'evicha Groznago, 1563–1567 gg.," in *Russkaia istoricheskaia biblioteka* (hereafter *RIB*), vol. 3 (St. Petersburg, 1876), pp. 192–93.

112. *Novgorodskiia letopisi (tak nazvannye novgorodskaia vtoraia i novgorodskaia tret'ia letopisi)* (St. Petersburg: Arkheograficheskaia kommissiia, 1879), p. 348.

113. Makarii, *Bol'shoi* (or, *Velikie Minei chetii,* in some variants) *chet'i minei,* vol. 1 (September–November), November 24, vol. 3, no. 9, pt. 1, listing no. 176, St. Petersburg: Akademiia nauk, 1868.

114. Ibid., no. 176, p. 1447; Gorskii and Nevostruev, *Opisanie slavianskikh rukopisei,* otdel vtoroi, *Pisaniia sviatykh ottsev,* pt. 3, *Raznye bogoslovskie sochineniia,* no. 319, *ll.* 132ob-146 (p. 605), and no. 324, *ll.* 460–473 (p. 674).

115. The coincidental mention of Athanasios in Capgrave and *Chet'i minei* almost certainly has no larger significance. It is impossible to imagine that Makarii had access to Capgrave, or even knew of it. In any case, the two texts are very different: Capgrave wrote in verse, Makarii in prose. Capgrave's work ran to hundreds of stanzas, Makarii's had far fewer paragraphs, etc.

116. Gorskii and Nevostruev, *Opisanie slavianskikh rukopisei,* vol. III, pt. 2, 605. See also Petrov, *O proiskhozhdenii . . . Prologa,* p. 26, which finds references to Athanasios in sixteenth-century prologs.

117. The Latin text is "Haec ego Athanasius, notarius simulque servus dominae meae Aecaterinae, conscripsi ejus commentaria in omni diligentia."

118. A small disclaimer is in order here. The Viteau edition includes a Latin translation of the Greek original on which I base the textual comparisons.

119. "In the year 305 of the reigning impious and evil emperor, Maxentius, there was a great false belief in idols."

120. J. L. Scharpe and F. Vyncke, eds., *Bdinski zbornik. An Old-Slavonic Menologium of Women Saints* (Bruges: De Tempel, 1973), pp. 29, 34, 148–62.

121. From Makarii, *Bol'shoi chet'i minei,* November 24.

3—*The* Terem *Chapel and the Romanov Women*

1. I. Tokmakov, "Kratkii istoricheskii ocherk tserkvi Sv. Velikomuchenitsy Ekateriny, chto na bol'shoe ordynke v moskve," *Moskovskie tserkovnye vedomosti,* no. 48 (November 28, 1882), p. 698.

2. Semen Zvonarev, ed., *Sorok sorokov. Al'bom ukazatel' vsekh moskovskikh tserkvei,* vol. 2 (Moscow: YMCA Press, 1988), p. 495.

3. Shuiskii's sister-in-law Ekaterina Grigor'evna was said to have attended services there.

4. *Novyi letopisets* (*PSRL,* vol. 14), 1965 p. 125.

5. *Skazanie Avraama Palitsyna,* ed. L. V. Cherepnin, O. A. Derzhavina, and E. V. Kolosova (Moscow: Akademiia nauk SSSR, 1955), p. 225.

6. Tokmakov, "Kratkii istoricheskii ocherk tserkvi sv. Velikomuchenitsy Ekateriny," pp. 698–99.

7. Ibid., p. 699. Chester Dunning's exhaustive account of this period makes no mention of a battle around St. Catherine's church, and his sober characterization of the leading figures on the Muscovite side is considerably less heroic than Palitsyn's. But he confirms the general point that these battles of spring and summer 1612 constituted a decisive moment in enabling the militias to begin dislodging Polish control of Moscow. Chester S. L. Dunning, *Russia's First Civil War: The Time of Troubles and the Founding of the Romanov Dynasty* (University Park, PA: Pennsylvania State University Press, 2001), pp. 434–39.

8. A. I. Uspenskii, ed., *Moskovskaia tserkovnaia starina. Trudy komissii po osmotru i izucheniiu pamiatnikov tserkovnoi stariny goroda moskvy i moskovskoi eparkhii,* vol. 4 (Moscow: A. I. Snegirev, 1905), no. 16, p. 1.

9. *PSRL,* vol. 6, 1853, p. 223; and several secondary accounts.

10. Uspenskii, *Moskovskaia tserkovnaia starina,* vol. 2 (1904), p. 47. The order decreeing the reconstruction and reconsecration is in "Dopolneniia k dvortsovym rozriadam," *Chteniia* (1882), bk. 3, p. 483.

11. Uspenskii, *Moskovskaia tserkovnaia starina*, p. 50, provides the date for the dedication. But the various court diaries show the opening having occurred only eleven days (November 28, 1627) after the reopening of St. Catherine's. They also record the tsaritsa attending services there, unmistakable evidence that the chapel had been consecrated on the earlier date. "Dopolneniiia k dvortsovym rozriadam," pp. 484–85, 497, etc.

12. Uspenskii, *Moskovskaia tserkovnaia starina*, pp. 47–49. The tsaritsy ordered the interior and iconostasis redone or repaired at least three times during the seventeenth century. In 1664, Mariia Il'inichna ordered the iconostasis redone in the same style as the Dormition Cathedral. In 1687, Sofia brought in Flemish artists to paint new icons and redesign the iconostasis, including adding new ornamentation to the icon of St. Catherine.

13. Ibid., pp. 124–26, 171–73.

14. S. P. Bartenev, *Bol'shoi Kremlevskii Dvorets. Ukazatel' k ego obozreniiu* (Moscow: Sinodal'naia Tipografiia, 1909), p. 48.

15. "Dela tainogo prikaza," *RIB*, vol. 23 (1904), pp. 985, 1008, 1091, 1092.

16. Ivan Zabelin, *Domashnyi byt russkikh tsarits v XVI–XVII st.* (Moscow: Tipografiia Gracheva i kompanii, 1863), pp. 130, 156, and passim.

17. Paul of Aleppo, *The Travels of Macarius, Patriarch of Antioch* (London: Oriental Translation Committee, 1829), p. 407.

18. Ibid., p. 408.

19. Uspenskii, *Moskovskaia tserkovnaia starina*, p. 49

20. Zabelin notes that in 1651 this case was in need of repair, an indication that it had been in the chapel for some time.

21. Pavel Svin'in, *Ukazatel' glavneishikh dostopamiatnostei sokhraniaiushchikhsia v masterskoi oruzheinnoi palate* (St. Petersburg: Smirdin, 1826), p. 81, item no. 298.

22. Zabelin, *Domashnyi byt*, p. 304.

23. Ibid., pp. 305–20; Ivan Zabelin, *Materialy dlia istorii, arkheologii, i statistiki goroda moskvy*, pt. 1, *Materialy dlia istorii, arkheologii, i statistiki moskovskikh tserkvei, sobrannye iz knig i del prezhdebyvshikh patriarshikh prikazov V. I. i G. I. Kholmogorovymi* (Moscow: Gorodskaia Tipografiia, 1884), pp. 181–82.

24. "Dopolneniia k dvortsovym rozriadam," pp. 653, 670, 677, 691, 757, 761, 814–15, 877, and passim. The frequency of the entries is inconsistent, sometimes listing several days in a week, other times going a week or two with no entries at all. Consequently, one cannot calculate how often the tsaritsa attended any particular church, but the proportion of entries for the St. Catherine church is greater than for any other.

25. Ibid., pp. 811–12 (April 21, 1633); Zabelin, *Materialy*, pp. 182, 286.

26. Thyrêt, *Between God and Tsar*, pp. 132–38.

27. Uspenskii, *Moskovskaia tserkovnaia starina*, pp. 198–200.

28. Ibid., p. 218ff. lists the various clergy implicated in the streltsy revolts, none of whom were connected to St. Catherine's.

29. "Ustav Moskovskikh Sviateishikh Patriarkhov Rossiiskikh . . .," *DRV*, vol. 10, 1789; reprinted 1970, pp. 90–94.

30. Ibid., p. 93. The entry for 1688, for example, relates that the patriarch conducted a small mass at the cathedral and sent the Vologda archbishop and the abbot of Znamenskii Monastery to Ascension Convent for vespers. They proceeded to St. Catherine's, accompanied by the ruling figures, in this case the tsar and tsarevna,, to read the liturgy, and then they all went to Chudov Monastery at which the Ustiug archbishop conducted a service. Finally, they returned to St. Catherine's to hear a sermon (*pouchenie*), presumably the patriarch's.

31. Brailovskii, "Odin iz pestrykh," p. 117.

32. "Dopolneniia k dvortsovym razriadam," pp. 595, 604, 654, 672, 677, and passim.

33. P. M. Stroev, *Vykhody gosudarei tsarei i velikikh kniazei Mikhaila Fedorovicha, Alekseia Mikhailovicha, Fedora Alekseevicha vseia Rusi samoderzhetsev, s 1632 po 1682 god* (Moscow: Tipografiia Avgusta Semena, 1844), pp. 323, 380, 439; N. D. Izvekov,

Moskovskiia kremlevskiia dvortsovye tserkvi i sluzhivshiia pri nikh litsa v XVII veke (Moscow: Tipografiia Snegirovoi, 1906), p. 50. Izvekov maintained that the tsar's miraculous vision of St. Catherine in 1658 inspired him to have the baptisms done in St. Catherine's. Although plausible, the statement's source is unknown.

34. Zabelin, *Domashnyi byt*, p. 317.

35. "Dopolneniia k dvortsovym razriadam," pp. 814–15, 875, 877.

36. *PSZ*, vol. 1, no. 235, August 24, 1658, p.460, "Ob'iavlenie o konchine i pogrebenii Tsarevny Tatiany Mikhai'lovny," and August 23, 1658: "O prestavlenii i pogrebenii Tsarevny Tatiany Mikhailovny," *DRV*, vol. 10, 1789; reprinted 1970, pp. 214–16.

37. S. M. Solov'ev, *Istoriia Rossii s drevneishikh vremen*, bk. 3, vol. 15 (St. Petersburg: Tovarishchestvo 'Obshchestennaia Pol'za, 1911), pp. 1202, 1375.

38. "a Tsar' i Tsaritsa proshchalis', i tselovali u samoi grobnitsy ikony." *Dvortsovye razriady*, vol. 4, pp. 620–22.

39. Ivan Snegirev, *Pamiatniki moskovskoi drevnosti* (Moscow: Avgust Semen, 1842–1845), p. 214; "O osviashchenii tserkvei Sviatei Patriarkhom," *DRV*, vol. 11, 1787 pt. 45, p. 271.

40. *PSZ*, vol. 4, no. 2118, August 24, 1706, pp. 354–55, "Chin pogrebeniia Tsarevny Tatiany Mikhailovny," pp. 354–55. The document can also be found in *DRV*, vol. 14, 1789; reprinted 1970, pp. 111–22.

41. *PSZ*, vol. 3, no. 1438, 1834, p. 182, "Ob''iavlenie o prestavlenii i pogrebenii Tsarevicha Aleksandra Petrovicha."

42. "Tseremonial vo vremia prestavleniia blazhennyia pamiati Blagovernago Gosudaria, Tsarevicha i Velikogo Kniazia Alekseia Alekseievicha, vseia Velikiia i Malyia i Belyia Rossii," *DRV*, vol. 14, 1789; reprinted 1970, pp. 65–69.

43. See, for example, the regulation of 1687 governing processionals of the cross within the Moscow Kremlin. "O tom, kakie v onykh malykh i bol'shikh krestnykh khodakh i ot kuda imenno Sviatye obrazy, kresty, i prochie nositsia, i kolikoe chislo dlia pod''emu onykh Sviashchennosluzhitelei podlezhatel'no?" DRV, vol. 11, 1789; reprinted 1970, pp. 162–63.

44. *PSZ*, vol. 1, no. 372, March 9, 1665, pp. 609–11, "Tseremonial Tsarskogo vykhoda na prazdnik Tsvetonosnago Khristova Voskreseniia v Uspenskii Sobor."

45. N. F. Protsenko, *Monastyri v Rossii i sobory v Moskve* (Moscow: Tipografiia P. A. Glushkova, 1863), p. 17.

46. The first such mention comes on December 6, 1627, and then again on December 14 and 16. "Dopolneniia k dvortsovym razriadam," p. 485. See also Aleksandr Ratshin, *Polnoe sobranie istoricheskikh svedenii o vsekh byvshikh v drevnosti i nyne sushchestvuiushchikh monastyriakh i primechatel'nykh tserkvei v Rossii* (Moscow: Universitetskaia Tipografiia, 1852), p. 340; Zvonarev, *Sorok sorokov*, vol. 1 (1988), pp. 69–70.

47. "Dopolneniia k dvortsovym razriadam," p. 382.

48. Ibid., p. 417.

49. "Prikhodo-raskhodnye knigi kazennogo prikaza," in *RIB*, vol. 9 (1884), contains seven separate references to outlays for the St. Catherine church in 1613 and 1614, the earliest coming on November 22, 1613. See pp. 191, 198, 215, 227, 295, 328, 346.

50. Izvekov, *Moskovskiia kremlevskiia dvortsovye tserkvi*, p. 47; *PSRL*, vol. 6, 1853 p. 223.

51. *Patriarshaia ili Nikonovskaia letopis'*, *PSRL*, vol. 11, 1862, p. 172. E. E. Golubinskii also lists this reference, citing it as evidence for the existence of the chapel, a conclusion made problematic by the absence of this reference in any other chronicle accounts of this period. Golubinskii, *Istoriia russkoi tserkvi. Period vtoroi, moskovskii*, vol. 2, *Ot nashestviia Mongolov do mitropolita Makariia vkliuchatel'no* (Moscow: Sinodal'naia Tipografiia, 1911), p. 397.

52. The Semeonovskii Chronicle, for example (*PSRL*, vol. 18, 1913) contains a lengthy passage on 6907 (pp. 143–48) without any mention of a St. Catherine church.

Several others also mentioned the trip to Novgorod (Semeonovskiaia, Nikanorovskaia, Tipografskaia) although some placed it in a different year, but none of these noted a chapel of St. Catherine.

53. The classic study of the Russian veneration of St. Alexis remains V. P. Adrianova (Peretts), *Zhitie Alekseia Cheloveka Bozhiia v drevnei russkoi literature i narodni slovesnosti* (Petrograd: Tipografiia Ia. Bashmakov i kompanii, 1917; reprint, The Hague: Mouton, 1969).

54. Viktor Zhivov, "Dva prostranstva russkogo srednevekov'ia i ikh pozdneishie metamorfozy," *Otechestvennye zapiski*, no. 5 (20), 2004, pp. 16–18.

55. B. M. Kloss, *Nikonovskii svod i russkie letopisi XVI–XVII vekov* (Moscow: Nauka, 1980), p. 55.

56. V. N. Tatishchev, *Istoriia Rossiiskaia*, vol. 6 (Moscow: Nauka, 1966), p. 137. The source for this text is identified in the introduction (p. 7) of vol. 6.

57. Ibid., p. 138.

58. Ibid., pp. 138–39.

59. N. M. Karamzin, *Istoriia gosudarstva rossiiskogo*, vol. 7 (St. Petersburg: Izdanie Evgeniia Evdokimova, 1892), p. 101 and notes p. 43.

60. Ibid., p. 106.

61. D. S. Likhachev, *Chelovek v literature drevnei Rusi* (Moscow: Nauka, 1970), pp. 26, 39. See also Daniel E. Collins, "Early Russian Topoi of Deathbed and Testament," in *Medieval Russian Culture*, vol. 2, ed. Michael S. Flier and Daniel Rowland (Berkeley: University of California Press, 1994), pp. 134–59.

62. *PSRL*, vol. 13 (Tsarstvennaia kniga), 1904; reprinted 1965, p. 417; vol. 34 (Postnikovskii letopisets), 1978, p. 22: vol. 29 (Aleksandro-Nevskaia letopis'), 1965, p. 125; vol. 21 (Stepennaia kniga), 1908, p. 614; vol. 6 (Vtoraia Sofiiskaia letopis', 1853, p. 273). Both Zimin and Likhachev have dated these chronicles from the middle third of the sixteenth century: Vtoraia [second] Sofiiskaia (1530s and 1540s), Stepennaia kniga (late 1560s), Nevskaia letopis' (late 1560s), Tsarstvennaia kniga (1553). Likhachev termed the Nevskii Chronicle the official Moscow chronicle of the second half of the sixteenth century. D. S. Likhachev, *Russkie letopisi i ikh kul'turno-istoricheskoe znachenie* (Moscow-Leningrad: Akademiia nauk SSSR, 1947), p. 373; A. A. Zimin, *Russkie letopisi i khronografy kontsa XV–XVI vv. Uchebnoe posobie* (Moscow: Gos. Istoriko-arkhivnyi institute, 1960; reprint, The Hague: Mouton, 1969), pp. 18–25.

63. This text comes from the Postnikovskii letopisets, pp. 22–23. The other versions are almost identical, with only slight stylistic changes in phraseology.

64. Gail Lenhoff, "Temir Aksak's Dream of the Virgin as Protectress of Muscovy," *Die Welt der Slaven* 49 (2004), pp. 39–42. See also, David Miller, "Legends of the Icon of Our Lady of Vladimir: A Study of the Development of Muscovite National Consciousness," *Speculum* 43, no. 4 (1968), pp. 239–73.

65. Serhii Plokhy argues that Theotokos played a similar role in Ukraine, particularly as a symbol of Moscow's growing protectorate over it during the seventeenth century. Thus the tsar's emissary to Bogdan Khmelnitskii proclaimed in a speech, "And as the Immaculate Theotokos once covered the faithful in Constantinople with her miraculous cloak, [repelling] the enemies who armed themselves against the faithful by means of the almighty intercession wrought by her miraculous image, defeating some miraculously and putting others to shameful rout, so she is depicted among your regiments on this banner of the tsar's; when it is carried, she protects you against infidel arms and grants victory over them, keeping you and the whole Orthodox host and all the faithful safe from harm." Plokhy, *Tsars and Cossacks: A Study in Iconography* (Cambridge: Harvard University Press, 2002), p. 36.

66. Collins, "Early Russian Topoi," p. 135.

67. Ibid., pp. 140–46.

68. Aleksandro-Nevskaia letopis', *PSRL* vol. 29, 1853, p. 120; Patriarshaia ili Nikonovskaia letopis', *PSRL* vol. 14, 1965, p. 75.

69. Patriarshaia ili Nikonovskaia letopis', *PSRL* vol. 14, 1965, p. 76; Aleksandro-Nevskaia letopis', *PSRL* vol. 29, 1853, p. 126.

70. Letopisets nachala tsarstva tsaria i velikogo kniazia Ivana Vasil'evicha (*PSRL,* 1965 vol. 29), pp. 9, 10.

71. The homilies and most of the epistles remain unpublished, but Vasilii Zhmakin's exhaustive study of Daniil included extensive summaries of each of his writings. Nowhere does Zhmakin mention St. Catherine. Vasilii Zhmakin, *Mitropolit Daniil i ego sochineniia* (Moscow: Universitetskaia Tipografiia, 1881), pp. 259ff.

72. Ibid., p. 221.

73. D. M. Bulanin, *Perevody i poslaniia Maksima Greka. Neizdannye teksty* (Leningrad: Nauka, 1984), pp. 8, 25ff; *Sochineniia Prepodobnogo Maksima Greka* (Kazan, 1859), pt. 1, p. 36.

74. "Prenie Daniila mitropolita moskovskogo i vseia Rusi so inokom Maksimom sviatogurtsem," *Chteniia* (1847), bk. 7, pp. 6–7. For background on the linkages between the transvolgans and Maksim Grek, see A. S. Arkhangel'skii, *Nil Sorskii i Vassian Patrikeev. Ikh literaturnye trudy i idei v drevnei Rusi,* vol. 1: *Prepodobnyi Nil Sorskii* (St. Petersburg: Tipografiia I. Voshchinskogo, 1882) and Ia. S. Lur'e, *Ideologicheskaia bor'ba v russkoi publitsistike kontsa XV–nachala XVI veka* (Moscow-Leningrad: Nauka, 1960). See also A. I. Pliguzov, *Polemika v russkoi tserkvi pervoi treti XVI stoletiia* (Moscow: Izdatel'stvo Indrik, 2002), especially chaps. 3, 5, and 6.

75. The interrogation between Vassian and Daniil, "Sudnoe delo Vassiana Patrikeeva (1531 god, 11 maia)," is reprinted in N. A, Kazakova, *Vassian Patrikeev i ego sochinehiia* (Moscow: Akademiia nauk SSSR, 1960), pp. 285–318. This particular interchange is on p. 290.

76. In a less than exhaustive search, I could find only one reference to St. Catherine in his works, in an epistle written to V. M. Tuchkov-Morozov, in which she is one of many saints, including Fedor, Panteleimon, George, and Barbara, cited as Christian martyrs whose lives should be revered. Bulanin, *Perevody,* p. 202.

77. Sigismund von Herberstein, *Notes upon Russia.* A translation of *Rerum Moscoviticarum Commentarii* done by R. H. Major (London: Haklyut Society, 1851), p. 21.

78. There was one other Catherine, the sister-in-law of King Gustavus Adolphus II of Sweden, who came close to entering the Romanov family in 1623. A delegation had gone to Stockholm with the proposal that she marry Tsar Mikhail Fedorovich. Since her family was unwilling to allow her to convert to Orthodoxy, the proposal was not accepted. Martin, "Dynastic Marriage in Muscovy," pp. 79–80.

79. Herberstein, *Notes upon Russia,* pp. 32–39.

80. Antonova and Mneva, *Katalog drevnerusskoi rukopisi,* vol. 2, no. 855, p. 364.

81. Thyrêt, *Between God and Tsar,* pp. 24–28.

82. Ibid., p. 25.

83. The most extensive study of the Byzantine princely connection remains V. Savva, *Moskovskie tsari i vizantiiskie vasilevy. K voprosu o vliianii Vizantii na obrazovanie idei tsarskoi vlasti moskovskikh gosudarei* (The Hague: Mouton Reprints, 1969), especially chap. 1. Savva found little evidence to support the idea that Sofia had been the moving force behind Byzantine influence, other than Herberstein's second-hand accounts, and he was skeptical of many of the claims for adaptation of Byzantine ritual (his discussion of the Palm Sunday ritual is a case in point). He also noted that Ivan III never insisted upon being called "tsar,'" unlike his successors who demanded that it be made part of official protocol. Nevertheless, Ivan III was the first to employ the title, and as Savva demonstrated, its meaning surely derived, at least in part, from Byzantium. See also Michael Cherniavsky, "Khan or Basileus: An Aspect of Russian Medieval Theory," *Journal of the History of Ideas* 20, no. 4 (1959), pp. 459–76.

84. Tsarstvennaia kniga, *PSRL,* 1904, vol. 13, pp. 500–501; Patriarshaia ili Nikonovskaia letopis,' *PSRL,* 1963, vol. 13, pp. 204–05.

85. Dopolneniia k nikonovskoi letopisi, *PSRL,* 1862; reprinted 1963, vol. 13, pp. 310–311.

86. Ibid., p. 372.

87. "Dopolneniia k dvortsovym razriadem," pp. 484–85, entry for November 28, 1627.

88. Ibid., p. 539.

89. Ibid., p. 497.

90. Ibid., p. 657, 737, 875 (Evdokia), 673, 813 (Irina), 768 (Marfa).

91. Zabelin, *Materialy,* p. 285.

92. N. F. Protsenko, *Monastyri v Rossii i sobory v Moskve* (Moscow: Tipografiia Glushkova, 1863), p. 16; Ivan Zabelin, *Al'bom starinnykh vidov moskovskago kremlia* (Moscow: Tipografiia Kushnerev, 1904), p. 1.

93. Zabelin, *Materialy,* p. 285.

94. Quoted in I. Tokmakov, *Povest' o moshchakh sv. Velikomuchenitsy Ekateriny. Po skazaniiam XVII veka* (Moscow: Izdatel'stvo Segirovoi, 1881), p. 3.

95. "Ustav tserkovnykh obriadov, sovershavshikhsia v moskovskom Uspenskom Sobore," in *RIB,* vol. 3 (1876), p. 36.

96. Stroev, *Vykhody gosudarei tsarei,* p. 23.

97. Ibid., pp. 181–82, 285–87.

98. Ibid., pp. 4, 23, 146, 176, 193, 251, 271, 301, 316–17, 343, 366, 388, and passim.

99. "Dopolneniia k dvortsovym razriadam," p. 649 and passim.

100. S. A. Belokurov, *Dneval'nye zapiski prikaza tainykh del 1765–1783 gg.* (Moscow: Tipografiia moskovskogo voennogo okruga, 1908), p. 41.

101. The account of her numerous intercessions in 1613 details how she received an array of supplications from all ranks of people ("vlasti, i boiare, i stol'niki, i striapchie, i dvoriane, i vsiakikh chinov liudi pisali") beseeching her, as the mother of the tsar, to convince her son to stay on the throne, in spite of his stated reluctance to do so. Eventually, say the *razriadnye knigi,* she prevailed upon Mikhail to remain, and only then did she give him her blessing. *Razriadnye knigi, 1598–1638* (Moscow: Akademiia nauk, 1974), pp. 192, 204–5, 208–9, 217–27, 220.

102. "Dopolneniia k dvortsovym razriadam," *Chteniia* (1882), bk. 1, entries for the years 1613–1622, pp. 1–288, contain several such references.

103. Zabelin, *Domashnyi byt,* pp. 349–52, 357, 498.

104. I. A. Shliapkin, "Opisanie rukopisei suzdal'skogo efimieva monastyria," *Pamiatniki drevnei pis'mennosti* 9, no. 4 (1880), p. 70.

105. V. D. Nazarov et al., eds., *Akty rossiiskogo gosudarstva. Arkhivy moskovskikh monastyrei i soborov XV–nachalo XVII vv.* (Moscow: Ladomir, 1998), pp. 494, 510.

106. Arkheograficheskaia komissiia. *Akty sobrannye v bibliotekakh i arkhivakh rossiiskoiu imperatorskoiu arkheograficheskoiu ekspeditsieiu imperatorskoi Akademii nauk* (St. Petersburg, 1836), vol. 2, pp. 136–37.

107. V. V. Zverinskii, *Materialy dlia istoriko-topograficheskogo izsledovaniia o pravoslavnykh monastyriakh v rossiiskoi imperii* (St. Petersburg: V. Bezobravov i kompaniia, 1890), pp. 130–31.

108. I. M., *Palomnik kievskii, ili putevoditel' po monastyriam i tserkvam kievskim, dlia bogomoltsev poseshchaiushikh sviatniu Kieva* (Kiev: Universitetskaia Tipografiia, 1854), p 83.

109. *DRV,* vol. 11, 1789; reprinted 1970, pp. 283, 290, 294, 296, 297, 316, 317, 318, 320, 322, 324.

110. *Istoricheskie materialy dlia sostavleniia tserkovnykh letopisei moskvskoi eparkhii,* ed. V. Kholmogorov and G. Kholmogorov, 10 vols. (Moscow: Tipografiia Snegireva, 1881–1894).

111. Zverinskii, *Materialy,* p. 202.

4—Monasteries

1. http:/www.vidnoe.ru/town

2. André Berelowitch, "Chasse et rituel en Russie au XVIIe siecle: le Règlement de

la fauconnerie d'Alexis Mixajlovič," *Russes, slaves, et sovietiques. Pages d'histoire offertes à Roger Portal*. Edited by Céline Gervais-Francelle (Paris: Institut d'études slaves, 1992), pp. 88–95.

3. http:/www.Vidnoe.ru.

4. On the decline in pilgrimages, see *Pravoslavnye russkie obiteli* (1910; reprint, St. Petersburg: Voskresenie, 1994), pp. 309–10, and I. Tokmakov, *Ekaterininskaia pustyn' moskovskoi gubernii, podol'skogo uezda. Kratkii istoriko-arkheograficheskii ocherk* (Moscow: Gubernskaia Tipografiia, 1892), p. 3.

5. Tokmakov, *Ekaterininskaia pustyn'*, p. 5.

6. *Monastyri Sviatoi Ekateriny Sinai. Rossiia. Posviashchaetsia 340–letiiu Sviato-Eka-terininskogo muzheskogo monastyria v Rossii* (Moscow: Tovarishchestvo 'Rarog', 1998), p. 9.

7. *Monastyri Sviatoi Ekateriny Sinai*, p. 14.

8. RGADA, *f.* 396 (Oruzheinaia palata), *op.* 1, part 5, no. 121/1156, November 27, 1658, announcing the birth of Ekaterina Alekseevna; no. 170/6295, December 30, 1658, announcing the new church of St. Catherine; *Monastyri Sviatoi Ekateriny Sinai*, p. 7.

9. Quoted in Tokmakov, *Ekaterininskaia pustyn'*, p. 7.

10. See, for example, the announcement for the birth of Ekaterina Ioannovna, born on October 29 but named after Saint Catherine. *Dvortsovye razriady*, vol. 4, pp. 620–22.

11. Daniel Kaiser, "Naming Cultures in Early Modern Russia," *Harvard Ukrainian Studies* 19 (1995), p. 287.

12. *Dvortsovye razriady*, vol. 3, p. 149; vol. 4, p. 536; Tatishchev, *Istoriia rossiiskaia*, vol. 7, p. 171, and passim.

13. RGADA, *f.* 396, *op.* 1, pt. 5, no. 121/1156, pp. 1–2.

14. Tatishchev, *Istoriia rossiiskaia*, vol. 7, p. 171.

15. Stroev, *Vykhody gosudarei tsarei*, index.

16. Mazurinskii letopisets. *PSRL*, vol. 31 (1968), p. 170. The dating is based on a watermark from 1680 and *skoropis'* of the late seventeenth century (p. 4).

17. "V nyneshnem vo 167 godu Noiabria v 27 den', za molitv sviatykh otets, Bog prostil Tsaritsu nashu i Velikuiu Kniaziniu Mariiu Il'inichnu, a rodila nam Velikomu Gosudariu dshcher' Tsarevnu i Velikuiu Kniazhnu Ekaterinu Alekseevnu; a imianiny eia Noiabria v 24 den' . . ." *AAE*, vol. 4, no. 109 (St. Petersburg, Akademiia nauk, 1836).

18. *Chteniia* (1880), bk. 2, p. 10.

19. Ibid., p. 11.

20. Lenhoff, "Temir Aksak's Dream of the Virgin," p. 39ff.

21. The translation appears in William Palmer, *The Patriarch and the Tsar* (London: Truebner and Co., 1840), vol. 4, pp. 310–12.

22. A. A. Kruming, "Chet'i Minei sviatogo Dimitriia Rostovskogo. Ocherk istorii izdaniia," *Filevskie chteniia*, vol. 9, *Sviatoi Dimitrii Rostovskii. Issledovaniia i materially* (Moscow, 1994), p. 8. The English translation of the life and appendix is in the work, St. Demetrius of Rostov [Rostovskii], *The Great Collection of the Lives of Saints*, vol. 3, *November* (House Springs, MO: Chrysostom Press, 2001), pp. 163–69.

23. "Diariush," in *Sochineniia Sviatogo Dimitriia, mitropolita rostovskogo*, vol. 1 (Moscow: Sinodal'naia Tipografiia, 1841), pp. 672–73.

24. Rostovskii, "Diariush," pp. 480–82.

25. M. I. Semevskii, "Petr Velikii v ego snakh," in *Ocherki i rasskazy iz russkoi istorii XVIII veka* (St. Petersburg: Akademiia nauk, 1884), vol. 2, pp. 271–76. This essay has been republished in a photo print facsimile. See Semevskii, *Slovo i delo, 1700–1725. Ocherki i raskazy iz russkoi istorii XVIII v.* (1884; reprint, Moscow: Sovmestnoe predpriiatie Kh. G. S., 1991), pp. 271–76. To date the only systematic study of those dreams is James Cracraft's psychoanalytic effort, "Some Dreams of Peter the Great: A Biographical Note," *Canadian-American Slavic Studies* 8, no. 2 (Summer 1974), pp. 173–97. Cracraft muses that there may be more such dream transcriptions buried in Peter's private papers, but to date not even these are listed in the relevant archival inventories. A less

psychoanalytic, but equally speculative reading can be found in Elena Pogosian, *Petr I—arkhitektor rossiiskoi istorii* (St. Petersburg: Iskusstvo St. Petersburg, 2001), pp. 230–34. See also, E. V. Anisimov, *Vremia petrovskikh reform* (Leningrad: Nauka, 1989), p. 49.

26. Cracraft, "Some Dreams of Peter the Great," pp. 192–93.

27. *PSZ*, vol. 1, no. 160, July 12, 1655, p. 366, "Imennyi [ukaz] skazannyi vsiakikh chinov sluzhivym liudam, v pokhvalu ikh userdnoi sluzhby."

28. On Arsenios's teaching, see Adam Olearius, *The Travels of Olearius in Seventeenth-Century Russia*, trans. Samuel H. Baron (Stanford: Stanford University Press, 1967), pp. 238–39; Sergei Belokurov, *Adam Olearii o grekolatinskoi shkole Arseniia Greka v Moskve v XVII v.* (Moscow: Tipografiia L. and A. Snegirevykh, 1888). Although most commentators believed that the school prepared correctors for the *Pechatnyi dvor*, Belokurov (pp. 17–25) saw it as having a more ambitious agenda of preparing well-educated clergy for the realm overall, the predecessor of the Greco-Latin-Slavonic Academy established in 1687.

29. Several scholars have recounted Arsenios's life, but the source for most of these is V. Kolosov, "Starets Arsenii Grek," *ZMNP*, pt. 217 (1881), pp. 77–93. See also B. L. Fonkich, *Grechesko-russkie kul'turnye sviazi v XV–XVII vv.* (Moscow: Nauka, 1977), pp. 120–21, 144–45, 165; Paul Meyendorff, *Russia, Ritual, and Reform: The Liturgical Reforms of Nikon in the Seventeenth Century* (Crestwood, NY: St. Vladimir's Seminary Press, 1991), pp. 101–8.

30. Textual descriptions can be found in A. S. Zernova, *Knigi kirillovskoi pechati izdannye v Moskve v XVI–XVII vekakh. Svodni katalog* (Moscow: Biblioteka imeni Lenina, 1958), nos. 257 *(Sluzhebnik)*, 266 *(Skrizhal')*, 287 *(Anfologion)*. See also V. M. Undol'skii, *Ocherk slaviano-russkoi bibliografii. Khronologicheskii ukazatel' slaviano-russkikh knig tserkovnoi pechati s 1491-go po 1864-i g.* (Moscow: Tipografiia Gracheva i kompanii, 1871), nos. 707, 710, 752, and 758.

31. A. I. Sobolevskii, *Perevodnaia literatura moskovskoi Rusi XIV–XVII vekov. Bibliograficheskie materialy* (Moscow: Akademiia nauk, 1903), p. 326; Adrianova, *Zhitie Alekseia*, pp. 107–14. On Arsenii Sukhanov's assemblage of 498 books and manuscripts, see Fonkich, *Grechesko-russkie kul'turnye sviazi*, pp. 68–71. The inventory of Nikon's property ordered by the tsar in 1658 lists many of the books that Arsenios borrowed from among those collected by Sukhanov. "Perepisnaia kniga domovoi kazny Patriarkha Nikona," *Vremennik Imperatorskogo moskovskogo obshchestva istorii i drevnostei rossiiskikh,* bk. 15 (1852), pp. 117–31.

32. A summary of these proceedings may be found in Makarii, *Istoriia russkoi tserkvi,* vol. 7, pp. 187–94. Makarii's account constitutes a vigorous defense of the entire proceedings, and of Nikon in particular, a view not shared by many other scholars. But his summary of events is very close to his sources.

33. "Knig liturgii Ioanna Zlatoustago i o semi tainakh tserkovnykh vostoku i Afanasiia Aleksandrskago otvety o vsiakikh veshchei i o bozhestam pokrestnam znaemnii." RGIA, *f. 796, op. 58, d. 43,* p. 5ob.

34. *Biblion kaloumenon paradeisos* (Venice, 1641); *Biblion kaloumenon eklogion* (Venice, 1644); *Biblion kaloumenon thesaurus* (Venice, 1570). My thanks to Sylvia Dover for assisting with the Greek titles.

35. Arsenii Grek, *Anfologion* (Moscow: Pechatnyi dvor, 1660), p. 2.

36. The table of contents is listed in Zernova, *Knigi kirillovskoi pechati,* no. 266, pp. 82–83.

37. RGIA, *f. 796, op. 58, no. 43,* p. 5ob.

38. Makarii, *Istoriia russkogo raskola izvestnogo pod imenem staroobriadstva* (St. Petersburg: Tipografiia morskogo ministerstva, 1858), p. 183.

39. Of the nine copies listed in the Library of the Academy of Sciences, only one contains an inscription from the seventeenth century, from the Feodorovskii Monastery, and none contains seventeenth-century marginalia. Antonina Zernova's posthumously published study of 800 pre-eighteenth-century inscriptions found on six-

teenth- and seventeenth-century Moscow imprints in the Lenin Library does not list *Anfologion* among them, even though the library possesses several copies of it. The copy in the British Library, which I consulted for this section, contains extensive marginalia, but all in modern script. The surviving copies of *Skrizhal'*, by contrast, include several seventeenth-century inscriptions, and considerable evidence of the books being used. L. I. Kiseleva, ed., *Korpus zapisei na staropechatnykh kngakh*, vol. 1, *Zapisi na knigakh kirillovskogo shrifta napechatannykh v Moskve v XVI–XVII vv.* (St. Petersburg: Biblioteka Akademii nauk, 1992), pp. 99–100, 107–8; A. S. Zernova, "Nadpisi na knigakh moskovskoi pechati XVI–XVII vv. v sobranii otdela redkikh knig gosudarstvennoi biblioteki SSSR imeni V. I. Lenina," *Kniga. Issledovaniia i materialy* 62 (1991), pp. 130–31.

40. Adrianova, *Zhitie Alekseia*, p. 108.

41. Arsenii, *Anfologion*, pp. 1–2.

42. Ibid., p. 3.

43. Adrianova, *Zhitie Alekseia*, note 2, p. 108.

44. The recorded inscriptions from eight surviving copies of *Anfologion* in institutional libraries in Moscow include no marginalia from the seventeenth century. By contrast, its companion volume, *Skrizhal'*, of which a dozen copies survived, includes at least three seventeenth-century inscriptions. Kiseleva, *Korpus zapisei na staropechatnykh knigakh*, pp. 99–100, 107–8.

45. Arsenii, *Anfologion*, pp. 11–12.

46. *Monastyri Sviatoi Ekateriny Sinai*, p. 3. This icon remained at St. Katherine's until the monastery was closed in 1918, after which it was transferred for safekeeping to St. Nicholas Church in the village of Ermolino, near where the monastery had been built. In 1970, the icon was stolen and eventually sold in Germany. Private correspondence from Ierodeacon Feodor of the St. Catherine Monastery, April 8, 2002.

47. *RIB*, vol. 21, 1902, p. 1435. My thanks to Ann Kleimola for bringing this document to my attention.

48. Amvrosii, Archimandrite of the Novgorod Seminary, *Istoriia rossiiskoi ierarkhii*, pt. 4 (Moscow: Sinodal'naia Tipografiia, 1812), pp. 80–81.

49. Tokmakov, *Ekaterininskaia pustyn'*, pp. 8–9.

50. "Ustav Moskovskikh Sviateishikh Patriarkhov Rossiiskikh, ot sozdaniia mira 7176, a ot Rozhdestva Khristova 1668 . . ." *DRV*, vol. 10, 1789; reprinted 1970, p. 91.

51. Ibid., pp. 90–94. The entries for 1680 and 1681 state explicitly that in that year no one was sent from the Kremlin to Ermolino.

52. *DRV*, vol. 10, 1789; reprinted 1970, p. 93.

53. *RIB*, vol. 23 (1904), pp. 42, 151, 668, 1325, 1536, 1547, 1550, 1553, 1555, 1657.

54. *Monastyri Sviatoi Ekateriny Sinai*, p. 8. Early twentieth-century guidebooks refer to cross processionals on June 29 and August 15, in honor of Saints Peter and Paul and Dimitrii Rostovskii, after whom a later chapel was named. *Pravoslavnye russkie obiteli* (St. Petersburg: P. P. Soikin, 1910; reprint, St. Petersburg: Voskresenie, 1994), pp. 309–10.

55. Kapterev, "Russkaia blagotvoritel'nost' sinaiskoi obiteli," p. 363.

56. The account of the sacking of monasteries and holy sites in 1366 recurs in several chronicles. See "Sokrashennyi letopisnyi svod 1495 g.," *PSRL*, vol. 27 (1962), p. 328; *Vologodsko-Permskaia letopis'*, vol. 26, 1959, p. 119.

57. Piatnitsky, *Sinai, Byzantium, Russia*, p. 20; *Novgorodskie letopisi*, p. 35.

58. N. F. Kapterev, "Snosheniia ierusalimskikh patriarkhov s russkim pravitel'stvom s poloviny XVI do kontsa XVIII stoletiia," *Pravoslavnyi palestinskii sbornik* vol. 15 (1895), p. 7ff.

59. Ibid., p. 94; Kapterev, "Russkaia blagotvoritel'nost' sinaiskoi obiteli," pp. 364–67.

60. *PSRL*, vol. 27 (1962), "Leningradskii spisok Khrongrafa Nikanorovskoi letopisi." pp. 418-19.

61. Kapterev, "Snosheniia," p. 95.

62. Trifon Korobeinikov, *Puteshestvie moskovskogo kuptsa Trifona Korobeinikova s tovarishchami v Ierusalim, Egipet, i k Sinaiskoi gore v 1583 g.* (St. Petersburg, 1783); "Posol'stvo s gosudarevoiu zazravnoiu milostieiu vo Tsar' gorod i vo Aleksandriiu i vo Antiokhiu i v Erusalim, i v Sinaiskuiu goru Trifona Korobeinikova i Mikhaila Ograkova (1593 g.)," *DRV,* vol. 12, 1789; reprinted 1970, pp. 425–49; Kh. M. Loparev, ed., "Khozhdenie Trifona Korobeinikova 1593–94 gg.," *Pravoslavnyi palestinskii sbornik* vol. 11, no. 3, (1889) pp. 84-103.

63. Loparev, "Khozhdenie Trifona Korobeinikova," p. 67.

64. Ibid., p. 68.

65. "Posol'stvo," p. 442.

66. Paisiia Agiapostolito mitropolita ruskago, "Opisanie sviatoi gory sinaiskoi i eia okrestnostei v stikhakh," *Pravoslavnyi palestinskii sbornik* 12, no. 2 (1891), pp. 109–11.

67. "Puteshestvie Igumena Daniila po sviatym mestam v nachale XII-go stoletiia," in *Puteshestviia russkikh liudei po sviatoi zemle* (St. Petersburg: Tipografiia Sakharova, 1839), p. 6; V. N. Khitrovo, *Palestina i Sinai* (St. Petersburg: Tipografiia Maikova, 1876), pp. 1–2; A. S. Demin, "'Khozhdenie' igumena Daniila v Ierusalim (opyt kommentariia na temu 'Rossiia i Zapad')," *Germenevtika drevnerusskoi literatury,* vol. 8 (1996), pp. 62–69.

68. "Puteshestvie Stefana Novgorodtsa po sviatym mestam"; "Puteshestvie Ierodiakona Zosimy"; "Puteshestvie diakona Arsenii Selunskogo po sviatym mestam," all in *Puteshestviia russkikh liudei.* A more extensive bibliography of early Russian pilgrims' narratives can be found in Khitrovo, *Palestina i Sinai.* See also "Khronologicheskjoe obozrenie puteshestviia Russkikh k sviatym mestam," *ZMNP,* pt. 61 (1849), pp. 169–71.

69. N. F. Kapterev, *Kharakter otnoshenii Rossii k pravoslavnomu vostoku v XVI i XVII stoletiiakh* (Sergiev Posad: M. S. Elov, 1914; reprint, The Hague: Mouton, 1968), pp. 115–46, esp. pp. 134–35.

70. Ibid., pp. 77–78. Kapterev calculated with apparent bemusement that relics of St. Panteleimon were sent no fewer than 23 times, along with 14 of Chrysostom, 14 of St. Stephan, 7 of John the Baptist, and 5 of the apostle Andrew.

71. Kapterev, "Snosheniia," p. 95.

72. A photo reproduction of the codex was published in 1989. *An Orthodox Pomjanyk of the Seventeenth-Eighteenth Centuries,* ed. Moshe Altbauer (Cambridge: Harvard Ukrainian Research Institute, 1989), p. viii.

73. Kapterev, "Russkaia blagotvoritel'nost' sinaiskoi obiteli," pp. 397–98.

74. Kapterev, "Snosheniia," p. 267.

75. Iōan V. Dura, "Ho Dositheos Hierosolymōn kai hĕ prosphora autou eis tas Roumanikas choras kai ten ekklesian auton" (Ph.D. diss., Theological School, University of Athens, 1977), pp. 178–200; Iōan E. Anastasiou, *Sinaïtika tou 16 kai 17 aiōnos* (Thessalonika, 1970), pp. 68–70, 78–89, 104–8. My thanks to Nikolaos Chrissides for pointing out these texts, and to Themis Chronopoulos for assistance in translating the relevant passages.

76. Pianitsky, *Sinai, Byzantium, Russia,* p. 21.

77. My thanks to Sara Lipton for helping decipher the names.

78. Tokmakov, *Ekaterininskaia pustyn',* pp. 5–6; Kapterev, "Russkaia blagotvoritel'nost' sinaiskoi obiteli," pp. 387–90.

79. Ibid., p. 6.

80. Ibid.

81. Kapterev, "Russkaia blagotvoritel'nost' sinaiskoi obiteli" pp. 380ff.; Ekkehard Kraft, *Moskaus greichisches Jahrhundert. Russisch-greichische Beziehungen und metabyzantinischer Einfluss, 1619–1694* (Stuttgart: Franz Steiner Verlag, 1995), pp. 89–90.

82. *Opisanie dokumentov i del khraniashchikhsia v arkhive sviateishogo pravitel'stvuiushchogo sinoda,* vol. 3 (St. Petersburg: Sinodal'naia Tipografiia, 1878), appendix 39, p. 174.

83. Piatnitsky, *Sinai, Byzantium, Russia,* p. 21.

84. Kapterev, "Russkaia blagotvoritel'nost' sinaiskoi obiteli," p. 402.

85. Ibid., pp. 403–4.

86. Kapterev, "Snosheniia," pp. 269–85; Anastasiou, Sinaitika, pp. 108–12, 122–31.

87. Kapterev, "Snosheniia," pp. 285–318.

88. "Mazurinskii letopisets," p. 22.

89. S. O. Vialova, "Znachenie monastyria sv. Ekateriny na Sinae v istorii kul'tury," in *Nasledie monastyrskoi kul'tury. Remeslo, khudozhestvo, iskusstvo,* ed. I. A. Chudinova, vol. 2 (St. Petersburg: Rossiiskii institut istorii iskusstv, 1997), pp. 5–13.

90. *Puteshestvie vo Ierusalim Sarovskiia obshchezhitel'nyia pustyni ieromonakha Meletiia v 1793 i 1794 godu* (Moscow: Gubernskaia Tipografiia, 1798), pp. 62, 130–31, 174–76, 245.

91. Ioann Luk'ianov, "Puteshestvie v sviatuiu zemliu sviashchennika Ioanna Luk'ianova," *Russkii arkhiv* (1863) nos. 1–6, pp. 21–64; 113–59; 223–64; 305–44; 385–416. The discussions of Jerusalem and its environs are on p. 305ff.

92. Ibid., p. 320.

93. Arkhimandrit Antonin, "Iz zapisok sinaiskogo bogomoltsa," *Trudy kievskoi dukhovnoi akademii* (1872) vol. 8, p. 331.

94. Ibid. (1873) vol. 5, p. 277ff.

95. See, for example, the discussion of the monastery's newly acquired manuscripts in V. N. Beneshevich, "Otchet o poezdke v Sinaiskii monastyr' sv. Ekateriny letom 1908 goda," *Izvestiia Imperatorskoi Akademii nauk* (1908), no. 14, pp. 1145–48.

96. Grigorii Luk'ianov, "Serebrianaia raka sviatoi velikomuchenitsy Ekateriny—dar russkikh tsarei v sinaiskii monastyr' v 1688 godu," *Seminarium Kondakovianum* (1936), vol. 8, p. 155.

97. "Puteshestvie iz Konstantinoplia v Ierusalim i Sinaiskuiu Goru, nakhodivshagosia pri Rossiiskom Poslannike, Grafe Petre Andreeviche Tolstom, Sviashchennika Andreia Ignat'eva i brata ego, Stefana, v 1707 godu," in *Palomniki-pisateli petrovskogo i poslepetrovskogo vremeni, ili putniki bo sviatoi grad Ierusalim, Chteniia* (1873), bk. 3, pp. 51–53.

98. See, for example, Arkhimandrit [later Bishop] Porfirii Uspenskii, *Vtoroe puteshestvie v sinaiskii monastyr' v 1850 godu* (St. Petersburg: Morskoi kadetskii korpus, 1856), pp. 251–55, 282–84; N. Kondakov, *Puteshestvie na Sinai v 1881 godu. Iz putevykh vpechatlenii drevnosti sinaiskogo monastyria* (Odessa: Tipografiia P. A. Zelenogo, 1882), pp. 39–40 and passim.

99. *Tale of Boiarynia Morozova: A Seventeenth-Century Religious Life,* trans. and ed. Margaret Ziolkowski (Lanham, MD: Lexington Books, 2000), p. 68. Ziolkowski's perceptive analyses of this passage, demonstrating the parallels being drawn between the martyrdom of Catherine and the travails of Morozova are on pp. 15–17.

100. The complete text of Ignatii's *Confession* is reprinted in *Pamiatniki staroobriadcheskoi pis'mennosti,* ed. N. Iu. Bubnov, O. V. Chumicheva, and N. S. Demkova (St. Petersburg: Russkii Khristianskii Gumanitarnyi Institut, 2000), pp. 119–35, with commentary on pp. 136–38.

101. Makarii (Bishop of Archangel), "Istoricheskoe opisanie krasnogorskogo monastyria," *Chteniia* (1880), bk. 3, pp. 83–84.

102. S. P. Luppov, *Kniga v Rossii v XVII veke* (Leningrad: Nauka, 1970) pp. 98–101.

103. For more on the Solovki library and Meshcherinov, see M. V. Kukushkina, *Monastyrskie biblioteki russkogo severa* (Leningrad: Nauka, 1977), pp. 19–25.

104. Robert Crummey argues that early female martyrs of the Old Belief, unlike their male counterparts, did not engage in theological disputes over liturgy and instead debated their duties as mothers versus their duties to Christ. To the extent that St. Catherine functioned as a female identity figure for Old Believer women, however, there may have existed an implicit valorization of female reasoning within Old Believer

rhetoric. Robert O. Crummey, "The Miracle of Martyrdom: Reflections on Early Old Believer Hagiography," in *Religion and Culture in Early Modern Russia and Ukraine*, ed. Samuel H. Baron and Nancy Shields Kollmann (DeKalb: Northern Illinois University Press, 1997), p. 139.

5—*Dimitrii Rostovskii and the Militant Bride of Christ*

1. The sermon, which dates from the 1690s, was printed in 1762, possibly for the first time, with Dimitrii's other works cited here, in *Sochineniia Sviatogo Dimitriia, mitropolita rostovskogo*, vol. 3 (Moscow: Sinodal'naia Tipografiia, 1762), pp. 401–20.

2. A. A. Titov, ed., *Raskhodnaia kniga patriarshago prikaza kushan'iam podavavshimsia Patriarkhu Adrianu i raznago china litsam s sentiabria 1698 po avgust 1699 g.* (St. Petersburg: Tipografiia A. Katanskogo, 1890), pp. 63–64: "Noiabr' v 24 den', v chetvertok. Na prazdnik Ekateriny Khristovy muchenitsy, sviateishemu patriarkhu podavano v kel'iu stolovogo kushen'ia." The document lists the menu for other days, feast days and not, from which it is clear that Patriarch Adrian regularly set a large and generous table. This menu, however, is considerably more lavish than most.

3. Semen Polotskii, *Vecheria dushevnaia* (Moscow: Verkhniaia Tipografiia, 1683), pp. 108–16.

4. Lennart Kjellberg, *La langue de Gedeon Krinovskij, prédicateur russe du XVIIIe siècle* (Uppsala: Almqvist & Wiksells, 1957), p. 12.

5. Polotskii, *Vecheria dushevnaia*, p. 111.

6. Ibid., pp. 113–16.

7. The vast majority of Istomin's opus remains unpublished. Most of what he wrote exists in two very large *sborniki* originally kept in the Moscow Chudov Monastery and in more recent times in the manuscript division of the State Historical Museum (GIM) in Moscow, which, unfortunately, remains closed. Some texts were published in a 1983 collection, but none of the St. Catherine ones. S. N. Brailovskii extensively inventoried the *sborniki* as part of his lengthy biography of Istomin, and it is his work that identifies the St. Catherine material. Brailovskii, "Odin iz pestrykh." The references to the St. Catherine sermon are on pages 117 and 260, the latter with a notation from May 1688, an indication that the sermon was delivered on November 1687 or earlier.

8. Brailovskii, "Odin iz pestrykh," pp. 71, 123, and 209.

9. Ibid., p. 202. The text is as follows: "V liubvi ko Khristu byst' Ekaterina / ne prelsti iu veshch' na zemli edina / v filosofii ta deva iavisia / kto liubit mudrost' prositi iu tshchisia."

10. Ibid., p. 260.

11. *PSZ*, vol. 3, no. 1417, 1834, pp. 114–15, "Ob"iavleniia o rozhdenii i o kreshchenii Tsarevny Ekateriny Ioannovny."

12. This point has been made by several contemporary Russian literary specialists. See, in particular, A. S. Demin, *Pisatel' i obshchestvo v Rossii XVI–XVII vekov* (Moscow: Nauka, 1985), chaps. 6 and 7; and A. N. Robinson, "Simeon Polotskii i russkii literaturnyi protsess," in *Simeon Polotskii i ego knigoizdatel'skaia deiatel'nost'*, ed. A. N. Robinson et al. (Moscow: Nauka, 1982), pp. 7–45.

13. Bogdanov and Buganov, eds., *Pamiatniki obshchestvenno-politicheskoi mysli*, no. 23, "Stikhotvornoe privetstvo tsariu Petru Alekseevichu k dniu angela," no. 31, "Zhelatelno privetstvo tsaritse Evdokii Fedorovne Lopukhinoi k dniu angela," and no. 33, "Pozdravlenie zhelatelnoe tsaritse Natalii Kirillovne Naryshkinoi k dniu angela, pri podnesenii stikhotvornogo zhitiia sv. Adriana i Natalii," pp. 210, 231–32, and 242–43. Brailovskii, "Odin iz pestrykh," p. 71.

14. L. I. Sazonova, *Poeziia russkogo barokko* (Moscow: Nauka, 1991), pp. 148–49.

15. The most detailed and authoritative study of Dimitrii's Chet'i minei and his activities while composing it is (Protoierei) Aleksandr Derzhavin, "Chetii-minei Sviatitelia Dimitriia, mitropolita rostovskogo, kak tserkovnoistoricheskii i literaturnyi

pamiatnik," *Bogoslovskie trudy,* vol. 15 (1976), pp. 61–145, and vol. 16 (1976), pp. 46–141, based upon a dissertation that was completed in 1915 and finally defended in the 1950s. Derzhavin, vol. 15, pp. 88–89.

16. For a brief account of his career, see James Cracraft, *The Church Reform of Peter the Great* (London: Macmillan, 1971), pp. 138–39. The fullest biography remains I. A. Shliapkin, *Sv. Dimitrii Rostovskii i ego vremia (1651–1709 g.)* (St. Petersburg: Tipografiia A. Transhel', 1891), but some of the most interesting accounts of his life, by Novikov and Metropolitan Evgenii Bolkhovitinov, date to the late eighteenth and early nineteenth century. Nikolai Novikov, *Opyt istoricheskago slovaria o rossiiskikh pisateliakh* (St. Petersburg: Tipografiia Akademii nauk, 1772), pp. 56–62; Mitropolit Evgenii (Bolkhovitinov), *Slovar' istoricheskii o byvshikh v Rossii pisateliakh dukhovnogo china greko-rossiiskoi tserkvi* (Moscow: Palomnik, 1995), pp. 76–87.

17. E. Golubinskii, *Istoriia kanonizatsii sviatykh v russkoi tserkvi* (Sergiev Posad: Tipografiia A. I. Snegirovoi, 1894), p. 125; A. A. Titov, *Letopisets o rostovskikh arkhiiereiakh* (St. Petersburg: Tipografiia S. Dobrodeeva, 1890), pp. 27–32; I. Chistovich, "Neizdannye propovedi Stefana Iavorskogo," *Khristianskoe chtenie* (1867), pt. 2, p. 140.

18. Iakim Zapasko and Iaroslav Isaevich, *Pamiatki knizhkogo mistetstva. Katalog starodrukiv vidanikh na Ukraini,* vol. 1 (L'viv: Visha shkola, 1981), nos. 520 (1674), 556 (1678), 582 and 583 (1680), and 743 (1699).

19. "Russkie ili pache Rossiiskie narody tyezhe sut' Slaviane. Edinogo bo estestva ottsa svoego Iafeta i togozhde iazyka." In *Sinopsis, ili kratkoe opisanie o nachale Slavenskogo naroda,* vol. 4 of *Sochineniia Sviatogo Dimitriia, mitropolita rostovskogo* (Moscow: Sinodal'naia Tipografiia, 1841), p. 628.

20. Ibid., p. 632.

21. Ibid., p. 635.

22. "Pouchenie . . . na pamiat', izhe bo sviatykh ottsa nashego Petra, Mitropolita Vserossiiskago," in *Sochineniia Sviatogo Dimitriia,* vol. 3, pp. 436–45.

23. "Slovo na pamiat' sviatago Alekseia Mitropolita Moskovskago, i vseia Rossii," in *Sochineniia Sviatogo Dimitriia,* vol. 3, p. 27.

24. "Piramida ili stolp, bo blazhennoi pamiati prestavliashagosia vysotse k Bogu ego milosti gospodina ottsa Innokentia Gizelia . . . k vechnoi pamiati v god po pogrebenii ego," in *Sochineniia Sviatogo Dimitriia,* vol. 3, pp. 574–613. This essay has been reprinted in a new edition of Dimitrii's selected works. See *Keleinyi letopisets sviatitelia Dimitriia Rostovskogo s pribavleniem ego zhitiia, chudes, izbrannykh tvorenii i Kievskogo sinopsisa arkhimandrita Innokentiia Gizelia,* ed. E. A. Luk'ianov (Moscow: Palomnik, 2000), pp. 511–31.

25. "Vo veki pamiat' ego v blagoslovenie. Ne ot''idet pamiat' ego, i imia ego pozhivet v rod i rod; premudrost' ego povestvuiut iazytsy, i khvalu ego ispovest' Tserkov." The English is taken from a translation of the Vulgate, which contains these two books, neither of which is included in the King James Bible or most standard English-language Bibles. I have changed "wisdom" to "holy wisdom" in order to bring the English in line with *"premudrost'"* in the Russian text.

26. Derzhavin, "Chetii-minei," vol. 15, p. 111; Rostovskii, "Diariush," p. 482ff.

27. Derzhavin, "Chetii-minei," vol. 15, pp. 116–18.

28. Shliapkin, *Sv. Dimitrii Rostovskii i ego vremia,* pp. 441–45; *Opisanie izdanii napechatannykh pri Petre Pervom, 1689–1725,* ed. T. A. Bykova and M. M. Gurevich, 3 vols. (Moscow: Akademiia nauk, 1955–1958), vol. 1, p. 188. Large parts of it were published shortly after Dimitrii's death, but not the complete text.

29. Novikov, *Opyt,* p. 57.

30. Bolkhovitinov, *Slovar' istoricheskii,* p. 85.

31. Derzhavin's summary of the earlier Kievan projects is in "Chetii-minei," vol. 15, pp. 83–88.

32. Shliapkin, *Sv. Dimitrii Rostovskii i ego vremia,* pp. 236–39.

33. See the account, translated from an unnamed Russian source, in *Lives of Eminent Russian Prelates* (London: Joseph Masters, 1854), pp. 54–55.

34. A. A. Kruming plausibly surmises from the tale of Dimitrii's dream mentioned in the previous chapter that Dimitrii was working chronologically and had reached mid-November by November 1685. Since vol. 1 ends with November, Dimitrii would have been able to complete the draft relatively soon thereafter. Kruming, "Chet'i Minei sviatogo Dimitriia Rostovskogo. Ocherk istorii izdaniia," *Filevskie chteniia*, vol. 10, *Sviatoi Dimitrii, Mitropolit Rostovskii. Issledovaniia i materialy* (Moscow, 1994), pp. 5–52.

35. Rostovskii, "Diariush," p. 491; Shliapkin, *Sv. Dimitrii Rostovskii i ego vremia*, pp. 246–47; Kruming, "Chet'i Minei," p. 23.

36. The press runs of these volumes are not known, but typically menologies were published in runs of 600 or 1,200. For bibliographic information, see Zapasko and Isaevich, *Pamiatki knizhkogo mistetstva*, no. 655, and Bykova and Gurevich, *Opisanie izdanii*, vol. 1, no. 1, pp. 50-52.

37. The edition of "Diariush" used here is published in Dimitrii's *Sochineniia*, vol. 1, pp. 451–570. It can also be found in *DRV*, vol. 17, 1792; reprinted 1970, pp. 1–107.

38. Derzhavin, "Chetii-minei," vol. 15, pp. 101–6.

39. Ibid., p. 104.

40. Rostovskii, "Diariush," p. 482.

41. The following discussion is drawn largely from Kruming, "Chet'i Minei," pp. 11–18.

42. Derzhavin, pp. 97–98.

43. Ibid., p. 102; Kruming, "Chet'i Minei," pp. 9 and 42n7.

44. Derzhavin, "Chetii-minei," vol. 15, p. 99; Kruming, "Chet'i Minei," p. 9, says that only the September and October drafts survived.

45. Derzhavin, vol. 16, pp. 65–71, 97–98.

46. Ibid., vol. 16, pp. 93–94.

47. A brief discussion of texts and sources is in order here. On the whole I have worked with two variants of the vita, one in the 1762 Moscow edition of *Chet'i minei*, the other a translation of this same text into vernacular Russian and published by the Synod in 1902. The Russian text follows the Slavonic rather faithfully in most places, but occasionally it adds creative embellishment. When the two diverge I follow the Slavonic, as that was the version available to Dimitrii's contemporary readers. In addition there exists a recent, highly reliable English translation, part of an ongoing project by the Chrysostom Society to make many of Dimitrii Rostovskii's works available in English. To date the society has published 6 volumes, or the first half of the menology, covering the months September through February. This version follows the Slavonic text, but it simplifies some of the phraseology, and it omits a great deal of Dimitrii's marginalia and scriptural signifiers contained in the original. It also corrects some minor errors that Dimitrii had made. For example, where the original refers to the emperor throughout as Maximin (repeated in the Russian vernacular), the Chrysostom Society edition corrects it to Maxentius. The society's edition also omits the troparion and other concluding prayers that were a part of Dimitrii's complete text. The translations presented here rely on the Chrysostom Society version as a template, but with occasional modifications, based upon my own reading of the original and the modernized Russian text so as to remain faithful to some of the eccentricities of Dimitrii's writing. "Zhitie i stradanie sviatoi velikomuchenitsy Ekateriny," in *Zhitiia sviatykh na russkom iazyke izlozhennye po rukovodstvu chent'ikh minei sv. Dimitriia Rostovskogo*, pp. 659–60 (Moscow, 1902); Dimitrii Rostovskii, *Chet'i minei* (Moscow: Sinodalnaia Tipografiia, 1762), vol. 1; Saint Demetrius of Rostov [Rostovskii], *The Great Collection of the Lives of the Saints*, vol. 3, *November*, trans. Father Thomas Marretta (House Springs, MO: Chrysostom Press, 2001), pp. 542–61.

48. Ibid., pp. 663–64.

49. Ibid., p. 674 and elsewhere.

50. Ibid., p. 681.

51. Rostovskii, *Great Collection*, vol. 1, p. 102.

52. Ibid., p. 242.

53. Rostovskii, *Great Collection,* vol. 4, p. 266; vol. 6, p. 47.

54. Rostovskii, *Great Collection,* vol. 4, p. 555.

55. Rostovskii, *Great Collection,* vol. 2, pp. 30, 225, 405.

56. Rostovskii, *Great Collection,* vol. 5, p. 181.

57. Ibid., p. 395.

58. Rostovskii, *Great Collection,* vol. 6, pp. 43–50.

59. See, for example, the late seventeenth-century tempera-on-wood life icon reproduced in Vladimir Ivanov, *Russian Icons* (New York: Rizzoli, 1988), plate no. 101, in which St. Catherine stands in the center of the image looking up to a Christ holding a scroll in the upper right corner.

60. *Snimki s drevnikh ikon nakhodiashchikhsia v staroobriadcheskom pokrovskom khrame pri rogozhskom kladbishche v moskve* (Moscow: Tovarishchestvo Kushnerev, 1899), plate no. 26.

61. All the above citations come from the November 24 entry of the 1692 Moscow printing of the *Mineia sluzhebnaia,* pp. 283–300.

62. Rostovskii, "Diariush," pp. 460, 461, 472, 473 and elsewhere.

63. Rostovskii, "Diariush," p. 670.

64. M. A. Fedotova, "Ukrainskie propovedi Dimitriia Rostovskogo (1670–1700 gg.) i ikh rukopisnaia traditsiia," *TODRL,* vol. 51 (1999), pp. 278–88.

65. Shliapkin, *Sv. Dimitrii Rostovskii i ego vremia,* pp. 386–87.

66. The Book of Judith, on which this analogy is based, is considered apocryphal within Judaism and Protestantism, but is accepted within Deuteronomy by Orthodoxy. See Bruce M. Metzger and Michael D. Coogan, eds., *The Oxford Companion to the Bible* (Oxford: Oxford University Press, 1993), pp. 399–401.

67. Rostovskii, "Pouchenie," p. 407.

68. All the above quotes come from the 1762 edition of Dimitrii's collected works, "Pouchenie na pamiat' sviatyia velikomuchenitsy Ekateriny," in *Sochineniia Sviatogo Dimitriia, mitropolita rostovskogo,* vol. 3, pp. 404–14.

6—The Order of St. Catherine

1. This may not have been the first St. Catherine play performed at the Russian court. E. V. Barsov's chronology of theatrical performances refers to a performance on June 24, 1676, of "Sviataia Ekaterina muchenitsa misteriia," written by Abbott Geoffrey (Zhoffrua) of St. Albans, almost certainly a reference to a late English medieval mystery play of St. Catherine attributed to Geoffrey, who later entered the monastery at St. Albans. A later entry from September 17, 1689, referred to a performance in the *terem* in honor of Sofia Alekseevna's birthday of "Ekaterina muchenitsa," ascribed here to Sofia herself. This latter entry may be in error, however, since Barsov transposed the story of Arsen'eva, recounted below, to this performance. E. V. Barsov, "Khronika russkogo teatra," *Chteniia* (1882), bk. 2, pp. 19, 30; C. B. C. Thomas, "The Miracle Play at Dunstable," *Modern Languages Newsletter* 32 (1917), pp. 337–44.

2. The surviving text ("Komediia sv. Ekateriny") has been reprinted, along with extensive commentary in O. A. Derzhavina et al., eds., *P'esy stolichnykh i provintsial'nykh teatrov pervoi polovine XVIII v.* (Moscow: Nauka, 1975), pp. 158–59, 623–24. See also V. Vsevolodskii-Gerngross, *Russkii teatr ot istokov do serediny XVIII v.* (Moscow: Akademiia nauk, 1957), p. 152.

3. Quoted in I. A. Shliapkin, "Tsarevna Natal'ia Alekseevna i teatr eia vremeni," *Pamiatniki drevnei pis'mennosti* 128 (1898), p. xi.

4. "Liubov" was a woman's name that also means "love."

5. *Pokhodnyi zhurnal za 1710 god,* p. 17.

6. *Pokhodnyi zhurnal za 1711 god,* p. 4.

7. Juel, *Zapiski Iusta Iulia,* pp. 300–301; Wittram, *Peter I, Czar und Kaiser,* pp. 371–72.

8. Ia. E. Vodarskii, "Legendy prutskogo pokhoda Petra I (1711 g.)," *Otechestvennaia istoriia*, no. 5 (September-October 2004), pp. 3-26.

9. Ibid., p. 8.

10. Ibid., pp. 14-16.

11. Juel was one of the first to confirm at least the broad outlines of the account. See Juel, *Zapiski Iusta Iulia*, p. 373; Wittram, *Peter I, Czar und Kaiser*, pp. 391-92.

12. *Opisanie arkhiva Aleksandro-Nevskoi lavry za vremia tsarstvovaniia Imperatora Petra Velikogo* (St. Petersburg: Sinodal'naia Tipografiia, 1903), vol. 1, pp. 38, 759-60.

13. RGADA, *f.* 9, *op.* 1, *d.* 89, May 15, 1714, "Memoriia admiralteiskomu sovetniku L. V. Kikinu o postroike korablei"; *f.* 9, *op.* 1, *d.* 156, June 14, 1714, "Sobstvennoruchnyi Petra Velikogo chernovik ukaza . . . dannyi na korable 'Sv. Ekateriny'"; *f.* 142, *op.* 3, no. 202, "Prikaz Petra I o flagakh i devitsakh k nim dannoi na bortu korablia 'Sviataia Ekaterina' (1714)," p. 1; *f.* 142, *op.* 3, no. 201, "Prikaz Petra I o poriadke podkhoda korablei dannoi na bortu korablia 'Sviataia Ekaterina.'"

14. *SIRIO*, vol. 40 (1881), pp. 285-86.

15. Wortman, *Scenarios of Power*, vol. 1, pp. 42-78.

16. Michael Khodarkovsky, *Russia's Steppe Frontier: The Making of a Colonial Empire, 1500-1800*. (Bloomington: Indiana University Press, 2002), p. 2.

17. Ibid., pp. 36-39.

18. Kapterev, *Kharakter otnoshenii Rossii k pravoslavnomu vostoku*, pp. 349-82. See also Hans Rothe, *Religion und Kultur in den Regionen des russischen Reiches im 18. Jahrhundert*, Rheinisch-Westfälische Akademie der Wissenschaften, no. 267. (Opladen: Westdeutscher Verlag, 1984), pp. 7-14.

19. The Order of St. Anne technically was not Russian, since it had been established by Duke Karl Friedrich of Holstein-Gottorp. From the outset, however, it had intimate Russian connections. Named in honor of Anna Petrovna, the deceased daughter of Peter the Great, it began inscribing Russian members in 1742, and by 1761 its Russian membership ran into the dozens. V. A. Durov, *Ordena Rossii* (Moscow: Voskresenie, 1993), p. 106.

20. The founding date of the Order of St. Andrew is unknown. Some of the literature refers to 1698, but the first documentary reference to the order comes from the diary of the Austrian ambassador to Moscow, Johann Georg Korb, in an entry from 1699. Durov, *Ordena Rossii*, p. 9; G. V. Vilinbakhov, "K istorii uchrezhdeniia ordena Andreia Pervozvannogo i evoliutsiia ego znaka," in *Kul'tura i iskusstvo petrovskogo vremeni*, ed. G. N. Komelova (Leningrad: Avrora, 1977), pp. 144-58; Wortman, *Scenarios of Power*, vol. 1, p. 45; Johann-Georg Korb, *Diary of an Austrian Secretary of Legation at the Court of Czar Peter the Great*, trans. Count MacDonnell (London: Cass, 1863), vol. 1, pp. 272-73.

21. Both Just Juel and Johann Korb, the Austrian ambassador's secretary, mention Sheremetev's insignias, which as Korb observed, provoked derision and sarcasm among the Russian officers. Juel, *Zapiski Iusta Iulia*, p. 360; Korb, *Diary*, p. 176 and 276.

22. Adriaan Schoonebeek, *Istoriia o ordinakh ili chinakh voinskikh pache zhe kavalerskikh* (Moscow: Moskovskaia Tipografiia, 1710).

23. Durov, *Ordena Rossii*, pp. 132-35.

24. Hyginus Eugene Cardinale, *Orders of Knighthood: Awards of the Holy See* (London: Gerrards Books, 1985), pp. 63-66.

25. Ibid., p. 174.

26. Ibid., p. 182.

27. Schoonebeek, *Istoriia*, pp. 6-7.

28. Ibid., pp. 301-2.

29. More recent research suggests that this order, much like St. Catherine herself, was an apocrypha. Jennifer R. Bray, "The Medieval Order of St. Katherine," *Bulletin of the Institute of Historical Research*, vol. 56, no. 133 (May 1983), pp. 1-6.

30. Lewis, *Cult of St. Katherine*, p. 161.

31. *PSZ*, vol. 5, no. 2860, November 24, 1714, pp. 129-33.

32. Dmitrii Bantysh-Kamenskii, *Istoricheskoe sobranie spiskov kavalerov* (Moscow: Tipografiia N. S. Vsevolzhskogo, 1814), p. 135.

33. *Treasures of the Tsar, from the State Museum of the Moscow Kremlin* (Rotterdam: Museum Boymans-van Beuningen, 1995), p. 208; Bantysh-Kamenskii, *Istoricheskoe sobranie spiskov kavalerov,* p. 141.

34. See, as one example, the description of her at the canonization ceremony of Alexander Nevskii in Archimandrite Avgustin (Nikitin), *Pravoslavnyi Peterburg v zapiskakh inostrantsev* (St. Petersburg: Neva, 1995), p. 94. She is characterized as standing beside Peter wearing the Order of St Catherine on a white ribbon around her neck.

35. *PSZ,* vol. 5, no. 2860, November 24, 1714, p. 130.

36. "Ustav ordena Sv. Etateriny ili tak nazyvaemogo ordena svobozhdeniia," in Bantysh-Kamenskii, *Istoricheskoe sobranie spiskov kavalerov,* pp. 139-48.

37. Ibid., p. 141.

38. Ibid., pp. 141–42.

39. The issue of what constituted a princess of the blood was made more complex by the fact that Catherine was not yet acknowledged as Peter's spouse, at least not officially. Just Juel, who spent a good deal of time in Catherine's company in 1711, did not quite know how to address her, and he consulted with his ambassador on how best to apply protocol to an awkward situation. The ambassador advised that Catherine would soon become the tsar's wife, and that she should therefore be called "Your Majesty," even though she was technically not a princess of the blood because she was not yet wed. Just Juel, *Zapiski Iusta Iulia,* pp. 373–74.

40. Ustav, p. 141.

41. Ibid., p. 144.

42. Ibid., p. 146.

43. Ibid., pp. 146–48.

44. Ibid., p. 143.

45. The text of the induction can be found in Bantysh-Kamenskii, *Istoricheskoe sobranie spiskov kavalerov,* pp. 139–49.

46. Jack Edward Kollmann, Jr. "The Moscow *Stoglav* ('Hundred Chapters') Church Council of 1551," Ph.D. diss. (University of Michigan, 1978) p. 562.

47. *Stoglav,* D. S. Kozhanchikov, ed. (St. Petersburg: Akademiia nauk, 1863) pp. 224–25.

48. *Treasures of the Tsar,* p. 208.

49. Peter Henry Bruce, *Memoirs of Peter Henry Bruce, esq., a Military Officer in the Services of Prussia, Russia, and Great Britain* (London: F. Cass, 1970), p. 161. Similar accounts can be found in other foreign memoirs. See, e.g., F. C. Weber, *The Present State of Russia,* vol. 1 (New York: DaCapo Press, 1968), p. 81.

50. Voltaire, *Histoire de l'empire de Russie sous Pierre le Grand (par l'auteur de l'histoire de Charles XII),* vol. 2 (Paris, 1763), pp. 92–93, 261; Golikov, *Deianiia,* vol. 4, p. 389; Muller's notes on the order can be found in his personal archive: RGADA, *f.* 199 ("Portfeli Millera"), *op.* 1, no. 150, pt. 7, *d.* 8, p. 8.

51. An excellent reproduction of the *konkliuziia* can be found in M. Alekseeva, *Graviura petrovskogo vremeni* (Leningrad, Iskusstvo, 1990), p. 139.

52. Ibid., p. 181.

53. To give additional examples, an official portrait of Catherine and Peter, done in 1721 by I. F. Zubov, presents the sash and star prominently. Zubov's famous *konkliuziia* of the coronation also prominently displays the regalia.

54. Sergei Dubinin et al., eds., *Vse o den'gakh Rossii* (Moscow: Konkord, 1998), pp. 50–52, 269, 315.

55. Ibid., pp. 322–32.

56. The disregard for the prescribed numbers continued as long as the order remained in existence. In Paul's reign there were 50 inductees, in the reign of Alexander I—127, Nicholas I—139, and Alexander II—77. See the entry for the Order of St.

Catherine in Brokgauz-Efron, *Entsiklopedicheskii slovar'*, vol. 11 (St. Petersburg: I. A. Efron, 1894), pp. 568–69.

57. *Opisanie vysochaishikh povelenii po pridvornomu vedomstvu, 1723–1830* (St. Petersburg: Tipografiia departamenta udelov, 1886), pp. 24–25.

58. I. Pushkarev, *Opisanie Sankt Peterburga* (St. Petersburg: Tipografiia N. Grecha, 1839), p. 256.

59. *Istoriko-statisticheskoe svedenie o S. Peterburgskoi eparkhii*, vol. 6 (St. Petersburg: Eparkhial'nyi istoriko-statisticheskii komitet, 1878), pp. 316–18. V. V. Antonov and L. V. Sobak, *Sviatyni Sankta-Peterburga. Istoriko-tserkovnaia entsiklopediia*, vol. 1 (St. Petersburg: Izdatel'stvo Chernysheva, 1994), p. 254.

60. Zvonarev, *Sorok sorokov*, vol. 3 (1989), pp. 417–19.

61. P. F. Karabanov, "Stats damy i freiliny russkogo dvora v XVIII stoletii. Biograficheskie spiski," *Russkaia starina*, vol. 2 (1870), p. 469.

62. *Opisanie vysochaishikh povelenii*, pp. 36–37.

63. The entire tale can be found in Irina Bobrovitskaia, "Pervaia imperatorskaia korona Rossii," *Mir muzeia*, vol. 162 (July–August 1998), pp. 44–59.

64. *Zapiski Imperatritsy Ekateriny vtoroi* (St. Petersburg: A. S. Suvorin, 1907), pp. 40–41.

65. "Bumagi Imperatritsy Ekateriny II khraniashchikhsia v gosudarstvennom arkhive," *SIRIO*, vol. 7 (1871), pp. 7–67.

66. "Ekaterina Vtoraia, novyia svedeniia, pis'ma, i bumagi, kasaiushchiiasia eia roditelei i eia priezda v Rossiu," in *Osmnadtsatyi vek*, ed. P. I. Barten'ev, bk. 1 (1868), pp. 21–26.

67. Quoted from H. Montgomery Hyde, *The Empress Catherine and Princess Dashkov* (London: Chapman and Hall, 1935), pp. 85 and 95. Dashkova's own account can be found in any of the several editions of her memoirs. Ekaterina Dashkova, *Zapiski, 1743–1810* (Kaliningrad: Iantarnyi skaz, 2001), p. 90.

68. Roderick E. McGrew, *Paul I of Russia, 1754–1801* (London: Oxford University Press, 1992), p. 237.

69. Brokgauz-Efron, *Entsiklopedicheskii slovar'*, vol. 11, p. 568.

70. Wortman, *Scenarios of Power*, vol. 1, p. 60.

71. A. I. Granat, *Entsiklopedicheskii slovar'* (Moscow: Granat, 1912), vol. 19, entry on Ekaterina Alekseevna (Catherine I), opposite p. 620.

72. This portrait, done by Chemezov in 1761, is reproduced in *Zapiski, Imperatritsy Ekateriny vtoroi* opposite p. 526.

73. The term "ptentsy," literally "fledglings," is commonly employed to refer to the inner corps of Petrine loyalists, in particular those who owed their high standing directly to their service to Peter.

74. Karabanov, "Stats damy i freiliny russkogo dvora," pp. 469, 472–74, 487, 492.

75. "Ustav ordena Sv. Etateriny ili tak nazyvaemogo ordena svobozhdeniia," in Bantysh-Kamenskii, *Istoricheskoe sobranie spiskov kavalerov*, p. 142.

76. See, for example, the *mesiatsoslov* printed by the Academy of Sciences in 1802, which has the following notation for November 24: "Tezoimenitstvo Eia Imperatorskogo Velichestva Blagovernoi Gosudaryni Velikoi Kniazhny Ekateriny Pavlovny i kavalerskii prazdnik ordena Sviatyia Ekateriny." *Mesiatsoslov s rospis'iu chinovnykh osob v gosudarstve na leto ot rozhdestva Khristosa* (St. Petersburg, 1802).

77. F. V. Berkhgol'ts, *Dnevnik kamer-iunkera F. V. Berkhgol'tsa vedennii im v Rossii v tsarstvovanie Petra Velikogo s 1721-go po 1725 god*, pt. 3, 1723. (Moscow: Universitetskaia Tipografiia, 1903), p. 179. Bergholz described similar events for other years as well.

78. Ibid., pp. 142–43.

79. Ralph Hancock et al., eds., *Treasures of the Czars, from the State Museums of the Moscow Kremlin* (London: Booth-Clibborn Editions, 1995), p. 209.

80. Hancock, *Treasures of the Czars*, p. 208.

81. *The Russian Primary Chronicle. Laurentian Text* (Cambridge: Mediaeval Academy of America, 1953), p. 124. The quote comes from the entry describing Prince

Vladimir's death in 1015.

82. Turoboiskii's pamphlet has come in for quite a lot of commentary recently. See Wortman, *Scenarios of Power*, vol. 1, pp. 48–49; Zhivov, "Kul'turnye reformy," pp. 541–47. The original has been reprinted in B. P. Grebeniuk, *Panegiricheskaia literatura petrovskogo vremeni* (Moscow: Nauka, 1979), pp. 150–80. Zhivov cites several other examples of Petrine references to Constantine. The identity of Peter and Constantine continued unabated after Peter's death, reaching an apotheosis of sorts in 1810 when Golikov devoted an entire book to a comparison of the two. I. I. Golikov, *Sravnenie svoistv i del Konstantina Velikogo pervogo iz rimskikh khristianskogo imperatora s svoistvami i delami Petra Velikogo* (Moscow, 1810).

83. Zhivov, "Kul'turnye reformy," p. 547, "returned from the victory of Emperor Constantine," "the victory of Emperor Constantine over the Impious Roman Emperor Maxentius." Zhivov observes that almost all official flags and banners of this time bore the cross of Constantine.

7—The Saint's Living Image

1. Frederic de Bassewitz, "Zapiski Grafa Bassevicha, sluzhashchiia k poiasneniiu nekotorykh sobytii iz vremeni tsarstvovaniia Petra Velikogo (1713–1725)," *Russkii arkhiv* (1865) no. 3, pp. 116–17.

2. Campredon (Dispatches to the French Court) in *SIRIO*, vol. 40, 1881 p. 187.

3. See Thyrêt, *Between God and Tsar*, chap. 2, "Helpmate to the Tsar and Intercessor for the Realm."

4. Reprinted in *Vedomosti vremeni Petra Velikogo, 1708–1719 g.* (Moscow: Sinodal'naia Tipografiia, 1906), p. 273.

5. Ibid., pp. 287–88.

6. RGADA, *f.* 17, *op.* 1, no. 141, pp. 1 and 12.

7. *PSZ*, vol. 5, nos. 2860 and 2883 respectively.

8. *PSZ*, vol. 7, no. 4314, September 30, 1723, pp. 125–26, "Ob uchrezhdenii sobstvennoi Kantseliarii Gosudaryni Imperatritsy Ekateriny Alekseevny dlia votchinnykh del."

9. *PSZ*, vol. 5, no. 3296, p. 638, "Instruktsiia ili Nakaz Zemskim Kameriram v Guberniiakh i provintsiiakh." "Zemskoi nadziratel' sborov dolzhen Ego Tsarskomu Velichestvu i Eia Velichestvu Gosudaryne Tsaritse i vysokim Naslednikam vernoi, chestnoi, i pravdivyi sluga byt'."

10. *PSZ*, vol. 5, no. 3318, p. 671.

11. *PSZ*, vol. 5, no. 3436, p. 738.

12. *PSZ*, vol. 6, no. 3534 (General'nyi Reglament), February 28, 1720, pp. 141–42; no. 3571 (Nakaz Zemskim D"iakam), April 20, 1720, p. 182; no. 3622 (Instruktsiia Polkovniku i Astrakhanskomu Gubernatoru Volynskomu), pp. 223–24; no. 3708 (Reglament, ili Ustav Magistrata), January 16, 1721, p. 291; no. 3718 (Reglament, ili Ustav Dukhovnoi Kollegii), January 25, 1722, pp. 314–15.

13. *PSZ*, vol. 5, no. 3466, December 11, 1719, p. 763.

14. Bykova and Gurevich, *Opisanie izdanii*, vol. 2, no. 105; Pekarskii, *Nauka i literatura*, vol. 2, no. 336. The text has been reprinted in full in Feofan Prokopovich, *Sochineniia* (Moscow: Nauka, 1961), pp. 68–75. The quotes are taken from the 1961 volume and summarized in Grebeniuk, *Panegiricheskaia literatura petrovskogo vremeni*, pp. 83–84.

15. Prokopovich, *Sochineniia*, p. 71.

16. Ibid., p. 75.

17. Grebeniuk, *Panegiricheskaia literatura petrovoskogo vremeni*, pp. 82–83.

18. Pogosian, *Petr I*, pp. 130–31.

19. A. I. Bogdanov, *Istoricheskoe, geograficheskoe, i topograficheskoe opisanie S. Peterburga ot nachala zavedeniia ego, s 1703 po 1751 god* (St. Petersburg: Akademiia nauk, 1779), pp. 304, 321; S. G. Runkevich, *Aleksandro-nevskaia lavra, 1713–1913* (St. Petersburg: Sinodal'naia Tipografiia, 1913), p. 242.

20. *Vedomosti vremeni Petra Velikogo,* pp. 254–60.

21. I. Chistovich, "Neizdannye propovedi Stefana Iavorskogo," *Khristianskoe chtenie* (1867), pt. 1, p. 814.

22. Stefan Iavorskii, "Slovo pokhval'noe na Sviatoi velikomuchenitsy Ekateriny," in *Propovedi blazhennyia pamiati Stefana Iavorskogo preosviashchennago mitropolita riazanskogo i muromskogo,* vol. 2 (Moscow: Sinodal'naia Tipografiia, 1805), pp. 2–36.

23. Iavorskii, "Slovo na tuiu zhe sviatuiu velikomuchenitsy Ekateriny," *Propovedi,* pp. 37–65.

24. Ibid., p. 41.

25. Ibid., p. 63.

26. Ibid., p. 64.

27. Gavriil Buzhinskii, *Propovedi Gavriila Buzhinskago (1717–1727),* ed. E. V. Petukhov (Iur'ev, 1898), pp. 261–77, 467–80, 481–96.

28. Ibid., p. 467, 478, and elsewhere.

29. Ibid., p. 475, 495.

30. Ibid., p. 469 and elsewhere.

31. Ibid., pp. 274–75.

32. Ibid., p. 495.

33. Ibid., p. 479.

34. Ibid., pp. 275–76.

35. Ibid., p. 475.

36. See, for example, a Synodal decree of October 16, 1723, mandating that name day services of the imperial family take place on the actual saint's day, irrespective of the day of the week on which they fell. *PSPR,* vol. 3, no. 1122, p. 208.

37. *PSPR,* vol. 9, no. 2866, pp. 44–48 (March 13, 1735). The decree mandating attendance at church service on official holidays also included the name day of the empress. *PSZ,* vol. 6, no. 4052, July 16, 1722, pp. 739–40, "O pokazanii Sviashchennikam v knigakh o ispovedavshikhsia i ne iavivshikhsia na ispovede prikhozhan."

38. RGADA, *f.* 17, *op.* 1, no. 141, pp. 5–6.

39. *PSPR,* vol. 4, no. 1253, pp. 107–9; no. 1254, pp. 109–10; no. 1324, p. 175.

40. *PSPR,* vol. 9, no. 3069, pp. 452–53.

41. See, for example, the note written by the tsarevna Mariia Alekseevna to Menshikov in November 1717, in which she joins him in celebrating Catherine's name day, or the day of her angel, as it also was called. RGADA, *f.* 142, *op.* 1 *d.* 470.

42. S. M. Solov'ev, *Istoriia Rossii s drevneishikh vremen,* vol. 9 (Moscow: Nauka, 1963), pp. 565 and elsewhere. Here Solov'ev mentioned in passing that Menshikov chose her name day in 1724 to work with Makarov in approaching the empress to help them avoid paying a fine. Several other episodes like this appear in subsequent passages.

43. Note, for example, Feofilakt Lopatinskii's lost sermon, *Slovo na den' tezoimenitstva Ekateriny Alekseevny* (Moscow, 1722); Prokopovich, "Slovo pokhval'noe na tezoimenitstvo blagovernyia gosudaryni Ekateriny," in his *Sochineniia,* pp. 68–75; Buzhinskii, "Festo Sanctae Megalomartyris Ecatherinae codemque Patronae Serenissimae Imperatricis Rossiacae Ecatherinae Alexiadis. Sanct Piterburgi 1718, November 24," in *Propovedi,* pp. 261–77.

44. Titov, *Raskhodnaia kniga,* pp. 63–64. Quote is in note 2 of chap. 5.

45. Berkhgol'ts, *Dnevnik,* pt. 1, pp. 169–71. Bergholz's description is confirmed by the entries in the *Pokhodnyi zhurnal* for those days.

46. Berkhgol'ts, *Dnevnik,* pt. 2, p. 227. This mantra, apologizing to the reader for his inability to understand Russian, recurs numerous times in the diary. Thus, on April 29, 1722, he attended a baptismal service about which he said, "since I do not understand Russian and still less all these ceremonies, the clergyman standing next to me had to take responsibility for me every time and explain to me what to do next" (pt. 2, p. 148). On other occasions he did attempt to render the meaning of Russian words,

and as often as not, he got them wrong. For example, on July 27, 1721, Bergholz witnessed a ship being christened the *St. Panteleimon,* which he explains, meant "victory." As his Russian editor explained in a footnote, Panteleimon actually meant "all merciful" (pt. 1, p. 82). He made similar errors in describing where people were buried (e.g., stating that the tsaritsy were buried at the Church of the Archangel) and in retelling Russian church history, as in his confused account of the life of St. Sergius on his visit to the Trinity monastery (pt. 2, pp. 16, 178). It is certainly true that Bergholz had a wonderful eye for the visual, but beyond that, as these incidents show, he was very much out of his depth, and without a trained and fluent interlocutor—frequently Bassewitz—his interpretations of Russian culture and society stood on shaky ground.

47. Berkhgol'ts, *Dnevnik,* pt. 3, p. 179.

48. *Pokhodnyi zhurnal za 1724 god,* p. 24.

49. Ibid., pp. 22–23.

50. *PSPR,* vol. 3, nos. 1124 and 1125, pp. 208–9.

51. RGADA, *f. 7, op.* 1, *d.* 143.

52. Ibid., pp. 57, 76.

53. RGADA, *f. 7, op.* 1, *d.* 165, 187, 216, 223, 257.

54. *Opisanie arkhiva Aleksandro-Nevskoi lavry,* vol. 2 (1911), pp. 1219–20.

55. Pekarskii, *Nauka i literatura,* vol. 2, no. 584. The reference to the Synodal order comes from A. V. Gavrilov, *Ocherki istorii St. Peterburgskoi sinodal'noi tipografii,* 1911 p. 39.

56. A. S. Lavrov, *Koldovstvo i religiia v Rossii, 1700–1740 gg.* (Moscow, Drevlekhranilishche, 2000), pp. 191, 244. These continued to circulate widely well after Peter's death. Rovinskii cites several commercially produced images of St. Catherine, done by the Artem'ev firm in Moscow and by Zakharii Samoilovich, some of which contained lengthy verses of praise. D. Rovinskii, *Russkiie narodnye kartinki,* bk. 3, *Pritchi i listy dukhovnye* (St. Petersburg: Tipografiia Imperatorskoi Akademii nauk, 1881), pp. 602–5, 720–21.

57. Gregory Kaganov, *Images of Space: St. Petersburg in the Visual and Verbal Arts,* trans. Sidney Monas (Stanford: Stanford University Press, 1997), pp. 13–14.

58. Sazonova, *Poeziia russkogo barokko,* pp. 30–41.

59. Cathy Potter, "Preaching and Teaching the Faith in Seventeenth-Century Russia," in *Chteniia po istorii russkoi kul'tury,* ed. Iu. S. Borisov (Moscow: RAN, 2000), pp. 334–38; Paul Bushkovitch, *Religion and Society in Russia, the Sixteenth and Seventeenth Centuries* (Oxford: Oxford University Press, 1992).

60. Feofan Prokopovich, *Razsuzhdenie o bezbozhii* (Moscow: Universitetskaia Tipografiia, 1774), pp. 3–11.

61. Ibid., pp. 29–38.

62. Feofan Prokopovich, *Razsuzhdenie o knize solomonovoi naritsaemoi Pesni Pesnei, iako ona est' ne chelevecheskomu voleiu, no Dukha Sviatogo vdokhnoveniem napisana ot solomona* (Moscow: Lopukhin, 1764).

63. Piatnitsky, *Sinai, Byzantium, Russia,* pp. 220–21.

64. Igor' Grabar', *Istoriia russkogo iskusstva,* vol. 6, *Zhivopis',* pt. 1 *Do-Petrovskaia epokha* (Moscow: I. Krebel', 1910), pp. 313–20.

65. I. Snegirev, "Ob ikonnom portrete Velikogo Kniazia Vasiliia Ioannovicha," *Russkii istoricheskii sbornik,* vol. 1, bk. 2 (1837), p. 75; G. Filimonov, "Ikonnye portrety russkikh tsarei," *Vestnik obshchestva drevne-russkogo iskusstva pri moskovskom publichnom muzee,* nos. 6–10 (1875), pp. 42–43. *Stoglav,* p. 128.

66. Kollmann, "The Moscow *Stoglav,*" p. 278; *Stoglav,* p. 153.

67. Kollmann, "The Moscow *Stoglav,*" pp. 277–84; *Stoglav,* p. 130–31.

68. *Stoglav,* p. 131.

69. Filimonov, "Ikonnye portrety russkikh tsarei," pp. 57–61; Snegirev, "Ob ikonnom portrete Velikogo Kniazia Vasiliia Ioannovicha," *Russkii istoricheskii sbornik,* vol. 1, bk. 2 (1837), p. 67.

70. *Russkaia zhivopis' XVII–XVIII vekov. Iz sobraniia Gos. Russkogo Muzeia, Gos.*

Tret'iakovskogo Galerei, Muzei drevne-russkogo iskusstva imeni Andreia Rubleva. Katalog vystavki. (Leningrad: Russkii muzei, 1977), p. 96; *Liki russkoi ikony,* pp. 109–10.

71. Iu. K. Begunov, "Drevnerusskie traditsii v proizvedeniiakh pervoi chetverti XVIII v. ob Aleksandre Nevskom," *TODRL,* vol. 26 (1971), pp. 72–73.

72. Ibid., p. 72.

73. *Pokhodnyi zhurnal za July 1710.* Also cited in M. D. Karateev, *Velikii kniaz' Aleksandr Nevskii* (Moscow: I. D. Sytin, 1893), p. 232.

74. Grebeniuk, *Panegiricheskaia literatura petrovskogo vremeni,* p. 87; Wortman, *Scenarios of Power,* vol. 1, p. 62.

75. Gavrilov, *Ocherki istorii St. Peterburgskoi sinodal'noi tipografii,* 1911, p. XIX.

76. *SIRIO,* vol. 49, 1883, p. 44. Both Bassewitz's memoirs and diary of Bergholz confirm Campredon's account, but they place the decision a few weeks earlier. Bergholz's entry for January 3, 1722, noted that Peter had ordered German jewelers to fabricate up to forty insignias (Bassewitz referred to them as "crosses") for the new Aleksandr Nevskii Order, which Peter wanted to establish. Bassewitz, *Zapiski Iusta Iulia,* p. 251; Bergholz, Dnevnik, vol. 2, p. 10.

77. Demin, "'Khozhdenie' Igumena Daniila v Ierusalem," pp. 64–65.

78. On Chrysostom see the entry in Rostov's [Rostovskii], *The Great Collection of the Lives of the Saints,* vol. 5: for January 27, "A Narrative of the Translation from Comana to Constantinople of the Honored Relics of Our Father among the Saints John Chrysostom." On Ignatius see the entry for January 29, "Translation of the Relics of Saint Ignatius the God Bearer."

79. RGADA, *f.* 237, *op.* 1, no. 1 5493, p. 1. The entry for the translation of the relics of Boris and Gleb is on April 19 (O.S.)

80. Saint Demetrius of Rostov [Rostovskii], *The Great Collection of the Lives of the Saints,* vol. 5: *January,* p. 154.

81. *Sobranie pisem Tsaria Alekseia Mikhailovicha,* ed. K. T. Soldatenkov (Moscow: Petr Bartenev, 1856), pp. 222–23.

82. This account comes largely from the vita of Nikon, allegedly written in the 1680s by I. K. Shusherin, an aide to Nikon and later the tsarevna's chancellor of the cross. Other sources, including Nikon's interrogation in 1666, conform closely to this account. Ioann Shusherin, *Izvestie o rozhdenii i vospitanii i o zhitii sviateishogo Nikona patriarkha moskovskogo i vseia Rossii* (Moscow: Universitetskaia Tipografiia, 1871), pp. 21–23.

83. *PSPR,* vol. 3, no. 1065, pp. 101–3.

84. *PSPR,* vol. 3, no. 1072, pp. 108–10. RGADA, *f.* 237, *op.* 1, no. 5493, p. 1.

85. Paul Bushkovitch, "*The Life of St. Filipp:* Tsar and Metropolitan in the Late Sixteenth Century," in *Medieval Russian Culture,* ed. Michael S. Flier and Daniel B. Rowland, 2 vols. (Berkeley: University of California Press), pp. 32, 44–46.

86. Ibid., p. 45.

87. Viktor Zhivov, "Protest mitropolita Stefan Iavorskogo protiv uchrezhdeniia Sinoda i ego tserkovno-politicheskie pozitsii," in *Iz tserkovnoi istorii vremen Petra Velikogo* (Moscow: Novoe literaturnoe obozrenie, 2004), pt. 2, pp. 69-130.

88. *PSPR,* vol. 4, no. 1318, p. 148. This process is summarized in Cracraft, *The Church Reform of Peter the Great,* p. 211.

89. Durov, *Ordena Rossii,* pp. 22–23.

90. *PSPR,* vol. 6, nos. 1335 and 1347, pp. 181, 188.

91. *PSPR,* vol. 4, no. 1390, p. 248.

92. Runkevich, *Aleksandro-Nevskaia lavra,* p. 549; Begunov, "Drevnerusskie traditsii," pp. 75–78.

93. This account comes from Karateev, *Velikii kniaz',* pp. 234–35.

94. Berkhgol'ts, *Dnevnik,* pt. 4, p. 59; see also Pogosian, *Petr I,* p. 161.

95. Bassewitz, *Zapiski Iusta Iulia,* p. 252.

96. Berkhgol'ts, *Dnevnik,* pt. 4, pp. 59–60.

97. Bassewitz, *Zapiski Iusta Iulia,* pp. 251–53.

98. Berkhgol'ts, *Dnevnik,* pt. 4, pp. 60–61.

99. Ibid., pp. 61–62.

100. Michael Cherniavsky, *Tsar and People: Studies in Russian Myths* (New York: Random House, 1969), pp. 84–85; Cracraft, *The Church Reform of Peter the Great,* p. 211.

101. Irina Chudinova, *Penie, zvony, ritual. Topografiia tserkovno-muzykal'noi kul'tury peterburga* (St. Petersburg: "Ut", 1994), p. 83.

102. Begunov, "Drevnerusskie traditsii," pp. 78–80.

103. Bassewitz, *Zapiski Iusta Iulia,* p. 252.

104. Runkevich, *Aleksandro-Nevskaia lavra,* pp. 360–61.

105. Ibid., p. 358.

106. Ibid., p. 398.

107. RGIA, *f.* 740, *op.* 5, no. 98, p. 32.

108. For more details, see the official history of the monastery, *Istoricheskoe opisanie moskovskogo novodevich'ego monastyria* (Moscow: Tipografiia L. O. Snegireva, 1885), pp. 22, 45–51, 79–80.

109. Ibid., p. 46.

110. Ibid., p. 53.

8—The Archbishop and the Empress

1. "Koronatsionnye zhetony i medali," pp. 154–55.

2. M. Semevskii, *Tsaritsa Praskov'ia, 1664–1723. Ocherk iz russkoi istorii XVIII veka* (Leningrad: Khudozhestvennaia literatura, 1991), appendix, pp. 239–41.

3. *PSZ,* vol. 6, no. 3840, October 22, 1721, p. 446.

4. *PSZ,* vol. 6, no. 3869, December 23, 1721, p. 467, "O titule Gosudaryni Imperatritsy, Velikikh kniazhn i detei Ego Imperatorskogo Velichestva."

5. See, for example, *PSZ,* vol. 6, no. 3882, January 18, 1722, pp. 481–83, "Sinodskii ukaz. O vozneshenii Vysochaishikh Imian pri tserkovnosluzheniiakh po dannym formam." Also, *PSZ,* nos. 3893, 3896, 3900, 4012, and several others included oaths of office, all of which required servitors to swear allegiance to the empress.

6. Marina may have had as many as three separate coronations, a Catholic one in Cracow on November 29, 1605, a quasi-Orthodox one in Moscow's Dormition Cathedral on May 18, 1606, and then possibly a third one in Kaluga after her marriage to the second False Dmitrii. The Moscow coronation was politically the most sensitive of the three, both because it took place in the Dormition Cathedral, and because it made significant gestures toward Orthodoxy. Marina was led to the cathedral by a retinue that included an entire regiment of *streltsy,* twenty hundredsmen, and personal guards. The official diary of Marina's time in power noted that she dressed in Muscovite attire, wore a gown of velvet adorned with pearls and precious stones, and was anointed "according to the Greek custom" *("unkcya more Graeco").* One foreigner in attendance, the Saxon mercenary Conrad Bussow, explained that a dispute had arisen as to whether she would in fact wear Russian attire. Dmitrii and his Polish magnates wanted her to dress in Polish clothes, while the Muscovites insisted on Russian dress. According to Bussow, Dmitrii consented reluctantly, commenting that "It is only a matter of a single day." After the ceremony Marina threw coins to the crowd, as was customary in Moscow but not in Poland. She also may have accepted communion from Patriarch Ignatii in the Orthodox manner. At the time the attendance of the many Polish Catholics within the Dormition Cathedral discomfited the Muscovites, as did Dmitrii's obeisance to them in the ceremony. But they recognized Marina's gestures as a visible indication of her adoption of Orthodoxy. The Poles, by contrast, found the entire ceremony baffling and the Orthodox gestures inconsequential. Stanislav Nemoevskii described it as part Old Testament and part Tatar. *Dnevnik Mariny Mnishek,* trans. V. N. Kozliakov (St. Petersburg: Petropolie, 1995), pp. 52–53, 146, 172–74, 183–86; "Skazanie o Grishke Otrep'ev," *RIB,*

vol. 13 (1925), pp. 743–44; Conrad Bussow, *The Disturbed State of the Russian Realm,* trans. and ed. G. Edward Orchard (Montreal: McGill-Queen's University Press, 1994), pp. 60–61; A. P. Bogdanov, *Moskovskaia publitsistika poslednei chetverti XVII veka* (Moscow: RAN, 2001), pp. 23–25. Bogdanov argues that all the seventeenth-century coronations, including Marina's, perpetuated the myth of unchanging ritual, the seamless cloth from antiquity to the present. See also Daniel B. Rowland, "Mniszek, Marina," in *Modern Encyclopedia of Russian and Soviet History,* vol. 22 (Gulf Breeze, FL: Academic International Press, 1981), pp. 241–42.

7. Margeret, *Russian Empire,* p. 37. See also his further description of the coronation on p. 72.

8. The full text (*PSZ,* no. 4366) is taken from *Ukazy Petra Velikogo samoderzhtsa v rossiiskogo sostoiavshchiiasia s 1714, po konchinu Ego Imperatorskogo Velichestva, genvaria po 28 chislo 1725 godu* (St. Petersburg: Tipografiia Akademii nauk, 1739), pp. 742–43.

9. Madariaga, "Tsar into Emperor," pp. 37–38.

10. Ibid., pp. 34–39.

11. Judith Herrin, *Women in Purple: Rulers of Medieval Byzantium* (Princeton: Princeton University Press, 2001), p. 249; A. A. Vasiliev, *History of the Byzantine Empire* (Madison: University of Wisconsin Press, 1952), vol. 1, p. 333; Charles Diehl, *Byzantine Portraits* (New York: A. A. Knopf, 1927), pp. 181–215.

12. It is possible that one or more of the many unpublished *khrongrafy* supplied the apocryphal histories on which the decree was based. But this remains a question for future research. *Letopisets ellinskii i rimskii,* ed. Tvorogov, pp. 401, 474. In this chronograf, Zoia is described as having the crown *(venets)* and Martina is described simply as ruling, not with Heraclius but alongside her son Heraclion.

13. *Prodolzhatel' Feofana. Zhizneopisaniia vizantiiskikh tsarei* (St. Petersburg: Nauka, 1992), p. 150, "Venchaet tsar' Lev doch' Zautsy Zoiu, i blagoslavliaet ee dvortosvyi sviashchennik." The same text recounts that Eudoxia, whom Leo married in 900 after Zoia died, also was crowned ("zhenilsia i venchal ee.") The second Zoia, Leo's fourth wife, dwelled in the court uncrowned, however ("i byla Zoia chetvertoi tsarskoi zhenoi i prebyvala vo dvortse s tsarem nevenchannoi"), pp. 151, 152.

14. Procopius, *The Secret History* (London: Penguin Books, 1981), p. 70; James Allan Evans, *The Empress Theodora, Partner of Justinian* (Austin: University of Texas Press, 2002), pp. 5–6; see also A. A. Vasiliev, *Justin the First: An Introduction to the Epoch of Justinian the Great* (Cambridge, MA: Harvard University Press, 1950).

15. Vasiliev, *Justin the First,* pp. 60–61.

16. Walter E. Kaegi, *Heraclius, Emperor of Rome* (Cambridge: Cambridge University Press, 2003), pp. 106–7.

17. *Die slavische Manasses-Chronik,* ed. Joan Bogdan, *Slavische Propylaen,* vol. 12 (1966), pp. x, 181. The Chronicle of John Malalas, whose narrative ends with the mid-sixth century, made no reference to Lupicina/Euphemia in its lengthy sections on Justin and Justinian. *The Chronicle of John Malalas,* trans. Elizabeth Jeffreys, Michael Jeffreys, and Roger Scott (Melbourne: Australian Association for Byzantine Studies, 1986), pp. 230–307.

18. RGADA, *f.* 96, *kn.* 33, ll. 30–31.

19. *Biblioteka Petra I. Ukazatel'-spravochnik,* ed. E. A. Bobrova (Leningrad: BAN, 1978), no. 205, 1413.

20. RGADA, *f.* 96, *kn.* 66, *ll.* 375–76. My thanks to Lindsey Hughes and Olga Kosheleva for bringing this document to my attention and retrieving it from the archive.

21. Vasiliev, *History of the Byzantine Empire,* vol. 1, p. 235.

22. Martin, "Dynastic Marriage in Muscovy."

23. Christoph von Manstein, newly arrived at the Russian court, described the situation: "Peter II . . . gave orders for the liberation of his grandmother, the empress [sic] Eudoxia Feodorowna Lapouchin . . . He ordered her a court proportionate to her

rank, and invited her to Petersburg. But this princess having too great an aversion to that city, and not finding the ministry pliable enough to give her any share in the government, resolved to remain at Moscow, where she lived in retirement. The family of the Lapouchins, near relations to the empress, were also recalled from exile in which they had been for several years.

"These acts of grace had been carried out against the inclination of Menzikoff, at the suggestion of some of the members of the supreme council, who had found in a favorable moment means to soften the young monarch in favour of his grandmother, and of her near relations . . ." General Christof Hermann von Manstein, *Contemporary Memoirs of Russia, from the Year 1727 to 1744* (London: Longman, Brown, Green, and Longmans, 1856), p. 3.

24. *Istoricheskoe opisanie moskovskogo novodevich'ego monastyria*, p. 102.

25. See the footnote to the original manifesto in *PSZ*, vol. 5, p. 534.

26. See, for example, A. A. Andreeva, '*Mestnik Bozhii' na tsarskom trone. Khristianskaia tsivilizatsionnaia model' sakralizatsii vlasti v rossiiskoi istorii* (Moscow: RAN, 2002), pp. 198–206; N. A. Ogarkova, *Tseremonii, prazdnestva, muzyka russkogo dvora, XVIII-nachalo XIX veka* (St. Petersburg: Dmitrii Bulanin, 2004), pp. 13–14. For Ogarkova, the key point was that the archbishop was being placed in the position of Peter's assistant instead of acting as head of the church. The *opisanie* does not explicitly say that, however, and, as we shall see below, the crowning ritual lends itself to more than one reading.

27. Constantin VII Porphyrogénète, *Le livre des ceremonies*, vol. 2, bk. 1, trans. Albert Vogt (Paris: Société d'édition 'Les Belles Lettres', 1939), pp. 11–12. The text is reproduced in the Greek original with a side-by-side French translation. "Le patriarche fait une prière sur la couronne et lorsqu'il a achevé la prière, le patriarche prend la couronne, le remit à l'empereur et ce dernier la place sur la tête de l'Augusta."

28. "Iz 'Zapisok' Stanislava Nemoevskogo o venchanii na tsarstvo Mariny Mnishek," in *Dnevnik Mariny Mnishek*, p. 185.

29. *PSPR*, vol. 4, pp. 107–8, "Chin tserkovnyi v den' koronatsii Blagochestiveishei Velikoi Gosudaryni Imperatritsy Ekateriny Alekseevny." The instruction continues in this manner throughout.

30. *Zapiski Grafa Bassevicha*, pp. 245–47.

31. Berkhgol'ts, *Dnevnik*, pt. 4, p. 31.

32. Ibid., p. 39.

33. Feodosii's distress ran deeper than the coronation and it derived primarily from Peter's creation of the Synod, an act that in his mind completely subordinated the clergy to the state. Feodosii wondered aloud whether their prayers would now be heard, and he responded dismissively when asked what the appropriate coronation prayers would be. "Do whatever the Statute says," he is quoted by several eyewitnesses as having muttered. Comments such as these earned him an investigation by the Secret Chancery in 1725, for which he was found guilty but granted clemency by the empress. The entire affair is reproduced in "Novye materialy dlia istorii tsarstvovaniia Ekateriny I (1725): Podlinnoe delo novgorodskogo arkhiepiskopa Feodosiia," *Russkii arkhiv*, vol. 2, no. 6 (1864), pp. 160–207.

34. The letters are reproduced in an appendix to Kapterev, *Kharakter otnoshenii Rossii k pravoslavnomu vostoku*, pp. 556–57.

35. "Slovo v den' koronatsii Gosudaryni Imperatritsy Ekateriny Alekseevny," in Feofan Prokopovich, *Slova i rechi pouchitel'nye, pokhval'nye i pozdravitel'nye* (St. Petersburg: Sukhoputnyi shliakhetnyi kadetskii korpus, 1761), vol. 2, pp. 103–11.

36. Riccardo Picchio, "The Function of Biblical Thematic Clues in the Literary Code of 'Slavia Orthodoxa,'" *Slavica Hierosolymitana* 1 (1977), pp. 1–31.

37. Ibid., p. 6.

38. Prokopovich, *Slova i rechi*, vol. 2, p. 105. The deposition of Queen Vashti and the Coronation of Esther are told in the Book of Esther (chaps. 1 and 2), New International Edition (London: Hodder and Stoughton, 1984).

39. Prokopovich, *Slova i rechi*, vol. 2, pp. 106–7. See also Richard Wortman's summary of this passage. Wortman, *Scenarios of Power*, vol. 1, p. 74.

40. Feofan Prokopovich, "Slovo pokhval'noe nad voiskami sveiskimi pobede, presvetleishemu gosudariu tsariu i velikomu kniaziu Petru Alekseevichu, vseia velikiia i malyia i belyia Rossii samoderzhetsu, v leto gospodne 1709 mesiatsa iunia dnia 27 Bogom darovannoi," in *Sochineniia*, p. 24. The same trope recurs on p. 29 and elsewhere in the text, counterposed with its polar opposite, the Judas-like betrayal of Mazepa.

41. Wortman, *Scenarios of Power*, vol. 1, pp. 74–75.

42. Ilarion, "Sermon on Law and Grace," in *Sermons and Rhetoric of Kievan Rus'*, trans. and with an intro. Simon Franklin (Cambridge, MA: Harvard University Press, 1991), pp. 22–23.

43. N. Subbotin, ed., *Deianiia moskovskikh soborov 1666 i 1667 godov* (Moscow: Sinodal'naia Tipografiia, 1893), p. 13.

44. Eleonskaia, "Skazanie o kreshchenii Rusi . . .," p. 36.

45. Tomyris did appear in Russian translations, but less often than the others. Although many texts retell the reign of her enemy, King Cyrus of Persia, none of the variants of the Alexander tale include her, nor do stories of the history of Troy or the *khronografy*. In Peter's time, however, the image of Tomyris had been displayed on an early Russian triumphal gate, as described by Turoboiskii in his 1704 treatise. "On the left side [of the back side of the gates] stands Tomirisa, the fearless Scythian queen . . . Tomirisa is the emblem of Russian power courageously defeating the Swedish forces and liberating Ingermanland from them." Grebeniuk, *Panegiricheskaia literatura petrovoskogo vremeni*, p. 179.

46. Guido [delle Colonne] de Columnis, *Historia Destructionis Troiae*, ed. Nathaniel Edward Griffith (Cambridge: Mediaeval Academy of America, 1936).

47. O. B. Tvorogov, ed., *Troianskie skazaniia srednevekovye rytsarskie romany o troianskoi voine po russkim rukopisiam XVI–XVII vekov* (Leningrad: Akademiia nauk, 1972), pp. 62–64 and 129–31 (Pentheselia) and 71–103; and Tvorogov, *Drevnerusskie khronografy* (Leningrad: Nauka, 1975). Bykova and Gurevich, *Opisanie izdanii*, vol. 1, nos. 20, 59, 231. The *History of Troy* remained popular through the rest of the eighteenth century, going through eight separate Russian printings between 1745 and 1799 (*SK*, vol. 1, nos. 1261–1268).

48. Feofan Prokopovich, *Apologia sacrarum reliquarium patrum nostrorum* in his *Miscellanea Sacra* (Wroclaw, 1744), pp. 75–83.

49. Herodotus, *The Histories*, trans. Robin Waterfield (London: Oxford University Press, 1998), bk. 1, no. 214, p. 93. "Tomyris filled a wineskin with human blood and searched among the Persian corpses for Cyrus's body. When she found it, she shoved his head into the wineskin, and in her rage addressed his body as follows: 'Although I have come through the battle alive and victorious, you have destroyed me by capturing my son with a trick. But I warned you that I would quench your thirst for blood, and so I shall.' Of all the many stories that are told about Cyrus' death, this seems to me to be the most trustworthy."

50. *Artakserkovo deistvo. Pervaia p'esa russkogo teatra XVII v.*, ed. I. M. Kudriavtsev (Moscow: Akademiia nauk, 1957), p. 45.

51. See, for example, the seventeenth-century engravings by Francois Chauveau for Jacques du Bosc's *La Femme heroique*, in which Deborah, Judith, and Tomyris are presented together as warrior queens. Annette Dixon, *Women Who Ruled: Queens, Goddesses, Amazons in Renaissance and Baroque Art* (London: Merrell, 2002), pp. 44–45.

52. *Artakserkov deistvo*, pp. 308–9.

53. Dante Alighieri, *The Divine Comedy*, trans. Kenneth McKenzie (London: The Folio Society, 1979), "Hell," canto 5, pp. 21–22.

54. While on the first terrace of Purgatory, Virgil shows Dante a series of gravestones, including that of Cyrus, about whom "Queen Tomyris exclaimed: 'For blood you thirsted, blood shall fill you now.'" Alighieri, *The Divine Comedy*, p. 198.

55. Herodotus, *The Histories,* bk. 1, no. 216, p. 94.

56. On this, see the extensive commentaries by A. P. Bogdanov and E. V. Chistiakova in Andrei Lyzlov, *Skifskaia istoriia* (Moscow: Nauka, 1990), pp. 345–440.

57. Lyzlov, *Skifskaia istoriia,* p. 42.

58. Feofan Prokopovich, "The Justice of the Monarch's Right," in *Peter the Great,* ed. and trans. Anthony Lentin (Oxford: Headstart History, 1996), p. 245.

59. Tomyris' beheading of Cyrus further vividly called to mind Salome's beheading of John the Baptist, an event marked by a major fast on August 29th in the Russian church, hardly a happy image for the faithful to contemplate. See the discussion of John the Baptist's saint's day in Kollmann, "The Moscow *Stoglav,*" pp. 265–66.

60. Grebeniuk, *Panegiricheskaia literatura petrovskogo vremeni,* p. 179.

61. "Letopis' skazuiushchuiu Deianiia ot nachala mirobytiia do rozhdestva Khristova," in *Sochineniia Sviatogo Dimitriia,* vol. 4, pp. 323–46.

62. See, for example, the sermon on the Pentecost by Semen Polotskii in *Obed dushevnyi* (Moscow: Verkhniaia Tipografiia, 1681), pp. 452–53.

63. *Artakserkovo deistvo,* pp. 36–40.

64. Ibid., pp. 144–47.

65. Ibid., pp. 170–72.

66. Book of Esther: 1 and 2, NIE.

67. This discussion of Helena draws largely from Jan Willem Drijvers, *Helena Augusta, the Mother of Constantine the Great, and the Legend of Her Finding of the True Cross* (Leiden: E. J. Brill, 1992), esp. pp. 35–88, 182–83.

68. In addition to St. Helena's vita in the relevant menologic and service books, her life was recounted in the *khronograf* and in the sources that contributed to it. See, for example, V. M. Istrin, *Khronika Georgiia Amatola v drevnem slavianorusskom perevode,* vol. 1, *Tekst* (Petrograd: Rossiiskaia gosudarstvennaia akademicheskaia tipografiia, 1920), pp. 330–32, 339–40; *Letopisets ellinskii i rimskii,* ed. Tvorogov, pp. 298–303.

69. Thyrêt, *Between God and Tsar,* pp. 65–69.

70. Elizabeth Kristoforovich Zelensky, "'Sophia the Wisdom of God' as a Rhetorical Device during the Regency of Sof'ia Alekseevna, 1682–1689," Ph.D. diss. (Georgetown University, 1992), p. 278; Kenneth Hollum, *Theodosian Empresses: Women and Imperial Dominion in Late Imperial Antiquity* (Berkeley: University of California Press, 1982), pp. 79–111.

71. A. M. Panchenko et al., eds., *Russkaia sillabicheskaia poeziia XVII–XVIII v.v.* (Leningrad: Sovetskii Pisatel', 1970), p. 202.

72. *Chronicle of John Malalas,* bks. 8–18, trans. from the Church Slavonic by Matthew Spinka and Glanville Downey (Chicago: University of Chicago Press, 1940), pp. 87–88. The Russian text is in V. M. Istrin, "Khronika Ioanna Malaly v slavianskom perevode, knigi 11–14," *Sbornik otdeleniia russkogo iazyka i slovesnosti Imperatorskoi Akademii nauk,* vol. 90, no. 2 (1913), pp. 14–16. Both Tvorogov and Istrin state that the chronicle of Malalas was one of the fundamental sources for the Russian *khronograf,* along with the chronicles of Georgios Hamartolos and Georgi Syncelli. Tvorogov, *Drevnerusskie khronografy,* p. 1.

73. See the summary of this mutual enmity in Vasliev, *History of the Byzantine Empire,* vol. 1, pp. 94–96.

74. *Paul of Aleppo, the Travels of Macarius Patriarch of Antioch,* trans. from Arabic (London: Oriental Translation Committee, 1829), p. 49.

75. Bassewitz, *Zapiski Iusta Iulia,* pp. 156–58.

76. Theodora's early life and the sources for it are described at length in Evans, *Empress Theodora,* pp. 13–21. None of Procopius' lurid anecdotes appear in Malalas, but Evans gives them credence based upon the norms of the day for actresses.

77. *The Chronicle of John Malalas,* bk. 18, pp. 255–56. Evans, *Empress Theodora,* pp. 30–32. Procopius, who despised Theodora, saw this as a cynical financial arrangement and nothing more.

78. Evans, *Empress Theodora*, pp. 45–47; Vasiliev, *History of the Byzantine Empire*, vol. 1, p. 157.

79. Herrin, *Women in Purple*, pp. 72–74.

80. Vasiliev, *History of the Byzantine Empire*, vol. 1, p. 235.

81. Originally written in Greek, an abbreviated English translation of the work of Paisius appears in Palmer, *The Patriarch and the Tsar*, vol. 3, pp. 202–3.

82. Ligarides' career is conveniently summarized in Harry T. Hionides, *Paisius Ligarides* (New York: Twayne Publishers, 1972).

83. *Russkaia sillabicheskaia poeziia*, p. 202. The association between Sofia and Pulcheria is well documented in the scholarship. See Sazonova, *Poeziia russkogo barokko*, p. 149; Hughes, *Sophia, Regent of Russia*, p. 224; A. P. Bogdanov, "Tsarevna Sof'ia Alekseevna v sovremennykh poeticheskikh obrazakh," in *Kul'tura srednevekovoi moskvy XVII vek*, ed. B. A. Rybakov et al. (Moscow: Nauka, 1999), p. 313.

84. Sil'vestr Medvedev, *Sozertsanie kratkoe leto 1790, 91 i 92 v nikh zhe chto sodeiasia vo grazhdanstve* (Moscow: Universitetskaia Tipografiia, 1894), p. 58.

85. Brailovskii, "Odin iz pestrykh," p. 280.

86. *Zapiski Andreia Artamanovicha Grafa Matveeva*, in *Zapiski russkikh liudei. Sobytiia vremen Petra Velikogo* (St. Petersburg: Tipografiia Sakharova, 1841), pp. 7–8.

87. *Artakserkovo deistvo*, p. 40. Kudriavtsev speculates that the play was intended as a commentary on the concrete situation at the Muscovite court, and that all the leading roles may well have represented living individuals at court. He acknowledges that much of this is his own construction, but he insists that the conscious association of Esther and Natal'ia was beyond doubt and widely perceived.

88. *Pis'ma i bumagi Petra I*, vol. 1 (St. Petersburg: Gosudarstvennaia Tipografiia, 1887), p. 109; M. A. Il'in and V. P. Vygolov, "Moskovskie triumfal'nye vorota rubezha XVII–XVIII vv.," in *Materialy po teorii i istorii iskusstva*, ed. A. A. Fedorov-Davydov (Moscow: Moscow University, 1956), pp. 106–7. See also D. D. Zelov, *Ofitsial'nye svetskie prazdniki kak iavlenie russkoi kul'tury kontsa XVII–pervoi poloviny XVIII veka. Istoriia triumfov i feierverkov ot Petra Velikogo do ego docheri Elizavety* (Moscow: URSS, 2002), p. 16.

89. Il'in and Vygolov, "Moskovskie triumfal'nye vorota," pp. 108–9.

90. S. K. Bogoiavlenskii, *Moskovskii teatr pri tsariakh Aleksee i Petre* (Moscow: Tipografiia V. I. Voronova, 1914), p. 146.

91. Potter, "Preaching and Teaching the Faith in Seventeenth-Century Russia," pp. 330–31.

92. As an example of the dramatic differentiation between sermons and other panegyrics, one need only look at the index in Grebeniuk's *Panegiricheskaia literatura petrovskogo vremeni* and compare the many dozens of references to pagan gods in secular panegyrics with the veritable handful of references to Mars and Hercules in the sermons.

93. Petr Nikiforovich Krekshin, "Zapiski novgorodskogo dvorianina Petra Nikiforovicha" Krekshina, in *Zapiski russkikh liudei. Sobytiia vremen Petra Velikogo* (St. Petersburg: Tipografiia Sakharova, 1841), p. 8.

94. Prokopovich, *Sochineniia*, p. 34.

95. Ibid., p. 44.

96. Prokopovich, *Slova i rechi*, 1762 vol. 2, p. 108.

97. Prokopovich, *Sochineniia*, p. 131.

98. Ibid., pp. 142–46.

99. Iavorskii, "Kolesnitsa torzhestvennaia," in *Propovedi blazhennyia pamiati Stefana Iavorskogo*, vol. 2, pp. 156–76.

100. Grebeniuk, *Panegiricheskii literatura petrovskogo vremeni*, p. 241.

101. Ibid., p. 239.

102. Prokopovich, *Razsuzhdenie o knize solomonovoi naritsaemoi Pesni Pesnei*. An earlier edition had appeared in 1774. See the commentary in *SK*, vol. 3, no. 7739.

103. Prokopovich, *Razsuzhdenie o bezbozhii*, p. 11.

104. Ibid., pp. 26–35.

105. Prokopovich, *Veshchi i dela, o kotorykh dukhovnyi uchitel' narodu khristian-skomu propovedati dolzhen, inaia obshchaia vsem, i inaia nekim sobstvennaia*, in *Slova i rechi*, vol. 4 (1774), pp. 266–74. It also appeared in 1784 as a separate pamphlet, printed by Moscow University Press.

106. "O boze, iako est', suprotiv Afeistov ili bezbozhnikov." Prokopovich, *Veschi i dela*, p. 266.

107. Ibid., pp. 271–73.

108. Pekarskii, *Nauka i literature*, vol. 2, pp. 630–32; *PSPR*, vol. 4, no. 1307, pp. 141–42.

109. V. G. Borukhovich, *Apollodor, mifologicheskaia biblioteka* (Leningrad: Nauka, 1972), chap. 1, pt. 3, paragraph 3 (Tomyris) and chap. 5, pt. 1, paragraph 2 (Penthe-selia).

110. Iavorskii, "Slovo pokhval'noe," in *Propovedi*, pp. 29–30.

111. Ibid., p. 29.

112. V. M. Zhivov and B. A. Uspenskii, "Metamorfozy antichnogo iazychestva v istorii russkoi kul'tury XVII–XVIII veka," in *Iz istorii russkoi literatury*, ed. A. D. Koshelev, vol. 4 (Moscow: Shkola iazyki russkoi kul'tury, 1996), pp. 475, 484–500.

113. Prokopovich, "Slovo v den' koronatsii," p. 109.

114. "Koronatsionnye zhetony," p. 155.

115. Prokopovich, "Slovo v den' koronatsii," p. 110.

116. Ibid., p. 110.

117. Prokopovich, "Slovo v den' vospominaniia Koronatsii Eia Imperatorskogo Velichestva," in *Slova i rechi*, vol. 2, pp. 171–92.

118. Ibid., p. 177.

119. Ibid., p. 182.

120. Feofan Prokopovich, *Slovo v den' koronatsii Gosudaryny Imperatritsy Anny Ioan-novny v Moskve*, in *Slova i rechi*, vol. 3 (1765), pp. 73–81.

121. "There was also a prophetess, Anna, the daughter of Phanuel, of the tribe of Asher. She was very old; she had lived with her husband seven years after her marriage, and then was a widow until she was eighty-four. She never left the temple but worshiped night and day, fasting and praying. Coming up to [Mary and Joseph] at that very moment, she gave thanks to God and spoke about the child to all who were looking forward to the redemption of Jerusalem" (Luke 2: 36–38). Another more distant reference to widowhood would refer to Anna, the mother of Mary. The text for this Anna's widowhood comes from the Apocrypha of Saint James, the only early Christian writing that mentions her. "And [Joachim's] wife mourned in two mournings, and lamented in two lamentations, saying: I shall bewail my widowhood; I shall bewail my childlessness." Protoevangelium of St. James 2:1. According to some legends, Anna survived Joachim, and after her widowhood remarried.

122. Prokopovich, *Rech' kotoroiu Gos. Imperatritsa Anna I po koronatsii ot vsekh chinov pozdravlena im vuspeniem*, in *Slova i rechi*, vol. 3, pp. 47–51.

123. *PSPR*, vol. 4, no. 1353, pp. 194–95; no. 1357, p. 200, and others.

124. Archimandrite Gedeon of Spasskii Cathedral had requested and received permission from the Synod to publish his coronation sermon, but no trace of it exists. *Opisanie dokumentov i del khraniashchikhsia v arkhive sviateishago pravitel'stvuiushchago sinoda*, vol. 4, *1724* (St. Petersburg: Sinodal'naia Tipografiia, 1880), p. 177.

125. M. I. Sokolov, ed., *'Slava Rossiiskaia,' komediia 1724 goda predstavlennaia v moskovskom goshpitale po sluchaiu koronatsii Imperatritsy Ekateriny Pervoi* (Moscow: Universitetskaia Tipografiia, 1892), pp. 13–14. See also Vsevolodskii-Gerngross, *Russkii teatr*, p. 152.

126. Sokolov, *'Slava Rossiiskaia,'* pp. 14–15.

127. Because of the Latin-based medical curriculum, Russia recruited almost all of its native medical and surgical students from the most advanced classes (i.e., theology and philosophy) of the religious academies, which also required an extensive grasp of

Latin. Until the 1740s, the Moscow Academy supplied well over half of all medical students, and nearly all of those at the Moscow medical school.

128. Sokolov, 'Slava Rossiiskaia,' pp. 3–5, 10–15.

129. Ibid., pp. 23–25.

130. Ibid., pp. 27–29.

131. So sensitive were the authorities that, as Evgenii Anisimov has shown, merely mentioning the names of the imperial family in an unsanctioned setting could initiate a slovo i delo (lèse majesté) case. Anisimov, Dyba i knut, pp. 15ff. Anisimov's exhaustive study supercedes the older work by Semevskii, Slovo i delo, 1700–1725.

132. RGADA, f. 371 (Preobrazhenskii prikaz), op. 1, no. 14419, pp. 1-64.

133. Ibid., p. 5.

134. Ibid., p. 10.

135. Ibid., p. 22

136. Quoted in Ogarkova, Tseremonii, p. 18.

137. Bassewitz provided the most detailed account, including the celestial St. Catherine. But Campredon also noted how unusual these fireworks were, so large and long lasting that they filled the area with smoke. Bassewitz, "Zapiski Grafa Bassevitsa ..." p. 248; Campredon, "Memorandum to Count de Morville of May 26 [n.s.], 1724," SIRIO, vol. 42, 1882 pp. 219–20.

9—Sacralizing Female Rule

1. See, for example, Sergei M. Soloviev, History of Russia, vol. 32, ed. and trans. Gary Marker (Gulf Breeze, FL: Academic International Press, 2001), pp. 158–60.

2. PSZ, vol. 6, no. 3882, January 18, 1722, p. 481, "O voznoshenii Vysochaishikh Imian pri tserkovnosluzheniiakh po dannym formam."

3. The account originally appeared in 1726. The citations here come from the 1831 edition. Feofan Prokopovich, Kratkaia povest' o smerti Petra Velikogo (St. Petersburg: Tipografiia I. Glazunova, 1831).

4. Prokopovich, "The Justice of the Monarch's Right," p. 195.

5. Ibid., p. 187.

6. Zitser, Transformed Kingdom, pp. 4–5.

7. Prokopovich, "The Justice of the Monarch's Right," p. 203.

8. Ibid., p. 209.

9. Feofan Prokopovich, "Slovo pokhval'noe blagorodneishago gosudaria tsarevicha i velikogo kniazia Petra Petrovicha," in Sochineniia, pp. 39–40. The entire panegyric runs from pp. 38–48.

10. Ibid., p. 47.

11. Ibid., p. 43.

12. Taken from the New International Edition of the Bible, p. 540.

13. "Memorandum" of Campredon to de Morville, February 1725, in SIRIO, vol. 42, 1881 pp. 428–40.

14. Ibid., p. 430. Focusing entirely on Realpolitik, Campredon made no mention in this memorandum of Prokopovich or rituals of legitimation. His only reference to the clergy cynically observed that they had been pacified by the promise of lower taxes. Otherwise his concern lay with the powerful men of the Senate and the potentially more powerful men in arms.

15. This account comes entirely from Prokopovich, Kratkaia povest', pp. 15–18.

16. RGADA, f. 371 (Preobrazhenskii prikaz), op. 1, no. 14419.

17. RGADA, f. 371, op. 1, no. 14419, pp. 30, 42.

18. RGADA, f. 371, op. 1, no. 14419, pp. 63–64.

19. "Slovo v den' godishchnogo pominoveniia vo blazhennoi pamiati prestavlenogosia blagochestiveishogo velikogo Gosudaria Petra Velikogo," in Buzhinskii, Propovedi, pp. 578–95.

20. This sermon was translated and published in English in London in 1770. The English text renders the passage slightly differently and to my eye less effectively, "Peter the Great is alive again; he lives in Catherine the Second." Platon, Archbishop of Moscow, *A Sermon Preached by Order of Her Imperial Majesty on the Tomb of Peter the Great in the Cathedral Church of St. Peterbourg* (London, 1770), p. 4.

21. This passage has been cited before, albeit in passing. See Cherniavsky, *Tsar and People*, p. 86. Cherniavsky's source was E. F. Shmurlo, "Petr Velikii v otsenke sovremennikov i potomstva," *ZMNP*, [new series] pt. 35 (1911), pp. 315–40; 36 (1911) 1–37, 201–73; 39 (1912), pp. 1–40, 193–259.

22. Buzhinskii, "Slovo v den'," p. 581.

23. Bogdanov, "Tsarevna Sof'ia Alekseevna," pp. 37–38.

24. *Pokhodnyi zhurnal za 1725*, p. 26.

25. *Pokhodnyi zhurnal za 1726*, p. 10. (The entry refers to the portrait as *"rabota gosudarevaia"*).

26. Piatnitsky, *Sinai, Byzantium, Russia*, p. 325.

27. *Pokhodnyi zhurnal za 1725*, pp. 39–40.

28. Pogosian, *Petr I*, p. 312.

29. *Pokhodnyi zhurnal za 1726*, pp. 33–35.

30. See, for example, the congratulatory letter of V. Gennin, director of mining in Ekaterinburg, from December 18, 1726. V. Gennin, *Ural'skaia perepiska s Petrom i Ekaterinoi I* (Ekaterinburg: RAN, 1995), p. 368.

31. Pogosian, *Petr I*, p. 318.

32. RGADA, *f.* 235, *op.* 4, no. 458/6654, pp. 1–3.

33. RGADA, *f.* 235, *op.* 4, no. 480/6676, pp. 9–10.

34. *Opisanie dokumentov i del khraniashchikhsia v archive sviateishogo pravitel'stvuiushchego sinoda*, vol. 5, *1725 g.* (1897), pp. 514–15.

35. Shakhovskoi, Iakov Petrovich, *Zapiski Kniazia Iakova Petrovicha Shakhovskogo pisannye im samim* (Moscow: Tipografiia Vsevolozhskogo, 1810), pp. 66–67.

36. Rovinskii, "Slovar' russkikh gravirovannykh portretov," p. 46.

37. The entry for April 14, 1726, says simply that she emerged from the court at midnight in a carriage, carrying the scepter of her rule and dressed as an Amazon. *Pokhodnyi zhurnal za 1726*, p. 14.

38. *Pokhodnyi zhurnal za 1726*, pp. 3–4.

39. *Pokhodnyi zhurnal za 1725*, p. 42.

40. Konstantin Pisarenko, *Povsednevnaia zhizn' russkogo dvora v tsarstvovanie Elizavety Petrovny* (Moscow: Molodaia gvardiia, 2003), p. 609.

41. N. N. Firsov, *Vstuplenie na prestol Imperatritsy Elizavety Petrovny* (Kazan: Universitetskaia Tipografiia, 1888), pp. 146–48; P. P. Pekarskii *Markiz de-la Shetardi v Rossii, 1740–1742 godov.* (St. Petersburg: Tipografiia Isafata Ogritzko, 1862), pp. 393–97.

42. See, for example, the official calendar of 1738 in which St. Catherine's Day is listed as a saint's day but not as a day of official state celebration. In its place were the birthday, name day, and coronation day of Anna Ioannovna (January 28, February 3, and April 28, respectively) and the name day and birthday of Elizaveta Petrovna (September 5 and December 18) and Anna Petrovna (December 8 and 9). *Sanktpeterburgskii kalendar' na leto ot rozhdestva Khristova 1738, kotoroe est' prostoe leto, soderzhashche 365 dnei, sochinennyi na znatneishiia mesta rossiiskogo gosudarstva* (St. Petersburg: Akademiia nauk, 1737).

43. Anna's court records indicate that she hosted an annual banquet for the Order of the White Eagle on July 23, often in the company of the Polish ambassador. See, for example, *Zhurnal pridvornoi kantory 1734go goda*, p. 7, *1736go goda*, p. 27, and *1737go goda*, p. 28.

44. For example, during the late 1720s and 1730s, she spent a great deal of time at the Dormition Convent on her estate in Alexandrovskaia sloboda, praying, subsidizing, and cultivating relations with the nuns there lest she be confined to a convent at

some future date. N. S. Stromilov, *Tsesarevna Elisaveta Petrovna v Aleksandrovoi slobode i Uspenskii devichii monastyr' v to zhe vremia* (Moscow: Universitetskaia Tipografiia, 1874), pp. 13–24.

45. Pushkarev, *Opisanie Sankt Peterburga,* p. 207

46. Ibid., p. 208.

47. Ibid., p. 279.

48. Runkevich, *Aleksandro-Nevskaia lavra,* pp. 743–44.

49. E. V. Anisimov, *Zhenshchiny na rossiiskom prestole* (St. Petersburg: Norint, 1997), p. 222 and *Elizaveta Petrovna* (Moscow: Molodaia gvardiia, 1999), p. 97.

50. The association between Elizabeth and the service of Saints Zachariah and Elizabeth was long-standing. As early as 1722, Peter had expressed disapproval at the failure of some parishes to observe Elizabeth's name day, and he ordered a new printing of the service. In response, the Nevskii Monastery Press published 1,200 copies and the Synodal Press in Moscow printed nearly 16,000 copies. Pekarskii, *Nauka i literatura,* vol. 2, p. 561.

51. The use of the plural "emperors" *(imperatorov)* clearly refers to Peter and Catherine. M. S. Popov, *Arsenii Matveevich i ego delo* (St. Petersburg: Tipografiia M. Fronovoi, 1912), p. 255.

52. The discussion of the coronation sermon is based on the text as reprinted in the *Kamerfur'erskii zhurnal* (St. Petersburg: Ministerstvo Imperatorskogo dvora) for 1742. The sermon is reproduced on pp. 14–29, and a brief word of greeting *("kratkoe pozdravlenie")* is on pp. 80–87.

53. Victor M. Zhivov, "Gedeon (Georgii Andreevich Krinovsky)," in *Dictionary of Literary Biography,* vol. 150, *Early Modern Russian Writers, Late Seventeenth and Eighteenth Centuries,* ed. Marcus C. Levitt (Detroit: Bruccoli Clark Layman, 1995), p. 112. See also Kjellberg, *La langue de Gedeon Krinovskij,* pp. 12–13. Several of his sermons were published in a collection of 1760, see Gedeon Krinovskii, *Sobranie raznykh pouchitel'nykh slov* (Moscow, 1760).

54. On this group of preachers see P. Zavedeev, *Istoriia russkogo propovednichestva ot XVII veka do nastoiashchago vremeni* (Tula: Tipografiia N. A. Sokalova, 1879), pp. 72–81.

55. Amvrosii arrived in St. Petersburg in 1734 and served for several years as an instructor at the Nevskii Monastery, during which time Elizabeth got to know him. In 1742 she arranged for him to become the seminary's prefect and archimandrite of the New Jerusalem *(stauropigial)* monastery, as well as her court sermonizer. Dmitrii Bantysh-Kamenskii, *Zhizn' Preosviashchennogo Amvrosiia, Arkhiepiskopa moskovskogo i kaluzhskogo* (Moscow: Gubernskaia Tipografiia, 1813), pp. 6–11; Popov, *Arsenii Matseevich i ego delo,* pp. 255–57.

56. Quoted in N. Popov, "Pridvornye propovedi v tsarstvovanii Elisavety Petrovny," in *Letopisi russkoi literatury i drevnosti,* ed. Nikolai Tikhonravov, vol. 2 (Moscow: Grachev and Company, 1853), pp. 3–4.

57. Ibid., pp. 4–7.

58. RGADA, *f.* 17, *op.* 1, no. 165, p. 2.

59. Ibid., p. 7.

60. Ibid., p. 9.

61. Popov, "Pridvornye propovedi," p. 12

62. Ibid., p. 15.

63. Ibid., p. 14

64. P. N. Petrov, *Istoriia Sankt-Peterburga s osnovaniia goroda do vvedeniia v deistvie vybornogo gorodskogo upravleniia* (St. Petersburg: Tipografiia Glazunova, 1885), p. 450. See, also, the contemporary comments by Manstein that confirm the general understanding that Catherine's will had named Elizabeth. Manstein, *Contemporary Memoirs of Russia,* pp. 316–26.

65. Anisimov, *Elizaveta Petrovna,* p. 97.

66. *PSZ*, vol. 8, no. 5070, May 7, 1727, p. 790, "Manifest o konchine Imperatritse Ekateriny I i o vozshestvii na prestol Imperatora Petra II. Prilozhenie, Testament blazhennyia pamiati Imperatritsy Ekateriny I."

67. See the entries in *Kamerfur'erskii zhurnal* for 1743, pp. 14–15; 1744, pp. 103–8; 1745, pp. 126–30; 1746, pp. 105–6; etc.

68. See, e.g., *Zhurnaly tseremonial'nye, banketnye, i pokhodnye 1743 goda*, St. Petersburg, 1856 pp. 14–15.

69. Pushkarev, *Opisanie Sankt Peterburga*, p. 298; Herman Kajanus, *St Katarina svenska församlings i St Petersburg* (Ekenäs: Ekenäs Tryckeri Aktiebolag, 1980), pp. 11–15.

70. *Ekaterina Velikaia i Moskva. Katalog-vystavka 850–letiiu Moskvy posviashchaetsia iun'-sentiabr' 1997* (Moscow: Tret'iakovskaia galereia, 1997), p. 25, no. 64.

71. Bartenev, "Ekaterina Vtoraia, novyia svedeniia . . .," pp. 28–29.

72. Pushkarev, *Opisanie Sankt Peterburga*, pp. 292, 298.

73. Romual'da Khankovska, *Khram Sviatoi Ekateriny v Sankt-Peterburge* (St. Petersburg: Chistyi list, 2001), pp. 45–46.

74. Pushkarev, *Opisanie Sankt Peterburga*, p. 159.

75. Ibid., p. 232.

76. Ibid., p. 253.

77. Antonov and Kobak, *Sviatyni Sankta-Peterburga*, vol. 1, pp. 183–85.

78. *Istoriko-statisticheskoe svedenie o S.Peterburgskoi eparkhii*, vol. 2, 1878, p. 17.

79. Ibid., p. 90.

80. *Istoriko-statisticheskoe svedenie o S.Peterburgskoi eparkhii*, vol. 6 (1878), p. 261.

81. *DRV*, vol. 11, 1789; reprinted 1970, pp. 283–327. This list shows fifteen churches and chapels of St. Catherine in operation in Moscow.

82. Ibid., p. 185, 251; Zvonarev, *Sorok sorokov*, vol. 2 (1988), pp. 245–47; vol. 3 (1989), pp. 417–19; *Istoriko-statisticheskoe opisanie tambovskoi eparkhii* (Tambov: K. I. Zakrzhevskii, 1861), p. 267.

83. Ibid., pp. 160–65.

84. A. Vinogradov, *Istoriia kafedral'nogo uspenskogo sobora v gubernskom gorode Vladimire* (Vladimir: Gubernskoe pravlenie, 1905), pp. 61–63. O. Iu. Tarasov, *Ikona i blagochestie. Ocherki ikonnogo dela Rossii* (Moscow: Progress-kul'tura, 1995), p. 107, 312.

85. Petrov, *Istoriia Sankt-Peterburga*, lists celebrations in 1762, 1764, 1768, 1770, 1771 (pp. 659, 688, 753, 771, 785). After Catherine's death, Paul I kept the feast day on the official calendar, but without mention of his mother. Instead, November 24 was celebrated as the name day of his daughter, Grand Princess Ekaterina Pavlovna and as the holiday of the Order of St. Catherine. See *Mesiatsoslov s rospis'iu chinovnykh osob v gosudarstve*, p. xvi.

86. *Kamerfur'erskii zhurnal*, 1763, pp. 232–34.

87. *Sanktpeterburgskiia vedomosti*, 1777, no. 95 (November 28), first nn. page.

88. Ibid., nos. 97, 1777 (December 5) and 98 (December 8).

89. Petrov, *Istoriia Sankt-Peterburga*, pp. 679, 687, 688, 752, 784, 785, et al.

90. *Sluzhba na den' Sviatoi Velikomuchenitsy Ekateriny* (Moscow: Sinodal'naia Tipografiia, 1765). The inventory of the Synod's Moscow press indicates that 18 separate services were printed in 1765 in runs of 2,400 each, 1,200 in civil orthography and 1,200 in church orthography. RGIA, *f*. 796, *op*. 58, no. 23, p. 44.

91. Arsenii (Vereshchagin), *Slovo o istinnoi slave v vysokotorzhestvennyi den' tezoimenitstva E. I. V. vsemilostiveishei gosudaryni* (Moscow: Universitetskaia Tipografiia, 1779); the 1794 sermon was published in Tver in 1814.

92. Arsenii (Vershchagin), *Slovo v den' vkhoda vo khram Presvytiia Bogomateri, i na sovershenie novoustroennoi zimnei tserkvi vo imia Sviatyia Velikomuchenitsy Ekateriny pri vtorom kadetskom korpuse* (St. Petersburg: Sinodal'naia Tipografiia, 1804).

93. Slovo na den' tezoimenitstva Eia Imperatorskogo Velichestva 1784 goda noiabria 24-go dnia. This manuscript is part (pp. 176–84) of a bound and untitled volume of published and unpublished religious texts in the Rare Book Room of the State

Public Historical Library in Moscow. At the end of the text it contains the notation that it was orated in the presence of the empress, but it does not say where or by whom. The most likely candidate is Dmitrii Sergeevich Anichkov, the noted Moscow University professor and former seminarian who had orated similar speeches in Catherine's honor, and in her presence, throughout her reign. See the entry in *Slovar' russkikh pisatelei XVIII veka,* vol. 1, ed. N. D. Kochetkova et al. (Leningrad: Nauka, 1988), pp. 31–32; *SK,* vol. 1, no. 172 (1762); vol. 6, *Dopolneniia,* no. 380 (1783).

94. Matthew 25: 1–4, NIE.

95. Ibid., pp. 179–80.

96. Amvrosii (Serebrennikov), *Slovo v den' tezoimenitstva Eia Imp. Vel. Blagochest-niveishiia Gosudaryni Imperatritsy Ekateriny Alekseevny* (St. Petersburg: Sinodal'naia Tipografiia, 1786). This imprint is unrecorded in *SK.* On Amvrosii, see Bolkhovitinov, *Slovar' istoricheskii,* pp. 33–34.

97. Gavriil (Petr Petrovich Shaposhnikov), *Slovo v den' tezoimenitstva . . . imp. Ekateriny Alekseevny* (St. Petersburg: Voennaia kollegiia, 1777). *SK,* no. 1212.

98. *SK,* vol. 1, no. 172 (1762); vol. 6, *Dopolneniia,* no. 380 (1783).

99. Semen Efimovich Desnitskii, *Slovo na vysokotorzhestvennyi den' tezoimenitstva . . . imp. Ekateriny Alekseevny* (Moscow: Universitetskaia Tipografiia, 1775). *SK,* vol. 1, no. 1811.

100. *SK,* vol. 6, *Dopolneniia,* no. 254.

Epilogue

1. Wortman, *Scenarios of Power,* vol. 1, p. 85.

Works Cited

Unpublished Sources

ARCHIVES

Russkii Gosudarstvennyi Arkhiv Drevnykh Aktov (RGADA), Moscow
 Fond 7: Tainaia kantseliariia
 Fond 9: Kabinet Petra I
 Fond 17: Nauka, literatura, iskusstvo
 Fond 18: Dukhovnoe vedomstvo
 Fond 96: Snosheniia Rossii so Shvetsiei
 Fond 142: Tsarskie podlinnye pis'ma
 Fond 156: Istoricheskie i tseremonial'nye dela
 Fond 199: Portfeli Millera
 Fond 235: Patriarshii/Sinodal'nyi kazennyi prikaz
 Fond 237: Monastyrskii prikaz
 Fond 371: Preobrazhenskii prikaz
 Fond 396: Oruzheinaia palata
 Fond 1239: Moskovskii Dvortsovyi otdel

Russkii Gosudarstvennyi Istoricheskii Arkhiv (RGIA), St. Petersburg
 Fond 740: Departament obshchikh del
 Fond 796: Sinodskaia kantseliariia

Tsentral'nyi Gosudarstvennyi Arkhiv Moskvovskoi Oblasti (TsGAMO), Moscow
 Fond 1323: Ekaterinskaia pustyn' moskovskoi eparkhii

OTHER

Slovo na den' tezoimenitstva Eia Imperatorskogo Velichestva 1784 goda noiabria 24-go dnia. (This manuscript is part [pp. 176–84] of a bound and untitled volume of published and unpublished religious texts in the Rare Book Room of the State Public Historical Library in Moscow).
Zelensky, Elizabeth Kristofovich. "Monarchic Imagery in the Reign of Sof'ia Alekseevna." Paper presented at the meeting of the American Association for the Advancement of Slavic Studies (1993).

Published Primary and Secondary Sources

Acta Sanctorum Quotquot Toto Orbe Coluntur Vel a Catholicis Scriptoribus Celebratur . . . Propylius. Brussels: Victor Palme, 1940.

Adrianova [Peretts], V. P. *Zhitie Alekseia Cheloveka Bozhiia v drevnei russkoi literature i narodni slovesnosti.* Petrograd: Tipografiia Ia. Bashmakova i kompanii, 1917. Reprint, The Hague: Mouton, 1969.

Alekseeva, M. A. *Graviura petrovskogo vremeni.* Leningrad: Iskusstvo 1990.

———. "Portret tsarevny Sof'i gravera Tarasevicha." *Pamiatniki kul'tury. Novye otkrytiia* vol. 2, (1975).

Altbauer, Moshe, ed. *An Orthodox Pomjanyk of the Seventeenth–Eighteenth Centuries.* Cambridge: Harvard Ukrainian Research Institute, 1989.

Altbauer, Moshe, and Horace G. Lunt, eds. *An Early Slavonic Psalter from Rus'.* Vol. 1. *Photo Reproduction.* Cambridge: Harvard Ukrainian Research Institute, 1978.

Amvrosii, Archimandrite of the Novgorod Seminary. *Istoriia rossiiskoi ierarkhii.* Pt. 4. Moscow: Sinodal'naia Tipografiia, 1812.

Anastasiou, Iōan E. *Sinaïtika tou 16 kai 17 aiōnos.* Thessalonika, 1970.

Andreeva, A. A. *'Mestnik Bozhii' na tsarskom trone. Khristianskaia tsivilizatsionnaia model' sakralizatsii vlasti v rossiiskoi istorii.* Moscow: RAN, 2002.

Anisimov, Evgenii V. *Dyba i knut. Politicheskii sysk i russkoe obshchestvo v XVIII veke.* Moscow: Novoe literaturnoe obozrenie, 1999.

———. *Elizaveta Petrovna.* Moscow: Molodaia gvardiia, 1999.

———. *Vremia petrovskikh reform.* Leningrad: Nauka, 1989.

———. *Zhenshchiny na rossiiskom prestole.* St. Petersburg: Norint, 1997.

Antonin, Arkhimandrit. "Iz zapisok sinaiskogo bogomoltsa." *Trudy Kievskoi dukhovnoi akademii* (1872).

Antonov, V. V., and L. V. Kobak. *Sviatyni Sankta-Peterburga. Istoriko-tserkovnaia entsiklopediia.* Vol. 1. St. Petersburg: Izdatel'stvo Chernysheva, 1994.

Antonova, V. I., and N. E. Mneva, eds. *Katalog drevnerusskoi zhivopisi.* 2 vols. Moscow: Iskusstvo, 1963.

Arkhangel'skii, A. S. *Nil Sorskii i Vassian Patrikeev. Ikh literaturnye trudy i idei v drevnei Rusi.* Vol. 1, *Prepodobnyi Nil Sorskii.* St. Petersburg: Tipografiia I. Voshchinskogo, 1882.

Arkheograficheskaia komissiia. *Akty sobrannye v bibliotekakh i arkhivakh rossiiskoiu imperatorskoiu arkheograficheskoiu ekspeditsieiu imperatorskoi Akademii nauk.* Vol. 2. St. Petersburg, 1836.

Arsenii Grek. *Anfologion.* Moscow: Pechatnyi dvor, 1660.

Artakserkovo deistvo. Pervaia p'esa russkogo teatra XVII v. Edited by I. M. Kudriavtsev. Moscow: Akademiia nauk, 1957.

Bantysh-Kamenskii, Dmitrii N. *Istoricheskoe sobranie spiskov kavalerov.* Moscow: Tipografiia N. S. Vsevolzhskogo, 1814.

———. *Zhizn' Preosviashchennogo Amvrosiia, Arkhiepiskopa moskovskogo i kaluzhskogo.* Moscow: Gubernskaia Tipografiia, 1813.

Baring-Gould, S. *The Lives of the Saints.* Edinburgh: John Grant, 1914.

Barnes, Timothy D. *Athanasius and Constantius: Theology and Politics in the Constantinian Empire.* Cambridge: Harvard University Press, 1993.

Barsov, E. V. "Khronika russkogo teatra." *Chteniia* (1882), book 2.

Bartenev, S. P. *Bol'shoi Kremlevskii Dvorets. Ukazatel' k ego obozreniiu.* Moscow: Sinodal'naia Tipografiia, 1909.

Bassewitz, Frederic de. "Zapiski Grafa Bassevicha, sluzhashchiia k poiasneniiu nekotorykh sobytii iz vremeni tsarstvovaniia Petra Velikogo (1713–1725)." *Russkii arkhiv* (1865), no. 3.

Beatie, Bruce A. "Saint Katherine of Alexandria: Traditional Themes and the Development of a Medieval German Hagiographic Narrative." *Speculum* 52, no. 4 (1977).

Begunov, Iu. K. "Drevnerusskie traditsii v proizvedeniiakh pervoi chetverti XVIII v. ob Aleksandre Nevskom." *TODRL* 26 (1971).

Belokurov, Sergei A. *Adam Olearii o grekolatinskoi shkole Arseniia Greka v Moskve v XVII v.* Moscow: Tipografiia L. and A. Snegirevykh, 1888.

Belokurov, S. A. *Dneval'nye zapiski prikaza tainykh del 1765–1783.* Moscow: Tipografiia Moskovskogo voennogo okruga, 1908.

Beneshevich, V. N. "Otchet o poezdke v Sinaiskii monastyr' sv. Ekateriny letom 1908 goda." *Izvestiia Imperatorskoi Akademii nauk* (1908), no. 14.

Berelowitch, André. "Chasse et rituel en Russie au XVIIe siècle. Le Règlement de la fauconnerie d'Alexis Mixajlovicō." *Russes, slaves, et sovietiques. Pages d'histoire offertes à Roger Portal.* Edited by Céline Gervais-Francelle. Paris: Institut d'études slaves, 1992.

Berkhgol'ts, F. V. [Bergholz]. *Dnevnik kamer-iunkera F. V. Berkhgol'tsa vedennii im v Rossii v tsarstvovanie Petra Velikogo s 1721-go po 1725 god.* Moscow: Universitetskaia Tipografiia, 1903.

Biblioteka Petra I. Ukazatel'-spravochnik. Edited by E. A. Bobrova. Leningrad: BAN, 1978.

Bobrovitskaia, Irina. "Pervaia imperatorskaia korona Rossii." *Mir muzeia* 162 (July–August, 1998): 44–59.

Bogdanov, A. I. *Istoricheskoe, geograficheskoe, i topograficheskoe opisanie S. Peterburga ot nachala zavedeniia ego, s 1703 po 1751 god.* St. Petersburg: Akademiia nauk, 1779.

Bogdanov, A. P. *Moskovskaia publitsistika poslednei chetverti XVII veka.* Moscow: RAN, 2001.

———. "Tsarevna Sof'ia Alekseevna v sovremennykh poeticheskikh obrazakh." In *Kul'tura srednevekovoi Moskvy XVII vek*, edited by B. A. Rybakov et al. Moscow: Nauka, 1999.

Bogdanov, A. P., and V. I. Buganov, eds. *Pamiatniki obshchestvenno-politicheskoi mysli v Rossii kontsa XVII veka. Literaturnye panegiriki.* Moscow: Akademiia nauk, 1983.

Bogoiavlenskii, S. K. *Moskovskii teatr pri tsariakh Aleksee i Petre.* Moscow: Tipografiia V. I. Voronova, 1914.

Bolkhovitinov, Metropolitan Evgenii. *Slovar' istoricheskii o byvshikh v Rossii pisateliakh dukhovnogo china greko-rossiiskoi tserkvi.* Moscow: Russkii dvor, 1995.

Book of Margery Kempe, The. Translated by John Skinner. New York: Doubleday, 1998.

Borukhovich, V. G. *Apollodor, mifologicheskaia biblioteka.* Leningrad: Nauka, 1972.

Brailovskii, S. N. "Odin iz pestrykh XVII-go stoletiia." *Zapiski Imperatorskoi Akademii nauk po istoriko-filologicheskomu otdeleniiu* 5 (1902).

Bray, Jennifer R. "The Medieval Order of St. Katherine." *Bulletin of the Institute of Historical Research* 56, no. 133 (May, 1983).

Bross, Louise Smith. "'She is among all virgins the queen . . . so worthy a patron . . . for maidens to copy': Livio Agresti, Cardinal Federico Cesi, and the Compagnia delle Vergini Miserabili di Santa Caterina della Rosa." In *Confraternities and the Visual Arts in Renaissance Italy,* edited by Barbara A. Wisch and Dane Cohl Ahl. Cambridge: Cambridge University Press, 2000.

Brown, Peter. *The Cult of Saints: Its Rise and Function in Latin Christianity.* Chicago: University of Chicago Press, 1981.

Bruce, Peter Henry. *Memoirs of Peter Henry Bruce, Esq., a Military Officer in the Services of Prussia, Russia, and Great Britain.* London: F. Cass, 1970.

Bubnov, N. Iu. "Slaviano-russkie prologi." In *Metodicheskoe posobie po opisaniiu slaviano-russkikh rukopisei dlia Svodnogo kataloga rukopisei khraniashchikhsia v SSSR.* Vol. 1. Moscow: Akademiia nauk, 1973.

Bubnov, N. Iu., et al., eds. *Pergamennye rukopisi biblioteki Akademii nauk SSSR.* Leningrad: Nauka, 1976.

Bubnov, N. Iu., O. V. Chumicheva, and N. S. Demkova, eds. *Pamiatniki staroobriadcheskoi pis'mennosti.* St. Petersburg: Russkii Khristianskii Gumanitarnyi Institut, 2000.

Bulanin, D. M. *Perevody i poslaniia Maksima Greka. Neizdannye teksty.* Leningrad: Nauka, 1984.

Bumagi Imperatritsy Ekateriny II khraniashchikhsia v gosudarstvennom arkhive. SIRIO 7 (1871).

Bushkovitch, Paul. *"The Life of St. Filipp:* Tsar and Metropolitan in the Late Sixteenth Century."* In *Medieval Russian Culture,* edited by Michael S. Flier and Daniel B. Rowland. Vol. 2. Berkeley: University of California, 1984–1994.

———. *Peter the Great: The Struggle for Power, 1671–1725.* Cambridge: Cambridge University Press, 2001.

———. *Religion and Society in Russia, the Sixteenth and Seventeenth Centuries.* Oxford: Oxford University Press, 1992.

Bussow, Conrad. *The Disturbed State of the Russian Realm.* Translated and edited by G. Edward Orchard. Montreal: McGill-Queen's University Press, 1994.

Butler, Alban. *Butler's Lives of the Saints.* Collegeville, MN: Liturgical Press,1995.

Buzhinskii, Gavriil. *Propovedi Gavriila Buzhinskago (1717–1727).* Edited by E. V. Petukhov. Iur'ev, 1898.

Bykova, T. A., and M. M. Gurevich, eds. *Opisanie izdannii napechatannykh pri Petre Pervom, 1689–1725.* 3 vols. Moscow: Akademiia nauk, 1955–1958.

Bynum, Caroline Walker. *Jesus as Mother: Studies in the Spirituality of the High Middle Ages.* Berkeley: University of California Press, 1982.

———. "Women's Stories, Women's Symbols: A Critique of Victor Turner's Theory of Liminality." In *Fragmentation and Redemption: Essays on Gender and the Human Body in Medieval Religion.* New York: Zone Books, 1992.

Byzantium: Faith and Power, 1261–1557. Edited by Helen C. Evans. New Haven: Yale University Press, 2004.

Capgrave, John. *The Life of St. Catherine of Alexandria.* London: Kegan, Paul, Trench, Trübner & Co., 1893.

Cardinale, Hyginus Eugene. *Orders of Knighthood: Awards of the Holy See.* London: Gerrards Books, 1985.

Cherniavsky, Michael. "Khan or Basileus: An Aspect of Russian Medieval Theory." *Journal of the History of Ideas* 20, no. 4 (1959).

———. *Tsar and People: Studies in Russian Myths.* New York: Random House, 1969.

Chistovich, I. "Neizdannye propovedi Stefana Iavorskogo." *Khristianskoe chtenie* (1867), parts 1 and 2.

Chronicle of John Malalas. Translated by Elizabeth Jeffreys, Michael Jeffreys, and Roger Scott. Melbourne: Australian Association for Byzantine Studies, 1986.

Chronicle of John Malalas. Books 8–18. Translated from the Church Slavonic by Matthew Spinka and Glanville Downey. Chicago: University of Chicago Press, 1940.

Chteniia v Imperatorskom obshchestve istorii i drevnostei rossiiskikh pri moskovskom universitete. 264 vols. Moscow: Universitetskaia Tipografiia, 1846–1918.

Chudinova, Irina. *Penie, zvony, ritual. Topografiia tserkovno-muzykal'noi kul'tury Peterburga.* St. Petersburg: "Ut", 1994.

Collins, Daniel E. "Early Russian Topoi of Deathbed and Testament." In *Medieval Russian Culture,* edited by Michael S. Flier and Daniel Rowland. Vol. 2. Berkeley: University of California Press, 1984–1994.

Colonne, Guido delle. *Historia destructionis Troiae.* Edited by Nathaniel Edward Griffin. Cambridge: Mediaeval Academy of America, 1936.

Constantin VII Porphyrogénète. *Le livre des cérémonies.* Vol. 2, bk. 1. Translated by Albert Vogt. Paris: Société d'édition 'Les Belles Lettres,' 1939.

Coursault, René. *Sainte Catherine d'Alexandrie. Le myth et la tradition.* Paris: Editions Maison Neuve et Larose, 1984.

Cracraft, James. *The Church Reform of Peter the Great.* London: Macmillan, 1971.

———. "Some Dreams of Peter the Great: A Biographical Note." *Canadian-American Slavic Studies* 8, no. 2 (Summer 1974).

Cross, Anthony. "The Old Man from Cambridge, Mrs. Cross, and Other Anglo-Petrine Matters of Due Weight and Substance." In *Peter the Great and the West: New Perspectives,* edited by Lindsey Hughes. London: Palgrave, 2001.

Crummey, Robert O. "The Miracle of Martyrdom: Reflections on Early Old Believer Hagiography." In *Religion and Culture in Early Modern Russia and Ukraine,* edited by Samuel H. Baron and Nancy Shields Kollmann. DeKalb: Northern Illinois University Press, 1997.

Dante Alighieri. *The Divine Comedy.* Translated by Kenneth McKenzie. London: The Folio Society, 1979.

Dashkova, Ekaterina. *Zapiski, 1743–1810.* Kaliningrad: Iantarnyi skaz, 2001.

"Dela tainogo prikaza." *RIB* 23 (1904).

Delehaye, Pere Hippolyte. *The Legends of the Saints.* New York: Fordham University Press, 1962.

Demin, A. S. "'Khozhdenie' Igumena Daniila v Ierusalem (opyt kommentarii na temu 'Rossiia i Zapad')." *Germenevtika drevnerusskoi literatury* 8 (1995).

———. *Pisatel' i obshchestvo v Rossii XVI–XVII vekov.* Moscow: Nauka, 1985.

Derzhavin, (Protoierei) Aleksandr. "Chetii-minei Sviatitelia Dimitriia, mitropolita rostovskogo, kak tserkovnoistoricheskii i literaturnyi pamiatnik." *Bogoslovskie trudy* 15 (1976) and 16 (1976).

Derzhavina, O. A., et al., eds. *P'esy stolichnykh i provintsial'nykh teatrov pervoi poloviny XVIII v.* Moscow: Nauka, 1975.

Desnitskii, Semen Efimovich. *Slovo na vysokotorzhestvennyi den' tezoimenitstva . . . imperatritsy Ekateriny Alekseevny.* Moscow: Universitetskaia Tipografiia, 1775.

Diehl, Charles. *Byzantine Portraits.* New York: A. A. Knopf, 1927.

Dimitrii [Rostovskii], Saint, Metropolitan of Rostov. *Chet'i minei.* Moscow: Sinodal'naia Tipografiia, 1762.

———. *The Great Collection of the Lives of the Saints.* Vol. 3: November. 6 volumes to date. Translated by Father Thomas Marretta. House Springs, MO: Chrysostom Press, 2001.

———. "Piramida ili stolp, vo blazhennoi pamiati prestavliashagosia vysotse k Bogu ego milosti gospodina ottsa Innokentia Gizelia . . . k vechnoi pamiati v god po pogrebenii ego." In *Sochineniia Sviatogo Dimitriia.* Vol. 3. Moscow: Sinodal'naia Tipografiia, 1841.

———. *Sinopsis, ili kratkoe opisanie o nachale Slavenskogo naroda. Sochineniia Sviatogo Dimitriia, Mitropolita Rostovskogo.* Vol. 4. Moscow: Sinodal'naia Tipografiia, 1841.

———. *Sochineniia Sviatogo Dimitriia, mitropolita rostovskogo.* 4 vols. Moscow: Sinodal'naia Tipografiia, 1841.

———. *Zhitiia sviatykh na russkom iazyke izlozhennye po rukovodstvu chet'ikh minei sv. Dimitriia Rostovskogo.* Moscow, 1902.

Dixon, Annette. *Women Who Ruled: Queens, Goddesses, Amazons in Renaissance and Baroque Art.* London: Merrell, 2002.

Dnevnik Mariny Mnishek. Translated by V. V. Kozliakova. St. Petersburg: Petropolie, 1995.

"Dopolneniia k dvortsovym razriadam." *Chteniia* (1882), books 1, 3; (1883), books 2, 3.

Drevne russkoe shit'e. Edited by N. A. Maiasova. Moscow: Iskusstvo, 1971.

Drevneishie slaviano-russkie rukopisi XIII–rubezha XV/XVI vv. New York: Norman Ross Publishing; Moscow: Nauchnaia biblioteka MGU, 1998.

Drevniaia rossiiskaia vivliofika. 20 vols. Moscow: Tipograficheskaia kompaniia, 1788–1791. Reprint, The Hague: Mouton, 1970.

Drijvers, Jan Willem. *Helena Augusta, the Mother of Constantine the Great and the Legend of Her Finding of the True Cross.* Leiden: E. J. Brill, 1992.

Druzhinin, V. G. *Opisaniia russkikh staroobradtsev. Perechen' spiskov sostavlennyi po pechatnym opisaniiam rukopisnykh sobranii.* St. Petersburg: Tipografiia Aleksandrova, 1912.

Dubinin, Sergei, et al., *Vse oden'gakh Russii.* Moscow: Konkord, 1988.

Dunning, Chester S. L. *Russia's First Civil War: The Time of Troubles and the Founding of the Romanov Dynasty.* University Park, PA: The Pennsylvania State University Press, 2001.

Dura, Iōan V. "Ho Dositheos Hierosolymōn kai hē prosphora autou eis tas Roumanikas chōras kai těn ekklěsian autōn." Ph.D. diss., Theological School, University of Athens, 1977.

Durov, V. A. *Ordena Rossii*. Moscow: Voskresenie, 1993.

Dvortsovye razriady po vysochaishemu poveleniiu izdannye 2-m Otdeleniem Sobstvennogo Ego Imperatorskogo Velichestva Kantseliarii. 4 vols. St. Petersburg: Tipografiia 2-go Otdelennia, 1850–1855.

Einenkel, Eugen, ed. *The Life of Saint Katherine from the Royal MS. 17a xxvi with its Latin Original from the Cotton MS. Caligula A viii*. London: N. Trubner and Co., 1894.

Ekaterina Velikaia i Moskva. Katalog-vystavka 850–letiiu Moskvy posviashchaetsia iun'-sentiabr' 1997. Moscow: Tret'iakovskaia galereia, 1997.

"Ekaterina Vtoraia, novyia svedeniia, pis'ma, i bumagi, kasaiushchiiasia eia roditelei i eia priezda v Rossiu." In *Osmnadtsatyi vek. Istoricheskii sbornik*, edited by P. I. Barten'ev, bk. 1. Moscow, 1868.

Eleonskaia, A. S. "Skazanie o kreshchenii Rusi v literaturnykh obrabotkakh XVII-nachala XVIII veka." *Germenevtika drevnerusskoi literatury* 8 (1995).

Entsiklopedicheskii slovar'. Vol. 11. St. Petersburg: I. A. Efron, 1894.

Eusebius. *The History of the Church from Christ to Constantine*. Translated by G. A. Williamson. London: Penguin, 1989.

Evans, James Allan. *The Empress Theodora, Partner of Justinian*. Austin: University of Texas Press, 2002.

Fedotova, M. A. "Ukrainskie propovedi Dimitriia Rostovskogo (1670–1700 gg.) i ikh rukopisnaia traditsiia." *TODRL* 51 (1999).

Filimonov, G. "Ikonnye portrety russkikh tsarei." *Vestnik obshchestva drevne-russkogo iskusstva pri moskovskom publichnom muzee*, nos. 6–10 (1875).

Firsov, N. N. *Vstuplenie na prestol Imperatritsy Elizavety Petrovny*. Kazan: Universitetskaia Tipografiia, 1888.

Flier, Michael S. "Court Ceremony in an Age of Reform: Patriarch Nikon and the Palm Sunday Ritual." In *Religion and Culture in Early Modern Russia and Ukraine*, edited by Samuel H. Baron and Nancy Shields Kollmann. DeKalb: Northern Illinois University Press, 1997.

Flier, Michael S., and Daniel B. Rowland, eds. *Medieval Russian Culture*. 2 vols. Berkeley: University of California Press, 1984–1994.

Fonkich, B. L. *Grechesko-russkie kul'turnye sviazi v XV–XVII vv*. Moscow: Nauka, 1977.

Freski Spasa-Nereditsy. Leningrad: Gos. Russkii Muzei, 1925.

Gavriil (Archbishop) (Petr Petrovich Shaposhnikov). *Slovo v den' tezoimenitstva . . . imp. Ekateriny Alekseevny*. St. Petersburg: Voennaia kollegiia, 1777.

Gavrilov, A. V. *Ocherki istorii St. Peterburgskoi sinodal'noi tipografii*. St. Petersburg: Sinodal'naia Tipografiia, 1911).

General Menaion, or The Book of Services Common to the Festivals of Our Lord Jesus Christ of the Holy Virgin and of the Different Orders of Saints. Translated by Professor N. Orloff. London: J. Davy & Sons, 1899.

Gennin, V. *Ural'skaia perepiska s Petrom i Ekaterinoi I*. Ekaterinburg: RAN, 1995.

Giordani, Igino. *Saint Catherine of Siena—Doctor of the Church*. Boston: St Paul Editions, 1975.

Glagoleva, Olga E. "The Illegitimate Children of the Russian Nobility in Law and Practice, 1700–1860." *Kritika* 6, no. 3 (Summer, 2005).

Golikov, I. I. *Deianiia Petra Velikogo, mudrogo preobrazovatelia Rossii*. Vol. 4. Moscow: Universitetskaia Tipografiia, 1788; reprinted 1975.

———. *Sravnenie svoistv i del Konstantina Velikogo pervogo iz rimskikh khristianskogo imperatora s svoistvami i delami Petra Velikogo*. Moscow, 1810.

Golubinskii, E. E. *Istoriia russkoi tserkvi. Period vtoroi, moskovskii*. Vol. 2, *Ot nashestviia Mongolov do mitropolita Makariia vkliuchatel'no*. Moscow: Sinodal'naia Tipografiia, 1911.

Golubinskii, E. *Istoriia kanonizatsii sviatykh v russkoi tserkvi*. Sergiev Posad: Tipografiia A.

I. Snegirovoi, 1894.

Gorskii, A. V., and K. I. Nevostruev. *Opisanie slavianskikh rukopisei moskovskoi sinodal'noi biblioteki.* 5 vols. Moscow: Sinodal'naia Tipografiia, 1855–1917.

Grabar', Igor. *Istoriia russkogo iskusstva.* Vol. 6, *Zhivopis'.* Pt. 1, *Do-Petrovskaia epokha.* Moscow: I. Knebel'. 1910.

Granat, A. I. *Entsiklopedicheskii slovar'.* 58 vols. Moscow: Granat, 1910-1948.

Grebeniuk, V. P. *Panegiricheskaia literatura petrovskogo vremeni.* Moscow: Nauka, 1979.

Hancock, Ralph, et al., eds. *Treasures of the Czars from the State Museums of the Moscow Kremlin.* London: Booth-Clibborn Editions, 1995.

Haney, Jack V. *From Italy to Muscovy: The Life and Works of Maxim the Greek.* Munich: Wilhelm Fink Verlag, 1973.

Harbus, Antonina. *Helena of Britain in Medieval Legend.* Cambridge: D. S. Brewer, 2002.

Hassel, Julie. *Choosing Not to Marry: Women and Autonomy in the Katherine Group.* New York: Routledge, 2002.

Herberstein, Sigismund von. *Notes upon Russia.* A translation of *Rerum Moscoviticarum Commentarii* 1549 by R. H. Major. London: Haklyut Society, 1851.

Herodotus. *The Histories.* Translated by Robin Waterfield. London: Oxford University Press, 1998.

Herrin, Judith. *Women in Purple: Rulers of Medieval Byzantium.* Princeton: Princeton University Press, 2001.

Hionides, Harry T. *Paisius Ligarides.* New York: Twayne Publishers, 1972.

Hollum, Kenneth. *Theodosian Empresses: Women and Imperial Dominion in Late Imperial Antiquity.* Berkeley: University of California Press, 1982.

Holy Bible. New International Edition. London: Hodder and Stoughton, 1984.

http:/www.vidnoe.ru/town

Hughes, Lindsey. *Russia in the Age of Peter the Great.* New Haven: Yale University Press, 1998.

———. *Sophia Regent of Russia, 1657–1704.* New Haven: Yale University Press, 1990.

Hyde, H. Montgomery. *The Empress Catherine and Princess Dashkov.* London: Chapman and Hall, 1935.

Iavorskii, Stefan. "Kolesnitsa torzhestvennaia." In *Propovedi blazhennyia pamiati Stefana Iavorskogo preosviashchennogo mitropolita riazanskogo i muromskogo.* Vol. 2. Moscow: Sinodal'naia Tipografiia, 1805.

Ilarion. "Sermon on Law and Grace." In *Sermons and Rhetoric of Kievan Rus'.* Translated and with an introduction by Simon Franklin. Cambridge: Harvard University Press, 1991.

Il'in, M. A., and V. P. Vygolov. "Moskovskie triumfal'nye vorota rubezha XVII–XVIII vv." In *Materialy po teorii i istorii iskusstva,* edited by A. A. Fedorov-Davydov. Moscow: Moscow University, 1956.

Ioann Zlatoust v drevnerusskoi i iuzhnoslavianskoi pis'mennosti XI–XVI vekov. Katalog gomili. Edited by E. E. Granstrem, O. V. Tvorogov, and A. Valevichius. St. Petersburg: Dmitrii Bulanin, 1998.

Istoricheskie materialy dlia sostavleniia tserkovnykh letopisei moskvskoi eparkhii. Edited by V. Kholmogorov and G. Kholmogorov. 10 vols. Moscow: Tipografiia Snegireva, 1881–1894.

Istoricheskoe opisanie moskovskogo novodevich'ego monastyria. Moscow: Tipografiia Snegireva, 1885.

Istoriko-statisticheskoe opisanie tambovskoi eparkhii. Tambov: K. I. Zakrzhevskii, 1861.

Istoriko-statisticheskoe svedenie o S. Peterburgskoi eparkhii. 6 vols. St. Petersburg: Eparkhial'nyi istoriko-statisticheskii komitet, 1878.

Istrin, V. M. *Khronika Georgiia Amatola v drevnem slavianorusskom perevode.* Vol. 1, *Tekst.* Petrograd: Rossiiskaia gosudarstvennaia akademicheskaia Tipografiia, 1920.

———. "Khronika Ioanna Malaly v slavianskom perevode. Knigi 11–14." *Sbornik otdeleniia russkogo iazyka i slovesnosti Imperatorskoi Akademii nauk* 90, no. 2 (1913).

Ivanov, Vladimir. *Russian Icons*. New York: Rizzoli, 1988.

"Iz sochineniia kodina ob obriadakh konstantinopl'skago dvora i chinakh velikoi tserkvi." *Chteniia* (1883), book 1.

Izvekov, N. D. *Moskovskiia kremlevskiia dvortsovye tserkvi i sluzhivshiia pri nikh litsa v XVII veke*. Moscow: Tipografiia Snegirovoi, 1906.

Jagic, V. *Menaea Septembris, Octobris, Novembris. Sluzhebnye minei za sentiabr', oktiabr', noiabr' v tserkovno-slavianskom perevode po russkim rukopisiam, 1095–1097 gg.* St. Petersburg: Tipografiia Akademii nauk, 1886.

Jenkins, Jacqueline, and Katherine J. Lewis, eds. *St Katherine of Alexandria: Texts and Contexts in Western Medieval Europe*. Turnbout Belgium: Brepols, 2003.

Juel, Just. *Zapiski Iusta Iulia, datskogo poslannika pri Petre Velikom (1709–11)*. Moscow: Universitetskaia Tipografiia, 1899.

Kaegi, Walter E. *Heraclius, Emperor of Rome*. Cambridge: Cambridge University Press, 2003.

Kaempfer, Frank. *Das russische Herrscherbild von der Anfaengen bis zu Peter dem Grossen*. Recklinghausen: Verlag Aurel Bongers Recklinghausen, 1978.

Kaganov, Gregory. *Images of Space: St. Petersburg in the Visual and Verbal Arts*. Translated by Sidney Monas. Stanford: Stanford University Press, 1997.

Kaiser, Daniel. "Naming Cultures in Early Modern Russia." *Harvard Ukrainian Studies* 19 (1995).

Kalanus, Herman. *St Katarina svenska fōrsamlings i St Petersburg*. Ekenäs: Ekenäs Tryckeri Aktiebolag, 1980.

Kamerfur'erskie tseremonial'nye zhurnaly [including *pokhodnye zhurnaly*]. Vols.1–45. St. Petersburg: Ministerstvo Imperatorskogo dvora, 1853–1896.

Kamil, Jill. *The Monastery of Saint Catherine in Sinai*. Cairo: American University of Cairo Press, 1991.

Kapterev, N. F. *Kharakter otnoshenii Rossii k pravoslavnomu vostoku v XVI i XVII stoletiiakh*. Sergiev Posad: M.S. Elov, 1914.

———. "Russkaia blagotvoritel'nost' Sinaiskoi obiteli v XVI–XVIII stoletiiakh." *Chteniia v obshchestve liubitelei dukhovnogo prosveshcheniia* (October/November 1881).

———. "Snosheniia ierusalimskikh patriarkhov s russkim pravitel'stvom s poloviny XVI do kontsa XVIII stoletiia." *Pravoslavnyi palestinskii sbornik* 15 (1895).

Karabanov, P. F. "Stats-damy i freiliny russkogo dvora v XVIII stoletii. Biograficheskie spiski". *Russkaia starina* 2 (1870).

Karamzin, N. M. *Istoriia gosudarstva rossiiskogo*. St. Petersburg: Izdanie Evgeniia Evdokimova, 1892.

Karateev, M. D. *Velikii kniaz' Aleksandr Nevskii*. Moscow: I. D. Sytin, 1893.

Kazakova, N. A. *Vassian Patrikeev i ego sochinehiia*. Moscow: Akademiia nauk SSSR, 1960.

Kazhdan, Alexander. "Rus'-Byzantine Princely Marriages in the Eleventh and Twelfth Centuries." *Harvard Ukrainian Studies* 12–13 (1988/1989).

Keleinyi letopisets sviatitelia Dimitriia Rostovskogo s pribavleniem ego zhitiia, chudes, izbrannykh tvorenii i Kievskogo sinopsisa arkhimandrita Innokentiia Gizelia. Edited by E. A. Luk'ianov. Moscow: Palomnik, 2000.

Khanovska, Romual'da. *Khram Sviatoi Ekateriny v Sankt-Peterburge*. St. Petersburg: Chistyi list, 2001.

Khitrovo, V. N. *Palestina i Sinai*. St. Petersburg.: Tipografiia Maikova, 1876.

Khludov, Andrei I. *Opisanie rukopisei i katalog knig tserkovnoi pechati*. Moscow: Sinodal'-naia Tipografiia, 1872.

Khodarkovsky, Michael. *Russia's Steppe Frontier: The Making of a Colonial Empire, 1500–1800*. Bloomington: Indiana University Press, 2002.

"Khronologicheskoe obozrenie puteshestviia Russkikh k sviatym mestam." *ZMNP*, no. 61 (1849), pt. 6.

Kipling, Gordon, ed. *The Receyt of the Ladie Katheryne*. Oxford: Oxford University Press, 1990.

Kiseleva, L. I., ed. *Korpus zapisei na staropechatnykh kngakh.* Vol. 1, *Zapisi na knigakh kirillovskogo shrifta, napechatannykh v Moskve, v XVI–XVII vv.* St. Petersburg: Biblioteka Akademii nauk, 1992.

Kizevetter, A. A. "Ekaterina I." In *Entsiklopedicheskii slovar'* [Granat]. Vol. 19. Moscow, n.d.

Kjellberg, Lennart. *La langue de Gedeon Krinovskij, prédicateur russe du XVIIIe siècle.* Uppsala: Almqvist and Wiksells, 1957.

Kloss, B. M. *Nikonovskii svod i russkie letopisi XVI–XVII vekov.* Moscow: Nauka, 1980.

Kochetkova, N. D., et al., eds. *Slovar' russkikh pisatelei XVIII veka.* Vol. 1. Leningrad: Nauka, 1988.

Kolesnikova, V. S. *Russkie pravoslavnye prazdniki.* Moscow: Kron-press, 1996.

Kollmann, Jack Edward, Jr. "The Moscow *Stoglav* ('Hundred Chapters') Church Council of 1551." Ph.D. diss., University of Michigan, 1978.

Kolonial'naia politika moskovskogo gosudarstva v Iakutii XVII v. Leningrad: Nauka, 1936.

Kolosov, V. "Starets Arsenii Grek." *ZMNP* 217 (September, 1881).

Kondakarii v grecheskom podlinnike XII–XIII v. po rukopisi moskovskoi sinodal'noi biblioteki No. 437, s drevneishim slavianskim perevodom kondakov i ikosov kakie est' v perevode. Moscow: Tipografiia Kudriavtsevoi, 1879.

Kondakov, N. *Puteshestvie na Sinai v 1881 godu. Iz putevykh vpechatlenii drevnosti sinaiskogo monastyria.* Odessa: Tipografiia P. A. Zelenogo, 1882.

Korb, Johann-Georg. *Diary of an Austrian Secretary of Legation at the Court of Czar Peter the Great.* Translated by Count MacDonnell. London: Cass, 1863.

Korobeinikov, Trifon. *Puteshestvie moskovskogo kuptsa Trifona Korobeinikova s tovarishchami v Ierusalim, Egipet, i k Sinaiskoi gore v 1583 g.* St. Petersburg, 1783.

"Koronatsionnye zhetony i medali XVIII veka." *Chteniia* (1883), book 1.

Kraft, Ekkehard. *Moskaus greichisches Jahrhundert. Russisch-greichische Beziehungen und metabyzantinischer Einfluss, 1619–1694.* Stuttgart: Franz Steiner Verlag, 1995.

Krekshin, Petr Nikiforovich. *Zapiski novgorodskogo dvorianina Petra Nikiforovicha Krekshina.* In *Zapiski russkikh liudei. Sobytiia vremen Petra Velikogo.* St. Petersburg: Tipografiia Sakharova, 1841.

Krinovskii, Gedeon. *Sobranie raznykh pouchitel'nykh slov.* 4 vols. Moscow: Imeratorskaia Akademiia nauk, 1760.

Kruming, A. A. "Chet'i Minei sviatogo Dimitriia Rostovskogo. Ocherk istorii izdaniia." *Filevskie chteniia.* Vol. 10, *Sviatoi Dimitrii, Mitropolit Rostovskii. Issledovaniia i materialy* (1994).

Kukushkina, M. V. *Monastyrskie biblioteki russkogo severa.* Leningrad: Nauka, 1977.

Kuprianov, I. *Obozrenie pergamennykh rukopisei novgorodskoi sofiiskoi biblioteki.* St. Petersburg: Akademiia nauk, 1857.

Laven, Mary. *Virgins of Venice: Broken Vows and Cloistered Lives in the Renaissance Convent.* New York: Viking, 2002.

Lavrov, A. S. *Koldovstvo i religiia v Rossii 1700–1740 gg.* Moscow, Drevle Khranilishche, 2000.

Lazar, Lance G. "'E faucibus daemonis': Daughters of Prostitutes, the First Jesuits, and the Compagnia delle Vergini Misrabili di Santa Caterina della Rosa." In *Confraternities and the Visual Arts in Renaissance Italy,* edited by Barbara A. Wisch and Dane Cohl Ahl. Cambridge: Cambridge University Press, 2000.

Lenhoff, Gail. "Temir Aksak's Dream of the Virgin as Protectress of Muscovy." *Die Welt der Slaven* 49 (2004).

Letopisets ellinskii i rimskii. Edited by O. V. Tvorogov. St. Petersburg: Dmitrii Bulanin, 1999.

Letters of St. Catherine of Siena. Vol. 1. Translated and with an introduction by Suzanne Noffice. Binghampton, NY: Medieval and Renaissance Texts and Studies, 1988.

Lewis, Katherine J. *The Cult of St. Katherine of Alexandria in Late Medieval England.* Woodbridge: The Boydell Press, 2000.

————. "Pilgrimage and the Cult of St Katherine in Late Medieval England." In *St Katherine of Alexandria: Texts and Contexts in Western Medieval Europe*, edited by Jacqueline Jenkins and Katherine J. Lewis. Turnbout, Belgium: Brepols, 2003.

Librovich, Sigizmund. *Petr Velikii i zhenshchiny.* Iaroslavl and Leningrad: Mezhdunarodnyi fond istorii knigi, 1991.

Likhachev, D. S. *Chelovek v literature drevnei Rusi.* Moscow: Nauka, 1970.

————. *Russkie letopisi i ikh kul'turno-istoricheskoe znachenie.* Moscow-Leningrad: Akademiia nauk SSSR, 1947.

Lileev, M. I. "Opisanie rukopisei khraniashchikhsia v biblioteke chernigovskoi dukhovnoi akademii." *Pamiatniki drevnei pis'mennosti* 6 (1880).

Lives of Eminent Russian Prelates. London: Joseph Masters, 1854.

Loparev, Kh. M., ed. "Khozhdenie Trifona Korobeinikova 1593–94 gg." *Pravoslavnyi palestinskii sbornik* 11, no. 3 (1889).

Loseva, O. V. *Russkie mesiatsoslovy XI–XIV vekov.* Moscow: Pamiatniki istoricheskoi mysli, 2001.

Luk'ianov, Grigorii. "Serebrianaia raka sviatoi velikomuchenitsy Ekateriny—dar russkikh tsarei v sinaiskii monastyr' v 1688 godu." *Seminarium Kondakovianum* (1936), Vol. 8.

Luk'ianov, Ioann. "Puteshestvie v sviatuiu zemliu sviashchennika Ioanna Luk'ianova." *Russkii arkhiv* (1863), nos. 1–6.

Luppov, S. P. *Kniga v Rossii v XVII veke.* Leningrad: Nauka, 1970.

Lur'e, Ia. S. *Ideologicheskaia bor'ba v russkoi publitsistike kontsa XV-nachala XVI veka.* Moscow-Leningrad: Nauka, 1960.

Lyzlov, Andrei. *Skifskaia istoriia.* Edited by A. P. Bogdanov and E. V. Chistiakova. Moscow: Nauka, 1990.

de Madariaga, Isabel. "Tsar into Emperor: The Title of Peter the Great." In *Politics and Culture in Eighteenth-Century Russia.* London: Longman, 1998.

Makarii, Bishop of Arkhangelsk. "Istoricheskoe opisanie krasnogorskogo monastyria." *Chteniia* (1880), book 3.

Makarii, Metropolitan of Moscow. *Istoriia russkogo raskola izvestnogo pod imenem staroobriadstva.* St. Petersburg: Tipografiia morskogo ministerstva, 1858.

————. *Istoriia russkoi tserkvi.* Vol. 12. St. Petersburg: Tipografiia R. Golike, 1881.

————. *Velikie minei chet'i. Uspenskii spisok.* St. Petersburg: Akademiia nauk, 1868.

Manstein, Christof Hermann von. *Contemporary Memoirs of Russia from the Year 1727 to 1744.* London: Longman, Brown, Green, and Longmans. Reprint, London: Frank Cass and Co., 1968.

Margeret, Jacques. *The Russian Empire and Grand Duchy of Muscovy. A Seventeenth-Century French Account.* Translated and edited by Chester S. L. Dunning. Pittsburgh: University of Pittsburgh Press, 1983.

Martin, Russell E. "Dynastic Marriage in Muscovy, 1500–1729." Ph.D. diss., Harvard University, 1996.

Matter, E. Ann. "The Personal and the Paradigm: The Book of Maria Domitilla Galluzzi." In *The Crannied Wall: Women, Religion, and the Arts in Early Modern Europe,* edited by Craig E. Monson. Ann Arbor: University of Michigan Press, 1992.

McGrew, Roderick E. *Paul I of Russia, 1754–1801.* London: Oxford University Press, 1992.

Medvedev, Sil'vestr. *Sozertsanie kratkoe leto 1790, 91, i 92 v nikh zhe chto sodeiasia vo grazhdanstve.* Moscow: Universitetskaia Tipografiia, 1894.

Meehan-Waters, Brenda. "Catherine the Great and the Problem of Female Rule." *The Russian Review* 34, no. 3 (1975).

Mémoires secrets pour servir a l'histoire de la cour de Russie sous les règnes de Pierre-le-Grand et de Catherine I, d'apres les manuscripts originaux du sieur de Villebois, chef d'Escadre et Aide-de-Camp de S. M. le Czar Pierre I. Paris: E, Dentu, 1853, p. 76

Meniailo, V. A. "Agiologiia Velikomuchenitsy Ekateriny na Rusi v XI–XVII vekakh."

Iskusstvo khristianskogo mira. Sbornik statei. Vol. 4 (2000).

Mesiatsoslov s rospis'iu chinovykh osob v gosudarstve na leto ot rozhdestva Khristosa. St. Petersburg: Akademiia nauk, 1802.

Metzger, Bruce M., and Michael D. Coogan, eds. *The Oxford Companion to the Bible.* Oxford: Oxford University Press, 1993.

Meyendorff, Paul. *Russia, Ritual, and Reform: The Liturgical Reforms of Nikon in the Seventeenth Century.* Crestwood, NY: St. Vladimir's Seminary Press, 1991.

Miller, David. "Legends of the Icon of Our Lady of Vladimir: A Study of the Development of Muscovite National Consciousness." *Speculum* 43, no. 4 (1968).

Mineia obshchaia. Moscow: Sinodal'naia Tipografiia, 1790.

Mineia sluzhebnaia. Moscow: Pechatnyi dvor, 1692.

Monastyri Sviatoi Ekateriny Sinai. Rossiia. Posviashchaemsia 340–letiiu Sviato-Ekaterininskogo muzheskogo monastyria v Rossii. Moscow: Tovarishchestvo 'Rarog', 1998.

"Na koronatsiiu Ekateriny I." In *Pamiatniki literatury drevnei Rusi. XVII vek.* Vol. 3. Edited by V. P. Grebeniuk. Moscow: Khudozhestvennaia literatura, 1979.

Nazarov, V. D., et al., eds. *Akty rossiiskogo gosudarstva. Arkhivy moskovskikh monastyrei i soborov XV–nachalo XVII vv.* Moscow: Ladomir, 1998.

Nikitin, Archimandrite Avgustin. *Pravoslavnyi Peterburg v zapiskakh inostrantsev.* St. Petersburg: Neva, 1995.

Nikol'skii, A. I. "Sofiia Premudrost' Bozhiia." *Vestnik arkheologii i istorii* 17 (1906).

Nikol'skii, Konstantin. *Posobie k izucheniiu ustava bogosluzheniia pravoslavnoi tserkvi.* St. Petersburg: Sinodal'naia Tipografiia, 1907.

The Nikonian Chronicle. Vol. 5. Edited by Serge A. Zenkovsky. Princeton: Darwin Press, 1989.

Novgorod Icons of the Twelfth to the Seventeenth Century. Oxford: Phaidon; Leningrad: Aurora, 1980.

Novikov, Nikolai. *Opyt istoricheskago slovaria o rossiiskikh pisateliakh.* St. Petersburg: Tipografiia Akademii nauk, 1772.

"Novye materialy dlia istorii tsarstvovaniia Ekateriny I (1725). Podlinnoe delo novgorodskogo arkhiepiskopa Feodosiia." *Russkii arkhiv* (1864), no.2.

"O osviashchenii tserkvei Sviatei Patriarkhom," *DRV* 11.

Ogarkova, N. A. *Tseremonii, prazdnestva, muzyka russkogo dvora XVIII–nachalo XIX veka.* St. Petersburg: Dmitrii Bulanin, 2004.

Olearius, Adam. *The Travels of Olearius in Seventeenth-Century Russia.* Translated by Samuel H. Baron. Stanford: Stanford University Press, 1967.

Opisanie arkhiva Aleksandro-Nevskoi lavry za vremia tsarstvovaniia Imperatora Petra Velikogo. 2 vols. St. Petersburg: Sinodal'naia Tipografiia, 1903, 1911.

Opisanie dokumentov i del khraniashchikhsia v arkhive sviateishago pravitel'stvuiushchago sinoda. St. Petersburg: Sinodal'naia Tipografiia, 1878–1897.

Opisanie koronatsii eia Velichestva Imperatritsy Ekateriny Alekseevny. St. Petersburg: Senatskaia Tipografiia, 1724.

Opisanie slavianskikh rukopisei biblioteki sviato-troitskoi sergievoi lavry. Moscow: G. Riss, 1878.

Opisanie vysochaishikh povelenii po pridvornomu vedomstvu, 1723–1830. St. Petersburg: Tipografiia departamenta udelov, 1886.

Opisi imushchestva novgorodskogo sofiiskogo sobora XVIII–nachala XIX v. Moscow: Akademiia nauk, 1988.

Opisi novgorodskogo sofiiskogo sobora. Edited by E. A. Gordienko and G. K. Markina. Moscow: Akademiia nauk, 1968.

"Otryvok iz letopisi o vremenakh tsaria Ioanna Vasil'evicha Groznago, 1563–1567 gg." *RIB* 3 (1876).

Paisiia Agiapostolito mitropolita ruskago. "Opisanie sviatoi gory sinaiskoi i eia okrestnostei v stikhakh." *Pravoslavnyi palestinskii sbornik* 12, no. 2 (1891).

Palmer, William. *The Patriarch and the Tsar.* 4 vols. London: Truebner and Co., 1840.

Palomnik kievskii, ili putevoditel' po monastyriam i tserkvam kievskim, dlia bogomoltsev pose-shchaiushikh sviatniu Kieva. Kiev: Universitetskaia Tipografiia, 1854.

Panchenko, A. M. "Russkaia kul'tura v kanun petrovskikh reform." In *Iz istorii russkoi kul'tury.* Vol. 3, *XVII–nachalo XVIII veka.* Edited by A. D. Koshelev (Moscow: Shkola iazyki russkoi kul'tury, 1996).

Panchenko, A. M., et al., eds. *Russkaia sillabicheskaia poeziia XVII–XVIII vv.* Leningrad: Sovetskii Pisatel', 1970.

The 'Paterik' of the Kievan Caves Monastery. Translated by Muriel Heppell. Cambridge: Harvard University Press, 1989.

Paul of Aleppo. *The Travels of Macarius Patriarch of Antioch.* Translated from Arabic by F. C. Balfour. London: Oriental Translation Committee, 1829.

Pekarskii, P. P. *Markiz de-la Shetardi v Rossii 1740–1742 godov.* St. Petersburg: Tipografiia Isafata Ogritzko, 1862.

———. *Nauka i literatura v Rossii pri Petre Velikom.* 2 vols. St. Petersburg: Obshchestven-naia pol'za, 1862.

"Perechen' iz chinovnoi knigi o venchanii na tsarstvo tsaria Alekseia Mikhailovicha s ukazaniem otmen, sdelannykh pri koronatsii tsarei Ivana i Petra Alekseevichei": 23: "Patriarkh tvoril Tsariu slovo uchitel'noe," and "Perechen' iz chinovnoi knigi o venchanii na gosudarstvo tsaria Feodora Alekseevicha." *Chteniia* (1883), book 1.

"Perepisnaia kniga domovoi kazny Patriarkha Nikona." *Vremennik Imperatorskogo moskovskogo obshchestva istorii i drevnostei rossiiskikh.* Book 15 (1852).

Petrov, N. *O proiskhozhdenii i sostave slaviano-russkago Prologa (inozemnye istochniki).* Kiev: Tipografiia Ermeeva, 1875.

Petrov, P. N. *Istoriia Sankt-Peterburga s osnovaniia goroda do vvedeniia v deistvie vybornogo gorodskogo upravleniia.* St. Petersburg: Tipografiia Glazunova, 1885.

Piatnitsky, Yuri, et al., eds. *Sinai, Byzantium, Russia: Orthodox Art from the Sixth to the Twentieth Century.* London: St. Catherine Foundation, 2000.

Picchio, Riccardo. "The Function of Biblical Thematic Clues in the Literary Code of 'Slavia Orthodoxa.'" *Slavica Hierosolymitana* 1 (1977).

Pisarenko, Konstantin. *Povsednevnaia zhizn' russkogo dvora v tsarstvovanie Elizavety Petro-vny.* Moscow: Molodaia gvardiia, 2003.

Pis'ma i bumagi Imperatora Petra Velikogo. 13 vols. St. Petersburg: Gosudarstvennaia Ti-pografiia, 1887–1975.

Pis'ma tsarevicha Alekseia Petrovicha k ego roditeliu gosudariu Petru Velikomu, gosudaryne Ekaterine Alekseevne, i kabinet-sekretariu Makarevu. Odessa: Gorodskaia Tipografiia, 1849.

Platon, Archbishop of Moscow (Ievshin). *A Sermon Preached by Order of Her Imperial Majesty on the Tomb of Peter the Great in the Cathedral Church of St. Peterbourg.* London, 1770.

Pliguzov, A. I. *Polemika v russkoi tserkvi pervoi treti XVI stoletiia.* Moscow: Izdatel'stvo In-drik, 2002.

Plokhy, Serhii. *Tsars and Cossacks: A Study in Iconography.* Cambridge: Harvard University Press, 2002.

Pogosian, Elena. *Petr I—arkhitektor rossiiskoi istorii.* St. Petersburg: Iskusstvo, 2001.

Polnoe sobranie russkikh letopisei (PSRL). Moscow: Akademiia nauk, 1949–.

    Vols. 3 and 4: Novgorodskiia letopisi (tak nazvannye novgorodskaia vtoraia i novgorodskaia tret'ia letopisi).

    Vol. 6: Vtoraia Sofiiskaia letopis'.

    Vol. 13: Tsarstvennaia kniga; Patriarshaia ili Nikonovskaia letopis'; Dopolnenie k nikonovskoi letopisi.

    Vol. 14: Novyi letopisets.

    Vol. 21: Stepennaia kniga.

    Vol. 26: Vologodsko-Permskaia letopis'.

    Vol. 27: Leningradskii spisok Khrongrafa Nikanorovskoi letopisi.

Vol. 29: Letopisets nachala tsarstva tsaria i velikogo kniazia Ivana Vasil'evicha; Aleksandro-Nevskaia letopis'.

Vol. 31: Mazurinskii letopisets.

Vol. 34: Postnikovskii letopisets.

Polotskii, Semen. *Obed dushevnyi.* Moscow: Verkhniaia Tipografiia, 1681.

———. *Vecheria dushevnaia.* Moscow: Verkhniaia Tipografiia, 1683.

———. *Virshi.* Minsk: Mastatskaia literature, 1990.

Pomerantsev, N. N., and S. I. Maslenitsyn, eds. *Russkaia dereviannaia skul'ptura.* Moscow: Izobrazitel'noe iskusstvo, 1994.

Popov, Aleksei. *Pravoslavnye russkie akafisty.* Kazan: Imperatorskii universitet, 1903.

Popov, M. S. *Arsenii Matveevich i ego delo.* St. Petersburg: Tipografiia M. Frolovoi, 1912.

Popov, N. "Pridvornye propovedi v tsarstvovanii Elisavety Petrovny." In *Letopisi russkoi literatury i drevnosti.* Vol. 2. Edited by Nikolai Tikhonravov. Moscow: Grachev and Company, 1853.

"Posol'stvo s gosudarevoiu zazravnoiu milostieiu vo Tsar' gorod i vo Aleksandriiu i vo Antiokhiu i v Erusalim, i v Sinaiskuiu goru Trifona Korobeinikova i Mikhaila Ograkova (1593 g.)." *DRV 12.*

"Postroenie chasovni v derevne Zarubina." In *Predaniia russkogo severa,* edited by N. A. Krinichnaia. St. Petersburg: Nauka, 1991.

Potter, Cathy J. "Preaching and Teaching the Faith in Seventeenth-Century Russia." In *Chteniia po istorii russkoi kul'tury,* edited by Iu. S. Borisov. Moscow: RAN, 2000.

Pravoslavnye russkie obiteli. St. Petersburg: P. P. Soikin, 1910. Reprint, St. Petersburg: Voskresenie, 1994.

"Prenie Daniila mitropolita moskovskogo i vseia Rusi so inokom Maksimom sviatogurt-sem." *Chteniia* (1847), book 7.

"Prikhodo-raskhodnye knigi kazennogo prikaza." *RIB* 9 (1884).

Procopius. *The Secret History.* London: Penguin Books, 1981.

Prodolzhatel' Feofana. Zhizneopisaniia vizantiiskikh tsarei. St. Petersburg: Nauka, 1992.

Prokopovich, Feofan. *Apologia sacrarum reliquarium patrum nostrorum,* in his *Miscellanea Sacra.* Wrotaw, 1744.

———. "The Justice of the Monarch's Right." In *Peter the Great,* edited and translated by Anthony Lentin. Oxford: Headstart History, 1996.

———. *Kratkaia povest' o smerti Petra Velikogo.* St. Petersburg: Tipografiia I. Glazunova, 1831.

———. *Razsuzhdenie o bezbozhii.* Moscow: Universitetskaia Tipografiia, 1774.

———. *Razsuzhdenie o knize solomonovoi naritsaemoi Pesni Pesnei, iako ona est' ne che-lovecheskoiu voleiu, no Dukha Sviatogo vdokhnoveniem napisana ot Solomona.* Moscow: Lopukhin, 1784.

———. *Slova i rechi pouchitel'nye, pokhval'nye i pozdravitel'nye.* 4 vols. St. Petersburg: Sukhoputnyi shliakhetnyi kadetskii korpus, 1761–1777.

———. *Slovo v den' koronatsii Gosudaryny Imperatritsy Anny Ioannovny v Moskve,* in his *Slova i rechi,* vol. 3.

———. *Sochineniia.* Edited by I. P. Eremin. Leningrad: Akademiia nauk, 1961.

———. *Veshchi i dela, o kotorykh dukhovnyi uchitel' narodu khristianskomu propovedati dolzhen, inaia obshchaia vsem, i inaia nekim sobstvennaia.* In his *Slova i rechi,* vol. 4 (1774). It also appeared in 1784 as a separate pamphlet, printed by Moscow University Press.

Protsenko, N. F. *Monastyri v Rossii i sobory v Moskve.* Moscow: Tipografiia P. A. Glushkova, 1863.

Pushkarev, I. *Opisanie Sankt Peterburga.* St. Petersburg: Tipografiia N. Grecha, 1839.

"Puteshestvie Igumena Daniila po sviatym mestam v nachale XII–go stoletiia." In *Puteshestviia russkikh liudei po sviatoi zemle.* St. Petersburg: Tipografiia Sakharova, 1839.

"Puteshestvie iz Konstantinopla v Ierusalim i Sinaiskuiu Goru, nakhodivshagosia pri

Rossiiskom Poslannike, Grafe Petre Andreeviche Tolstom, Sviashchennika Andreia Ignat'eva i brata ego, Stefana, v 1707 godu." In *Palomniki-pisateli petrovskogo
i poslepetrovskogo vremeni ili putniki vo sviatoi grad Ierusalim. Chteniia* (1873), book 3.

*Puteshestvie vo Ierusalim Sarovskiia obshchezhitel'nyia pustyni ieromonakha Meletiia v 1793 i
1794 godu.* Moscow: Gubernskaia Tipografiia, 1798.

Puteshestviia russkikh liudei po sviatoi zemle. St. Petersburg: Tipografiia Sakharova, 1839.

Pyliaev, M. I. *Staryi Peterburg.* St. Petersburg: Izdatel'stvo Suvorina, 1889.

Ratshin, Aleksandr. *Polnoe sobranie istoricheskikh svedenii o vsekh byvshikh v drevnosti i
nyne sushchestvuiushchikh monastyriakh i primechatel'nykh tserkvei v Rossii.* Moscow:
Universitetskaia Tipografiia, 1852.

Razriadnye knigi, 1598–1638. Moscow: Akademiia nauk, 1974.

Robinson, A. N. "Simeon Polotskii i russkii literaturnyi protsess." In *Simeon Polotskii i
ego knigoizdatel'skaia deiatel'nost',* edited by A. N. Robinson et al. Moscow: Nauka,
1982.

Rogov, A. I. "Minei (spravka)." In *Metodicheskoe posobie po opisaniiu slaviano-russkikh
rukopisei dlia Svodnogo kataloga rukopisei khraniashchikhsia v SSSR.* Vol. 1. Moscow:
Arkheograficheskaia komissiia, 1973.

Rothe, Hans. *Religion und Kultur in den Regionen des russischen Reiches im 18. Jahrhundert.*
Rheinisch-Westfälische Akademie der Wissenschaften, no. 267. Opladen: Westdeutscher Verlag, 1984.

Rousset de Missy, Jean. *Mémoires du règne de Catherine Impératrice et Souveraine de toute la
Russie.* The Hague: Rousset, Chez Alberts & Vander Kloot, 1728.

Rovinskii, D. A. "Slovar' russkikh gravirovannykh portretov." *Zapiski Imperatorskoi
Akademii nauk* 21 (1872).

———. *Russkiie narodnye kartinki.* Book 3, *Pritchi i listy dukhovnye.* St. Petersburg: Tipografiia Imperatorskoi Akademii nauk, 1881.

Rowland, Daniel B. "Marina Mniszek." In *Modern Encyclopedia of Russian and Soviet History.* Vol. 22. Gulf Breeze, FL: Academic International Press, 1981.

Runkevich, S. G. *Aleksandro-nevskaia lavra, 1713–1913.* St. Petersburg: Sinodal'naia Tipografiia, 1913.

Russian Primary Chronicle. Laurentian Text. Cambridge: Mediaeval Academy of America,
1953.

Russkaia istoricheskaia biblioteka. 39 vols. St. Petersburg: Akademiia nauk, 1872–1927.

*Russkaia zhivopis' XVII–XVIII vekov. Iz sobraniia Gos. Russkogo Muzeia, Gos. Tret'iakovskogo
Galerei, Muzei drevne-russkogo iskusstva imeni Andreia Rubleva. Katalog vystavki.*
Leningrad: Russkii muzei, 1977.

"Russkii svodnyi ikonopisnyi podlinnik XVIII v." *Vestnik obshchestva drevne-russkogo
iskusstva pri moskovskom publichnom muzee* (1876), no. 11–12.

Sands, Tracy R. "The Saint as Symbol: The Cult of St Katherine of Alexandria among
Medieval Swedish High Aristocracy." In *St Katherine of Alexandria: Texts and Con-
texts in Western Medieval Europe,* edited by Jacqueline Jenkins and Katherine J.
Lewis. Turnbout Belgium: Brepols, 2003.

*Sanktpeterburgskii kalendar' na leto ot rozhdestva Khristova 1738, kotoroe est' prostoe leto,
soderzhashche 365 dnei, sochinennyi na znatneishiia mesta rossiiskogo gosudarstva.* St.
Petersburg: Akademiia nauk, 1737.

Sanktpeterburgskiia vedomosti (1777), no. 95 (November 28).

Savva, V. *Moskovskie tsari i vizantiiskie vasilevy. K voprosu o vliianii Vizantii na obrazovanie
idei tsarskoi vlasti moskovskikh gosudarei.* The Hague: Mouton Reprints, 1969.

Sazonova, L. I. *Poeziia russkogo barokko (vtoraia polovina XVII–nachalo XVIII v.)* Moscow:
Nauka, 1991.

Sbornik Imperatorskogo russkogo istoricheskogo obshchestva. 134 vols. St. Petersburg: Imper-
atorskoe istoricheskoe obshchestvo, 1874–1916.

Scharpe, J. L., and F. Vyncke, eds. *Bdinski zbornik. An Old-Slavonic Menologium of Women
Saints.* Bruges: De Tempel, 1973.

Schoonebeek, Adriaan. *Istoriia o ordinakh ili chinakh voinskikh pache zhe kavalerskikh.* Moscow: Moskovskaia Tipografiia, 1710.

Schulenberg, Jane Tibbetts. "Saints' Lives as a Source for the History of Women, 500–1100." In *Medieval Women and the Sources of Medieval History*, edited by Joel T. Rosenthal. Athens, GA: University of Georgia Press, 1990.

Semevskii, M. I. "Petr Velikii v ego snakh." In *Ocherki i rasskazy iz russkoi istorii XVIII veka.* St. Petersburg: Akademiia nauk, 1884.

———. *Slovo i delo, 1700–1725. Ocherki i raskazy iz russkoi istorii xviiiv.* St. Petersburg: Tipografiia V. S. Balasheva, 1884. Reprint, Moscow: Sovmestnoe predpriiatie Kh. G. S., 1991.

———. *Tsaritsa Praskov'ia, 1664–1723. Ocherk iz russkoi istorii XVIII veka.* Leningrad: Khudozhestvennaia literatura, 1991.

Serebrennikov, Amvrosii. *Slovo v den' tezoimenitstva Eia Imp. Vel. Blagochestniveishiia Gosudaryni Imperatritsy Ekateriny Alekseevny.* St. Petersburg: Sinodal'naia Tipografiia, 1786.

Shakhovskoi, Iakov Petrovich. *Zapiski Kniazia Iakova Petrovicha Shakhovskogo pisannye im samim.* Moscow: Tipografiia Vsevolozhskogo, 1810.

Shliapkin, I. A. "Opisanie rukopisei suzdal'skogo efimieva monastyria." *Pamiatniki drevnei pis'mennosti* 9, no. 4 (1880).

———. *Sv. Dimitrii Rostovskii i ego vremia (1651–1709 g.)* St. Petersburg: Tipografiia A. Transhel', 1891.

———. "Tsarevna Natal'ia Alekseevna i teatr eia vremeni." *Pamiatniki drevnei pis'mennosti* 128 (1898).

Shmidt, S. O., ed. *Svodnyi katalog slaviano-russkikh rukopisnykh knig khraniashchikhsia v SSSR XI-XIII vv.* Moscow: Nauka, 1984.

Shmurlo, E. F. "Petr Velikii v otsenke sovremennikov i potomstva." *ZMNP* 35 (1911), 36 (1911), 39 (1912).

Shusherin, Ioann. *Izvestie o rozhdenii i vospitanii i o zhitii sviateishogo Nikona patriarkha moskovskogo i vseia Rossii.* Moscow: Universitetskaia Tipografiia, 1871.

Skazanie Avraama Palitsyna. Edited by L. V. Cherepnin, O. A. Derzhavina, and E. V. Kolosova. Moscow: Akademiia nauk SSSR, 1955.

"Skazanie o Grishke Otrep'ev," *RIB* 13 (1891).

Slavische Manasses-Chronik, Die. Edited by Joan Bogdan. *Slavische Propylaen* 12 (1966).

Sluzhba na den' Sviatoi Velikomuchenitsy Ekateriny. Moscow: Sinodal'naia Tipografiia, 1765.

Smirnov, P. S. "Vzgliad raskola na perezhivaemoe vremia v pervoi chetverti XVIII veka." *Khristianskoe chtenie* 229, pt. 1 (1909): 685–86.

Snegirev, Ivan. "Ob ikonnom portrete Velikogo Kniazia Vasiliia Ioannovicha." *Russkii istoricheskii sbornik* 1, bk. 2 (1837).

———. *Pamiatniki moskovskoi drevnosti.* Moscow: Avgust Semen, 1842–1845.

Snimki s drevnikh ikon nakhodiashchikhsia v staroobriadcheskom pokrovskom khrame pri rogozhskom kladbishche v Moskve. Moscow: Tovarishchestvo Kushnerev, 1899.

Sobolevskii, A. I. *Perevodnaia literatura moskovskoi Rusi XIV–XVII vekov. Bibliograficheskie materialy.* Moscow: Akademiia nauk, 1903.

Sobranie pisem Tsaria Alekseia Mikhailovicha. Edited by K. T. Soldatenkov. Moscow: Petr Bartenev, 1856.

Sochineniia Prepodobnogo Maksima Greka. Kazan', 1836.

Sokolov, M. I., ed. *'Slava Rossiiskaia,' komediia 1724 goda predstavlennaia v moskovskom goshpitale po sluchaiu koronatsii Imperatritsy Ekateriny Pervoi.* Moscow: Universitetskaia Tipografiia, 1892.

Solov'ev, S. M. *Istoriia Rossii s drevneishikh vremen.* Vol. 9. Moscow: Nauka, 1963.

———. *Istoriia Rossii s drevneishikh vremen.* 6 bound Vols. (containing volumes 1-29) St. Petersburg: Tovarishchestvo 'Obshchestennaia Pol'za, 1911–1916.

Soloviev, Sergei M. *History of Russia.* Vol. 32. Edited and translated by Gary Marker. Gulf

Breeze, FL: Academic International Press, 2001.

Stoglav. Edited by D. E. Kozhanchikov. St. Petersburg: Akademiia nauk, 1883.

Stoliarova, L. V. *Drevnerusskie nadpisi XI–XIV vekov na pergamennykh kodeksakh.* Moscow: Nauka, 1998.

Stroev, P. M. *Vykhody gosudarei tsarei i velikikh kniazei Mikhaila Fedorovicha, Alekseia Mikhailovicha, Fedora Alekseevicha vseia Rusi samoderzhetsev (s 1632 po 1682 god.)* Moscow: Tipografiia Avgusta Semena, 1844.

Stromilov, N. S. *Tsesarevna Elisaveta Petrovna v Aleksandrovoi slobode i Uspenskii devichii monastyr' v to zhe vremia.* Moscow: Universitetskaia Tipografiia, 1874.

Strong, Phil. *Marta of Muscovy: The Fabulous Life of Russia's First Empress.* Garden City, NY: Doubleday, Doran & Company, 1945.

Strong, Roy. *Splendour at Court: Renaissance Spectacle and Illusion.* London: Weidenfeld and Nicolson, 1973.

Subbotin, N., ed. *Deianiia moskovskikh soborov 1666 i 1667 godov.* Moscow: Sinodal'naia Tipografiia, 1893.

Svin'in, Pavel. *Ukazatel' glavneishikh dostopamiatnostei sokhraniaiushchikhsia v masterskoi oruzheinnoi palate.* St. Petersburg: Smirdin, 1826.

Svodnyi catalog russkoi knigi grazhdanskoi pechati XVIII v., 1725–1800. 5 vols. plus addendum. Moscow: Biblioteka imeni Lenina, 1962–1967.

Tale of Boiarynia Morozova, a Seventeenth-Century Religious Life. Edited and translated by Margaret Ziolkowski. Lanham, MD: Lexington Books, 2000.

Tanner, Berngard. *Opisanie puteshestviia pol'skago posol'stva v Moskvu v 1678 godu.* Moscow: Universitetskaia Tipografiia, 1891.

Tarasov, O. Iu. *Ikona i blagochestie. Ocherki ikonnogo dela Rossii.* Moscow: Progress-kul'tura, 1995.

Tatishchev, V. N. *Istoriia Rossiiskaia.* Moscow: Nauka, 1966–1968.

Thomas, C. B. C. "The Miracle Play at Dunstable." *Modern Languages Newsletter* 32 (1917).

Thyrêt, Isolde. *Between God and Tsar: Religious Symbolism and the Royal Women of Muscovite Russia.* DeKalb: Northern Illinois University Press, 2001.

Titov, A. A. *Letopisets o rostovskikh arkhiiereiakh.* St. Petersburg: Tipografiia S. Dobrodeeva, 1890.

———., ed. *Raskhodnaia kniga patriarshago prikaza kushan'iam podavavshimsia Patriarkhu Adrianu i raznago china litsam s sentiabria 1698 po avgust 1699 g.* St. Petersburg: Tipografiia A. Katanskogo, 1890.

Tokmakov, I. *Ekaterininskaia pustyn' moskovskoi gubernii, podol'skogo uezda. Kratkii istoriko-arkheograficheskii ocherk.* Moscow: Gubernskaia Tipografiia, 1892.

———. *Istoricheskoe opisanie vsekh koronatsii rossiiskikh tsarei, imperatorov, i imperatrits.* Moscow, 1896.

———. "Kratkii istoricheskii ocherk tserkvi Sv. Velikomuchenitsy Ekateriny, chto na bol'shoe ordynke v Moskve." *Moskovskie tserkovnye vedomosti,* no. 48 (November 28, 1882).

———. *Povest' o moshchakh sv. Velikomuchenitsy Ekateriny po skazaniiam XVII veka.* Moscow: Izdatel'stvo Segirovoi, 1881.

Travels of Sir John Mandeville. Translated and with an introduction by C. W. R. D. Moseley. Middlesex, UK: Penguin Books, 1983.

Travers, P. L. *Mary Poppins Comes Back.* New York: Harcourt, Brace and World, 1963.

Treasures of the Tsar, from the State Museum of the Moscow Kremlin. Rotterdam: Museum Boymans-van Beuningen, 1995.

Trial of Jean D'Arc. Translated by W. P. Barrett. New York: Gotham House, 1932.

"Tseremonial vo vremia prestavleniia blazhennyia pamiati Blagovernago Gosudaria, Tsarevicha i Velikogo Kniazia Alekseia Alekseievicha, vseia Velikiia i Malyia i Belyia Rossii." *DRV* 14, 1790; reprinted 1970.

Tvorogov, O. V. *Drevnerusskie khronografy.* Leningrad: Nauka, 1975.

————., ed. *Letopisets ellinskii i rimskii. Tekst.* St. Petersburg: RAN, 1999.

————., ed. *Troianskie skazaniia srednevekovye rytsarskie romany o troianskoi voine po russkim rukopisiam XVI–XVII vekov.* Leningrad: Akademiia nauk, 1972.

Ukazy Petra Velikogo samoderzhtsa v rossiiskogo sostoiavshchiiasia s 1714, po konchinu Ego Imperatorskogo Velichestva, genvaria po 28 chislo 1725 godu. St. Petersburg: Tipografiia Akademii nauk, 1739.

Undol'skii, V. M. *Ocherk slaviano-russkoi bibliografii. Khronologicheskii ukazatel' slaviano-russkikh knig tserkovnoi pechati s 1491-go po 1864-i g.* Moscow: Tipografiia Gracheva i kompanii, 1871.

Uspenskii, A. I. *Piat' vnov' otkrytykh ikon kisti Simona Ushakova.* Moscow: I. Efimov, 1901.

————, ed. *Moskovskaia tserkovnaia starina. Trudy komissii po osmotru i izucheniiu pamiatnikov tserkovnoi stariny goroda Moskvy i moskovskoi eparkhii.* Vol. 2. Moscow: A. I. Snegirev, 1904.

Uspenskii, B. A. *Tsar' i imperator. Pomazanie na tsarstvo i semantika monarshikh titulov.* Moscow: Iazyki russkoi kul'tury, 2000.

Uspenskii, Porfirii (Arkhimandrit). *Vtoroe puteshestvie . . . v sinaiskii monastyr' v 1850 godu.* St. Petersburg: Morskoi kadetskii korpus, 1856.

"Ustav Moskovskikh Sviateishikh Patriarkhov Rossiiskikh, ot sozdaniia mira 7176 a ot Rozhdestva Khristova 1668. . . ." *DRV* 10, 1789; reprinted 1970.

"Ustav tserkovnykh obriadov, sovershavshikhsia v moskovskom Uspenskom Sobore." *RIB* 3 (1876).

Van Dam, Raymond. *Saints and Their Miracles in Late Antique Gaul.* Princeton: Princeton University Press, 1993.

Vasiliev, A. A. *History of the Byzantine Empire.* 2 vols. Madison: University of Wisconsin Press, 1952.

————. *Justin the First: An Introduction to the Epoch of Justinian the Great.* Cambridge: Harvard University Press, 1950.

Vedomosti vremeni Petra Velikogo, 1708–1719 g. Moscow: Sinodal'naia Tipografiia, 1906.

Vereshchagin, Arsenii. *Slovo o istinnoi slave v vysokotorzhestvennyi den' tezoimenitstva E. I. V. vsemilostiveishei gosudaryni.* Moscow: Universitetskaia Tipografiia, 1779.

————. *Slovo v den' vkhoda vo khram Presvytiia Bogomateri, i na sovershenie novoustroennoi zimnei tserkvi vo imia Sviatyia Velikomuchenitsy Ekateriny pri vtorom kadetskom korpuse.* St. Petersburg: Sinodal'naia Tipografiia, 1804.

Vialova, S. O. "Znachenie monastyria sv. Ekateriny na Sinae v istorii kul'tury." In *Nasledie monastyrskoi kul'tury. Remeslo, khudozhestvo, iskusstvo,* edited by I. A. Chudinova. Vol. 2. St. Petersburg: Rossiiskii institut istorii iskusstv, 1997.

Vilinbakhov, G. V. "K istorii uchrezhdeniia ordena Andreia Pervozvannogo i evoliutsiia ego znaka." In *Kul'tura i iskusstvo petrovskogo vremeni,* edited by G. N. Komelova. Leningrad: Avrora, 1977.

Villebois, Théophile Hallez-Claparède, comte de. *Mémoires secrets pour servir á l'histoire de la cour de Russie sous les règnes de Pierre-le-Grand et de Catherine Ire.* Paris: E. Dentu, 1853.

Vinogradov, A. *Istoriia kafedral'nogo uspenskogo sobora v gubernskom gorode Vladimire.* Vladimir: Gubernskoe pravlenie, 1905.

Viteau, Joseph. *Passions de saints Ecaterine et Pierre d'Alexandrie, Barbara et Anysia.* Paris: Librairie Emile Bouillion, 1897.

Vitsen, Nikolaas. *Puteshestvie v Moskoviiu, 1664–1665. Dnevnik.* St. Petersburg: Symposium, 1996.

Vlasova, O. M., ed. *Permskaia dereviannaia skul'ptura.* Perm: Permskoe knizhnoe izdatel'stvo, 1985.

Vodarskii, Ia. E. "Legendy prutskogo pokhoda Petra I (1711 g.)." *Otechestvennaia istoriia* (September-October 2004), no. 5.

Voltaire. *Histoire de l'empire de Russie sous Pierre le Grand (par l'auteur de l'histoire de Charles XII).* Geneva, 1763.

Voragine, Jacobus de. *The Golden Legend of Jacobus de Voragine*. New York: Arno Press, 1969.

Vsevolodskii-Gerngross, V. *Russkii teatr ot istokov do serediny XVIII v.* Moscow: Akademiia nauk, 1957.

Walsh, Christine. "The Role of the Normans in the Development of the Cult of St Katherine." In *St Katherine of Alexandria: Texts and Contexts in Western Medieval Europe*, edited by Jacqueline Jenkins and Katherine J. Lewis. Turnbout, Belgium: Brepols, 2003.

Weber, Friedrich Christian. *The Present State of Russia*. Vol. 1. New York: DaCapo Press, 1968.

Winstead, Karen A. *Virgin Martyrs: Legends of Sainthood in Late Medieval England*. Ithaca: Cornell University Press, 1997.

Wisch, Barbara A., and Dane Cohl Ahl, eds. *Confraternities and the Visual Arts in Renaissance Italy*. Cambridge: Cambridge University Press, 2000.

Wittram, Reinhard. *Peter I, Czar und Kaiser. Zur Geschichte Peters des Grossen in seiner Zeit*. Göttingen: Vandenhoecken & Ruprecht, 1964.

Wortman, Richard S. *Scenarios of Power: Myth and Ceremony in Russian Monarchy*. Vol. 1. Princeton: Princeton University Press, 1995.

Zabelin, Ivan E. *Al'bom starinnykh vidov moskovskago kremlia*. Moscow: Tipografiia Kushnerev, 1904.

———. *Domashnyi byt russkikh tsarits v XVI–XVII st.* Moscow: Tipografiia Gracheva i kompanii, 1863.

———. *Materialy dlia istorii, arkheologii, i statistiki goroda Moskvy*. Pt. 1, *Materialy dlia istorii, arkheologii i statistiki moskovskikh tserkvei, sobrannye iz knig i del prezhdebyvshikh patriarshikh prikazov V. I. And G. I. Kholmogorovymi*. Moscow: Gorodskaia Tipografiia, 1884.

Zapasko, Iakim, and Iaroslav Isaevich. *Pamiatki knizhkogo mistetstva. Katalog starodrukiv vidanikh na Ukraini*. Vol. 1. Lviv: Visha shkola, 1981.

Zapiski Andreia Artamanovicha Grafa Matveeva. In *Zapiski russkikh liudei. Sobytiia vremen Petra Velikogo*. St Petersburg: Tipografiia Sakharova, 1841.

Zapiski Imperatritsy Ekateriny vtoroi. St. Petersburg: A. S. Suvorin, 1907.

Zapiski Iusta Iuli, datskogo poslannika pri Petre Velikom (1709–11). Moscow: Universitetskaia Tipografiia, 1899.

Zavedeev, P. *Istoriia russkogo propovednichestva ot XVII veka do nastoiashchago vremeni*. Tula: Tipografiia N. A. Sokalova, 1879.

Zelensky, Elizabeth Kristoforovich. "'Sophia the Wisdom of God' as a Rhetorical Device during the Regency of Sof'ia Alekseevna, 1682–1689." Ph.D. diss., Georgetown University, 1992.

Zelov, D. D. *Ofitsial'nye svetskie prazdniki kak iavlenie russkoi kul'tury kontsa XVII-pervoi poloviny XVIII veka. Istoriia triumfov i feierverkov ot Petra Velikogo do ego docheri Elizavety*. Moscow: URSS, 2002.

Zernova, A. S. *Knigi kirillovskoi pechati izdannye v Moskve v XVI–XVII vekakh. Svodni catalog*. Moscow: Gos. Biblioteka imeni Lenina, 1958.

———. "Nadpisi na knigakh moskovskoi pechati XVI–XVII vv. v sobranii otdela redkikh knig gosudarstvennoi biblioteki SSSR imeni V. I. Lenina." *Kniga. Issledovaniia i materialy* 62 (1991).

Zhivov, Viktor M. "Dva prostranstva russkogo srednevekov'ia i ikh pozdneishie metamorfozy." *Otechestvennye zapiski*, no. 5, Vol. 20, 2004.

———. "Gedeon (Georgii Andreevich Krinovskii)." In *Early Modern Russian Writers, Late Seventeenth and Eighteenth Centuries*, edited by Marcus C. Levitt. Dictionary of Literary Biography, vol. 150. Detroit: Bruccoli Clark Layman, Gale Research, 1995.

———. *Iz tserkovnoi istorii vremen Petra Velikogo*. Moscow: Novoe literaturnoe obozrenie, 2004.

———. "Kul'turnye reformy v sisteme preobrazovanii Petra I." In *Iz istorii russkoi kul'tury*.

Vol 3, *XVII-nachalo XVIII veka,* edited by A. D. Koshelev. Moscow: Shkola iazyki russkoi kul'tury, 1996.

Zhivov, Viktor M., and Boris A. Uspenskii. "Metamorfozy antichnogo iazychestva v istorii russkoi kul'tury XVII–XVIII veka." In *Iz istorii russkoi literatury,* edited by A. D. Koshelev. Vol. 4. Moscow: Shkola iazyki russkoi kul'tury, 1996.

———. "Tsar' i Bog: Semioticheskie aspekty sakralizatsii monarkha v Rossii." In *Iazyki kul'tury i problemy perevodimosti,* edited by B. A. Uspenskii. Moscow: Nauka, 1987.

Zhmakin, Vasilii. *Mitropolit Daniil i ego sochineniia.* Moscow: Universitetskaia Tipografiia, 1881.

Zhurnal pridvornoi kantory (for the years 1734, 1736, 1737). St. Petersburg.

Zimin, A. A. *Russkie letopisi i khronografy kontsa XV–XVI vv. Uchebnoe posobie.* Moscow: Gos istoriko-arkhivnyi institute, 1960. Reprint, The Hague: Mouton, 1969.

Zitser, Ernest A. *The Transfigured Kingdom: Sacred Parody and Charismatic Authority at the Court of Peter the Great.* Ithaca: Cornell University Press, 2004.

Zverinskii, V. V. *Materialy dlia istoriko-topograficheskogo izsledovaniia o pravoslavnykh monastyriakh v rossiiskoi imperii.* St. Petersburg: V. Bezobravov i kompanii, 1890.

Zvonarev, Semen, ed. *Sorok sorokov. Al'bom ukazatel' vsekh moskovskikh tserkvei.* 3 vols. Moscow: YMCA Press, 1988–1989.

Index

Sources of Figures

Images found in this volume are from a wide assortment of sources. Great thanks are extended to all:

p. 11—T. A. Anan'eva, *Semen Ushakov* (Leningrad, 1971).

p. 49—N. N. Pomerantsev and S. I. Maslenitsyn, *Russkaia dereviannaia skul'ptura* (Moscow, 1994).

p. 54—State Art Gallery of Novosibirsk.

p. 86—*Snimki s drevnykh ikon nakhodiashchikhsia v staroobriadcheskom pokrovskom khrame pri rogozhskom kladbishche v Moskve* (Moscow, 1899).

p. 119—*Russkaia zhivopis' XVII–XVIII vekov. Iz sobraniia Gosudarstvennnogo russkogo muzeia, Gos. Tret'iakovskogo galereia, muzeia drevne-russkogo iskusstva* (Katalog vystavki, Moscow, 1972).

pp. 128, 159, & 171—D. A. Rovinskii, *Materialy dlia russkoi ikonografii St. Petersburg, 1890,* Vol. 7, no. 279; Vol. 2, no. 63; & Vol. 7, no. 280.

p. 158—State Hermitage Museum, Drevniaia zhivopis' number 1368.

p. 172—*Pamiatniki russkoi kul'tury pervoi chetverti XVIII veka* (Moscow, 1966).

p. 206—P. N. Petrov and S. N. Shubinskii, *Al'bom 200-letniago iubileia Petra Velikogo* (St. Petersburg, 1872).

p. 220—Tretiakov Gallery, Moscow.